1,000,000 Books

are available to read at

Forgotten Books

www.ForgottenBooks.com

Read online
Download PDF
Purchase in print

ISBN 978-0-282-48459-0
PIBN 10853355

This book is a reproduction of an important historical work. Forgotten Books uses
state-of-the-art technology to digitally reconstruct the work, preserving the original format
whilst repairing imperfections present in the aged copy. In rare cases, an imperfection in
the original, such as a blemish or missing page, may be replicated in our edition. We do,
however, repair the vast majority of imperfections successfully; any imperfections that
remain are intentionally left to preserve the state of such historical works.

Forgotten Books is a registered trademark of FB &c Ltd.
Copyright © 2018 FB &c Ltd.
FB &c Ltd, Dalton House, 60 Windsor Avenue, London, SW19 2RR.
Company number 08720141. Registered in England and Wales.

For support please visit www.forgottenbooks.com

1 MONTH OF FREE READING

at
www.ForgottenBooks.com

By purchasing this book you are eligible for one month membership to ForgottenBooks.com, giving you unlimited access to our entire collection of over 1,000,000 titles via our web site and mobile apps.

To claim your free month visit:
www.forgottenbooks.com/free853355

* Offer is valid for 45 days from date of purchase. Terms and conditions apply.

English
Français
Deutsche
Italiano
Español
Português

www.forgottenbooks.com

Mythology Photography **Fiction**
Fishing Christianity **Art** Cooking
Essays Buddhism Freemasonry
Medicine **Biology** Music **Ancient Egypt** Evolution Carpentry Physics
Dance Geology **Mathematics** Fitness
Shakespeare **Folklore** Yoga Marketing
Confidence Immortality Biographies
Poetry **Psychology** Witchcraft
Electronics Chemistry History **Law**
Accounting **Philosophy** Anthropology
Alchemy Drama Quantum Mechanics
Atheism Sexual Health **Ancient History**
Entrepreneurship Languages Sport
Paleontology Needlework Islam
Metaphysics Investment Archaeology
Parenting Statistics Criminology
Motivational

PRECIOUS STONES:
FOR CURATIVE WEAR;
AND OTHER REMEDIAL USES.
LIKEWISE THE NOBLER METALS.

PRECIOUS STONES:

FOR CURATIVE WEAR;
AND OTHER REMEDIAL USES:

LIKEWISE
THE NOBLER METALS.

BY

W. T. FERNIE, M.D.

Author of "Herbal Simples," "Animal Simples," "Kitchen Physic," "Meals Medicinal," etc.

"O! mickle is the powerful grace that lies
In herbs, plants, *Stones*, and their true qualities."

Charity be a Precious Stone, Devotion is its lustre; if Charity be a rich Balm, Devotion is its odour;—yea; the odour of sweetness which comforts Men, and rejoices Angels."
"Philothea."—*St. Francis de Sales*, 1762.

BRISTOL: JOHN WRIGHT & CO.
LONDON: SIMPKIN, MARSHALL, HAMILTON, KENT & Co., Ld.

1907.

R
133
.F4
1907

JOHN WRIGHT AND CO.,
PRINTERS AND PUBLISHERS, BRISTOL.

To the lasting lustre of—"Our Island Home;"—
"First Flower of the Earth; and first Gem of the Sea."

"This Precious Stone, set in the Silver Sea,
(Which serves it in the office of a wall,
Against the envy of less happier lands;)
This blessed spot, this earth, this Realm, this England;
This land of such dear souls, this dear, dear land."

AD LECTOREM.

"Qui cupis emunctim Gemmarum scire medullas,
Huc venias; totum continet iste liber.
Occultas enim Lapidum cognoscere vires,
Quorum causa latens effectus dat manifestos,
Egregium quiddam volumus, rarumque videri;
Scilicet hinc solers medicorum cura juvatur
Auxilio lapidum morbos expellere docta."

TO THE READER.

"Gems would you cleanse from their dross, and fathom their innermost virtues,
Come to our Book, and find them fully disclosed in its pages;
Sympathies scarce understood; yet effects which are visible plainly;
These to reveal, and expound, is a task which should win us distinction.
Hence may the curative skill of the doctor be splendidly aided,
Taught that the wearers of Stones which are Precious can baffle diseases."

"And thou shalt make the Breast-Plate of Judgment with cunning work." "And thou shalt set in it settings of Stones, even four rows of Stones: the first row shall be a Sardius, a Topaz, and a Carbuncle. And the second row shall be an Emerald, a Sapphire, and a Diamond. And the third row a Ligure, an Agate, and an Amethyst. And the fourth row a Beryl, and an Onyx, and a Jasper; they shall be set in Gold, in their inclosings." "And thou shalt put in the Breast-Plate of judgment the Urim, and the Thummim; and they shall be upon Aaron's heart when he goeth in before the Lord."

"The Priest, having put on his robes, went into the Holy Place, and stood before the veil which separated this from the Holy of Holies. Then the Priest enquired of God in a low voice; and fixing his eyes upon the Breast-Plate he received the answer to his question by Urim, and Thummim."—Rabbins allege that the answer was given by certain letters engraven on the Stones in the Breast-Plate emitting a bright light, so as to be read by the High Priest into words. Josephus says that when the Jewels shone with peculiar radiance the answer was to be regarded as affirmative; but when dim, as negative. Authorities declare that the Urim, and the Thummim signified "Light, and Truth." Ælian tells that the High Priest among the Egyptians, as superior Judge, wore round his neck an image of Sapphire, which was called "Truth."

PREFACE.

> "And this our life, exempt from public haunt,
> Finds tongues in trees, books in the running brooks,
> *Sermons in Stones;* and good in everything."

To say a few prefatory words about ourselves, as now

> "Talking of Stones, Stars, Plants, of Fishes, Flies;
> Playing with Words, and idle Similes;"

—at this the close of our literary endeavours, we cannot do better than quote the quaintly pertinent reflections (by far better expressed for the purpose than any phrases of ours could be) of "the most learned Theophrastus Paracelsus, first written in the German tongue, and afterwards published in the English, by John Hester, Practitioner in the Art of Distillation, 1633": "At the beginning,—some ten, or more, years back,—casting about with ourselves, we were cumbred with a hundred odde crotchets, all as farre beyond the compasse of our reach, as they were short of the condition of our liking; till at length, in the midst of this muse we met in our mind with two such minions as in our conceit were the only Paragons of the rest; the one, sweet and odoriferous, adorn'd with flowers, and hearbs, beautified with delicate spices, sole Lady, and Regent of all pleasant things that grow upon the face of the Earth; the other, gallant, and gorgeous, garnish'd with Gold, and Silver, bedect with Jewels, sole Ladie, and Governesse of all the rich Mines, and Minerals that are in the bowels of the Earth. These we vowed to serve, and to honour, (even, if required, to the losse of life, and limme); neyther have we greatly broken promise with them, though they have not kept touch with us. Goodly, and many golden mountains they promised us; who have but scantily performed hitherto but as leaden mole-hills. Still, howsoever, the bargaine stands between them and us; we are neither disposed to excuse them, nor excuse ourselves. We agreed upon wages, and we weare their Liveries; their Cognisance,—such as it is,—we beare where we are not ashamed to shew it: divers, and sundry other affayres have they employed us about; in the which we have faithfully, painfully, and chargeably applied ourselves, and attained, by their instructions, many their hidden secrets, as well in Hearbs, and Spices, as in Mettals, and Mineralls. The latter part of which we have now diligently collected together, and (for the non-payment meantime of our board wages at their hands) we are forced to set them, with the residue of our skill, to sale; with offer unto thee (Good Readers) of preferment to the best things we have: yet at a farre easier price than they have cost us, being no lesse than our '*Summa Summarum;*' cast up; and the final balance of our account set down!"

Adopting this timely argument, let us briefly add that, having done our best during a decade of past years to discuss *Herbal Simples*, *Animal Simples*, and *Dietetics;* we here with *Precious Stones*, and *Certain Metals*, bring our life's labours to a termination as regards seeking the suffrages of the public further in print. Like the Dwarf, in " The Showman's Story," told so humorously, but yet so pathetically, by Charles Dickens, (extra Xmas Number, 1858)—" The Little Man, having walked three times round the cairawan, will now retire behind the curtain."

Not that we would make our final bow as the comic actor of the Company : wherefore, now doffing the Cap, and Bells, out of due respect to our present audience, we take a more serious view of the situation, and seek to come forward hand in hand with some established favourites of the generous literary public to support us on this occasion. Asking—for the nonce—the paramount assistance of dear, quaint, learned, eccentric Charles Lamb, the Prince of convivial Essayists, that he shall grasp us by the right hand of good-fellowship; and invoking that piously endearing, yet unsanctimonious, homely Saint, Robert Herrick, the human-hearted poet of Devon, to lend us his happy-phrased eloquence, on our left ; we venture to withdraw from the boards with a modicum of hoped-for applause, granted, if not to ourselves, at least to these distinguished brethren of the Sock, and Buskin, who come from Elysian Fields to lend us their gracious help.

—"Bespeaking kindly attention," saith Elia ; (with his familiar use of old-fashioned language, much to the point), "shall we confess a truth ? I begin to count the probabilities of my duration ! In proportion as the years lessen, and shorten, I set more count upon their periods ; I am not content to pass away 'like a weaver's shuttle.' These metaphors solace me not, nor sweeten the unpalatable draught of mortality. I care not to be carried with the tide ; and I reluct at the inevitable course of destiny. I am in love with this green earth; the face of town, and country; the unspeakable rural solitudes ; and the sweet security of streets : I would set up my tabernacle here : I am content to stand still at the age to which I am arrived; I, and my friends ! "

" Sun, and sky, and breeze, and solitary walks, and

summer holidays, and the greenness of fields, and the delicious juices of meats, and fishes, and society; and the cheerful glass; and candle-light; and fireside conversations; and innocent vanities, and jests; and even irony itself! Do these things go out with life?" "Can a ghost laugh, or shake his gaunt sides when you are pleasant with him?" "And you, my midnight darlings, my Folios! Must I part with the intense delight of having you (huge armfuls) in my embrace? Must knowledge come to me, if it come at all, by some awkward experiment of intuition, and no longer by the familiar processes of reading?" "Shall I enjoy friendships there, wanting the smiling indications which point me to them here; the recognisable face; the 'sweet assurance of a look'?"——"But, there! Avaunt, thou grim phantom of sadness! Out on thee, we say! Away with your puling fears just now expressed! Another cup, say we, of the generous juice of the grape! —So have they passed like a cloud! clear washed-away by a spell of true Helicon; the only Spa for all such moping hypochondries!"

Thus recites, as akin to our purpose, the gentle Elia, (straight from the table of the Gods), lending us the lustre of his peerless prose, which "Shakespeare himself might have written, and a Hamlet might have quoted," (as Leigh Hunt so aptly pronounces).—Forthwith, in opportune verse, Herrick, our erstwhile Poet-Preceptor, takes up his cue melodious :—

"MAY GOD BLESS THE BOOK!"

"For every sentence, clause, and word,
That's not inlaid with Thee, O Lord,
Forgive me, God: and blot each line
Out of this Book that is not Thine!

> But if, midst all, Thou findest one,
> Wanting Thy Benediction,
> That one, of all the rest, shall be
> The glory of my Book, and me!"
>
> "DEUS PROPITIETUR!"
>
> "Si quid in his fuerit, sententia, clausula, verbum
> Quod non te sapiat, vel tua, sancte Deus,
> O, precor, ignoscas, damnataque carmina dele;
> Quodcumque indignum vivere, dispereat!
>
> Si tamen exciderit de tot modo versibus unus,
> Quem sinis æthereas, Maxime, adire domos,
> Illud carmen erit, dum spiritus hos regit artus,
> Et, vati, et tremulæ gloria summa lyræ."—

Thus, with all diffidence be it said, we ask the advent of these sainted supporters. For, what, in his *Wisdome*, has told the Sonne of Sirach? "Burthen not thyselfe above thy power whiles thou livest; and company not with one that is mightier than thyselfe; for howe agree the kettle and the earthen pot together? for, if the one be smitten against the other, it shall be broken!" But none the less courageously, we dare to challenge this Scriptural admonition! "Albeit, our name," saith again the *Wislom of Solomon*, "shall be forgotten in time; and no man shall have our works in remembrance."—" Come on, therefore; let us enjoy the good things that are present; and let us speedily use the creatures (of gladness) like as in our youth." "Let us fill ourselves with costly wine; and let no flower of the spring pass by us. Let us crown ourselves with rosebuds before they be withered; let us leave tokens of our joyfulness in every place; for this is our portion; and our lot is this."

"And heere shall be our Apocryphal ending," (as the "Finis"—last chapter—puts it in the *Bookes of the*

Maccabees.) "If we have done well, and as is fitting the story, it is that which we desired; but if slenderly, and meanly, it is that which we could attain unto. For, as it is hurtful to drink wine, or water, alone; and as wine mingled with water is pleasant, and delighteth the taste; even so, speech, finely framed, delighteth the ears of them that read the story."

So therefore, hand in hand with loyal upholders from the land of Shades, we make our obeisance to our Ladye, the Public, and bow ourselves off the Boards.

Jack Point, Strolling Jester, shall furnish our parting ditty, in sadly-humorous strain :—

"We have a Song to sing, O!
Oh! 'tis the song of a merry man; moping mum!
Whose soul is sad; whose glance is glum;
Who sips no sup; who craves no crumb,
 As he sighs for the love of a ladye."=(the indulgent public.)

"We have a Song to sing, O!
 And a doleful ding, ding, dong!
'Tis sung to the knell of a Church-yard bell,
 And a doleful ding, ding, dong!
Heigh day! Heigh day! Misery me! Misery me!
—But his pains are o'er, and he'll sigh no more;
 For, *he lives in the love of the ladye!*"

RICHMOND, SURREY,
Month of the Turquoise: 1907.

CONTENTS.

	PAGE
ABRAHAM'S Precious Stone	25
Adamant (Diamond),	64, 65, 66, 73, 321, 322
ADDER-STONE	348–349
Ætites (Eagle Stone)	214
Æsculapius	350
AGATE	68, 310–312
Aladdin	89
Alcahest	178
ALCHEMY	203, 373–387
ALUMINA	278
AMBER	263, 322–329, 348, 352
AMETHYST (stone)	169–173
,, Flower	172
Amianthus	46
Ammonia	423
AMULETS	45, 50–54, 180, 294, 384
Animal Stones	7
Antipathies	9
Antique Silver	410, 411
Apostle Stones	44, 45
AQUA-MARINE	116, 128, 131, 132
Arabian Nights	88, 90, 91, 94, 95
Archaus (of Helmont)	265
ARMENIAN STONE	331, 332
Artificial Stones	54, 55
ASBESTOS	346
BACILLI	436
BALAS RUBY	145
Bananas	429–432
Benjamin, tribe of	173

	PAGE
BERYL	4, 116, 130–132, 204, 309, 314
BIRTH-STONES	38–43
BEZOAR STONE	339, 340
Blood, to test	153
BLOODSTONE	4, 174, 257
BRASS	439
Bread	117–120
BREASTPLATE OF HIGH PRIEST, Preface,	21–24, 45, 104, 314, 351
Brilliants	69
Byron (Heaven and Earth)	349
CABOCHON, EN	40, 158
CAIRNGORM	179
CALCIUM	355, 356
Cameos	132, 218
Cancer (Crab) in Zodiac	46
Carat	71, 75
CARBUNCLE STONE	157–159, 355
CARNELIAN	138, 310
CAT'S EYE	126, 131, 311
Charcot, Dr.	217, 416, 418
CHRYSOBERYL	126, 131
CHRYSOLITE	4, 163, 276
Chrysoprase	164, 172, 310
Cooking Utensils	434
COPPER	421–442, 472
CORAL	288–291, 385
Corundums	126, 140, 142
Cramp Rings	108, 109, 380
Crown Jewels	40
CRYSTAL ROCK	164, 200–205, 215, 222

CONTENTS.

Crystal Gazing 15, 20, 204–208, 214–217
Cullinan Diamond 76, 353

DACTYLOTHECA - - 27
Daniel, Prophet, Statue of 474
DAYS FOR THE PRECIOUS STONES - - 38
Dee, Dr. 107, 203, 377
DIAMOND - 64–95
DIVINING ROD 397, 419
DRAGON STONE - 137

EAGLE-STONE (Ætites) 214, 341–345
Eastern Love of Precious Stones 23, 30–33, 91, 92
Elizabeth, Queen 6, 104, 107, 203, 312
EMERALD 2, 43, 116, 117, 125, 127–138, 354
Ephod of High Priest 21, 24, 64, 115
EPITOME OF PRECIOUS STONES - 352, 353

FLINT-SILICA 258, 279, 283
Foxglove - - 123

GALACTIDES - 346
GARNETS 156–158, 159–163
GEMS 1–4, 35, 36, 46, 309
Generative Powers of Diamond - - 67
GOLD - -360–399, 471
,, forms of - 382
Grosseteste, Bishop 5, 27, 28
Gyges, Ring of - 107, 108

HÆMATITIS (Bloodstone) 253, 254, 264
Haunted Houses 50, 410, 411

HELIOTROPE 180–186, 198, 199, 333
Henson, Mr., Lapidary - 317
HERRICK, ROBERT—Preface 196
Horace (and Mæcenas) - 52
HYACINTH STONE 3, 160, 161, 311

IMITATION Stones 54–56, 144 (Jasper 174,) 264, 267, 275, 30 5, 310
Inherited Qualities of Precious Stones - 49
INTRODUCTION - 1–13
IRON 109, 152, 168, 185, 206, 257, 468, 469, 473
Ivan the Terrible 46, 47

JACINTH - - 161
Jackdaw of Rheims 99, 100, 101
JADE - - 284–286
JARGOON - - 163
JASPER 3, 173, 199, 263
JET - - 347, 348
Jew's Eye - - 59
Jewish Time, how reckoned 43
,, Amulets - 52

KAISER (TALISMAN OF) - 108
Kilmansegg, Legend of 388–391
KOHINOOR DIAMOND 74, 75

LAMB, CHARLES (Elia) Preface, 230, 243, 329, 449
Lambert, Daniel - 63
LAPIS LAZULI 2, 96, 329–332
LEAD - -442–452, 473
LIME - - 332
LOADSTONE 206, 318–322
Lunar Caustic - 400, 404
LYCHNITES (Lamp Stone) 159

CONTENTS.   xvii

	PAGE
MAGIC	- 10, 11, 346
MAGNESIA	129, 146, 355
MALACHITE	166, 263, 422
Marbodus	173, 182, 193
Metallurgy	- - 360
METALS	11, 12, 357–360, 416–419, 455, 471
„ Epitome of	471–473
Mind, dual	- - 14
Mirfield	- 122, 138
Mistletoe	- 393–396
Montague, Lady Mary	91–94
MONTHS OF PRECIOUS STONES	- 37, 44
MOONSTONE	- 332–339

Nessus, Shirt of	26, 27
November (Hood)	- 44

OCCULT POWERS OF PRECIOUS STONES 8, 9, 24, 51, 239, 259, 293
Odours - 224, 227, 228
ONYX - 179, 312–316, 329
OPAL - 39, 248–253
ORIENTAL TOPAZ - 164
„ **AMETHYST (Sapphire)** 170
Outward Remedies 26, 177, 280, 287

PARACELSUS, Preface 178, 279–283, 310, 376, 415
PEARLS 294–305, 307
Pepys (Precious Stones) 77, 78
PEWTER 459, 460, 461
Pewter Wort - - 460
Pigeons' Blood Ruby 140, 141, 165
PLATINUM 373, 420, 472
POINT, JACK Preface
POISONS COUNTERACTED BY PRECIOUS STONES 21, 70

	PAGE
PRECIOUS STONES	4, 8, 14, 23, 29, 48
„ Multiply in Earth	- 67
„ **Epitome of Virtues**	352–356
„ List of	- - 67
„ of the Months	- 37
„ of the Days of Week	38
„ of the Apostles	- 44
„ of the Zodiac	- 45
Psychometry	- 14–18
Pythagoras	- - 47

QUARTZES 169, 178, 199

RADIUM 180, 254–261, 419
Rajah of Borneo's Diamond - 71, 77
Revised Old Testament - 351
RINGS of Cardinals 98, 99, 340
„ of Queen Elizabeth 104, 105, 106, 107
„ of Saint Mark - 108
„ Cramp 108, 109, 416
„ Occult - - 111
„ Poison - 340, 341
ROCK CRYSTAL 159, 164, 253
Rosary, and Scapular 53, 169
RUBY 48, 54, 87, 138–156
„ Balas 145, 154–156
„ Bohemian - 179

Salamander Stone - 214
San Graal - - 133
SAPPHIRE 2, 5, 57, 95–103, 109–115, 353
SARD 52, 313–315
SARDONYX 4, 179, 314, 315
Sentiment, lack of, about Precious Stones - 35
SERPENT STONE 56–58
SILICA, *See* **FLINT.** 258, 279, 283
SILVER 399–420, 472

	PAGE
Sinbad the Sailor	88
SMARAGDUS (Emerald)	127, 128
SOLOMON, WISDOM OF—	Preface
Soul Stones	47
SPINEL	142, 145
Spirits in Stones	49, 50, 282
SPIRITUAL VIRTUES OF PRECIOUS STONES	48, 256, 416
SPURIOUS STONES	56, 85
Stone Eater	59, 60
,, to Lick for Cure	63
Stone, to Dissolve	61, 97
SULPHUR	358, 444, 455
Sympathies	48, 230, 416
TALISMANS	50, 51, 111, 127
Telepathy	10, 16, 17, 217, 416
TIN	452–468, 473
Tinfoil	466

	PAGE
TOADSTONE	337–339
TOPAZ	3, 85, 163–168
,, Oriental	139
TOURMALINE	145, 146, 154
Tumours, against, Sard	314
TURQUOISE	30, 37, 263–273
URIM AND THUMMIM	22, 24
V*ANADIUM*	165
VERDIGRIS	422, 423, 439
Vinegar	459
Virtues of Precious Stones,	19, 20, 56, 352–356
W*OUNDS*, to Heal—	
,, ,, Loadstone	320
,, ,, Sard	314
,, ,, Tinfoil	467
ZINC	370, 371, 468–473

CORRECTIONS.

On Page 258, third line from top, for *triturations* read *trituration*.

On Page 314, fourteenth line up from bottom, for *caelam* read *coenum*.

On Page 415, bottom line, for *mind* read *maid*.

On Page 435, sixteenth line from top, for *making* read *using*.

PRECIOUS STONES:

FOR CURATIVE WEAR;

AND OTHER REMEDIAL USES.

LIKEWISE THE NOBLER METALS.

INTRODUCTION.

QUITE recently a leading Medical Journal has pertinently asked—" Is it not of timely interest to enquire,—having before our notice the results of modern investigations into radio-activity, and force-rays,—whether, after all, Precious Stones may not be capable of exerting therapeutic influences? The astute Physician should not altogether overlook the part taken by Gems in the kaleidoscopic variation of human sentiments, and the evolution of personal sympathies." "It may be that the practice of wearing Gems in olden times as amulets, and charms, to ward off disease, and other evils, was really the origin of their after-use as remedial agents, which grew to a considerable extent in the Middle Ages." Galen records that the Egyptian King Nechepsus wore a green Jasper cut into the shape of a dragon surrounded with rays, which being thus applied over the region of his digestive organs was found to be wonderfully strengthening to their functions. Again, the Diamond, though long suspected of exercising poisonous properties, if taken internally, was, nevertheless, believed to endow its wearer with courage, and to make him "more fearless than careful." The Ruby was worn to ward off the plague and pestilence; having, also, according to Cardamus, the virtue of making its wearer prudent, and of banishing idle, foolish thoughts. When taken internally this gem was believed to make the body capable of resisting decay. The Emerald was used medicinally in early times as an astringent, being warranted to cure dysentery, the plague, the falling sickness, and the bitings of venomous creatures. It was also reputed to stop hæmorrhages; to strengthen the memory, and to remove acrid humours. This stone was administered in the form of fine powder, of which the dose was from six to thirty grains. Taking up his parable, we remind our readers that, as an old writer puts it, "the Emerald takes away foolish fears, as of devils, and hobgoblins, with folly, and anger, so as to cause good conditions."

Extraordinary virtues were likewise attributed to the Sapphire in ancient times by medical men of those days. This stone was supposed to have sexual distinctions; the pale blue being held to be the male, and the dark blue variety representing the female. Medicinally the sapphire stones "fortified the heart, counteracted the effects of poisons, purified the blood, and dried up ulcers on the eyes." Similarly, powdered Rubies were given, in doses of from ten to forty grains, to "sweeten the sharpness of the humours, to strengthen the vitals, to drive away melancholy, and to restore lost strength." Again, Lapis Lazuli, "the Stone of beautiful blue," was employed to "purge melancholy, and fortify the heart," forming, so as to produce these salutary effects, an ingredient in many compound medicines of that date. The Jacinth too (in olden times called the "Hyacinth"), when ground to powder, was given to stimulate the heart, and as an antidote to poisons. A certain wonderful confection thereof, which was believed to be a sovereign remedy for many bodily ills, was made in France. It was composed of Jacinth, Coral, Sapphire, Topaz, Pearls, and Emerald, together with Gold, and Silver leaf, and several herbs of power. "This preparation," says Pomet (1712), "is much used in Florence and Languedoc, where you meet with but few persons not having a pot thereof."

The Topaz, reduced to powder, was mixed with rosewater, and taken to prevent bleeding: whilst for staying bleeding at the nose the stone itself was applied within, or to the side of that organ. The Amethyst was the stone of temperance and sobriety, being said to restrain the wearer from strong drinks, and from indulging in too much sleep. It was further believed to quicken the wits, and to drive vapours from the head.

Pearls were administered in cases of consumption, and were commended, when powdered, in ten-grain doses, for giving strength to the heart. They were further esteemed for fortifying the nerves, curing weak eyes, preserving the body sound from the decay of old age, and even resisting the plague, when taken in doses of six grains, in water sweetened with manna. Amber was given to cure coughs; while Red Coral was "an excellent purifier of the blood, correcting derangements of the liver."

Jasper was adopted by the early physicians as an astringent, being curative of epilepsy, and the stone.

The Beryl helped "defluxions of the throat:" whilst the Sardonyx made men cheerful, averting melancholy. The Chrysolite was reputed to ward off fevers; the Onyx, moreover, when worn round the neck, prevented epileptic fits. The Opal was thought to cure weak eyes; and the Bloodstone was frequently carried by warriors, that it might arrest bleeding from a wound.

By "Precious Stones" are meant, according to the general acceptation of this term, minerals remarkable for hardness, lustre, beauty of colour, and transparency, as well as for their rarity in nature. But, beyond these manifest endowments, the Gems proper, together with several other stones of less commercial value, are to be highly prized, as of yore by the ancients, on account of their so-called spiritual powers, and their subtle health-restoring virtues. A main purpose of the volume now undertaken is to vindicate on sound, and even scientific, grounds the confidence reposed by our forefathers in Precious Stones for remedial uses, whether by outward wear, or by other such means as were inspired by nature and gleaned by simple experience. "The estimation in which these Flowers of the Mineral Kingdom have been held from the very earliest ages, alike by the most refined, and the most barbarous nations is little short of wonderful; insomuch that Gems do really seem to exercise occult charms which cause them to have always been widely coveted from the first." It is noteworthy that tropical countries are far more prolific in affording Precious Stones than other parts of the globe; wherefore it would seem as if those lands on which the sun shines with most power and splendour produce Gems the more abundantly; perhaps, too, the volcanic changes to which these lands are subject have something to do with the matter! The said Gems are found mostly in the older formations, such as Granite, Gneiss, etc., and in the beds of rivers, whither they have been brought by torrents, and generally accompanied by some of the precious metals. Furthermore, several kinds of Gems are frequently found together. The various mineral components which enter into the formation of these Gems are plentiful throughout the globe.

In primitive English days "Christiani fidem in verbis; Judæi in lapidibus pretiosis; et Pagani in herbis ponere solebant." Christians were wont to pin their faith on words (of Holy Writ); the Jews trusted in precious stones; the Pagans relied upon herbs of the field.

This trust in the curative virtues of certain Precious Stones was transmitted from the early ages to a comparatively late period. In the Church of Old Saint Paul's, London, was a famous Sapphire, which had been given by Richard de Preston, Citizen and Grocer of that City, for the cure of infirmities in the eyes of all those thus afflicted who might resort to it. So likewise had Robert Grosseteste, a former Bishop of Lincoln, when at Oxford, invented charms for expelling diseases, with certain words for exorcising fiends, and other mysterious characters of marvellous power which were inscribed on valuable Gems.

Vincentius (A.D. 434) said, when making mention of the Jasper, "Other, some Stones are also found figured and marked with the figure of a man bearing on his necke a bundle of hearbs and flowers; with the estimation and value of them noted that they have in them a facultie, or power restrictive, and will in an instant, or moment of time, staunch blood." "Such a kind of Stone (as it is reported) Galen wore on his finger."

As far back as in the year 1320, Nostradamus (quoting Pierre de Boniface, a noted Alchemist) wrote. "the Diamond renders a man invisible; the Agate of India, or Crete, eloquent, prudent, amiable, and agreeable; the Amethyst resists intoxication; the Carnelian appeases anger; the Hyacinth provokes sleep, etc." More recently, in the time of our lion-hearted Queen Elizabeth, it was said by Bishop Vaughan, in reference to her assumed power of healing scrofulous patients by the Royal touch, that she did it by virtue of some precious stone then in the possession of the English Crown, which Stone was endowed with this marvellous gift. "But," as Harrington drily observes, "had Queen Elizabeth been told that the Bishop ascribed more virtue to her Jewels (though she loved them dearly) than to her person, she would never have made him Bishop of Chester!"

According to Dr. Rowland's *Compleat Chymical Dispensatory*, as translated from the Latin of Dr. John Schroder (1669), the "Precious Stones, or Gemms, as classified in those days, were the Amethist, Carneolus, Sarda or Sardonyx, Chrysolite, Granate, Hyacinth, Rubin Oriental, Saphyre, Smaragde, Pearl, and Bezar Stone, East and West.

"Of which Gemms five were chiefly called Precious: the Granate, Hyacinth, Saphyre, Sardonix, Smaragde." "The Less Precious Stones were the Eaglestone, Alabaster, Amiantus, or Alum Plumous, Armenian Stone, Calaminaris, Crystal, Blood-stone, Jew-stone, Lyncurius, Lapis Lyncis, Load-stone, Marble, Nephritickstone, Osteocol, or Bone-Binder, Pumex-stone, Shiver-stone, Serpentine, Flint, Smirgle, Selenitis, or Specular-stone, Spunge-stone, Talce, (and Stone from a Man)."

Animal Stones, so called, were likewise formerly used medicinally; such as " stones or eyes, of Crabs, Carps, Pearches, Trouts; also Mother-of-Pearl, Egg-Shells, and Ostridge Egg-Shells." " All kinds of Stones taken from the Heads of Fishes, powdered, and drunk in Wine, were found to abate the Cholick, and to break the stone in the kidneys."

Again, other stones were found in certain creatures, and in many parts of them; yet " they are rare; and, besides Bezoar stone, there are scarce any in the Apothecaries' shops." " But it would be good to have some ready that break the stone in Man."

The curative virtues were held to be " stronger in Minerals than in Vegetable remedies," " because they are nearer the first original, and therefore more united, and by consequence stronger; for, strength united is stronger." " They are not given so that their Acrimony might be hurtful, but mixed with other things, serving the Physitian's intention, whereby the Acrimony is abated, and amended; so Chalcitis is put into Treacle; and Garlick into Sauce."

" The Operations, or Preparations by which Stones were to be made medicinal were chiefly these—(1) Poudering; (2) Calcination; (3) Purification, or Edulcoration; (4) Liquation; (5) Destillation, or Volatilisation; and sometimes (6) Syrupisation."

" Stones are best *Poudered*, first by grinding, then by Levigation, and sprinkling convenient water while you levigate, and bringing it into a pulp, and drying it in the Sun."

"*Calcination* is that by which Stones come to be Medicinal; and it is called rather a Solution. This is done by fire, simple, or restinct; or by Corrosion, and that with common Salt, or Sulphur, etc." "*Solution* of both Precious, and Vulgar Stones is made by divers Menstruums, whereinto the calcined stones are cast, and set in a hot place, so often have the Menstruum repeated till no more will be dissolved."

"*Liquation* is when the Salt of the Stones is set in a Glass, in a moist place, to turn to Liquor."

"*Volatilisation* is done when the Stones are dissolved, and digested with Spirits of Wine, fourteen days and nights, and destill'd often by a Retort."

"*Syrupisation* is made when you bring the Solution to a Syrup (with proper Juyce, as that of Citrons, or Barberries), with Sugar, and some convenient Water."

But with respect to Minerals, and Metals, whilst these General Faculties are self-evident, their Occult Faculties are not openly declared. "Our Ancestors were commonly busied in finding out only the Manifest Faculties. The Moderns have studied the Occult." Thus wrote Dr. Schroder, more than two centuries ago. With what fourfold force do his arguments apply in these advanced days of progressive scientific research, and of wonderful recent discoveries! Just one highly significant note is interposed by Schroder, which bears on our subject of Precious Stones, and the Nobler Metals. "You may see such Simples as make vehement evacuations, to grow rather in mountains, and in stony places, or between Rocks; where is the Natural seat of Metallick Spirits."

A later Work, *Magus;* or *The Celestial Intelligencer;* by Francis Barrett, Professor of Chemistry (1801):

dwells on "The occult Properties of Metals; Herbs; and Stones." But the Author is not entitled to equal acquiescence with his teachings as is Dr. Schroder; seeing that he claims excessive faith in Planetary Influences; and the pursuits of Alchemy; (e.g. by searching for the "Philosopher's Stone," which should convert whatever baser metal it might touch into Gold.)

Certain Metals are alleged by this fanciful writer, "Magus," to exercise natural "Antipathies." These are said to obtain through "an obstinate contrariety of Nature; such as the Sapphire Stone against hot bile, feverish heats, and diseases of the eyes. The Amethyst against drunkenness; the Jasper against the bloody flux; the Emerald against lust; Agates against poison; Coral against the black choler, and pains of the stomach; the Topaz against spiritual heats, such as covetousness, and all manner of love excesses."

In this way "a Diamond," saith he, "disagrees with a Loadstone, insomuch that being present it suffers no Iron to be drawn thereto." Thus likewise, "a Lion fears lighted torches, and is tamed by nothing sooner; a Horse fears a Camel so much that he cannot endure a picture of that beast; a Snake is afraid of a naked man, but pursues one clothed; Amber attracts all things to itself except Garden-Basil, and substances smeared with Oil, whereto it has a natural antipathy."

Vindicating his special doctrines and arguments as advanced in this Book (from which we have quoted the above occult teachings), Professor Barrett has defended his allegations and beliefs in a plausible Preface, certain parts of which read as follows:—

"We have not forgot to give the most clear and rational illustration of sympathy and antipathy;

attraction and repulsion. We have proved how cures are performed by virtue of sympathetic powers, and medicines, by Seals, rings, and Amulets, even at unlimited distances.

"We know how to communicate with any person, and to give him intimation of our purpose, at a hundred, or a thousand miles distance; but then a preparation is necessary, and the parties should have their appointed seasons, and hours for that purpose; likewise both should be of the same firm constancy of mind. And we have given methods by which a man may receive true and certain intimation of future things (as by dreams) of whatsoever his mind has before meditated upon, himself being properly disposed. All of which matters we have collected out of the Works of the most famous Magicians, such as Zoroaster, Hermes, Apollonius, Simon of the Temple, Trithemius, Agrippa, Porta (the Neapolitan), Dee, Paracelsus, Roger Bacon, and a great many others.

"Our endeavour has been to point out the difference of these several arts, so as to free the name of Magic from any scandalous imputation: seeing this is a word originally significative, not of any evil, but of every good and laudable science, such as a man might profit by, and become both wise and happy: and the practice is so far from being offensive to God, or man, that the very root and ground of all magic takes its rise from the Holy Scriptures; viz., 'The fear of God is the beginning of all wisdom'; which fear of God is the beginning of Magic; for, Magic is wisdom; and on this account the Wise Men were called 'Magi.' The Magicians were the first Christians; they were the first to acknowledge the glory, and majesty of our Saviour;

therefore let no one be offended at the venerable and sacred title of Magician, a title which every wise man merits while he pursues that path which Christ Himself trod; namely, Humility, Charity, Mercy, Fasting, Praying, etc.: for the true Magician is the truest Christian, and nearest disciple of our blessed Lord, Who set the example we ought to follow; since He says, 'If ye have faith, as a grain of mustard-seed, ye shall say unto this mountain, Remove hence to yonder place: and it shall remove.'"

Concerning Metals (about which, of the nobler sort, the Second Part of the present Manual treats), Dr. Schroder's *Chymical Dispensatory* goes on to say, "They are brought into three ranks, according to their conformity, and disparity of hardness; and according to their conveniency of preparations." "The First are the Noblest Metals; as Gold, and Silver." "The Second are the more ignoble, and hard; as Iron, and Copper." "The Third are the most ignoble, and soft; as Lead, and Tin."

"Metals are to be prepared by: (1) Purgation; (2) By Calcination; (3) By Volatilisation (by which the Metal is made of a spiritual nature); (4) By Extraction (whence come Tinctures); (5) By Sublimation (whence are Flowers); (6) By Salification (whence comes Salt)."

In the fifteenth, and sixteenth centuries, amongst British Professors of Physic, all their knowledge of Chemistry was very primitive. Furthermore, gross superstition prevailed, insomuch that Alchemy and Astrology occupied the minds and attention of these said Professors almost exclusively. Nevertheless, there were, even in those days, some few doctors of real learning, and repute, who found valid reasons for attributing medicinal and curative virtues to certain Precious Stones, and Metals.

Dr. John Schroder, "that most famous, and faithful Chymist," produced in 1669, "*The Compleat Chymical Dispensatory;* in Five Books; treating of All Sorts of Metals, Precious Stones, and Minerals; How rightly to Know Them. And How they are to be used in Physick; with their several Doses." "The like work being very proper for all Merchants, Druggists, Chirurgions, and Apothecaries; also for such ingenious persons as study Physick, or Philosophy." This learned Volume was written in Latin; and was afterwards Englished by William Rowland, Doctor of Physick, who had previously translated Hippocrates, Rivierus, Bartholinus, Platerus, Sennerius, Rulandus, Crato, and other ancient classical writers. It was "printed, and sold at the Sign of the 'Two Angels, and Crown,' in Little Brittain."

"To you, Noble Merchants," wrote Dr. Rowland, "I have presented this Work because during my long captivity in Algiers, Tunis, and Alexandria I received many favours from you, wherefore I studyed how I might in point of Gratitude do something with my Pen which might not only eternize your Names, but make you more acquainted with all things of the Creation wherein you Trade; as Metals, Precious Stones, and other Minerals; that you might be more quick sighted therein. And that you might (when you are constrained to be your own Physitians, as Travellers are used to be) be able to cure yourselves, and preserve the health of others." "With these Remedies (by God's assistance)

I have cured many, and doubt not but they will grow more and more in request. . . . It is *Medicina adepta : itaque, carpere vel noli nostra, vel ede tua.* Commend it; or Come, mend it."

"As for you, my Countrymen, that study Physick, and philosophy in your Mothr Tongue (not with intent to deceive the People by damnable Fortune-Telling, or Witchcraft), I humbly desire your kind acceptance of this my last Work in this kind of Physick.

"The Lord bless, and preserve you in all the wayes of Health, and Happiness : and give you both inward and outward riches, according to your publick Spirits, for the Honour of our God, King, and country. So prayeth your truly loving Countryman, and ready Servant, William Rowland."

And so piously beseecheth the present author. "The writing of 'Precious Stones, and Noble Metals,'"—as Kingsley said of *Westward Ho*, has "done him good." He has been "living among the primitive books of old Hebrew faith, Classic lore, and Elizabethan learning; among grand, devout, beautiful, silent men."

PRECIOUS STONES.

PRECIOUS stones are incorporated into all religions, being made to represent the noblest meanings, and the divinest attributes. Savage, and civilised nations alike hold them as among the most precious circumstances of human life. These morsels of ordinary materials, these mere crystals, composed of the commonest clays, and earths, have been deemed even sometimes by wise men more precious than liberty or life : who have felt themselves more richly endowed through the gift of gems than if they had become possessed of half the virtues, and all the knowledge possible to man. Perhaps we shall some day know the full meaning of this universal fascination, and learn the secret of the mysterious affinity so evidently existing between man and jewels.

It is more than possible, indeed, highly probable, that what the advanced mental science of to-day terms, after a pedantic fashion, " Psychometry," is largely concerned in this universal fascination exercised by precious stones. The said scientific art implies a supposed power of the human mind to discern the past history of inanimate objects by occult telepathic perceptions. The double constitution of the human mind, as recognised nowadays by all authorities, bears immediately upon this fundamental question. Broadly speaking, every man has two minds : the one " objective ; " the other " subjective." The former (objective) takes cognisance of the ordinary daily outside objective world, through the five bodily senses. The latter (subjective) perceives by intuition. This latter is the storehouse of memory, never forgetting any incident, however trifling, of the past individual life; nor omitting to record the same indelibly on its tablets of reserve. But, in order that this "subjective" mind may exercise its highest functions, whether of remote memory, or of recalling emotions long since absolutely forgotten, it can only act thus when the "objective" senses are, for the time being, in abeyance.

Probably our readers will think the above disquisition dry, and repellent at the commencement of a book such as our present projected treatise, which makes a promise of being light, and entertaining,—rather than scientific, and of stiff reading. But we straightway undertake, that, after advancing the argument thus adduced, our style shall be altogether free from any such philosophic pedantry. Nevertheless, this abstruse text was essential to be insisted on as embodying the main principle on which our descriptive, and discursive pages throughout the book will actually depend.

It was in former times a very common belief that all the nobler gems are sexual: also that they possess various mystic, yet intelligent qualities which bind them up in close relation with man. Thus they were all thought to represent certain spiritual, and moral virtues which would confer kindred powers on their wearers; also to detect the presence of poison; some of them turning dark, and obscure, and turbid; others pale, and sickly; some even shattering themselves to pieces in passionate despair, and abhorrence at the touch thereof.

When coming presently to the consideration of Crystals (among Precious Stones), and the strange faculty of Crystal-gazing, which certain persons can undoubtedly exercise, under proper conditions,—we shall dwell more at length (whilst without any prolix discourse) on this pertinent subject of double mentality.

But here it may be asked pointedly, to start with, what are some of the circumstances calculated to eclipse for the while that protective power, and guidance which our ordinary commonsense of every day life affords, and maintains, throughout its incidents, and course. Let us explain that chief among such circumstances are to be reckoned imminent drowning, febrile delirium, and some forms of insanity. The late Professor Denton produced during the latter part of his life a work which specially discusses, after a fashion easily comprehended. this science of Psychometry, under the plainer title of "The Souls of Things." Therein he has alleged confidently a power of the human mind to discern the past lifelong history of inanimate objects by telepathic (distance-reading) aid. Together with his sister, his wife, and some other persons who had been found to possess this telepathic power in a remarkable degree, Professor Denton made a long series of experiments. The particular branch of science to which the Professor devoted his usual daily life was geology: outside which he was also well versed in general knowledge and learning. His wife and sister were likewise highly cultivated persons, being particularly interested in those branches of learning in which the gifted Professor excelled. It was the habit of the Professor to select a geological specimen, or some fragment of a structure possessing historical interest, and to submit the same to his "hypnotised" coadjutors, so as to elicit their version of its history. His wife would then readily enter a partially "subjective" condition of mind, so that—

the relic being placed upon her head—she would at once pronounce a very plausible, and often times a most wonderfully accurate, history of the scenes which had been enacted within its former ancient environment. Thus, if the object happened to be a geological specimen, she would launch out into a glowing description of its surroundings when found; furthermore, going back into its history, before the earth's crust was formed, she would trace it down through the various geological changes it had experienced, until she finally landed it in the Professor's cabinet. Again, a piece of mortar, let us say from the ancient dwelling of Cicero, would be handed to her, and she would render a vivid description of the domestic life of those persons who had occupied the mansion, and would describe the several historic events which might have been witnessed from the former habitat of the said piece of mortar. And, so as to eliminate the factor of geological knowledge already possessed on her part, and thus perhaps emotionally reproduced, the professor would wrap the specimen in a piece of paper beforehand, and would in this way carefully conceal from her ordinary objective knowledge its particular character. But the result was always alike; she would read the history of the specimen under these guarded conditions with the same apparent accuracy as before. Again, the Professor did not forget that Telepathy (the faculty of distance-viewing which some persons can bring to bear under favourable conditions) was an element necessary to be likewise eliminated. The possibility that she might be thus reading what was in his own mind at the time, must also be therefore provided against. To secure which end he wrapped a considerable number of specimens in separate packages as nearly alike as they could be made, so that it was not possible for him to know them apart. One specimen after another would then be handed to her; and each would be described with the same accuracy as before. This was considered a supreme test; and the doctrine that "things," in common with "men," have (thus to say) "souls," was thought to have been demonstrated.

Our present contention is, that, granting the said hypothesis of the Professor to be true, Gems and Precious Stones retain within themselves a faithful and accurate record, even to its smallest detail, of physical conditions, and acquired properties, from the primitive time of their original molecular beginning; and that, if we allow a suspension for the while of the wearer's ordinary perceptions, as commonly exercised, the Precious Stone in use will continue to assert meantime its long-remembered virtues, for his, or her, welfare (or the reverse), mental, and bodily.

Thus the salutary sunlight stored up from past ages, in tropical regions, the electric endowments from volcanic furnaces, the marine boons derived from many waters, and the remedial virtues of many curative herbs, may come to react, healthfully, and beneficially, for the good of the fortunate owner, and for that of the modestly confident wearer. Reasoning after which convincing, yet plain-sailing fashion, we may readily comprehend how to a right-minded wearer, when debilitated by the wearisome exactions of a London season, the Diamond, by its adamantine brilliancy, representing, as it does, the sublimated sunshine of many tropical æons, may be found to supply renovated strength and vigour; how the Corundum group of Gems (including the Sapphire, the Ruby, and the Oriental Amethyst: each identical in composition, though possessing diversities of colour, and of optical properties) may exercise for the benefit, or restoration to health, of invalid owners the tonic effects of Aluminium oxide, their common basis of structure; how the Ruby (composed essentially of Alumina, one part, and Magnesia one part), may, by virtue of its metallic oxides, of Iron, Copper, and Chromium, renovate the bloodless patient, bringing back the rich hue of convalescence, together with vital force, "renewed like the eagle's"; how the Turquoise, by its phosphates, may confer fresh brain-powers; how the Brazilian Topaz may endow the bony skeleton during youthful growth with a continuous solidity of frame (developing on into the adventurous miner, or the bold, successful colonist), by virtue of its Silicon, and its Fluorine,—thus steadily incorporated; how the Garnets likewise (employed as inlaid stones in Celtic, and Anglo-Saxon jewellery) by their oxides of Iron, and Magnesium, can prove of admirable help to bloodless wearers. Why the vitreous Opal—containing, as it does, from nine to ten parts of water when lustrous and bright (but liable to become dry, and therefore dull; and, moreover, because fragile of texture, soon growing greasy)—is for these several reasons unpopular, and deemed unlucky for those persons who venture to adopt it; why Amber has deservedly gained an antiseptic reputation (as against such bacterial maladies as whooping cough, putrid sore throat, etc.) because of its innate sulphur; why Pearls (as secreted by the mantle of the Pearl-Oyster from the depths of the Persian Gulf, or of Australian seas) whilst charming to view because of their iridescent sheen, have become credited from earliest times with salutary marine influences, as exerted for the physical welfare of their owners, and wearers.

But the indispensable conditions for realising any of the advantages which have now been discussed as possible, and even probable, from a personal use of these specified Gems must comprise absolute purity of life, with a frank, open, guileless, receptive mind. These said essential requirements will be dealt with more fully, and explicitly, when we come to consider the Crystals (Beryl, Aquamarine, and Chrysoberyl), as intimately associated with the practice of Crystal-gazing, and with the professors of that art. From earliest days these professors have insisted that the Crystal-reader, or gazer, must be a boy, or a young virgin, of unsophisticated mind, innocent of sexual desires, fearing God, and His Angels, whilst given to pious prayer, and praise. Under such auspicious conditions the "subjective" mind dominates, whilst the ordinary objective faculties are (favourably) in complete abeyance.

It need scarcely be added that to wear costly jewels merely for ostentatious display, or because attempting to indicate thereby the implied wealth of their owner, must gravely depreciate the intrinsic worth of any such Gems (almost priceless though they may be) for influencing the character, or welfare, beneficially, of their possessor. Moreover, in such a case the jewels would visibly suffer a loss of their natural lustre, or of their acquired perfect polish. And an intelligible reason is thus afforded which explains the well-known circumstance that jewels which have got to betray a lack of their lustre, and brilliancy, because habitually worn by an owner who is sick, or sorry, or under the pressure of adversity, will recover their pristine brilliancy, and beauty of colour, with a conspicuous attractiveness, if lent for temporary wear to a differently constituted, and more happily circumstanced friend, who is blithehearted, sincere, and of childlike simplicity of motive, and purpose.

> "Integer vitæ, scelerisque purus
> Non eget Mauri, jaculis neque arcu;
> Nec venenatis gravida sagittis,
> Fusce, pharetra."

> "Fuscus; the man of life upright, and pure,
> Needeth not javelin, nor bow of Moor:
> Nor arrows tipped with venom deadly sure
> Loading his quiver."

The belief that certain Precious Stones can exercise the virtue of betraying the presence of poison by sweating, is mentioned by Holinshed (1577). In speaking about the death of King John, he says : " And thereupon the King suspected them (the Pears) to be poisoned; indeed this by reason that such precious stones as he had about him cast forth a certain sweat, as it were bewraeing the poison," etc., etc.

Plato (B.C. 400) supposed the origin of Precious Stones to be the vivifying spirit abiding in the stars, which converts the most vile and putrid matter into the most perfect objects.

As already stated, the Twelve Stones which were in the Breast-plate of the High Priest were : the Sard, the Topaz, the Carbuncle, or Ruby, the Emerald, the Sapphire, the Diamond, the Ligure, the Agate, the Amethyst, the Beryl, the Onyx, and the Jasper. On the shoulder-knot were likewise two Onyx stones, engraved with the names of the twelve tribes, to each of which one or the other of these stones was consecrated. The Shekinah in the Breast-plate became obscured with a sombre darkness which came over the Stones when the anger of the Lord was kindled. [One account tells that it was a special stone among the twelve—the Sapphire—which was the sensitive agent of this adverse manifestation. But when the Lord was graciously at peace with His people, the light of Heaven shone brightly on the stones of the sacred Ephod.

The Jews had a tradition that when, on the Day of Atonement, the High Priest asked forgiveness by the Almighty for the sins of the whole nation, then if such forgiveness was granted, the stones in the Urim and Thummim shone forth most brightly; but if forgiveness was withheld, then the Precious Stones became black of colour. By reason of these occult phenomena the Magi of the East, believing that remarkable virtues must have been inherent in the contexture of Precious Stones which formed the Breastplate of the High Priest, adopted a research into this occult knowledge of Gems as a branch of their magical system. From that remote date even down to the present time Precious Stones worn as jewels have been believed to indicate the state of health of their possessor, or of the donors thereof. If the stones turned dull, their owners were conjectured to be ill, or in danger; and when becoming actually opaque or colourless, they gave rise to the most dismal forebodings.

Camillus Leonardus, a Physician of Pisaro, in Italy, wrote (1502) *The Mirror of Stones*, as dedicated to Cæsar Borgia, his patron. Treating therein about the virtues of jewels, he said, " Whatever can be thought of as beneficial to mankind may be confirmed to them by the virtues of Stones." " Yet this is to be noted, that in Precious Stones there is sometimes one virtue, sometimes two, sometimes three, and sometimes many; and that these virtues are not caused by the beauty of the Stones, since some of them are most unsightly, and yet have a great virtue; and sometimes the most beautiful have none at all, and therefore we may safely conclude, with the most famous doctors, that there are virtues in Stones as well as in other things; but how this is effected is variously controverted." "Do we not witness the magnet attract iron? the sapphire curing a grievous carbuncle? and the like in many others?"

"There is," saith the Author of *Precious Stones: their History and Mystery* (1880), "a strange fascination in Precious Stones. It is not surprising that they should have been held in peculiar veneration by the ancients, when other objects, infinitely less attractive and important, were supposed to be endowed with supernatural attributes; but it is a matter for wonder why the mysterious properties ascribed to them should have survived the growth of ages, and still find believers." "In the region of faith which our forefathers respected, a man fortified with the protecting ægis of a charmed Jewel would brave the greatest perils; and, probably through the force of his conviction as to its efficacy, would pass unscathed through dangers where another person, without having such helpful influences realised in his imagination, would straightway succumb."

Some such a potent reason as this may actually underlie the well known Oriental passion of Eastern chiefs for rare and costly jewels. Mysticism, and an insight into the occult, are special attributes of the Oriental mind: whilst the "astral conditions recognised thereby (under which the ordinary mental perceptions are subordinated, and the objective mind gains a temporary ascendency) prevail."

That precious stones possess occult powers, and can exercise physical virtues, is a fact beyond all dispute. These faculties are independent of the mere beauty, lustre, splendour, rarity, and hardness of the gems, though such endowments make them supremely prized. Biblical history affords the earliest attestation of these mystic, even spiritual attributes. As related in the Book of Exodus, it was through a divine inspiration exercised on the heart of the High Priest when wearing the Ephod (of gold, of blue, of purple, and of scarlet) with its two stones upon the shoulders, whereupon was bound the Breastplate of Jewels, and whereto—by its hem—golden bells, and pomegranates (blue, and purple, and scarlet,) were attached, that Aaron became enabled to interpret the Urim and Thummim before the Lord in the Holy place. "And they shall be upon Aaron's heart when he goeth in before the Lord; And it shall be upon Aaron to minister." Such were the marvellous influences of Precious Stones combined together, in four rows, as ordained by divine command, and worn over the human heart, in the patriarchal times of Moses and Aaron. Modern speculation cannot but ask, in all devoutness, would the like combination of Precious Stones, set (piously, and prayerfully) by a modern Master-Jeweller, and worn by the hierarch of a Christian Church, inspire him with any similar special spiritual power, and zeal? settings of Stones, even in four rows; a Sardius (Cornelian), a Topaz, and a Carbuncle; an Emerald, a Sapphire, and a Diamond; a Ligure, an Agate, and an Amethyst; a Beryl, and an Onyx, and a Jasper?

Turning—somewhat abruptly, it may seem—to a secular instance of wondrous qualities developed by Precious Stones when combined in a single Jewel, we read concerning *"Mr. Isaacs"* (otherwise Abdul Hafiz-ben-Isak) in that remarkable Eastern story by Marion Crawford, 1899 : " Though Mr. Isaacs was endowed with exceptional gifts of beauty by a bountiful nature, these were by no means what first attracted the attention of the observer." " I was enthralled, and fascinated by his eyes. I once saw in France a jewel composed of six precious stones, each a gem of great value, so set that they appeared to form but one solid mass, yielding a strange radiance that changed its hue at every movement, and which multiplied the sunlight a thousandfold. Were I to seek a comparison for my friend's eyes, I might find one in this masterpiece of the jeweller's art. They were dark, and of remarkable size ; there was a depth of life, and vital light in them that told of the pent-up force of a hundred generations of Persian Magii. They blazed with the splendour of a god-like nature, needing neither meat, nor strong drink to feed its power."

" Every Precious Stone has its special virtue," as Madame De Barrera, 1860, learnedly testified ; " the more precious the Stone, the more powerful its virtues." Of Pharmacopœias, the oldest one counted amongst its most sovereign remedies a costly compound called the " Five Precious Fragments," which consisted of powdered Rubies, Topazes, Emeralds, Sapphires, and Hyacinths. Antiquity and the Middle Ages believed as implicitly in the influence of Stones, (and Plants) as in that of the heavenly bodies. There is an Oriental tradition that Abraham wore a precious stone round his neck which preserved him from disease, and which cured sickness if looked upon. When the patriarch died God placed this stone in the Sun; hence arose the Hebrew proverb, "When the Sun rises the disease will abate." The Oriental Ruby, or Carbuncle of the ancients, gave warning by a change in its colour if misfortune threatened the wearer, becoming much darker in hue. When the peril, or evil was averted the stone resumed its former brilliant tint. Wolfganogus Gabelschoverus relates the following incident: "On the fifth day of December, 1600 after the birth of Christ Jesus, as I was going with my beloved wife (of pious memory) from Stutgard to Caluna, I observed by the way that a very fine Ruby which I wore mounted in a gold ring (the which she had given me) lost repeatedly, and each time almost completely, its splendid colour, and that it assumed a sombre blackish hue, which blackness lasted not one day, but several; so much so that, being greatly astonished, I drew the ring from my finger, and put it into a casket. I also warned my wife that some evil followed her, or me, the which I augured from the change in the Ruby. And truly I was not deceived; for, within a few days she was taken mortally sick. After her death the Ruby recovered its pristine colour, and brilliancy."

Even in the primitive times of the Roman Empire this principle of physical effects, for good, or evil, resulting to the body through outward instrumentalities acting immediately on its exterior, next the skin, was recognised, and believed in. The old classic fable of Nessus, and his shirt, is an illustration in point. When wounded to the death by an arrow shot from across a river by Hercules, to avenge the rape of his wife, (Dejinira), this Nessus craftily gave to Dejinira his shirt stained with blood from the mortal wound, alleging with his dying breath that the shirt would insure conjugal fidelity for the future on the part of its wearer. Long afterwards, being accorded the shirt by Dejinira, Hercules clothed himself therewith, and died straightway from its fatal effects on his body.

Somewhat similarly in modern English times a curative power became attributed to the noted piece of linen which was said to have been dipped in the blood of the martyred King Charles the First, immediately after his decapitation on Whitehall scaffold. Sir William Wilde, when a boy, saw this "Foil-a-ree," or "King's blood;" by which name the rag thus exsanguined with the Royal blood was then known. "Hundreds of persons came to be touched with the "Foil-a-ree," by Abbot Prendergast (the Revd. Peter Prendergast), last Lord Abbot of Cong. Sir William, whose father lived in Connaught, has left these facts on record forty years ago; adding that, when last heard of, the very same rag (as curative of the King's Evil) was in the possession of a family near Ballandine : "so that it is more than probable the 'Foil-a-ree' is preserved to this day, near Aughrim, in Connaught." Again, Mark Antony exclaimed, we remember, in his famous funeral oration over the body of Julius Cæsar :—

"Let but the commons hear this testament—[the Will]—
"And they would go and kiss dead Cæsar's wounds,
And dip their napkins in his sacred blood."

A collection of Gems and Precious Stones in ancient Rome bore the name of a "dactylotheca." Robert Grosseteste, Bishop of Lincoln (1235-1254), when at Oxford, invented charms for expelling diseases, which were inscribed on Precious Stones. This excellent Bishop was learned, not only in theology, but likewise in both law and medicine. "Probably no one had a greater influence than himself on English literature for the two centuries following his time."

Roger Bacon said of him, "*Solus unus ut Dominus Robertus Lincolniensis Episcopus præ aliis hominibus scivit scientias; cujus comparatio ad omnes doctores modernos est velut comparatio Solis ad Lunam quando eclipsatur.*"

This Bishop Grosseteste (who died 1524) was buried in the Transept of Lincoln Cathedral with great honour. It was said that a miraculous oil issued from his tomb; wherefore one of the Canons was regularly appointed custodian thereof.

Tyssington pronounced respecting the said Prelate that, "at the table of bodily refreshment he was hospitable, eloquent, courteous, pleasant, and affable; at the spiritual table devout, tearful, and contrite." To a preaching Friar, whose health was broken, the Bishop commended an old Salernitan maxim:—

"Si tibi deficiant medici,—medici tibi fiant
Hæc tria; mens hilaris, requies, moderata dieta."

"If doctors fail, trust more to Nature's care—
Good spirits, quietude, and frugal fare."

To another Friar, oppressed with melancholy, he gave counsel to drink a cup of good wine; quoting the Latin line: "*Gignit et humores melius vinum meliores.*"

But, far better than any alcoholic drink for realising the refrain of that familiar old song, "Away with Melancholy," will it be to follow the cheery advice of our modern writer, Dickens, and to put the trust in animal spirits as inspired by all the beauties and delights of out-door nature—(*Barnaby Rudge*, chapter xxv.):—

" Ye men of gloom, and austerity, who paint the face of Infinite Benevolence with an eternal frown; read in the Everlasting Book, wide open to your view, the lesson it would teach. Its pictures are not in black and sombre hues, but bright and glowing tints; its music, save when ye drown it, is not in sighs and groans, but songs, and cheerful sounds. Listen to the million voices in the summer air, and find one dismal as your own. Remember, if ye can, the sense of hope, and pleasure which every glad return of day awakens in the breast of all your kind who have not changed their nature; and learn some wisdom (even from the witless Barnaby) when their hearts are lifted up they know not why, by all the mirth and happiness it brings."

Rabbi Benoni—already told about—of the fourteenth century, who was said to be one of the most profound alchemists of his time, affirmed, with respect to Precious Stones, that " the Agate quenches thirst, if held in the mouth, and soothes fever; the Amethyst banishes the desire for drink, and promotes chastity; the Garnet preserves health, and joy; the Sapphire impels to all good things, like the Diamond; the red Coral is a cure for indigestion when kept constantly next the person; Amber is curative of sore throat, and glandular swellings; the Crystal promotes sweet sleep, and good dreams; the Emerald strengthens friendship, and constancy of mind; the Onyx is a demon imprisoned in stone, who wakes only of a night, causing terror, and disturbance to sleepers who wear it; the Opal is fatal to love, and sows discord between the giver and receiver; the Topaz is favourable for all hæmorrhages, and imparts strength, with good digestion; the Loadstone, Sapphire, and Diamond, are each capable of producing somnambulism;

and when combined into a talisman, they attract such powerful planetary spirits as render the bearer almost invisible."

Marlowe in his (Rich) *Jew of Malta*, 1633, has told about Eastern superiority as to its wealth, and magnificence of Precious Stones, and rare Gems:—

"Give me the Merchants of the Indian Mines,
That trade in Metal of the purest mould;
The wealthy Moor that in the Eastern rocks
Without control can pick his riches up,
And in his house, heap Pearls like pebble-stones;
Receive them free, and sell them by the weight.

Bags of fiery Opals, Sapphires, Amethysts,
Jacinth, hard Topaz, grass-green Emeralds,
Beauteous Rubies, sparkling Diamonds,
And seld-seen costly Stones, of so much price
As one of them, indifferently rated,
And of a carect of this quantity,
May serve, in peril of calamity,
To ransom great Kings from captivity."

"In olden times," writes Harry Emanuel, F.R.G.S., *On Diamonds and Precious Stones*, 1867, " the Monarchs of the East, with their fondness for display, and pomp, decorated—as likewise they now do,—their horse-trappings, their thrones, and their persons with gems; long even before they knew how to cut these: and they attributed—as also at the present day—magical and talismanic powers thereto. This belief has been, and still remains, shared by almost every nation. Even in our own country many persons nowadays wear about them a Turquoise, in the full belief that it preserves them from contagion." This gem, the Turquoise, in old Roman times was conceived to have an affinity with its possessor, or master, and to change colour as his state of health varied; and it is a positive fact that some Turquoises do alter in colour under differing conditions;

the supposed cause of such variation being atmospheric mutations, and gradations of temperature.

During the visit of the (then) Prince of Wales to India in 1876, Sir Jung Bahadur, when presented, was thus described by one who witnessed the ceremony.

"No Gnome King, in a gorgeous Pantomime, ever shone, in the midst of electric, or magnesium light, and blue fire, half so splendidly as the Nepaulese Minister. His skull-cap, "parsemi" with Pearls, was surrounded with a triple row of Emeralds, Rubies, and Diamonds, together with pendants of the same. From his Aigrette, representing the Sun (which was an enormous Ruby) rose the double-eyed Peacock's feather. This was again surmounted by a beautiful plume of Bird of Paradise feathers, curved backwards. His tunic, of purple satin, lined with the softest and finest fur, was embroidered exquisitely, and set with rich Pearls. Over his breast he wore the Riband of the Bath, and Star of India. His sword was Diamond-hilted; the sheath rich with Jewels."

It is still true that Eastern peoples venerate, while they delight in, the mystic phantasies of the mineral world: the hieroglyphic Agate; the luck-assuring "Cat's-eye;" the ominous Moonstone; the unlucky Tourmaline, and the Carbuncle, each aglow with malignant fire. All the human affections and passions are believed by them to be under the influence of Gems; each Gem again having its tutelary sprites, who direct its powers, for good, or evil. From the cradle to the grave, in sickness, or in health, in prosperity, or adversity, the Oriental takes counsel of a Jewel, or seeks its help; and no circumstance of his life is without its precedent of subjection to the potent agencies of the "Precious Stones."

But far more magnificent in his royal display of costly jewels, rich raiments, and splendid caparisons, was the famous Tudor progenitor of our present Monarch (if the chroniclers of that time—1540—may be believed), the uxorious Henry VIII, who, as Hall relates, when he met his new bride, the Princess Anne of Cleves, on Blackheath, January 3rd, " was all ablaze with gold, and jewellery."

" The King's Highness was mounted on a goodly courser, trapped in rich cloth of gold, traversed lattice-wise square, all over embroidered with gold of damask, pearled on every side of the embroidery; the buckles, and pendants were all of fine gold. His person was apparelled in a coat of purple velvet, somewhat made like a frock, all over embroidered with flat gold of damask, with small lace mixed between, of the same gold; and other laces of the same so going traverse-wise; which garment was a rich guard, very curiously embroidered; the sleeves, and breast were cut, lined with cloth of gold, and ty'd together with great buttons of Diamonds, Rubies, and Orient Pearl; his sword, and sword-girdle, adorned with stones, especial Emerodes; his night-cap garnished with Stone; but his bonnet was so rich with jewels that few men could value them. Beside all this, he wore, in baudrick-wise, a collar of such Balystes, and Pearls, that few men ever saw the like. And, notwithstanding that this rich apparel, and precious jewels were pleasant to the Nobles, and all other being present to behold, yet, his princely countenance, his goodly personage, and royal gesture, so far exceeded all other creatures being present that in comparison of his person all his rich apparel was little esteemed."

The Royal Pair were conducted in splendid state to Greenwich, and on to Westminster, where they were married. A few months afterwards they were divorced; and on August the 8th of the same year, Catherine Howard was declared Queen of England.

Lord Curzon, in describing the Palace of the late Shah of Persia, as it was during 1889, helps to confirm this impression of Oriental love for precious stones, the precious metals, and a profuse display of splendid gems about their palaces, and their persons.

He tells of Royal crowns, superb tiaras, a throne covered with Rubies and Emeralds, a globe of Jewels worth three hundred thousand pounds, and a glass case containing a vast heap of Pearls. There was also the Peacock Throne, encrusted with Diamonds, of fabulous value; and the celebrated "Sea of Light"—sister Diamond to the Koh-i-noor. Moreover, an occult faith in special virtues attached to these rich possessions still obtains implicitly in the Eastern mind.

Later on, Mr. Fraser, visiting the same Palace, found himself surrounded by a mass of wealth unequalled in the world. "Down each side of the room were chairs covered entirely with sheeted gold; and at intervals were tables of gold (but nailed with the commonest of cheap, black-headed tacks). The Throne itself, which has been valued at five million pounds sterling, and is probably worth more than two million pounds, is a great camp-bed structure encrusted from end to end, and from top to bottom, with Diamonds. At the back is a star of Brilliants which makes the eyes blind."

Again, Mr. T. P. O'Connor, writing about the new Shah, 1907, says that this new Sovereign, Mahomed Ali, "succeeds to what is without doubt the most magnificent kitchen in the whole world : more like a palace than a kitchen; as the ceiling is of costly lacquer, and the pillars which support it are of marble, and onyx. The stoves, poker, and tongs, and even the coffee-mill, are of solid silver; and all that is not made of silver is formed of copper, heavily gilt. The dishes, and the plates, likewise the knives, and forks and spoons, are all made of solid gold; and the plates, and dishes are, in addition, set with hundreds of precious stones. The value of the Shah's kitchen, and dining-room, has been estimated by a European traveller, who knows Teheran well, as at least a million sterling."

The inventory of jewel-treasures left by the late Shah of Persia shows their value to be about ten millions sterling. The old crown of the Persian dynasty holds a Ruby as large as a hen's egg. A belt, studded with Diamonds, worn only on great State occasions, is appraised at several hundred thousand pounds. A wonderful silver vase is decorated with a hundred superb Smaragds. A sword with a Diamond-covered scabbard is worth a quarter of a million sterling. One remarkable object among the collection is a square block of Amber (of four hundred cubic inches) which is said to have dropped from the skies in the time of Mahomet.

At Teheran, these jewels left by the late Shah have been valued by his successor; a thing that has never been done before. Among the same are several Diamonds which have not their equals in the world. The ancient crown of the Persian sovereigns, which the Shah only wears on State occasions, is covered with valuable precious stones, and is worth something like half a million sterling.

But, notwithstanding this widespread fascination,

as to the innate immaterial essences of power for good, or ill, which Precious Stones most indubitably exercise on their possessors, and wearers, (these psychic qualities being the true secret of their supreme value, and their marvellous attractiveness from all time,) the man of mere hard matter-of-fact, short-sighted chemical science, (so-called), is either actually blind, or else in his arrogance wilfully adverse.

Thus, in a Handbook on *Precious Stones*, considered in their scientific, and artistic relations, as " Printed for the Committee of Council on Education " (South Kensington Museum,) 1891. By A. H. Church, of Oxford ; Professor of Chemistry in the Royal Academy of Arts,"—it is stated (in Chapter I), " As Precious Stones have simply to be looked-at, and worn, or used in decorative work, it will be readily understood why no occult property is of much moment in determining their value ! Individual, and learned amateurs may indeed value a Stone according to what they know of its History, its Romance, its Memories, or the curiousness of its components ; but in nine hundred and ninety-nine cases out of a thousand any enhancement of value through such causes is out of the question." " Still, from the Mineralogical, and Chemical points of view, it is perhaps legitimate to import some elements of interest when appraising the right of a Stone to be called ' Precious ' for its place in the list of Gems " !

Almost all Gems conceal their true physical beauties whilst in a natural state. The Diamond in the rough is most unattractive ; and would be thrown away by a casual observer as a worthless pebble ; its perfections are hidden by a hard crust which can only be removed by its own powder.

"The deep velvety hue of the Sapphire, the glowing brilliant red of the Ruby, the still clear green of the Emerald, and the delicate strata of the Onyx, alike, only display themselves in their true character after the lapidary has expended his skill in cutting them into facets, and polishing them; on the perfection of which operations depend in a great measure the physical beauty of the Gems." "Many pure, and perfect Jewels have been irretrievably spoilt by unskilful hands." Precious stones come under the name of "*Gems*" when cut, and polished by the Lapidary. Marbodus has said (1740):—

"Gemmis a Gummi nomen posuere priores,
   Quod transplenderent Gummi splendentis ad instar."
"Jewels of old were *Gems*—thus named from *Gums*,
   Which shine transplendent: so do precious Stones."

In an old Poem; translated 1750:—flowers are given the preference:—

"Quid cupis Gemmas? quid avarus, et spe
   Fessus? insana nimis alto quæris?
 —Carpe contentus facili rubentes
   Tramite flores."
"If Gems we seek, we only tire,
   And lift our hopes too high;
 —The constant Flowers that line our way
   Alone can satisfy."

True it is that thus hath moralized a former Philosopher, sad of spirit! But none the less hopefully, and interestedly we turn our present best attention to the comprehensive, and promising subjects of "Precious Stones," and "The Nobler Metals."

A certain belief, which is more or less superstitious, and which hails from Poland, is of late gaining credit in this country, even amongst educated, and sensible persons, that each month in the year is associated with, and under the influence of, some one, or another Precious Stone : which particular influence is exercised throughout life upon every individual, according to the special virtues, or evil tendencies attached to his, or her particular natal stone of the month. (One established catalogue of such Mascots, or personal monthly natal stones, limits them to only ten months of the year.) Thus :

For *January* — the Jacinth, or Garnet (whose possessors are likely to be faithful, and true).

February—the Amethyst.

March—the Bloodstone.

April—the Sapphire ; or the Diamond (which endows with the virtues of love, joy, and purity).

May—the Emerald.

June—the Agate : Chrysoprase (emblematic of eloquence, and good luck).

July—the Cornelian ; or the Ruby (protecting from harm by aught which is poisonous).

August—the Sardonyx.

September—the Chrysolite : or (according to some authorities) the Sapphire.

October—the Aqua-Marine ; or the Opal.

November—the Topaz : Cat's Eye (Chryso-beryl).

December—the Turquoise ; or the Malachite.

(It may be noted that the Turquoise is credited with the property of securing friendly regard ; thus coming to verify the traditional saying that " he, or she, who owns a Turquoise will never want a friend.")

Again, a fashion has more recently come back into vogue of claiming some particular lucky Stone for each day in the week. We are now told by those persons who hold this modern revived notion, that every weekday has its separate Stone, which forebodes good, or evil for that day's proceedings; insomuch that those who believe most firmly, (or, superstitiously) in this creed, even go so far as to refuse to embark upon a journey, to start any new scheme, or venture even to give any social entertainment, without donning a brooch, or putting on a ring, or a bangle containing the protective jewel of the particular week-day. Sunday is, of all days, that upon which the Ruby should be worn; and the deeper its colour the more propitious the Gem.

On Monday, the Moon-stone should be worn; so as to woo good luck; though this is not thought to be the most fortunate of Jewels. On Tuesday, mishaps may be thwarted by adopting pink, and white, Coral as personal adornments; Emeralds are favourable to Wednesday; and Cat's Eyes to Thursday. On Friday, the woman who puts on her Diamonds may rest content to believe she has done her best towards courting good luck throughout this day, which is so commonly regarded as an ominous one. On Saturday, the Sapphire, if worn as a personal ornament, will ensure happiness, and success; this beautiful Stone being regarded as the truer harbinger of prosperity than any of the other seven.

This same cult of Birth Stones has become again of late accredited, and practised, by persons even of note, and education. February, the Amethyst month, comes in for special distinction, including, as it proudly does, the birthday of our much loved Princess Royal, whose Mother, the Queen, possesses matchless Amethysts, which she wore for the first time, it is said, at the wedding of Prince, and Princess Alexandra, of Teck.

The Queen never wears Opals; though she owns a casket of very beautiful specimens. The traditional characteristic attributes of the Amethyst are pronounced to be a power of preserving from strong passions; and of securing mental tranquillity. One of Queen Alexandra's favourite trinkets is a peculiar pendant, made of a large gold nugget, upon the top of which is a little hunchback, in green Enamel. By touching a secret spring the nugget flies open, and reveals a small Jade heart, made from New Zealand Greenstone, (sometimes called the Paunamu Stone). This Jewel was given by the late Duke of Clarence to his mother; who frequently wears it, and calls it her *porte bonheur*.

Certain other persons who are more or less well known in Society, and the birthdays of whom occur in December, swear by the Turquoise (the particular endowments conferred by which are "brilliant good fortune, with success, and happiness in every circumstance of life"). For example, Lady Wicklow, Lady Margaret Sackville, and Miss Helen Henniker, are observed to always wear some Turquoise ornaments.

Again, the Opal, often deemed unlucky, but credited, nevertheless, with the virtue of inspiring hope, though linked with misfortune, is said to bring special good fortune to those of its wearers who were born in the month of October. Among notabilities who lay claim to this distinction are the Queen Victoria Eugenie, of Spain; the Lady Deerhurst, and Lady Arabella Romilly. Likewise Madame Sara Bernhardt wears Opals, because she was born in October; though her favourite "Mascots" are a girdle of Cameos, and a necklace of nuggets, which was given to her by miners in California. New Zealand Jade is much favoured by some women who are well known in Society; Mary, Lady Gerard, is seldom seen without a bracelet of this Stone, which is the birth-stone dedicated to September; as also is the Chrysolite, contributing prudence, and preserving from folly. Mrs. Brown Potter was born in May, the Emerald month. She wears, for luck, an Emerald ring, and often an Emerald necklace. To "love, and to be successful in love," are the privileges secured by the wearers of this precious Stone.

Because they are a relic of Orientalism, stones set *en Cabochon* (not cut, but only polished) are in high favour nowadays with the Russian Royal Family. The Czar, Czarina, and the Duchess of Saxe-Coburg Gotha, make a point of giving *Cabochon* stones when sending presents to their friends. Those persons who admire such settings find these Russian Sapphires, and Rubies, with their gleaming uncut polish, incomparable. It was our King Edward, with Queen Alexandra, who started the fashion of getting old Jewels re-set after this fashion.

In the matter of Crown Jewels nowhere are there so many fine stones to be seen as in St. James's Palace; and there, the Diamond reigns supreme. Again, the Georgian Sapphire which was placed in the front of the bandeau supporting King Edward's Crown is the largest in the world. Queen Alexandra always makes the great Koh-i-noor Diamond (which belonged before the Indian Mutiny to Maharajah Dhuleep Singh, deposed,) her principal ornament at all the Courts, following in this the example of the late Queen Victoria. It was set for the Coronation in the front of Queen Alexandra's Crown; which was formed exclusively of

Diamonds; but immediately after, it reverted to its old place as a brooch. King Edward's companion Coronation Jewel, the wonderful Black Prince Ruby, has a history. It was presented to the Black Prince by Don Pedro; was lost on the French field of battle; and, when found, had the bad fortune to be delivered into the hands of the rough Court Jewellers of those times, who felt so little respect for such marvellous gems that they actually drilled three holes through the Ruby, to hold the Prince's feathers. The two Queens of Italy have a fondness for wearing Pearls, both black and white; their collection of these Jewels being the finest in the world.

"Dumb Jewels often in their silent kind,
More than quick words, do move a woman's mind."
Two Gentlemen of Verona.

Ancient faiths held that planetary influences (such as we now consider magnetic, and electric) radiate into space, and become focussed by their responding Precious Stones; to some one of which each month of the year is specially dedicated: and a belief follows that persons wearing a stone to which the particular month in which his, or her birthday occurs, stands dedicated, will be thus rendered subject to the planetary influences (good, or bad) by which such month is regulated in its course. Thus the creed, now revived, of suitable Birthday Stones, selected in accordance with this doctrine, is amply justified.

LUCKY BIRTH STONES.
A TIME-HONOURED RHYME.

"By her in January born
No gem save Garnets should be worn;
They will ensure her constancy,
True friendship, and fidelity.

PRECIOUS STONES.

The February-born shall find
Sincerity, and peace of mind,
Freedom from passion and from care,
If they the Amethyst will wear.

Who in this world of ours, her eyes
In March first opens, shall be wise.
In days of peril, firm and brave,
And wear a Bloodstone to her grave.

She who from April dates her years,
Diamonds shall wear, lest bitter tears
For vain repentance flow; this stone,
Emblem for innocence, is known.

Who first beholds the light of day,
In spring's sweet flowery month of May,
And wears an Emerald all her life,
Shall be a loved, and happy wife.

Who comes with summer to this earth,
And owes to June her hour of birth,
With ring of Agate on her hand,
Can health, wealth, and long life command.

The glowing Ruby shall adorn
Those who in warm July are born;
Then will they be exempt and free
From love's doubt, and anxiety.

Wear Sardonyx, or for thee
No conjugal felicity;
The August-born without this stone,
'Tis said, must live unloved, and lone.

A maiden born when autumn leaves
Are rustling in September's breeze.
A Sapphire on her brow should bind;
'Twill cure diseases of the mind.

October's child is born for woe,
And life's vicissitudes must know;
But lay an Opal on her breast,
And hope will lull those foes to rest.

Who first comes to this world below,
With drear November's fog, and snow,
Should prize the Topaz's amber hue,
Emblem of friends, and lovers true.

If cold December gives you birth,
The month of snow, and ice, and mirth,
Place on your hand a Turquoise blue;
Success will bless whate'er you do."

It is worthy of note that in calculating, by name, and rotation, the several week-days, all Jews, from the time of Moses, and the Old Testament, have employed a different scheme of reckoning from that with which we are familiar. Thus, their Monday ends in the evening, when Tuesday begins. Again, on Tuesday evening Wednesday commences; and so on, with the seven days throughout the week. As we read in Genesis, "The evening, and the morning, were the first day," etc.

A large Emerald without a flaw in its structure is almost unattainable; which Stone (appertaining to the Beryl family), whilst already a favourite, promises to become still more highly, and generally prized. (Similarly, when seen through a powerful magnifying glass almost every Diamond reveals minute flaws, and disfigurations on its surface). Thus also perfect specimens of the Ruby, the Sapphire, and the Oriental Amethyst,—all of which belong scientifically to the same family,—are rare, and very costly. The beautiful colour of the Sapphire should be of a deep, rich, cornflower blue, easily distinguishable from the inferior Gem.

With respect to other personal qualities which are thought to be bestowed throughout individual lives by the Birth Stones of the several months, the Bloodstone grants to persons born in March, courage, and success in danger, and in hazardous enterprises. The Sapphire endows persons, whose birth took place in April, with a pacific disposition, with piety, and purity of soul.

To the fortunate owners of a birthday in July, the Cornelian, or the Ruby, bespeaks philosophical capabilities; with a forgetfulness of evils, or a cure thereof. Furthermore, the Topaz secures friendship, and fidelity for such well-fated folk as can claim a birthday in dark, gloomy November. These said possessions must be specially valuable, and opportune at so forlorn a season ; which was described (as may be remembered), with much tender regret, in a pathetic key, by Thomas Hood, as affording :—

> " No sun ; no moon ;
> No morn ; no noon ;
> No dawn ; no dark ; no proper time of day !
> No sky : no earthly view ;
> No distance looking blue ;
> No warmth ; no cheerfulness ; no healthful ease ;
> No comfortable feel in any member ;
> No shade ; no shine ; no butterflies ; no bees ;
> No fruits ; no flowers ; no leaves ; no birds ;
> *No-Vember* ! "

(As to the symbolic relations which obtain between the several months, and the particular Gem, or Gems, dedicated protectively to each, some doubt exists with respect to May, and June ; July, and August. Thus, certain authorities give the Agate to May ; and the Emerald to June ; also the Cornelian to August ; and the Onyx to July.)

Another calendar of the leading Gems as emblematic of the Twelve Apostles, has gained general acceptance, and is commonly recognised. To Andrew is dedicated the bright blue Sapphire, as symbolical of his heavenly faith. To Bartholomew, the Red Cornelian, as signifying his martyrdom. To James, the White Chalcedony, as indicative of his purity. To James-the-Less, the Topaz, emblematic of delicacy. To John, the Emerald, emblematic of his youth, and gentleness. To Matthew, the Amethyst, emblematic of sobriety. (Matthew was at one time a "publican," but he became a sober man, under the leaven of Christianity.)

To Matthias, the Chrysolite, because pure as sunshine. To Peter, the Jasper; hard, and solid; as the Rock of the Church. To Philip, the friendly Sardonyx. To Simeon, of Cana, the Pink Hyacinth; denoting a sweet temper. To Thaddeus, the Chrysoprase, emblematic of serenity, and trustfulness. To Thomas, the Beryl, as indefinite in lustre, being thus expressive of his doubting faith.

The Zodiac Stones of the old Romans denoted a particular Stone dedicated to each Zodiacal Month. Thus the Jacinth, or the Garnet, stood for January (Aquarius); the Amethyst for February (Pisces); the Bloodstone for March (Aries); the Sapphire for April (Taurus); the Agate for May (Gemini); the Emerald for June (Cancer); the Onyx for July (Leo); the Cornelian for August (Virgo); the Chrysolite for September (Libra); the Aqua-marine for October (Scorpio); the Topaz for November (Sagittarius); and the Ruby for December (Capricorn). These Zodiac Stones were set all together in an amulet to be worn as a talismanic ornament. A like notion (taken evidently from the Twelve Stones in the Breast-Plate of the Jewish High Priest) is still maintained by not a few believers throughout Eastern Countries.

Whether or not such an Amulet, of imitative, Sacerdotal Stones has served to exercise any personal influence, benignant, or malign, on its wearer, we have no traditional lore to tell us. But it is quite justifiable to suppose that on a person of pure life, and sanctified motives, the Amulet (Breastplate) would coruscate with additional brilliancy under pious exaltation, or joyful conditions of health, and spirits; whilst, if despondency, and sorrow were depressing the vitality, the contexture of Jewels might loom darkly, and obscurely, bowing the downcast head.

The Sign of "Cancer, the Crab," in the Zodiac, was designated in old prescriptions thus—O.c, as indicating *Oculi Cancrorum*, or Crabs' eyes, from which a medicinal tincture was made (1690), the powdered (calcareous) eyes being dissolved in "best vinegar," which was then filtered. Two tablespoonfuls were given twice daily, for curing ulcers. It is noteworthy that the Emerald being the Monthly (June) Zodiacal Stone associated of old with the sign Cancer, was thought to exercise for its wearer a similar virtue in the healing of sores, and the dispersion of acrid humors.

Tavernier John Baptist, *temp.* Louis XIV. (1650), testifies that his Travels through Hindostan, and the East, afforded him great insight into the production, and cultivation there, of Precious Stones. He found that certain Gems were used, when powdered, for medicinal purposes, and were believed to be sovereign in their effects.

Even at this day large quantities of Seed-Pearls are thus employed in China, and the East, for divers remedial purposes.

In the recorded "List of Queen Mary's Jewels at Fotheringay Castle, two curative Precious Stones are mentioned: the one "medicinable against poison; the other medicinable for the colic."

Dean Stanley has related in his *Eastern Churches* how "The old Emperor, Ivan the Terrible (1584), caused the waiters to reach out his staff royal, a unicorn's horn, garnished with very faer Diamonds, Rubies, Sapphires, Emeralds, and other precious stones, rich in value (costing seven thousand marks, sterling, from David

Gower, of Onsburghe). 'Seek out,' said he, 'some spiders!' He then made his Physician, Johannes Lloff, scrape with the staff a circle on the table, putting within it one spider, which quickly died; and so likewise one other, some others which were outside the circle running apace from it. 'Alas!' said he, 'it is too late! It will not preserve me.' 'Behold these precious stones! This Diamond is the Orient's richest, and most precious of all others; but I never affected it. It restrains fury, and luxury; it confers abstinence, and chastity. The least parcel of it, taken in powder, will poison a horse, when given in its drink; much more a man!' Pointing next to the Ruby, 'This,' quoth he, 'is most comfortable to the heart, vigour, and memory of man, clarifying congealed, and corrupt blood!' Then, pointing at the Emerald, said, 'This precious stone, being of the nature of the rainbow, is an enemy to uncleanness.' 'The Sapphire I greatly delight in; it preserveth, and increaseth courage, joys the heart, is pleasing to all the vital senses; precious, and very sovereign for the eyes, cheers the sight, takes away bloodshot; strengthens the muscles, and the strings thereof.' Finally, taking the Onyx in hand, 'All these are God's wonderful gifts; secrets in nature; and yet he reveals them for man's use and contemplation, as friends to grace, and virtue, and enemies to vice. But I faint. Carry me away till another time!'"

"The Pythagoreans," saith Leonardus (1502), "held that certain virtues are communicated to Precious Stones by the Soul; and that Souls can enter into, and depart from them by the animal operations. So it was the Souls of the Stones extended themselves originally from the place of the Stone's natural residence, and then passed onward to man, thus impressing their innate virtues on the substance of man."

In the Prologue of Bartholomew Anglicus, *On the Properties of Things,* a reminder of the same doctrine is thus conveyed : " Reciteth this also the blessed Apostle Paul, in his Epistles, saying, that by things visible, which be made, and are visible, man may see, and know, by his inward intellectual sight, the divine, celestial, godly things which be invisible to this our natural sight. 'For, by Him (the image of the Invisible God) were all things created that are in heaven, and that are on earth, visible, and invisible.' "

"There are," tells Bacon, in his *Sylva Sylvarum,* "many things that operate upon the spirits of man by secret sympathy, and antipathy." " That Precious Stones have virtues in the wearing has been anciently, and generally received ; so much is true that Gems have fine spirits, as appears by their splendour ; and, therefore, they may operate on the spirits of men, to strengthen, and exhilarate them." " It is manifest, moreover, that light, above all things, rejoices the spirits of men ; and, probably, varied light has the same effect, with greater novelty : which may be one cause why precious stones exhilarate."

Emerson has rhymed gracefully to the same romantic effect :—

> "They brought me Rubies from the mine,
>   And held them to the sun ;
> I said 'They're drops of frozen wine,
>   From Eden's vats that run.'
> I look'd again ;—I thought them hearts
>   Of friends to friends unknown ;
> Tides that should warm each neighbouring life
>   Are lock'd in sparkling stone.

> But fire to thaw that ruddy snow,
> To break enchanted ice,
> And give love's scarlet tides to flow,—
> Whence shall that sun arise ?"

"In good sooth," adds De Boot, "I am fain to confess that supernatural effects are after this fashion produced, God having permitted that it should be so. Those, therefore, who would attract good spirits to inhabit their Gems, and would benefit by their presence therein, let them have the martyrdom of our Saviour, the actions of His life, which teach virtue by example, graven upon their Jewels; and let them often contemplate them piously. Without doubt, by the grace of God, and the assistance of good spirits, they will find, that not in the Stone only, or the graven image, but from God, are its admirable qualities."

Proverbially—"Great minds know each other at first sight." From the same stand-point, only with regard to domestic rather than pious affections, it may be reasonably conjectured that the family Diamonds, and other such heirlooms, handed down from grandsires, and grand-dams, or otherwise fondly inherited, and highly prized, retain within their substance ancestral virtues, and excellent personal qualities, which are possible of self-realisation (under particularly favourable conditions) by their fortunate present inheritors. But not when these costly Jewels are worn ostentatiously in public, or for the vain purpose of causing envy, or mere worldly admiration. It must be rather when modestly chosen as adornments at home, or within the family circle, in the true spirit of memorial love, and of a meek desire to win esteem by unpretending gracefulness, that the Jewels will set free for a while the spiritual tendencies which they still derive, in a measure, from their worthy, and noble-minded owners in past times. Haunted Jewel-houses are they; just as (to quote from Longfellow's notable verse) :—

"All houses wherein men have lived, and died,
　Are haunted houses.—Through the open doors
The harmless phantoms on their errands glide,
　With feet that make no sound upon the floors.

We meet them at the doorway, on the stair;
　Along the passages they come, and go;
Impalpable impressions on the air;
　A sense of something moving to, and fro.

There are more guests at table than the hosts
　Invited; the illuminated hall
Is thronged with quiet, inoffensive ghosts,
　As silent as the pictures on the wall.

The stranger at the fireside cannot see
　The forms I see, nor hear the sounds I hear;
He but perceives what is; while unto me
　All that has been is visible, and clear.

The spirit-world around this world of sense
　Floats like an atmosphere, and everywhere
Wafts through these earthly mists, and vapours dense
　A vital breath of more ethereal air."

Similarly, from remote times, Amulets, and Talismans were worn about the person, being suspended from the neck, or bound round some part of the body; these being believed to be invested with virtues all but supernatural. Two thousand years ago they were dispensed by the priests; and afterwards by those who practised medicine, alchemy, and astrology. An Amulet consisted of some certain ornament in stone, or metal, carved, or painted. Talismans were likewise objects usually of one of the precious stones, or of metal, worn about the person, to ward off danger, ill-luck, or the "evil eye," as well as for their reputed medicinal virtues. By their means it was thought possible to commune with the world of spirits. Pliny mentions their virtue; while

Galen, Dioscorides, Cardamus, and other ancient writers on medicine, speak of their value in repelling disease.

"The Amulets, and Talismans held in the highest esteem," as we learn from "*The Mystery and Romance of Alchemy and Pharmacy*," 1897, were those in the form of Precious Stones. They were supposed to be influenced in some mysterious way by the Planets, and to be the abode of spirits.

Amongst Highland superstitions that of the Evil Eye still finds its confident, and timorous votaries. Cattle, and all kinds of property, are believed to suffer thereby. It will deprive cows of their milk, and milk of its nourishing properties, rendering it unfit for food. This superstition can certainly lay claim to great antiquity. Virgil, Ossian, and other classic writers have alluded fearsomely to its existence, and its disastrous effects!

"Nescio quis teneros oculus mihi fascinat agnos."

M. Victorien Sardou, the veteran French Dramatist, has related not long ago that on the day he sought admission into the Société des Auteurs Dramatiques, he met a singular-looking old man, with hooked nose, and reddish beard, excessively thin, and with a strikingly piercing glance, suggesting altogether, one of the fantastic figures of Hoffman. It was Jacques Offenbach, who, it appears, was credited with possessing the "evil eye." Sardou adds, that he was no more superstitious then than he is now; but the fact remained, nevertheless, that until five years after this ill-omened encounter he was not able to bring a single piece to success. A charm against the evil eye consisted formerly of a quill filled with mercury, sealed at each end, and worn bound to the body.

Equally superstitious, as it would appear, are the Highland means resorted-to for the cure of calamities thus caused; such as the use of certain charms, the repetition of strange, uncouth rhymes, the putting live trout in some of the spoiled milk, and many other such credulous appliances.

Witches were formerly believed capable of killing with the "evil eye," slaying with lightning, passing through key-holes, riding through the air on broomsticks, and performing many other weird marvels. Epileptic seizures were attributed to the malign influence of witches, who were said to make two covenants with the devil: one public, and the other private. The devil was supposed to bestow Amulets upon them, and mischievous philtres.

Among the Bedouin tent-dwellers of Palestine it is customary even now to suspend over a child's primitive wooden cot, or cradle, a blue bead for averting the evil eye.

"That invisible Corpuscles may pass from Amulets," saith the Honble. Robert Boyle, "or from other external remedies, into the Blood, and Humours, and there produce great changes, will scarcely seem improbable to him who considers how perspirable, according to Hippocrates, a living body is; and the Vegetable, and Animal bodies may well be supposed to send forth expirations, since even divers Minerals are found to do the like; as may appear by the odorable steams of rub'd Brimstone, and Amber, without their sensibly losing anything, either of their bulk, or weight."

Mæcenas, the famous patron of Quintus Flaccus Horatius, was a passionate lover of Gems, and Precious Stones (B.C. 28). "Not merely," (C. W. King, 1885), "for their native beauties, but, like the great Julius, for the higher value of the genius therein enshrined." This is made evident by the lines attributed to Mæcenas on the departure of Horace, for the loss of whose devoted companionship not even the sight of his darling Jewels could console him :—

"Lugens, O mea vita! te Smaragdos,
Beryllos mihi, Flacce, nec nitentes,
Nec percandida Margarita quæro;
Nec quos Thyrica lima perpolivit,
Anellos, nec Iaspios lapillos."

"Whilst I thine absence, O my life, deplore,
Emeralds, and lustrous Beryls charm no more;
No more, my Flaccus, can the brilliant white
Of Orient Pearls my soul, as erst, delight;
Nor can my favourite Rings my grief beguile,
Nor Jaspers, polished by the Thyrian file."

Medical practice among the ancient Jews consisted chiefly in Amulets used externally. And even still, modern Jews are remarkably given to entertain such beliefs, and practices. Some wear an Amulet which consists of a small piece of parchment with a few cabalistic words written upon it by one of their Rabbis. Others have a bulb of Garlic hanging about them, tied up in a small shred of linen; whilst, again, others carry a small piece of their Passover cake in this, or that pocket. In the Roman Catholic religion the Scapular, the Rosary, and treasured relics worn about the person, come under the designation of Amulets; from the use of which talismans important bodily benefits are expected. Scapulars are generally required to be suspended from the neck. Similarly, relics of Saints are employed for the cure of diseases. Lightfoot, when writing about Hebrew women, says that in former times, "There was no people in the whole world that more used, or were more fond of Amulets. According to Oriental writers these were frequently formed of Gold, Silver, and Precious Stones.

"There is little doubt" (*Alchemy and Pharmacy*) "that the modern custom of wearing precious stones in rings, and as charms for pendants to watch-chains, originated in the amulet, and the talisman. Who can say that faith in such charms has yet altogether died out? The belief in keeping a crooked sixpence, or a broken ring, is evidence of a peculiar vein of superstition which runs through most of us, and which, strange though it may seem, the advance of science, and education, has not altogether dispelled."

In a Lecture on "Precious Stones," delivered recently before the Society of Arts, Professor Miers explained the process by which crystallized Gem-stones, true in many respects, can be produced by artificial means.

Diamonds, for instance, of such a character, can be produced by dissolving charcoal in molten iron, in an electric furnace, and cooling under pressure: the resultant crystals being mere specks; but they probably represent the actual process by which true Diamonds have been generated in meteorites.

By similar means the Ruby has been successfully reproduced in Paris, on a scale sufficiently large to be used in jewellry. The crystals thereof are made by raising to a very high temperature a mixture of alumina, potassium carbonate, and calcium fluoride; the red colour being obtained by adding a trace of potassium chromate. Then, by maintaining the temperature for about a week, crystals weighing one-third of a carat are obtained without any great difficulty. "These Stones," said the Lecturer, "cannot be distinguished from natural Rubies by any of the known tests. They possess the specific gravity, the refraction, and the double refraction of the natural stone; and in the Polariscope they show the same uni-axal interference figure."

"Other Minerals have been likewise constituted by artificial means. Turquoise has been successfully made by compressing powdery artificial Phosphate of Aluminium into a compact mass: and the only respect in which it (and the others described above) differ from the natural stones is, that they have been formed by a different process." "These daring, unabashed men of science," comments a leading writer, "can now-a-days, and do, manufacture Stones, however trivial in size, and value, which are no mere imitations of the veritable treasures of the Mine, but rather the Gem itself, the authentic handiwork of the Creator, parodied, plagiarised, and vulgarised by venturesome man!" "Who is to say they will never go further? Who can safely predict that, since they can certainly produce, and submit to every imaginable analytical test, these tiny specimens which are so perfect, they may not eventually turn out Rubies as big as raspberries, and Diamonds as large as ten, or a dozen Koh-i-noors crystallised into one?"

Further (we reply) they perhaps may go in these spiritless materialistic proceedings; but the innate virtues, and intrinsic mystic worth of true Precious Stones have been altogether overlooked by them, and disregarded.

Neither the merely mechanical results vaunted by Professor Miers, nor the flippant, well-nigh profane, inferences of his would-be humorous commentator, pay the slightest heed, or respect, to those rich endowments of spiritual influence, of remedial virtues, and of transcendental soul, so to speak, which place the secret treasures of precious Stones, such as have been sublimated to perfection throughout long ages of time, on a pinnacle of supreme excellence inaccessible to mere Art, and defiant of audacious science. Every page of this our Book, we make bold to say, vindicates our assertions, and justifies the lofty claims of Nature's Jewels as priceless beyond compare, and as possessing occult, immaterial properties of an order far beyond the reach of chemistry, though ever so ambitious, and learned.

But none the less important is it that a wise knowledge should be kept always in view by those persons who own, or seek to acquire, Precious Stones of irreproachable character, and of indisputable truth, regarding the imitative perfection which has been attained as concerns lustre, colour, hardness, form, and response to analysis in the chemist's laboratory, by substitutions now achieved which the most expert lapidary fails to detect. Else, indeed, dire will be the disappointment, fraught too, it may be, with grave consequences, of the unsuspecting seeker after health, cure, comfort, or welfare, in implicit reliance on the aid, and influences of personal jewels, believed-in beyond all doubt.

Among the Arabians, serpents, either from the brilliancy of their eyes, or because they inhabit the cavities of the earth, were formerly supposed to possess precious stones of inestimable value. Allusions to such Serpents' Stones are frequently found as made by the early writers. In the *Gesta Romanorum* (1362) it is stated that the Emperor Theodosius, The Blind, ordained that the cause of any aggrieved person should be brought before him by ringing a bell placed in a public part of his Palace. A serpent had its nest near the spot where the bell-rope hung; and, in the absence of this serpent, a toad took possession of its nest. The serpent, on its return, by twining itself round the rope managed to ring the bell for justice, when, by the Emperor's special command, the toad was killed. A few days afterwards, while the Emperor was reclining on his couch, the serpent entered the chamber, bearing a precious stone in its mouth; and, crawling up to the Emperor's face, laid it on his eyes; then glided out of the apartment. The monarch found his sight restored from that moment.

It is more than probable that underlying this mythical story there is a basis of positive fact; as is the case with most of the old classic fables, and likewise with the familiar Fairy tales of our childhood. By virtue of some particular Gem worn in contact with his eyes the fortunate Emperor Theodosius was enabled to recover his powers of sight. Most likely this potential Gem was the Sapphire, famous from all time for remedying defective vision. For instance, as we tell elsewhere, and more in detail, there was formerly in the Church of Old Saint Paul's, London, a famous Sapphire kept expressly for helping infirmities of the eyes of all persons thus afflicted who might resort to it. In St. Alban's Abbey is preserved a Stone which was presented by the Bishop of Ardfert, Ireland, of a light airy colour, marked with white spots, and called the "Serpent's Stone, which was thought to be efficacious against Lunacy. This Stone is square in form, and encompassed with silver."

Worth a passing notice is the fact that quite recently a fashion has sprung up again of wearing Serpent-Jewellry for personal adornment. As a current fashionable Journal states—"The Serpent insinuates itself into lockets, rings, and bracelets, its venomous head alight with fiery Rubies, and baleful Emeralds; whilst its sinuous length is displayed in silver, as well as in gold."

When Martin Chuzzlewit and Mark Tapley, were making terms for a location in the "Walley of Eden," of which fanciful(but as yet unredeemed, and imaginary) settlement, glowing accounts, as if of a flourishing city already in full swing, had been given them by Mr. Scadder, Agent to the "Eden, and New Thermopylæ Land Corporation Company";—Mark fell into talk about "Eden" with a "military officer"! "As thick as scarecrows these officers be out here," says Mark to his master; "which scarecrows is a sort of militia themselves, being entirely coat, and wescot, with a stick inside."

"'Am I rightly informed, says the military gent, not exactly through his nose, but as if he'd got a stoppage in it, very high up, 'that you're a going to the Walley of Eden?' 'Well,' says he, 'if you *should* ever happen to go to bed there; you *may*, you know, in course of time, as civilization progresses; don't forget to take a axe with you.' I looks at him tolerable hard, says Mark.—'Fleas?' says I.—'And more,' says he.—'Wampires?' says I.—'And more,' says he. 'Musquitoes, perhaps?' says I.—'And more,' says he. 'What more?' says I.—'Snakes, more,' says he. 'Rattlesnakes! You're right, to a certain extent, stranger. There air some catawampous chawers (fleas) in the small way, too, out there, as graze upon a human, pretty strong: but don't mind them! They're company! It's snakes,' he says, 'as you'll object to; and whenever you wake, and see one, in an upright postoore, on your bed,' he says, ' like a corkscrew with the handle off, a sittin' on its bottom ring, cut him down, for he means wenom!'"

With reference to Jewels in general, the "Slang Dictionary" (Chatto & Windus, 1874) associates the vulgarism—" a Jew's eye," as signifying anything particularly valuable, with the French word *Joaille*, a Jewel.

In ancient times, when a king was short of cash, he generally issued orders for so many "Jews' Eyes," or equivalent sums of money. The Jews preferred paying the ransom, although often very heavy. Furthermore, it is notorious that at one time in this country an order often went forth to draw Jews' teeth, in the event of their refusing to contribute a certain sum to the Exchequer. Thus a probable supposition is, that if the teeth of a Jew brought in so much money, the value of a Jew's eye must be something far higher. Possibly, too, the *lex talionis* is here intimated :—" An eye for an eye ; and a tooth for a tooth."

With regard to a possible faculty for digesting stones, there is related in Hone's *Table Book* (1878), an account of a Stone-Eater, by Father Paulian. "In the beginning of May, 1760, was brought to Avignon a true Lithophagus, or Stone-Eater. He not only swallowed flints, of an inch and a half long, and a full inch broad, and half-an inch thick ; but other stones, which he could reduce to powder, such as marbles, pebbles, etc., he made up into a paste, taking this as seemingly a most agreeable, and wholesome food. I examined this man with all the attention I possibly could ; I found his gullet very large ; his teeth exceedingly strong ; his saliva very corrosive ; his stomach placed lower than ordinary. As to the vast number of flints he had swallowed, these were about five and twenty, one day with another. His keeper tells me that some physicians at Paris got him blooded; that the blood had little or no, serum ; and in two hours' time it became as fragile as Coral."

"In the Learned Sennertus's Paralipomena," says Robert Boyle, (*Experimental Philosophie,*) "we are told that in the end of the yeare 1632 there lived at that time, and belonging to a Noble Man of those Parts, a certain Lorainer, somewhat low, and slender, and about 58 years of age, who would swallow any substance, however nauseous, or distasteful ; Glass, Stones, Wood, Coals, Bones, pieces of Linen, or Woollen fabric ; the hairy feet of Animals, living creatures, Fish, when still leaping about, likewise hard Metals, Cups, and tin balls, which he was often seen to crush with his teeth, and to devour." "Some other examples of this nature we have also met with, especially that of the Glass-eater mentioned by Columbus." "And not long ago there was here in England a private souldier (who for aught I know is yet alive) very famous for digesting of Stones. And a very inquisitive Man that gave me the accuratest account I have met with concerning him, assures me that he knew him familiarly, and had the curiosity to keep in his company for twenty-four hours together, to watch him ; and not only observed that he eat nothing in that time, save Stones (or fragments of them) of a pretty bigness : but that his grosser excrement consisted chiefly of a sandy substance, as if the devoured stones had been in his body dissolved, and crumbled into sand. And indeed this memorable story seems to argue that a natural Menstruum appertaining to the human body, but not so corrosive as to fret the same, may dissolve Stones, Metals, and other compact substances."

"Since I have observ'd it to be the main thing that keeps judicious men from seeking, or so much as hoping to discover, noble dissolvents, that they are scarce to be persuaded that there can be considerably piercing Menstruums that are not proportionably corrosive to the bodily tissues, I will here acquaint you with a Liquor that may, I presume, assist you to undeceive some of these men. We take then ordinary Household Bread (I like that of Rye; but I have divers times us'd that of Wheat), and when it is cut into slices, and somewhat dryed, we almost fill a glass retort with it; and placing that in a Sand furnace; by degrees of fire we draw off what will be made to come over without much difficulty. The Oyl, as useless to our purpose, being by a Filter separated from the rest of the Liquor; we also by a gentle heat free the Spirit from some of its phlegm, which yet sometimes we find no great necessity to do. And still this Spirit, which you will easily believe is no such Corrosive as Aquafortis, or other distill'd Liquors of Mineral Salts, will work upon the hardest sorts of bodies, and perform things that Chemists, counted of the judiciousest, would not have us expect from the most sharp, and corrosive Menstruums now in use. For with this we have in a short time, and that in the cold, drawn tinctures, not only from crude Corals, and some of the more open Minerals, but likewise from very hard Stones, such as Blood-Stone, and Granates (even unpowder'd); nay, and though Rubys seem to be the hardest Bodies yet known, save Diamonds (for I have learn'd from those that cut Precious Stones that they can grind other Gems with the powder of Rubies, but not these with any powder save their own, and that of Diamonds,) yet have even these afforded me in the cold a not ignoble Tincture."

"And, since, as we have now shown, one Liquor, prepared by Nature only, could dissolve that great variety of bodies mentioned above, why should it not be thought that some other Menstruum wherein Nature is skilfully assisted, and to the utmost heightened, by art, should not be able to dissolve concretes such as the Precious Stones, of different degrees of hardness? Why may not Nature, and Art, afford a Menstruum whose variety of parts and figures, and (perhaps also motion) may give it ingress into bodies of the most varying textures? Just as chemically, though Aqua Regia will dissolve Gold, but not Silver, and Aqua Fortis Silver, but not Gold; yet Quick-silver will dissolve both, (and Copper, Tin, and Lead, to boot)."

"As to the efficacy of the aforesaid Menstruum (concocted from Bread, as described,) I have found," says Robert Boyle, "that from some Minerals it will draw a much higher Tincture than from others; and from some scarce any at all; but that it will, if kept by itself, for many Moneths, continue clear, and limpid."

Helmont relates, "that the noted Irish physician, Dr. Butler, by slightly plunging a little stone which he possessed, into Almond Milk, or Oyl, imbued those liquors with such a sanative efficacy that a spoon-full of the former cured (and that without acquainting him with what was given him) a Franciscan Friar (a very famous Preacher) of a most dangerous Erysipelas in the arm, in one hour; and one drop of the latter being apply'd in his presence to the Head of an old Laundress that had been sixteen years troubled with an intolerable Hemicrania: Headache, (one-sided), the Woman was presently cured, and remained so to his knowledge for divers years."

He adds almost as strange a cure, done in one night, upon a maid of his wife's, by anointing the part affected with four drops of that oyl. He further tells us that the master of the Glass-house at Antwerp being troubled, and made unwieldy with too much fat, begged some relief of Dr. Butler. Who, having given him a small fragment of his little Stone, with orders to lick it nimbly with the tip of his tongue once every morning,—" I saw," says the Dr., "within three weeks the compass of his waist lessened by a span, without any prejudice to his health."

What an inestimable boon this stone might have proved to Daniel Lambert, the fat man of all time, whose epitaph in the burial ground at Stamford Baron runs as follows:—

" In Remembrance of that prodigy in nature, Daniel Lambert, a native of Leicester, who was possessed of an excellent, and convivial mind, and in personal greatness he had no competitor. He measured three feet one inch round the leg; nine feet four inches round the body; and weighed 52 stone 11lb. (14lb. to the stone). He departed this life on the 21st of June, 1809, aged 39 years."

And what more striking contrast to this ponderous character can be adduced (though from fiction) than that of Mrs. Todgers (in *Martin Chuzzlewit*) who presided over a boarding-establishment for commercial gentlemen, near the Monument, where " the gravy alone was enough to add twenty years to one's age " ? " What I have undergone in consequence," cried the worthy, worn, little woman. " no one would believe." " She had a lean, lank body, Mrs. Todgers, but a well-conditioned soul within it. Perhaps the Good Samaritan was lean, and lank, and found it hard to live! Who knows ? "

"Next, a gentleman in France, being not long since reported to have a fragment of this Stone, and to have cured several persons therewith of inveterate diseases, by letting them lick it; my noble friend, Sir Kenelm Digby, being then in France, was solemnly requested from thence to enquire into the truth of that report, and answered, ' that he could not upon examination finde it other than true.' "

THE DIAMOND.

The Diamond (*Adamas*, or "Indomitable," as it was called of old) is the hardest substance known. When worn in the Ephod of the Jewish High Priest, it gave token of the guilt, or innocence, of an accused person. If such person was guilty, the gem became dim and lustreless; though if guilty, even unto death, the stone flamed forth with a sullen flare of fierce blood-red. If, on the contrary, the accused person was innocent, then the Diamond shone out with its glory increased tenfold. This precious stone was held to symbolise innocence, justice, faith, strength, and the impassivity of fate. An ancient Black-letter book pronounces respecting the Diamond: "God hath indyed hym with greatter vertues than many other stones."

The material basis of the Diamond (carbon) is to be found almost everywhere: in the bread we eat, in our sugar, in the wood, and the coal which we burn; but then in an uncrystallised state, being opaque, and easily frangible. When crystallised as a diamond it is the hardest substance known (though the amorphous variety of diamond, a carbonate, whilst of precisely the same chemical composition, and of a nearly equal specific gravity, is black, lustreless, and degraded to the mere purpose of cutting, and polishing other gems).

The designation "Adamant," now transferred to the Blood Stone, was certainly bestowed on the Diamond in former times. Juvenal, without doubt, told thus of the Diamond as adorning the finger of Berenice:—

"Adamas notissimus, et Berenices
In digito factus pretiosior."

Whilst reputed to be an antidote to all poisons when worn as a finger-jewel, yet the Diamond, if swallowed, was considered, during the Middle Ages, to be the most deadly of substances. It was among the poisons administered to Sir Thomas Overbury when a prisoner in the Tower of London. Yet such is by no means the real fact. Garcius tells of slaves in the mines swallowing large diamonds for the purpose of stealing them, but without the least bodily injury being sustained by their so doing. He also writes of a woman known to him who administered doses of diamond-dust for many days together to her husband (troubled by dysentery), but without producing the least effect. The natives of India, says Harry Emanuel, "imagine that when diamond powder is taken into the mouth, it causes the teeth to fall out; also that it acts as a preservative against lightning."

Tavernier (1676) was the first to visit the famous diamond mines of Golcondah (Hindostan). Serapion (1473) ascribed to the Diamond a power of driving away lemures (ghosts), incubes (nightmares), and succubos (calamities); also of making men courageous, and magnanimous; he said further that if this gem be placed in proximity to a loadstone, it multiplies the power thereof. The Diamond is found of all colours: white, yellow, orange, red, pink, brown, green, blue, and opalescent.

Camillus Leonardus, in his *Mirror of Stones* (translated into English, 1750), wrote concerning the Adamant (Diamond): "It is a help to lunaticks, and such as are possessed with the devil; being bound to the left arm it gives victory over enemies; it tames wild beasts; it helps those who are troubled with phantasms, and the night-mare, making him that wears it bold, and daring in his transactions."

The Honble. Robert Boyle (1692) treating *Of Experimental Philosophie*, said, "Even in divers minerals, as we may see in nitre, chrystal, and several others, the figures that are admired are not produc'd by chance, but by something analogous to seminal principles, as may appear by their uniform regularity in the same sort of concretions, and by the practice of some of the skilfullest of the salt-peter men; who, when they have drawn as much nitre as they can out of the nitrous earth, cast not the earth away, but preserve it in heaps, for six or seven years; at the end of which time they finde it impregnated with new salt-peter, produced chiefly by the seminal principle of nitre implanted in that earth." " I shall here annex that memorable relation which I finde recorded by Hinschoten, and Garcias ab Horto, whereby it may appear that the seminal principles of precious stones, as of plants, are lodg'd in the bowels of the mine they grow in. Thus Diamonds are digged like gold out of mines. Where they digg'd one year the length of a man into the ground, within three or four years after there are found Diamonds again in the same place, which grew there. Sometimes they thus finde diamonds of 400, or 800 grains."

Garcias confirms this assertion; " Diamonds which ought to be brought to perfection, in the deepest bowels of the earth, and in a long tract of time, are almost at the top of the ground ; and in three, or four years' space, made perfect ; for, if you dig this year but the depth of a cubit, you will finde diamonds ; and after two years dig there you will finde diamonds again."

Such generative powers of self-multiplication were attributed to certain precious stones even by some of the old classical writers. Theophrastus (1530) has described a belief, which was common when he wrote, as to the faculty which some stones possess of generating others (though he did not attach much belief to this notion).

Another author, of about the same period, tells a strange anecdote to the same effect ; and accounts for this marvellous phenomenon by supposing that the peculiarly fine atmosphere which must have surrounded the parent gems facilitated a fresh formation in the new crystals thought to have been generated. His little story goes, that a noble lady had inherited two

Diamonds, which remained for many years hidden among her treasures; at the end of which period was discovered that from time to time these stones had given birth to several indisputable facsimiles.

The *Diamond* is phosphoric, and electric. Diamonds, and gold have always had a strange connection together; in Brazil they are found in close union. About some parts of that country gold can be picked up in the streets after a shower of rain; and diamonds have been discovered entangled in the roots of vegetables, also in the crops of chickens.

Ben Mansur, the Oriental writer, has likewise said, "The Diamond has a strange affinity for gold; small particles of which metal fly towards it. Furthermore, this precious metal is wonderfully sought-after by ants; which crowd over it, as though they would swallow it up."

According to the assertions of ancient philosophers (and of "Sinbad, the Sailor"), gems were obtained in former days by flinging beefsteaks down inaccessible precipices, for vultures, and eagles to fetch up the same with a fringe of diamonds adhering thereto.

Diamonds are often found coloured, and, when so, are valuable in proportion to the fulness, and richness of the tint. Even perfectly black diamonds have been discovered; but these are rare. The small, soft, and ill-complexioned Diamonds, neither purely colourless, nor richly tinged, are broken up for diamond-dust, worth fifty pounds the ounce; this is used for cutting cameos, and onyxes, as well as for polishing some of their inferior relations. The difference between "brilliant," "rose," and "table," diamonds consists only in the cutting.

Four hundred years ago all Diamonds were cut with four flat surfaces, these being Indian-cut, or "table" diamonds; later they were cut in the form of half a polyhedron resting on a plane section, this being the "rose-diamond." The Diamonds known as "brilliants" are cut into the form of two truncated pyramids, the upper, or bizel, being much more deeply truncated than the lower, or "collet"; and having thirty-two facets, inclined under different angles; while the lower has but twenty-four; each facet, both of the "bizel," and the "collet" side, having its distinctive name, and arbitrary proportion. This is the most effective, but most wasteful way of cutting diamonds, about one half the weight being lost in converting them into "brilliants," or "roses," from the rough. Old diamonds are cut with greater care than the quite modern, and are worth forty or fifty per cent more.

Concerning the Diamond—Sir John Mandeville (Paris, 1561) has advanced remarkable notions, partly derived from Pliny. "He directs that a man should carry the Diamonds on his left side; for it is of greater virtue than the right side; for the strength of their (the Diamonds) growing is towards the north, that is, the left side of the world; and the left part of the man is when he turns his face towards the East. And if you wish to know the virtues of the Diamond, I shall tell you, as they beyond the sea say, and affirm; from whom all science, and philosophy come. He who carries the Diamond upon him it gives him hardiness, and manhood, and it keeps the limbs of his body whole." "It gives him victory over his enemies, in Court, and in war, if his cause is just; and it keeps him that bears it in good wit; it preserves him from strife, and riot;

from sorrowe, and enchantments: from phantasies, and illusions of wicked spirits. And, if any cursed witch, or enchanter, would bewitch him that bears the Diamond, all that sorrow, and mischance shall fall to the offender, through virtue of that stone; and no wild beast dare assail the man who bears it on him. Also the Diamond should be given freely, without coveting, and without buying; and then it is of a greater virtue; and it makes a man stronger, and firmer against his enemies; and heals him that is a lunatic, and those whom the fiend pursues, or torments. And if venom, or poison be brought in the presence of the Diamond, anon it begins to grow moist, and to sweat. Nevertheless it often happens the good Diamond loses its virtue by sin, and for incontinence of him who bears it; and then it is needful to make it recover its virtue again, or else it is of little value."

With regard to the indestructibility of the Diamond, Ben Mansur has said, that one laid upon an anvil, instead of breaking is drawn into the anvil; so that the only plan of reducing it is to wrap it in lead. "Which statement is fabulous," declares Leonardus, "for I have seen many broke with the blow of a hammer." De Boot, when speaking of "precious stones" (as the abode of angels,) states that the Diamond is not only proof against fire, but actually improves by exposure to its action throughout several days. Furthermore, Diamonds resist the disintegrating action both of acids, and of alkalies.

Pliny imagined that the Diamond, though so hard as to be almost incapable of fracture with hammer, and anvil, nevertheless would become soft if immersed in goat's blood. "*Hæc tamen hircino calefacta cruore fatiscit.*" This precious stone, though it is combustible, cannot be fused. An application of heat to the various gems produces very different results; some change their colour; some swell, and decrepitate; some burn away; in some, globules are produced; in some, an enamel; in some, dust; and in some, phosphorescence may be observed.

Benvenuto Cellini in his *Memoirs* relates how his life was preserved by the roguery of an Apothecary who, being employed to pulverise a Diamond with the intention of poisoning him, by mixing the powdered stone in a Salad, substituted in its place a piece of Beryl as cheaper.

At one time a marvellous curative power was supposed to exist in a Diamond belonging to the Rajah of Matara, in the Island of Borneo; the Malays believing that by drinking water in which this Diamond had been put to lie for a while every disease among them might be cured. So greatly was this precious stone esteemed that the Governor of Batavia offered the Rajah an enormous sum of money for it, besides two ships of war, fully equipped; but this offer was refused; not only because of such faith in the healing powers of the stone, but also because it was believed that the safety of the dynasty depended upon its continued custody.

"Adamantine," or the hard, unbreakable, structural part of the diamond, lies between the metallic and the resinous lustres. This Gem, as well as the other more valuable precious stones, is bought, and sold, by "Carat" weight; the "Carat" being divisible into four grains of the Diamond-substance. The origin thereof is to be sought in certain small leguminous seeds which, when once dry, remain constant in weight. But the carat is not of absolutely the same significance in all countries.

The European Diamond trade is now centred in Antwerp, and Amsterdam; some factories having been also established in the United States of America. In Diamond-cutting the first rough formation is termed "brutage"; the rough stones being then embedded in liquid Aluminium, within moulds. Having become thus fixed when cool, they are taken from the moulds, and cloven with a circular saw, into the cutting edge of which some diamond dust with oil is forced; next one stone is rubbed against another until the required formation is achieved; each stone is first fixed in cement for this purpose,—the cement being then set by plunging it into cold water. The "diamond-dust" which is produced by thus rubbing the two stones together falls into a copper box, called an "égrisoir," placed immediately below the diamonds which are being worked. This dust is carefully preserved. Finally a stone is polished into facets, on a revolving disc of soft steel, rotating horizontally at a speed of some three thousand revolutions to the minute. In olden times Diamond cutters contented themselves with thus producing as large a number as possible of small facets on the surface of a stone. But since then it has become manifest that for obtaining the best results, and the most sparkling lustre, a Diamond must be cut into a regular form, so that one facet-surface may reflect on another, thereby bringing out the hidden light, and beauty of the stone. Because the molten metal within a mass of which the stones are fixed for polishing is composed mainly of lead, therefore the exceedingly rapid revolution of the wheel makes this part of the occupation very unhealthy, by reason of the lead-poisoning produced. As each Diamond has sixty-four facets requiring to be smoothed, it takes a workman about two weeks to polish one stone. The Diamond has to be set, and reset, in the molten lead eighteen times.

A Diamond which is perfectly free from colour is of "the first water," and is the most highly valued. Likewise Diamonds of a slight rose tint are highly esteemed; and next to these, green-tinted stones are reckoned best.

Among the Greeks a first mention of the Diamond is made about three centuries before Christ, under this designation—"Adamas"—(the unsubduable)—because of its extreme hardness, and its having the power of resisting fire. Our name for this stone is from the old "diamas" (as occurring in Albertus Magnus; and other writers, of the thirteenth century). Seneca said of it—"*Non secari, aut caedi, vel deteri potest.*" Formerly the more highly coloured Rubies and Emeralds, and Sapphires, were often preferred before the Diamond. Even in the sixteenth century Benvenuto Cellini assigned it only the third rank in value. Solomon, as we well know, appraised the Ruby as the gem of highest value. "Who can find a virtuous woman? for her price is far above rubies." In the East diamonds are showered on an infant at the christening by the sponsors.

The most famous Diamonds are "The Premier," of three thousand and thirty carats; "Excelsior," of nine hundred and seventy-one carats; "Great Mogul," of seven hundred and eighty carats; "Regent," of four hundred and ten carats; "Koh-i-noor," of nine hundred carats (before cutting); and, quite recently discovered, (1905) at Johannesburg, the largest Diamond known in the world, the "Cullinan," found by Mr. F. Wells, on the Premier Mine, near Pretoria. It weighs three thousand, and twenty-four carats, being of splendid quality, and singularly free from defects. This magnificent Stone was safely transported to England, and deposited in the strong room of the South African Standard Bank. It was insured for five hundred thousand pounds, and is valued at a million pounds sterling. The "Great Mogul," or "Agra" Diamond, was discovered about the middle of the seventeenth century. This Stone was taken at the Battle of Agra (1626), and stolen from the King of Delhi, at the time of the Indian Mutiny. It somehow reached England, and was sold at Christie's in February, 1905, for five thousand, and one hundred pounds. Report has said that the Agra Diamond was smuggled out of India by being placed within a horse-ball, which a horse was made to swallow. As to the "Regent," or "Pitt," Diamond, this was bought by Pitt, the Governor of Fort Saint George, in Golcondah, for one hundred and thirty-five thousand pounds, from Jamel-Chund, a Hindoo Merchant, who was said to have stolen it :—

"Asleep, and naked as the Indian lay,
An honest factor stole the gem away."

The Koh-i-noor, or "Mountain of Light," is the eighth, or smallest, of the Paragon Diamonds, (all Diamonds weighing above a hundred carats being styled "Paragon.") This was originally the largest Diamond known up to that time, weighing, uncut, nine hundred carats. It belonged at first to the Great Mogul.

Since the "Mountain of Light" came into the possession

of the English it has been cut as a brilliant, being thus enhanced in value, and beauty, though diminished in weight. The old " Iron " Duke of Wellington was the first to place it in the mill; and it took thirty-eight days to be cut by a lapidary working twelve hours a days, without intermission.

The carat grain used in weighing diamonds is different from the Troy grain, five diamond grains being equal to four Troy grains. Four carat grains make one carat; and six carats, or twenty-four grains, one pennyweight.

Respecting the " Koh-i-noor " we have already given some particulars. When Sir John Lawrence—the hero of Lahore, in the Indian Mutiny days,—was Lieutenant Governor of the Punjab, he had in his keeping no less a treasure than this famous Koh-i-noor; and no one could have taken better care of so precious a charge. Nevertheless there came a day when the great Jewel was missing. The house was searched throughout; the police were consulted; the servants were closely examined; and native fakirs pressed into the investigation; but all to no purpose! When Sir John was absolutely in despair, the Diamond reappeared; and of all places, from an old cigar-box, which was beside the Lieutenant-Governor's bed.

Tradition carries back the existence of this precious Stone in the memory of India to the year 57 B.C. The Hindoos profess to trace curses, and ultimate ruin brought inevitably upon its successive possessors ever since it was first wrested from the line of Vikramalitya.

During 1850, in the name of the East India Company (since, in its turn, defunct), Lord Dalhousie presented the Koh-i-noor to Queen Victoria. The Brahmins will hardly yet relinquish their belief in the malignant powers exercised by this stone.

Respecting the giant "Cullinan" Diamond, one of our leading Journals said with grim humour, at the time of its publicly announced discovery,—" the other day a South African Mine-Manager happened to see something gleaming in the primeval clay belonging to his Imperial "limited liability" Company. With a pardonable curiosity he put in his thumb, and pulled out a plum, which turned out to be the biggest uncut Diamond in the world. From that moment the poor fellow, who had, after all, done nothing amiss, had to be protected by a small battalion of police, all of whom doubtless wanted, like the rest of humanity, to murder him, because he was, through no fault of his own, the victim of singularly unhappy circumstances. Finally, the Diamond was brought to England, insured for half a million golden sovereigns, and deposited—for better, or worse—in the strong room of a Bank. Presumably it will be sold to adorn the swan-like throat, or dark love-locks, of some American million-heiress; and finally it will end its career at Monte-Carlo; where it will be deposited as security for a loan negotiated at this oft-fatal pawnshop, in favour of some bankrupt duke who sees no reason why his imported wife should not wear paste." "And what of the ladies who will wear upon their hearts this dangerous penalty of past volcanic energy? Think of having the effect of an earthquake lingering in your tiara! Not one woman will be the prettier, or the happier, or the gentler, because this glittering eye of a snake has been unearthed from its lair. Wherever that Diamond goes, there will its glint be reflected back in envious glances at the wearer. If the said fateful Diamond should come your way, my fair friend, sell it! If no one will buy it, then present it to your worst enemy, and pray to be forgiven! If your worst enemy won't have it, bribe her with all the pocket-money you can screw out of your husband. If finally your enemy sends the stone back to you, by parcel post, then stamp upon it with the heel of your dainty slipper, stamp it to powder; and give it as fuel to your housemaid when she has run out of firewood."

In a large Star, Cross, and Chain, worn on grand gala days by the Prince of Brazil, as Sovereign of the Portuguese Orders of Knighthood, the central Diamond of the Star is valued alone at eight hundred thousand pounds.

Diamonds, when rubbed together, have a peculiar indescribable sound, of a grating character, which is significant of their distinctive nature. This accurately denotes the gems whilst still in the rough.

The Rajah of Mattan in Borneo possessed (as stated) a large Diamond which was shaped like an egg, with an indented hollow near its smaller end. It was found in that island, being of the finest water, and weighing more than two ounces. All attempts to polish diamonds were baffled until 1456, when young Berguin of Bruges effected this by rubbing two stones together.

Samuel Pepys has told, in his inimitable Diary, how, on March 4th, 1660, " My Lord (Sir Edward Mountagu, first Earl of Sandwich) went this morning on his journey to Hinchingbroke;—before his going he did give me some jewels to keep for him, viz., that the King of Sweden did give him, with the King's own picture in it, most excellently done; and a brave George; all of diamonds." Again on November 16th, 1664 : " To Eriffe ; where Madame Williams did give me information of Wm. How's having bought eight bags of precious stones, taken from about the Dutch Vice-Admirall's neck; of which there were eight dyamonds which cost him four thousand pounds sterling, in India; and hoped to have made twelve thousand pounds here for them. So, I on board; where Sir Edmund Pooly carried me down into the hold of the India ship, and there did show me the greatest wealth lie in confusion that a man can see in the world,—pepper scattered through every chink, you trod upon it; and in cloves and nutmegs I walked above the knees; whole rooms full. And silk in bales, and boxes of copper-plate, one of which I saw opened."

On July 31st, 1665, Pepys "ended this month with the greatest joy that ever I did any in my life." It was the occasion of Mr. Philip Carteret's marriage to Miss Jemima Mountagu: "though we drove (again from Hinchingbroke) hard with six horses we met them coming from church, which troubled us; but that trouble was soon over, hearing it was well done; they both being in their old cloaths; my Lord Crew giving her away, there being three coach fulls of them. The young lady mighty sad, which troubled me; but yet I think it was only her gravity, in a little greater degree than usual.—At night to supper, and so to talk; and, (which methought was the most extraordinary thing,) all of us to prayers, as usual, and the young bride, and bridegroom too; and so, after prayers, soberly to bed; only I got into the bridegroom's chamber while he undressed himself; and there was very merry, till he was called to the bride's chamber; and into bed they went. I kissed the bride in bed; and so the curtaines drawne with the greatest gravity that could be, and so good night. But the modesty, and gravity of this business was so decent that it was to me indeed ten times more delightful than if it had been twenty times more merry, and joviall."

Sir Thomas Fuller, whose long career has been bound up with Cape Colony, had the distinction, shared only by one or two others, of getting the first glimpse of the first Diamond found in South Africa. The finder (whether on the North, or the South side of the Orange River, has been a disputed point) was a herd-boy. At first this was thought to be a Crystal; then someone sent it up to the Government; at whose instance the French Consul, who was an expert in precious stones, was invited to inspect the small box which contained this supposed "Crystal." As soon as the French Consul saw the stone he at once declared it to be a Diamond. "Take note," he exclaimed, "that at three paces I pronounce it to be a Diamond." Which Diamond weighed seven carats, and resembled a piece of Camphor in appearance. The stone was sold for five hundred pounds.

Captain Gronow (*Anecdotes and Reminiscences*, 1842) relates that "on the day after the Coronation of George IV. (1820), Mr. Hamlet, the jeweller, came to see the house in which Mr. Coutts, the wealthy Banker, then lived (in Stratton Street). Mr. Coutts was at dinner, but admitted the jeweller, who exhibited to him a most magnificent Diamond Cross, which had been worn on the previous day by the Duke of York. This Jewel at once attracted the attention of Mrs. Coutts (Harriet Mellon: afterwards Duchess of St. Albans), who loudly exclaimed "How happy I should be with such a splendid Ornament!" "What is it worth?" asked Mr. Coutts. "I could not allow it to pass out of my possession for less than fifteen thousand pounds," said the wary tradesman. "Bring me a pen and ink"— was the only answer given by the doting husband; and he at once drew a cheque for that amount upon the Bank in the Strand. Then with much delight the worthy old gentleman placed the Jewel upon the fair bosom of the lady:—

"Upon her breast a sparkling cross she wore,
Which Jews might kiss, and infidels adore!"

Within recent times the Diamond has been triturated to a fine powder, and administered therapeutically, in varying doses. It is the "Adamas" of the "Pharmacopœia Homœopathica Polyglotta." Likewise the Emerald (Smaragdus) has been similarly triturated (together with sugar of milk) for medicinal uses, in America. One of our leading practical chemists says he should be more inclined to attribute whatever curative results follow the exhibition of these finely triturated stones "to the Carbon liberated by thermochemical action on the sugar of milk, than to inherent virtues of the precious stones themselves, as developed by such minute subdivision." "The friction of the harder on the softer substance is enormous; and thus we have seen triturations of glass made together with sugar of milk, and still in our possession, which show the carbonising effects of this vitreous substance on the milk-sugar, in a very marked manner." It is a fact well known to Frenchmen that white sugar, when pounded in a mortar with a pestle, gives quite a different taste to "*eau sucrée*" made therewith, than loaf sugar does when used in lumps for the same purpose.

Nevertheless it is quite allowable to suppose that the aggregate of such beneficent qualities, as tropical sunlight, richly endowed streams, mighty volcanic transmutations, and other wonder-working operations of Nature, may lie immeasurably condensed within the imprisonment of a precious Stone;—a Diamond, for instance,—constituting its (so to speak) spiritual essence; this being capable of practical reproduction for health-giving uses under long-continued trituration, or as acted upon by individual physical influences. Though a somewhat abstruse doctrine, the hypothesis is fully borne out by indisputable analogous facts. Professor Doppler, of the Halle University, has shown that "the power of remedial agents may be measured by extension of surface, i.e., of the aggregate surface of all its ultimate molecular constituents, in a state of absolute separation from one another. By disuniting these atomic constituents the actual surface of a body (for our argument, a precious Stone) may be increased from a square inch to several thousand square feet. And such a potentialising separation is to be effected by mixing the substance, already finely pulverised, with an additional quantity of inert sugar of milk, then renewing the process of grinding in a mortar until a homogeneous product has become patiently acquired. The trituration with sugar of milk is resorted-to in order to prevent any reunion of the atoms by virtue of the attraction of affinity which their immediate contact with each other might excite." "In making the successive triturations we shall find that electricity becomes developed on the surface of the atoms thus endowed with a high degree of expansiveness. That such electricity is thus generated may be ascertained very readily by any one who will make these triturations in the dark. After the first trituration but little is seen thereof : it becomes much more intense when making the second trituration ; and still more so during the third. An electric light is readily perceived ; and the crackling of a multitude of little sparks may be heard." "Nature and history furnish many proofs that very small bodies may after this fashion produce powerful effects. The greatest philosophers believe in the infinitely small." Furthermore, is it chimerical to suppose that the sublimated salutary qualities kept packed with almost supernatural closeness within the hard crystallised compass of a gem can be liberated, for good, or bad ends, by certain insensible, but none the less actual, processes ?

As already stated, the Diamond reflects light most strongly. Because of this property (which is similarly possessed by fatty, and unctuous bodies), Sir Isaac Newton supposed that the Diamond might really be " an unctuous substance coagulated." It is moreover probable that Diamonds are of vegetable origin, since, when they are burnt,—at a very high temperature,— carbonic di-oxide is produced. Seeing, likewise, that Diamonds are found in the sands, and gravel, of certain localities, these stones may then be from a meteoric source, and have dropped from the skies in such shape, being literally, " a gift from heaven." Diamonds, according to the older writers, are the distinctive talisman for Saturday (Saturn's day), because they are produced from the black Carbon of Saturn.

The first Diamond necklace made in Europe was given by Charles of France to Agnes Sorel, and was called a " carcanet,"—(an iron collar),—because the sharp edges of the gem hurt the neck of the favourite. So hard is the Diamond in its texture that it must be shaped, and worked in the lapidary's hands only by one of its fellow stones:—" Diamond cut Diamond."

The protective virtue of this superlative Precious Stone has always been commonly believed among all civilised nations. Napoleon the Great had a Diamond set in the hilt of his sword, with a confident assurance that it would secure for him protection, and victory. The Third Napoleon always wore a lucky ring which had belonged to the First Napoleon. The Prince Imperial refused to have this ring removed from his father's finger after death; so that it was buried thereon. Since which time—remarkably enough—the House of Bonaparte have had a succession of misfortunes. President Kruger had an unlucky Diamond, which first belonged to Chaka, the Zulu chief. Chaka's brother assassinated him, and possessed himself of the Diamond. It had changed hands fifteen times before it became the property of Kruger,—each previous owner having died a violent death. Kruger's own misfortunes were associated with this Stone by many persons.

De Boot's notion as to the beneficial effects on the health, and spirits which may be looked-for under the influence of varied light has been verified recently by ascertained facts. Thus M. Redard, Professor of Medicine in the Geneva University, has made a communication lately on this subject to the National Institute at Geneva. He states that each of the primary colours has a definite, and characteristic effect on the human organism. Red light is found to be more or less irritating; with yellow light the general effect is depressing; while blue light proves calming, and produces a sense of well-being. Professor Redard puts his conclusions, as thus stated, to practical effect regarding blue light; under exposure to which a sufficient measure of insensibility to pain can be induced as to allow the performance of minor surgical operations (such as are connected with dentistry, for instance) painlessly. For this effect nothing more is required than an electric light (of sixteen candle power), a blue glass globe, and a sheet of blue satinette. The lamp is fixed in front of the patient's eyes, at a distance of a few inches; and the patient is directed to stare at it, keeping his eyes wide open. His head, and the lamp, are then covered with the blue cloth, so as to exclude all natural light; and he is assured that, if he keeps on staring, he will be unconscious of any pain during the operation which is about to be performed. Then, if the cloth is removed after the lapse of from two to three minutes, the patient will be found in a condition of general insensibility to pain, sufficiently deep for the performance without pain, of any brief surgical operation. The idea naturally occurs to one's mind that this result is actually brought about through such self-suggestion as is now named hypnotism. But this supposition is negatived by Professor Redard's statement that he has failed to produce the same phenomena with either yellow, or red light. Nevertheless a consensus of opinion, medical, and lay, testifies to the importance of wearing red in a tropical country when exposed to the sun's direct rays. Dr. Olpp, for instance, by wearing a red-lined hat suffered far less headache through prolonged exposure to the sun than before resorting to this measure. The Chinese Mandarins in the South, for their official duties out of doors, invariably protect themselves by a baldachin of red hue. Again, there is the red fez of the Turk, the preference for red in the Indian's turban, the partiality for red head-kerchiefs evinced by the native women of South West Africa ; and the red oil used by the Papuan tribes for lubricating their limbs, and anointing their bodies.

It has been found by a series of experiments carried on at the Finsen Institute, Copenhagen, that light affects the blood materially. Darkness will reduce its total amount by three per cent ; decreasing at the same time the quantity of blood in the heart. And red light has a precisely similar effect. But blue light augments the amount of blood, whilst increasing the quantity contained by the heart. Animals born in the dark, or in red light, have a greater weight than those born under ordinary conditions but only half the amount of blood.

As to the genuine character of precious Stones, Mr. Harry Emanuel tells that " the tourmaline is sometimes mistaken for the ruby ; the pink topaz for the balas ruby ; and occasionally the white sapphire, as likewise the white topaz, pass for the Diamond,—even with those persons who profess to be acquainted with Gems. But the tables of " hardness," " specific gravity " ; and " electrical properties," should prevent any one from falling into such errors, since nothing can be more easy than from these given data to ascertain to which class any particular Stone belongs." A special endowment of the Diamond, by which its genuineness, or its spurious character, may be determined, is its single refraction of transmitted light. This particular property among precious stones appertains only to the Diamond, the Garnet, and the Spinel Ruby. Furthermore, a ready method, which is fairly reliable, for telling whether or not Stones are genuine, is to touch them with the tip of the tongue ; when the true stone will give a colder sensation than the false stone, because being a better conductor of heat. Various methods are attempted for testing the genuineness of Diamonds; most of the same being only feasible by an expert; nevertheless the test by light is very reliable, and simple enough to be easily applied by an amateur. The Gem should be held at arm's length, about ten inches from the light of a candle, or lamp, in a straight line with the eye. If the Diamond is real it will give out only a single bright ray of refraction.

Diamantino is the city of the Diamond mines in Brazil. A negro is reported to have found a diamond there of nine carats among the roots of some vegetables which he pulled up in his garden.

If a manufactured diamond contains a flaw, (being thus " off colour,") its value is diminished. To ascertain if the flaw exists, the gem should be breathed-on until its lustre is temporarily abolished, when any such imperfection may be easily detected.

Other precious Stones besides the Diamond are sensibly affected by mutations of light, and heat, when telling on their substance. Topazes, when exposed to a low red heat in a sand bath, become of a fine pink hue; but they lose much of their first brilliancy after being exposed to any bright light for a length of time. Opals, as is well known, are peculiarly sensitive to extremes of heat, and cold; whilst at the same time they are the most brittle stones which occur. The prismatic reflections to which they owe their beauty are entirely due to the minute seams, and clefts which are distributed over their surface, and which emit rays of light in every direction. Rubies, again, are to be included amongst those Gems which are most readily affected by strong light. Experiments have been made on two such stones, of equally intense colouring, the one being exposed to continuous light during the daytime, whilst the other remained shut up within an hermetically sealed box. Of the two, that which was kept in the light was found to have lost an evident amount of colouring after a few years, when compared with the other specimen, it being in this way deprived of some of its value. Nevertheless Rubies, as well as Sapphires, and Emeralds, are less prone to discoloration than many other stones; and are less susceptible to sudden changes of temperature, or extremes of heat, and cold.

The Diamond, when worn of old, was believed to make a man "rather fearless than careful." A jacinth had the reputation of being able to strengthen the heart; and was often worn close to that organ, fashioned into the form of some animal, or saint. The Sapphire was supposed to possess a divine gift of sharpening the intellect; and was also worn as a preventive against the bites of venomous animals. The Emerald was worn in a ring to prevent giddiness, and strengthen the memory. Garcius adds, "it takes away foolish fears of devils, and hobgoblins, folly, and anger." Great faith was placed in the Ruby as an amulet to ward off plagues, and pestilences. Cardamus says, "it has the power of making the wearer cheerful, whilst banishing idle, and foolish thoughts." The Amethyst was supposed to promote temperance, and sobriety, to cause the wearer to abstain from strong drinks, and from taking too much sleep. By other writers this stone is said also to quicken the wit, and repel vapours from the head. The Chrysolite was thought to ward off fevers; whilst the Onyx, worn round the neck, was supposed to prevent an attack of epilepsy. The Opal was believed to cure weak eyes; and the Topaz to cure inflammations, and keep the wearer from sleep-walking. Lapis-Lazuli, worn as a jewel, acts similarly to the Sapphire; in ancient medicine it was given as a purgative. In the Talmud it is said that Noah had no other light in the Ark than that furnished by precious Stones.

Readers of *The Arabian Nights*, whether as a fascinating delight of childhood, or as a mental recreation in after life, will remember the Story of Sinbad, the Merchant of Bagdad, who acquired great wealth by his commercial enterprise, and activity. How he went seven voyages; which he related to a poor discontented porter, named Hindbad, the object being to show this man that wealth must be gained by perseverance in trade, and personal exertion. It happened to Sinbad in his second voyage that he was left during sleep, on a desert island, where he discovered a "Roc's egg," fifty paces in circumference. He fastened himself to one of this huge bird's claws, and was deposited in the "Valley of Diamonds." Next day some merchants came to the top of the crags; and threw into the valley large joints of raw meat;—to which the Diamonds stuck. And when the eagles picked up the meat, the merchants scared these birds from their nests, and bore off the diamonds. Sinbad fastened himself to one of the pieces of meat; being thus carried by an eagle to its nest; from which he was rescued by the merchants, having laden himself with diamonds, which he brought home triumphantly.

Again, in the story of "Aladdin and the Wonderful

Lamp" (by means of which the "son of a poor Chinese tailor,—obstinate, disobedient, and mischievous," eventually became enormously rich, and married the Sultan's daughter), we are told that at first both he, and his mother were reduced to poverty through his indolence. One day an African Magician accosted Aladdin, pretending to be his uncle, and sent him down into a cavern, to bring up therefrom the Wonderful Lamp: but giving him at the same time a "ring of safety." Aladdin secured the Lamp, but would not hand it to the Magician until he was out of the cave; whereupon the Magician shut him up in the cave, and departed for Africa. Aladdin, wringing his hands in despair, happened to rub the "magic ring," when the Genius of the "ring" appeared before him, and asked what were his commands. Aladdin requested to be delivered from the cave; and then returned home. Being in want of food the mother of Aladdin began to scrub the Lamp, intending to sell it; when the Genius of the Lamp again appeared, and promptly supplied for their wants a sumptuous feast. Having thus learnt the merits of the Wonderful Lamp, Aladdin obtained, as has been said, untold wealth; built a superb Palace; and married Badroulboudour, the Sultan's daughter. At the top of the said Palace was a Saloon containing twenty-four windows, (six on each side), all but one of the same being enriched with diamonds, rubies, and emeralds. The solitary exception was left for the Sultan to complete; but all the jewellers in his Empire were unable to make such a window as would match the others. Aladdin straightway commanded the "slaves of the Lamp to complete the work."

Incidentally from these famous tales (each of which

conveys a useful lesson, though seldom is this perceived by the ordinary readers of the well-known stories) we may gather profitable instruction, besides being delightedly amused by all the glamour, and fascination of Fairy Legends. To somehow teach these lessons to the youngsters at Christmastime, when the splendid pantomimes are produced, year after year, each magnificent show being designed to illustrate one or another of the "Arabian Nights'" entertainments, would vastly enhance the value of these occasions. Though, of course, for the mummers to prove didactic, (like good Mr. Barlow, in *Sandford and Merton* :—Thomas Day, 1795)—or for the Clown to preach a sermon, in place of "Hot Codlins," or "Tippitywitchet," would lamentably spoil all the fun of the Fair!

The most charming edition extant of *The Thousand and One Nights*, commonly called *The Arabian Nights' Entertainments*, is the rare set of three volumes translated from the Arabic, by Edward William Lane; having been published by Charles Knight, in the year 1841. It is, moreover, delightfully illustrated with several hundred wood engravings, by William Harvey. The Introduction runs this: "In the name of God, the Compassionate; the Merciful." "Praise be to God, the Beneficent King, the Creator of the Universe, who hath raised the heavens without pillars, and spread out the earth as a bed !—and blessing, and peace be on the lord of Apostles, our lord, and master, Mohammed, and his Family; blessing, and peace, enduring, and constant, unto the day of judgment."

"The lives of former generations are a lesson to posterity; that a man may review the remarkable events which have happened to others, and be admonished, and may consider the history of people of preceding ages, and of all that hath befallen them; and be restrained."

"Extolled be the perfection of Him who hath thus ordained the history of former generations to be a lesson to those which follow! Such are the *Tales of a Thousand and one Nights*, with their romantic stories, and their fables." This recital of a *Thousand and one Nights*, was originally derived from a Persian, or perhaps, an Indian, source, and was most probably translated in the time of the Caliph Mansour, who came to the throne, A.D. 754: that is to say, thirty years before the reign of the Caliph Haroun Alraschid (786–809), who was afterwards made to play so large a part in the histories. "In reading these fascinating Tales, which abound so sumptuously with Eastern magnificence, luxury, wealth, splendour, priceless gems, costly banquets, and every possible refinement which boundless riches might produce,—it may be thought that they are thus embellished to an extravagant, and impossible extent. Nevertheless the tales were written by an author of the country which they so graphically depict; and (except as to the Enchantments, which are flights of Oriental fancy, and imagination), they are a true representation of Persian manners, and doings, at the time supposed."

Quite worthy of reference as corroborative of the statement thus advanced is the following extract from the Diary of Lady Mary Wortley Montague (1720)—(who first introduced inoculation against small-pox)—in which she gives an account of her visit to the Sultana Hafiten, who became the favourite of Sultan Mastapha, after the death of Fatima. This highly descriptive passage affords, on personal veracious evidence, a glowing picture of the splendour, magnificence, and richness of Eastern dresses. "I was led into a large room, with a sofa extending the whole length of it, covered with pale blue figured velvet, on a silver ground, with cushions of the same; where I was desired to repose until the Sultana appeared, who had contrived this manner of reception so as to avoid rising at my entrance: though she made me an inclination of the head when I rose up to her. She did not seem to me to have ever been so beautiful as the fair Fatima, (whom I saw at Adrianople,) though she had the remains of a fine face, more decayed by sorrow than time. Her dress was something so surprisingly rich that I cannot forbear describing it. She wore a vest called 'dualma,' which differs from a caftan by longer sleeves, and folding over at the bottom. It was of purple cloth, straight to her shape, and thick set, on each side, down to her feet, and round the sleeves, with pearls, of the best water, being of the same size as their buttons usually are, about the bigness of a pea. And to these buttons large loops of diamonds were fastened in the form of those gold loops so common on birthday coats. This habit was tied at the waist with two large tassels of smaller pearls, and round the arms embroidered with large diamonds. Her shift was fastened at the bottom with a large diamond shaped like a lozenge: her girdle, as broad as the broadest English ribbon, was entirely covered with diamonds: round her neck she wore three chains which reached to her knees; one, of large pearls, at the bottom of which hung a fine coloured emerald, as big as a turkey egg: another consisting of two hundred emeralds, close joined together, of the most lively green, perfectly matched, every one as large as a half-crown piece, and as thick as three crown pieces; and another of small emeralds, perfectly round. But her ear-rings eclipsed all the rest. They were two diamonds shaped exactly like pears; as large as a big hazel nut. Round her talpoche she had four strings of pearls, the whitest, and most perfect in the world, fastened with two roses, consisting of a large ruby for the middle stone; and round them twenty drops of clear diamonds to each. Besides this, her headdress was covered with bodkins of emeralds, and diamonds. She wore large diamond bracelets, and had five rings on her fingers;—except Mr. Pitt's, the largest diamonds I ever saw in my life. 'Tis for jewellers to compute the value of all these things; but, according to the common estimation of jewels in our part of the world, her whole dress must be worth a hundred thousand pounds sterling. The magnificence of her table answered very well to that of her dress. The knives were of gold; and the hafts set with diamonds. But the only articles of luxury which grieved my eyes were the table-cloth, and napkins, which consisted all of tiffany, embroidered with gold, after the finest manner, in natural flowers. It was with the utmost regret that I made use of these costly silken napkins, which were as finely wrought as the finest handkerchiefs that ever came out of the country. You may be sure that they were entirely spoilt before dinner was over. The Sherbet (which is the liquor they drink with their meals) was served in china bowls, but the covers, and salvers were of massive gold. After dinner water was brought in gold basins, together with towels (of the same kind as the napkins), which I very unwillingly wiped my hands upon; and coffee was served in china, with gold spoons. When I took my leave of her I was complimented with perfumes, as at the Grand Vizier's, and was presented with a very fine embroidered handkerchief. Her slaves were to the number of thirty, besides ten little ones, the eldest not above seven years old. These were the most beautiful girls I ever saw; all richly dressed: and I observed that the Sultana took a great deal of pleasure in these lovely children, which are a vast expense; for there is not a handsome girl of that age to be bought under a hundred pounds sterling. They wore little garlands of flowers; and their own hair braided with all their head-dresses; but their habits were entirely of gold stuff."

"It is our duty," says Sir Richard Burton, in his unparalleled, and scholarly edition of *The Thousand Nights, and a Night*,—twelve volumes,—"to read the 'Arabian Nights,' and to try to understand the life portrayed there so vividly; and this duty is not an unpleasant one! We all, when we were children, knew something of the mere husk of the tales; we peopled our fancied East with brave Princes, and tender Princesses, with jewelled palaces, and mystic islands, heroes, and robbers, genii, and magicians;—but to the adult mind *The Nights*, in a fuller revelation, offer a perspective which is even more amazing. 'The Tales not only teach, but inspire; and many romantic writers of the modern school have acknowledged their debt to even an imperfect translation of the Tales." Thackeray has told us in a charming passage how *The Nights* fascinated, and inspired him. In the Life of Charles Dickens we read that the dormant imagination of the future novelist was roused to action by *The Thousand*

Nights; and Balzac never turned to them in vain when his prodigious imagination needed a spur. "Shahrazad's Tales" preserve their charm for us in even greater measure than *The Pilgrim's Progress*, or *Gulliver's Travels;* for, although the mature mind finds in them an accurate, and detailed picture of the Moslem World, yet they retain a romantic interest altogether without parallel.—"He that hearkens Eastward hears

> "Bright music from the world where shadows are;
> Where shadows are not shadows."
> *Algernon Charles Swinburne.*

Tennyson has told, in graceful verse, about his "Recollections of the *Arabian Nights*."

> "On many a sheeny summer morn,
>   Adown the Tigris I was borne,
>   By Bagdat's shrines of fretted gold,
>   Its high-walled gardens, green, and old;
>   True Mussulman I was, and sworn;
>   For it was in the golden prime
>   Of good Haroun Alraschid.
>
> "Six columns, three on either side,
>   Pure silver, underpropt a rich
>   Throne of the massive ore, from which
>   Down droop'd in many a floating fold,
>   Engarlanded, and diaper'd
>   With inwrought flowers, a cloth of gold:
>   Thereon—his deep eye laughter-stirred
>   With merriment of kingly pride,—
>   Sole star of all that place, and time,
>   I saw him in his golden prime,
>   The Good Haroun Alraschid!"

THE SAPPHIRE.

NEXT to the diamond in hardness, beauty, and value, comes the Sapphire: the "holy Sapphire," which is found to render its bearer "pacific, amiable, pious, and devout, confirming the soul in good works "; which refuses to shine for the beautifying of the unchaste, or the impure; and which, by the mere force of its own pure rays, kills all noxious and venomous creatures.

The Sapphire in its true colour is blue; blue as an Italian sky, blue as the deep blue sea. But it may also be red, and yellow, and violet, and green, and hair-brown, such a brown as the Venetian painters loved, with a golden light striking through it.

Sometimes the stone is bluish-grey, and blackish; the Sapphire also sometimes changes colour by artificial light. Sapphires of the finest blue come from Ceylon. The composition thereof is pure Alumina, for the most part.

Next to the diamond the Sapphire is the hardest known mineral. Its splendid colour of deep translucent blue is probably due to the presence of oxide of cobalt; which chemical salt is invariably used when making imitations of the gem. The Sapphire of the ancients is our "Lapis Lazuli."

Epiphanius said, "It is medicinal; for, being powdered it heals the sores following pustules, and boils, if smeared over them, being thus applied mixed with milk to the ulcerations."—" It is written also in the Law that the vision seen by Moses in the Mount, and the Law given there unto him were made out of the Stone, Sapphire." The chemical constituents of the Sapphire are (being virtually pure alumina, coloured through admixture with oxide of iron, cobalt). "Alumina, 98·5; lime, 0·5; silica, 0·0; oxide of iron, 1·0." The gem is highly electric.

Dr. John Schroder wrote (in Latin, 1669) concerning the Sapphire, "It is of a sky-blue colour; clear, and transparent. Some stones are blue and white; these are called the males; the others are the females. The colour is easily taken out by fire." "The vertues of the Saphyre are—it is cold, dry, and astringent: it dryes up rheums in the eyes, and takes away their inflammation, being used in collysiums, or to anoint the eyelids. It is good in all fluxes of the belly, the dysentery, the hepatick flux, the hæmorrhoids, and other bleedings; it cures internal ulcers, and wounds, strengthens the heart, and refreshes it; is an enemy to all poisons; it likewise cures melancholy."

"A whole Stone laid to the forehead stops bleeding at the nose, and when applied to inflammations abates them. Being brought into little balls, as big as peas, and polished, and put in the eyes, it takes out anything that is fallen-in, dust, or gnats; and preserves the eyes from the small pox, and other diseases." "A Saphyre is prepared the common way, by levigation, with cordial water." "Others dissolve the fine dust of a Saphyre in pure vinegar, and juyce of limons, and give the solution, with some other cordial."

Furthermore, Mr. Boyle in his treatise already named, goes on to say, " I am not of their minde that reject the internal use of leaf-gold, rubys, sapphyrs, emeralds, and other gems, as things that are unconquerable by the heat of the stomack. For, I think the stomack acts not upon medicines barely by means of its heat, but is endow'd with a subtle dissolvent by which it may perform divers things not to be done by so languid a heat alone. And I have with liquors of differing sorts (easily drawn from vegetable substances, and perhaps unrectified) sometimes dissolved, and sometimes drawn, tinctures from gems, and that in the cold.

But what I chiefly consider is on this occasion that 'tis one thing to make the possibility probable that gold, rubys, sapphyrs, etc., may be wrought upon by the humane stomack; and another thing to show both that they are wont to be so, and that they are actually endowed with those particular, and specifick vertues that are ascribed to them." Among the Alchemists—Paracelsus, of Basel, invented, about the year 1520, such a solvent liqueur, called "The Great Secret."

The Middle Ages had a strange passion for gold. Small fragments of this metal were intermixed with many of their choice drinks; which metallic additions not only flattered a refined taste, but were further supposed to be of value in curing disease. One of their earliest liqueurs — "Aqua d'Oro"—contained incorporated gold-leaves. This "Golden Water" was introduced into France from Italy by Catherine de Medicis.

When a new Cardinal is elected by the Pope in the Roman Catholic Church, he receives with much pomp, and ceremony, at a public Consistory, a red hat; and, subsequently, when bestowing on him his title, the Pope puts on the ring-finger of the Cardinal's right hand a gold ring, set with a Sapphire. This is done according to a Bull of Gregory XV., to show that "the Church is now his spouse, and that he must never abandon her." Judging by the show of Ecclesiastical Rings (mainly Papal) to be seen amongst antique objects at the South Kensington (now "Victoria and Albert") Museum, these finger jewels, though sacerdotal, were made most commonly in their day from some base metal, bronze, or brass-gilt, and not of gold.

They are thick, clumsy, block-shaped, hump-backed, Rings, furnished in several instances with mock Sapphires, of pretentious blue paste; or even simply of opaque glass. The shabby, pretentious grandeur of these adornments, associated of old with Cardinals, and other high dignitaries of the opulent Romish Church, is surprising.

In those most fascinating (whilst somewhat broad) *Legends of Mirth, and Marvel*, by Thomas Ingoldsby, Esquire (Revd. Thomas Barham), 1840: (rhymed with marvellous facility, and humorous to the last degree), the talented Author has translated—"De Illust. Ord. Cisterc,"—a tale well known to every admirer of the best English literature,—" The Jackdaw of Rheims."

The classical argument on which this most popular tale is founded, runs as follows:—*Tunc miser Corvus adeo conscientiæ stimulis compunctus fuit, et execratio eum tantopere excarnificavit, ut exinde tabescere inciperet, maciem contraheret, omnem cibum aversaretur, nec amplius crocitaret; pennæ præterea ei defluebant, et alis pendulis omnes facetias intermisit; et tam macer apparuit ut omnes ejus miserescent.—Tunc Abbas sacerdotibus mandavit ut rursus furem absolverent; quo facto, Corvus, omnibus mirantibus, propediem convaluit, et pristinam sanitatem recuperavit.*"

To begin-with, a feast is capitally versified, whereat the Lord Primate is served by a goodly company of " Bishop, and Abbot, Monk, and Friar: many a Knight, and many a Squire "; the Jackdaw sitting demurely enough meantime on the Cardinal's chair. Presently, " In and out through the motley rout this little Jackdaw kept hopping about; here and there, like a dog in a fair." Then :—

"The Feast was over; the board was clear'd;
The flawns, and the custards had all disappeared;
And six little singing-boys;—dear little souls!
In nice clean faces, and nice clean stoles,
  Came, in order due,
    Two by two,
Marching that grand refectory through,
A nice little boy held a golden ewer,
Emboss'd, and filled with water as pure
As any that flows between Rheims and Namur,
Which a nice little boy stood ready to catch
In a fine golden hand-basin made to match.
Two nice little boys, rather more grown,
Carried Lavender-water, and Eau-de-Cologne;
And a nice little boy had a nice cake of soap,
Worthy of washing the hands of the Pope.—
  One little boy more
  A napkin bore,
Of the best white diaper, fring'd with pink,
And a Cardinal's hat marked in ' permanent ink.'

The great Lord Cardinal turns at the sight
Of these nice little boys dressed all in white;
From his finger he draws
His costly Turquoise;
And, not thinking at all about little Jackdaws,
  Deposits it straight
  By the side of his plate,
While the nice little boys on his Eminence wait;
Till, when nobody's dreaming of any such thing,
That little Jackdaw hops off with the Ring."

Here the clever author of this most amusing Legend makes a manifest mistake about the kind of precious stone which is invariably chosen for a Cardinal's official ring. As we have already stated, a Sapphire is appointed by the Romish Church for this symbolical purpose.

To the remainder of " The Jackdaw of Rheims " it is needless to refer. All readers of *The Ingoldsby Legends* know how, when the ecclesiastical ring was not to be found, high nor low, the irate Cardinal " rose with a dignified look; he call'd for his candle, his bell, and his book." Then, " In holy anger, and pious grief, he solemnly cursed the rascally thief." Eventually, when "the day was gone; and night came on, the sacristan saw, on crumpled claw, come limping a poor little lame Jackdaw; which feebly gave vent to the ghost of a 'caw'; and turn'd his bald head, as much as to say, 'Pray be so good as to walk this way.'"

> "Slower, and slower,
> He limped on before,
> Till they came to the back of the belfry door,
> Where the first thing they saw,
> Midst the sticks and the straw,
> Was the ring, in the nest of that little Jackdaw."

This being happily so, the bird was forgiven; the terrible curse removed; the poor little bird "was so changed in a moment, 'twas really absurd; he grew sleek, and fat; in addition to that, a fresh crop of feathers grew thick as a mat":—

> "He hopp'd now about,
> With a gait devout;
> At Matins, at Vespers he never was out;
> While many remarked, as his manners they saw,
> That they never had known such a pious Jackdaw!
> He long lived the pride
> Of that country side;
> And, at last, in the odour of sanctity, died."

Francis Barrett ("Magus," 1801) has said, "A Sapphire, or a stone that is of a deep blue colour, if it be rubbed on a tumour wherein the plague discovers itself, (before the party is too far gone;) and if, by and by it be removed from the sick, the absent jewel attracts all the poison, or contagion therefrom." "And thus much is sufficient to be said concerning its occult natural virtues." The Sapphire frequently becomes dull by candle-light; though a really fine stone will retain its blueness then, as well as by daylight.

When the Russian Grand Duke Sergius was assassinated (March 6th, 1905), among the articles found on the scene of his assassination was a curious stone, perfectly black in colour, which, on examination, proved to be a large Sapphire, from a ring worn by the Grand Duke. It was supposed to have lost its colour through the effects of flame from the bomb.

The Hebrew name for this gem is "Sapphir"; the Chaldaic, "Sapirinon"; the Greek, "Xaffiros"; the Latin, "Sapphirus."

To the Sapphire has been ascribed the magical properties of preventing wicked, and impure thoughts; whilst being such an enemy to poison, that if put into a glass with a spider, or venomous reptile, it kills the same. Saint Jerome, in his exposition of Isaiah, chapter xxx., says, that "the Sapphire procures favour with princes, pacifies enemies, and gives freedom from enchantment, or captivity." In classical times this gem was sacred to Apollo, and was worn when enquiring of the Oracle at his shrine. It was esteemed as a remedy against fevers; whence arose the old distich :—

"Corporis ardorem refrigerat interiorem
Sapphirus, et Cypriæ languida vota facit."

Boetius tells that, on account of its attachment to chastity, it was formerly worn by priests. This Stone is frequently mentioned in the Bible as being of great value, and exquisite beauty. "The superstitious assigned thereto the virtue of preserving the sight, and invigorating the body as well as the soul."

"One precious stone," says Mr. Streeter, "is notorious more than all for its beneficent, kindly influence. It is the great rival of the Diamond; it is the Sapphire, of that indescribably beautiful blue of the field-cornflower, bearing with it ever the tint of the heaven under which it glistens with matchless beauty." To the Sapphire Stone the throne above the Cherubim is likened in Holy Writ.

The Sapphire, furthermore, in former times had the virtues ascribed to it by common consent, if worn about the person—of healing boils, of amending the manners, and of restoring impaired sight. According to Bartholomew Anglicus (1250), it was thus pronounced, "The Sapphire is a precious stone, and is blue in colour, most like to heaven in fair weather, and clear; and is best among precious stones,—and most apt and able to fingers of kings. Its virtue is contrary to venom, and quencheth it at every deal. And if thou put an addercop (viper) in a box, and hold a very Sapphire of Ind at the mouth of the box, any while, by virtue thereof the addercop is overcome, and dieth as it were suddenly. And this same I have seen oft proved in many and divers places."—The "cop" or head, of an adder has on its top a characteristic "blotch," something like the "death's head and thigh-bones" of the "death's head moth." Vipers were formerly held in estimation as a medicine. Pliny, Galen, and others extolled their flesh for the cure of ulcers. Quite recently in the French tariff they were subject to a duty of four shillings per pound. In Italy a stew, or jelly, of vipers (*Pelias berus*) is regarded as a luxury.

Leonardus wrote (1750): "The Sapphire heals sores; and is found to discharge a carbuncle with a single touch."

The old-time commendation of the Sapphire for sacerdotal wear, as inspiring chastity, most probably arose through the remarkable coldness of this stone to the touch, by reason of its great density. Epiphanius similarly records its power of extinguishing fire, because of a natural antagonism to heat.

Even the pious, sober-minded, grave St. Jerome wrote that the Sapphire "conciliates to its wearer the condescension of princes, quells his enemies, disperses sorcery, sets free the captive, and actually assuages the wrath of God himself."

September asserts its right to the Sapphire; which was one of the Stones in the Breast-Plate of Aaron, the High Priest of God. It has, therefore, been ever associated with sacred things; perhaps, also, because its pure azure symbolizes heaven's blue serenity.

Of Sapphires (the jewel for September, as ruled by Taurus), as to their colour—the true cornflower blue, *bleu de roi*, is the most valuable shade, and quite uncommon. They should be worn on Wednesday, the day for all blue stones.

It was Prometheus (the first to wear a ring, set with such a stone from the Caucasus) who stole fire from heaven for man.

A Sapphire ring was intimately concerned, according to history, with the death of our lion-hearted Queen Elizabeth. The circumstances have been related by Miss Agnes Strickland (*Lives of the Queens of England*, 1851), as follows: " The Queen, on March 24th, 1602, when mortally ill, exhausted by her devotions, had, after the Archbishop left her, sunk into a deep sleep, (from which she never woke), and, at about three in the morning it was discovered she had ceased to breathe. Lady Scrope gave the first intelligence of this fact by silently dropping a Sapphire ring to her brother, who was lurking beneath the window of the chamber of death, at Richmond Palace. This ring remained known for long afterwards in Court tradition as the 'blue ring,' which had been confided to Lady Scrope by James as appointed for a certain signal to announce the Queen's decease. Sir Robert caught the token, fraught, as it was, with the destiny of the Island empire, and departed, at fiery speed, to tell the tidings in Scotland. Thus, the spirit of the mighty Elizabeth passed away, after all, so quietly, that the vigilance of the self-interested spies by whom she was surrounded was baffled; and no one knew the actual moment of her departure."

Another story,—of an historical ring again associated with Queen Elizabeth,—likewise related by Miss Strickland, may be of equal interest here to our readers. It concerns a ring which the Queen was said to have bestowed upon Essex, the ill-fated Earl, in a moment of fondness, as a pledge of her affection; with an intimation that, should he ever forfeit her favour, if he would send this ring back to her, the sight of it would ensure her forgiveness. When Essex lay under sentence of death he determined to try the virtue of the ring by returning it to the Queen, and claiming the benefit of her promise: but knowing he was surrounded by the creatures of those who were bent on taking his life, he was fearful of trusting the ring to any of the attendants. At length, looking out of his window, he saw early one morning a boy whose countenance pleased him, and whom he induced by a bribe to carry the ring (which he threw down to him from above), to the Lady Scrope, his cousin, who had taken so friendly an interest in his fate. The boy, by mistake carried it to the Countess of Nottingham, the cruel sister of the fair, and gentle

Scrope; and, as both these ladies were of the royal bedchamber, the mistake might easily occur.

"The Countess conveyed the ring to her husband, the Lord Admiral, who was the deadly foe of Essex, and told him the message; but he bade her suppress both.

"The Queen, unconscious of the accident, waited, in the painful suspense of an angry lover, for the expected token to arrive; but, not receiving it, she concluded that Essex was too proud to make this last appeal to her tenderness; and, after having once revoked the Warrant, she ordered the execution to proceed."

No European sovereign ever manifested so inordinate a passion for personal ornament as did Queen Elizabeth. Furthermore, she employed precious stones profusely towards other purposes besides those of self-adornment; for instance, on the occasion of her visit to Tilbury:—

> "He happy was that could but see her coach,
> The sides whereof, beset with Emeralds,
> And Diamonds; with sparkling Rubies red,
> In checkerwise, by strange invention,
> With curious knots embroidered in Gold."

Queen Elizabeth, with all her masculine good sense, was surprisingly superstitious! "Her Majesty," says Lady Southwell, "being then in very good health, one day Sir John Stanhope, Vice-Chamberlain, came, and presented her with a piece of gold, of the bigness of an angel, full of characters; which piece, as it was stated, an old woman in Wales had on her deathbed bequeathed to the Queen; and, thereupon, Sir John discoursed how the said testatrix, by virtue of the piece of gold, lived to the age of one hundred and twenty years; and, when come to that age, having all her body withered, and consumed, and nature failing to nourish her, she died, commanding the same piece of gold to be carefully sent to her Majesty; alleging further, that as long as she might wear it on her body she could not die. The Queen, in full confidence, took the said gold, and hung it about her neck." Finally, on January 14th, 1602, the Queen, having sickened two days before of a cold, and being forewarned of Dee, who retained his mysterious influence over her mind to the last, to "beware of Whitehall," removed to Richmond, "which," she said, "was the warm winter-box to shelter her old age."

In a letter from Lord Chancellor Hutton (September 11th, 1586), concerning an epidemic then prevailing in England, was enclosed a ring, for Queen Elizabeth, to wear between her breasts, which would have the virtue to " expell infectious airs."

Whilst discoursing about these historical rings we may hark back to a date long prior to the times of English kings, and queens, so as to learn how originated the noted "Ring of Gyges," which has remained proverbial since early classical days, 718 B.C. It would seem, according to Plato, that Gyges, a Lydian, thinking to avenge the Queen, who had been grossly insulted by King Candaulus, her husband, descended into a deep chasm of the earth, where he found a brazen horse, the sides of which he opened; and within the horse's body he discovered the carcase of a gigantic man, from whose finger he took the brass ring, which has become traditionally famous. This ring, when put on his own finger, but with its stone turned inwards, rendered Gyges invisible. (and has become a byword for any such faculty ever since). By means of the said strange endowment Gyges introduced himself, as the myth alleges, to the Queen of Candaulus, slew her husband, then married her, and usurped the Crown of Lydia. What particular Precious Stone this famous legendary ring held classical lore does not reveal.

The German Emperor is said to repose some faith in the talismanic properties of a ring which he always wears, and from which he would not part. This jewel is a large, dark, rather ugly-looking stone, in a heavy setting of dull gold; and the Kaiser wears it on the middle finger of his left hand. It is stated to be an heirloom in the family of Hohenzollern, having been at one time the property of the great Saladin.

Rings have for hundreds of years played an important part in the life of the City of Venice. Saint Mark is believed to have saved the city at one time from destruction by a raging storm; and, in proof of his intervention, to have given a ring from his finger to the boatman, whom he had persuaded to challenge the storm with him. He then bade the said fisherman direct the authorities of the city to look in the sanctuary for the Ring of St. Mark, which they would not be able to find. The fisherman did as he was bid, showing the ring, whilst relating his story to the City Rulers. A solemn thanksgiving was ordered for the preservation of the city: and the fisherman was pensioned for life.

With respect to the Cramp Rings still kept in memory as associated with Good Friday, the story goes, that on the said day a certain king of England gave a ring from his finger to a beggar, who was asking alms "for the love of Saint John, the Evangelist." Many years afterwards this ring was brought back to the king as a gift from the Holy Land; and was placed by him in Westminster Abbey, where it remained for several centuries, and was supposed to cure all those afflicted with cramp, or with the falling sickness (epilepsy), who touched the ring. From this, it is said, the quondam English custom arose of hallowing "Cramp Rings" on Good Friday; whereby "the Kynge's Majestie hath a great helpe in this matter, by halowyng Crampe Ringes, and so given without money, or petition."— *Breviary of Health*, 1567. Such rings, warranted sovran against epilepsy, were inscribed "Marie Jesu," in the fifteenth century.

There was a clause in the Will of the late Napoleon the Third, to the effect that—"With regard to my son, I desire that he will keep as a Talisman the seal which I used to wear attached to my watch." The ill-fated Prince Imperial obeyed this injunction, and always carried the seal, suspended by a string round his neck; but, alas! it brought him anything but good luck. At the time of his death this seal was, probably, carried off by the Zulus, who stripped his body. The inscription engraved thereon was (in Arabic characters), if translated: "The Slave Abraham relying on the Merciful" (God).

The Sapphire is identically the same stone as the Ruby. It differs in name on account of the colour, which varies from white to the deepest blue, or even black. It has the same hardness, composition, electrical properties, and other such attributes as the Ruby. The difference between a white Sapphire and a Diamond can be easily ascertained by taking the specific gravity, or by testing the hardness with another Sapphire, or Diamond. Sapphires contain small quantities of magnesia, (as likewise do rubies), with oxide of iron, and silica. In "*The General History of Druggs*, (1712), by the Messrs. Lemery and Tournefort,"—when treating of Stones, they say, concerning the Sapphirus, or Saphir, "used in physick are the fragments, or pieces which the lapidaries cut off from the Saphirs, which are much about the size of large pin-heads, reddish, or blackish; but the red are to be prefer'd, because the black are full of iron-stone; by which we may perceive they have some analogy to the Loadstone, for they will be attracted like iron." "There are a great many virtues attributed to the Saphirs which they have not; as the fortifying the heart, and other noble parts, purifying the blood, resisting of Poyson; their true properties are to stop fluxes, sweeten the blood, and dry up ulcers of the eyes."

To serve utilitarian purposes Sapphire Stones are put into the works of watches, for some of the wheels to rotate upon as hard, durable pivots.

On their signet-rings both the Phœnicians and the Asiatics manifested a persistent partiality for the old Egyptian Scarabæi, or Beetles. It may be that as the received symbol of the Sun this insect commended itself to the Phœnicians (who were exclusive worshippers of that luminary, under the name of Baal): the Beetle having acquired this distinction amongst the Egyptians from its habit of forming globes, types of the world, as receptacles for its eggs; thus symbolizing the creation, by the Divine Author of its being. Ælian states further, that amongst the Egyptians their warriors wore beetles in their rings, as a badge of their profession; because the insect typified manliness, being, according to the popular belief, exclusively of the male sex.

"Rings," Magus, (Francis Barrett, (1801), has said in his *Occult Philosophy*, "when they are opportunely made, impress their virtues upon us, insomuch that they affect the spirit of him that carries them, with gladness, or sadness; and render him bold, or fearful; courteous, or terrible; amiable. or hateful; inasmuch also as they fortify us against sickness, poisons, enemies, evil spirits, and all manner of hurtful things."

"I have read in Philostratus Jarchus that a Prince of the Indians bestowed seven Rings, marked with the virtues, and names of the Seven Planets, on Apollonius; of which he wore one every day, distinguishing according to the names of the days; by the benefit of which Rings he lived above one hundred and thirty years, as also always retained the beauty of his youth." "In like manner Moses, the Lawgiver, and Ruler of the Hebrews, being skilled in the Egyptian Magic, is said by Josephus to have constructed Rings of Love, and Oblivion."

"The manner of making Talismanic Rings is this. When any star ascends (auspiciously) in the horoscope, with a fortunate aspect, or conjunction of the moon, we proceed to take a Stone, and Herb, that are under the star, and we likewise make a ring of the metal that is corresponding to the star; and, in the ring, beneath the stone put the herb, or root, not forgetting to inscribe the image, name, and character, as also the proper suffume, (a decoction of root, herb, flower, seed, etc.: the smoke of which is conveyed into the body from a close-stool)."

About a century ago it was customary to wear the Marriage-ring on the thumb; though at the nuptial ceremony it was placed on the fourth finger. The fashion of wearing a ring on the thumb is very ancient in England. During Elizabeth's reign, grave persons, such as aldermen, wore a plain gold ring upon the thumb. Brome, in his Play, "The Antipodes" (1638) wrote, "A good man in the city wears nothing rich about him, but the gout, or a thumb-ring." In Chaucer's "Squier's Tale," it is said, respecting the rider of the brazen horse:—

".... Upon his thumb he had of gold a ring."

THE HUSBAND'S PETITION.

" Thou wil't not sure deny me
   My first, and fond request?
—I pray thee by the memory
   Of all we cherish best;
By all the dear remembrance
   Of those delicious days
When hand in hand we wandered
   Along the summer braes:

" By the great vow which bound thee
   For ever to my side;
And by the Ring that made thee
   My darling, and my bride;—
—Thou wilt not fail, nor falter,
   But bend thee to the task;
—A boiled sheep's Head on Sunday,
   Is all the boon I ask."—
                    Bon Gaultier Ballads.

Incidentally, as connected with the subject of finger rings, the general aspect of the hands is closely confronted. Thus, the secret of a woman's age is more often revealed by the appearance of her hands than by her features, or her figure. Brittle nails, to wit, and prominent veins on the hands, are sure signs of advancing years.

According to a Rabbinical saying—"Man is born with his hands clenched; he dies with his hands wide open. Entering life he desires to grasp everything; leaving the world he is compelled to relinquish all that he has possessed."

"Look in a man's eyes for honesty; around his mouth for weakness; at his chin for strength; at his hands for temperament; at his nails for cleanliness."

As a useful hint we would say that mutton-tallow is invaluable as a cure for split nails. The fingers should be soaked in warm water; after doing which, the nails are to be rubbed with a small lump of the tallow, and polished by a chamois leather.

A curious fact, not generally known, which relates to the leg of mutton is, that strictly observant Jews do not eat that portion of the limb which is supposed to be signified by the "sinew which shrank" (Genesis xxxii. 32), "which the children of Israel eat not to this day." The "sinew" thus particularised is thought to be the "popliteus" muscle, or some such a tendinous part, immediately adjacent thereto; from which part the leg of mutton is first "purged" by a Jewish butcher before being sold.

Robert Boyle tells, "I know also a very happy Physitian who assures me that he hath very often cured, both in himself, and in others, the Chilblains, when they come to be broken, by barely strowing on the sore parts the fine powder of Quinces, thinly sliced, and dry'd." Devout Mohammedans in Jerusalem regard tallow which drips from the candles lighted by fire descending from heaven once a year on Easter Eve, at the Church of the Holy Sepulchre, as marvellously curative for sores, or wounds.

Marbodus (1555) has elegantly embodied the virtues exercised by the Sapphire, thus :—

"Nam corpus vegetat, conservat, et integra membra;
Et qui portat eum nequit ulla fraude noceri.
Corporeis etiam morbis lapis iste medetur.

Contritis lateri, super illitus ulcera sanat;
Tollit et ex oculis sordes, ex fronte dolores;
Et vitiis linguæ simili ratione medetur.
Sed qui gestat eum castissimus esse jubetur."

Regarding the significant, and characteristic hue of the Sapphire, (and of other Precious Stones), colour superstitions still hold good in some of our remote rural districts. Thus, in the East of England, folks say:—

"Blue is true; Red's brazen;
Yellow's jealous; White is love;
Green's forsaken; And Black is death."

That " true Blue will never stain " is proverbial; as signifying that a really noble heart will never disgrace itself. A cognate reference is made here also to the blouses, and aprons of blue worn by butchers, because the colour thereof does not show blood-stains. Surely, by reason of this distinction the butcher should himself be immaculate; above the least suspicion of a spurious " sweetbread," for instance; or of South Down mutton from a Colonial source.

When young Copperfield, as a small boy, first went to school (Dr. Strong's) at Canterbury, a certain youthful butcher was the terror of Canterbury boys. " He seemed to have derived preternatural strength from the beef-suet with which he anointed his hair; a broad-faced, bull-necked, young butcher, with rough red cheeks, an ill-conditioned mind, and an injurious tongue." His main use of that tongue was to disparage Dr. Strong's young gentlemen, saying publicly, that " if they wanted anything he'd give it them." The consequence was that Copperfield resolved to fight this young butcher.

" After several sanguinary rounds, which went all

against Copperfield, he found himself finally queer about the head, and seeming to wake from a giddy sleep; with the sight before him of the young butcher walking off (whilst congratulated by two other butchers, and the sweep, and the publican), and putting on his coat as he went; from which it was justly augured the victory was his."

Some fifteen, or more years afterwards, Copperfield, being now come to man's estate, and having business to execute at Canterbury, travelled down thither at night by the Dover mail. Getting with difficulty into his hotel in the middle of the night, he went "shivering to bed, through various close passages, which smelt as if they had been steeped for ages in a solution of soup, and stables." "Early next morning he sauntered through the dear old streets, and strolled into the country for an hour, or so. Returning by the main street he saw among those who were now stirring in their shops his ancient enemy the butcher, advanced by this time to top-boots, and a baby; and in business for himself. He was nursing the baby, and appeared to be a benignant member of society."

The "Robe of the Ephod" was to be in colour significantly "all of blue." This colour blue predominated in the Tabernacle. It is peculiarly a heavenly colour; according to the Old Testament Scriptures. Moses and the Elders saw under the feet of the "God of Israel" "as it were a paved work of a Sapphire Stone, and as it were the body of heaven in His clearness." Purple was the Royal colour (of the House of David). —"Three blue beans (bullets, or small shot) in a blue bladder," made in former times a toy-rattle for a baby.

THE EMERALD.

The Emerald is found principally in South America, which is its real nursery. It is esteemed by the priests as a holy Gem; as likewise by the Jewish Rabbis; being worn by the former in a ring, by the latter in the Ephod, or breast-plate. "The Emeraude passeth all grene thynges of grenesse," saith an old black-letter book sententiously; "the finest come from the flode of Paradyse terrestre." "That Emeraude that is most clennest, and passynge grene, he is most gentyll, precyous, and best." It is said that the Emerald is born white, and ripens in the mine to its mature perfectness of meadow-green, first assuming this verdancy in the part nearest the rising sun. The chemical composition of the Emerald is sixty-two, and a fraction, of silica; fifteen, and a fraction, of glucina (a sweet earth); sixteen, and a fraction, of alumina, with a dash of the oxides of iron, and chrome. Its crystal is a long six-sided prism, which was formerly believed to restore sight, and memory: it sent evil spirits howling into space; changed colour when the lover was faithless, passing from the hue of the spring-leaf to that of the sere; and, if unable to do its possessor good, or to avert evil, it shivered into a thousand atoms, broken by despair. "So delightful," quoth Leonardus, "is the Emerald in its colour that there is scarce any jewel that affords more refreshment to the eyes."

The Emerald is in truth a *beryl*, of which Gem there are two other varieties, humble cousins of the Emerald,— the precious Beryl, or Aqua-marine, and the common Beryl. In general the Beryl is of a sea-green colour, or a pale blue, partaking both of Emerald and Sapphire combined, but not equal to either. Sometimes it is golden yellow, and sometimes white. It cures liver complaints, and the jaundice ; reconciles married folks, chases away idleness, and stupidity ; and is held sacred to the month of October ; but it is of no such special value unless it has risen from Beryl to Emerald, or has lightened from the opaque, and lustreless mammoth of the mines to the clear, and dainty sea-water Gem. Concerning this stone ("Smaragdus") Marbodus has said—

"Emendat fessos viridi mulcedine visus."

And again :

"Infirmus oculis, in quis jacet unda, medetur."

The Emerald—Smaragdus—(so Messrs. Gould, Homœopathic Chemists, London, report,)—has been triturated with sugar of milk in America for curative purposes. They further go on to state : " The friction of the harder on the softer substance is enormous, and serves to show its carbonising effect on the sugar in a very marked manner, by turning it lightly brown."

It may thus be fairly assumed that, on the same principle, with regard to our Bread, if the wheat from which it is made be ground between mill-stones, after the old-fashioned way, the colour of the Bread baked therefrom, which is known to become dark, is rendered so by this thermo-chemical action liberating the Carbon. Such bread—" Stan-Myln " (Stone-ground) was always made in home-baking days with flour of wheat-grains, including their germ, or embryo ; which germ is characterized by its special richness in proteid, and fat,—each in a soluble form. But now-a-days, so as to produce white bread for fastidious consumers, by the modern processes of roller-milling, the wheat germ is purposely left out therefrom. A supposition is advanced that the oil which is contained so abundantly in the germ is apt to become rancid, and to spoil the flour; also that at the same time the soluble proteids which are present in the germ, being apt to act upon the starch of the flour, serve to convert part thereof into soluble dextrin, and sugar; these darkening the colour of the bread in the oven. But this plausible conjecture is really not tenable. Rancid bread in the good old home-baking days was a thing unknown; indeed, the said household bread, of appetisingly brownish hue, with its sweet, nutty flavour, would remain quite excellent for eating, a full fortnight, or longer, after its baking. Far more likely is it that the said dark colour of such bread (offending the dainty folk of these Sybarite times) is due to the salutary "carbonising" which we have described.

Moreover, the positive fact should be borne in mind that this carbonising materially increases the easy digestibility of the loaf. An important increment of mineral food-salts, over and above what white bread is able to afford, is at the same time secured. Regarding this whole subject (which is assuredly of vital importance) *The Lancet*, in a comparatively recent article on "The Purity of Bread," has taught uncompromisingly what a much better "staff of life" is the old-fashioned loaf, made from stone-crushed flour, than the modern unnatural snow-white bread, with this quality of deceptive whiteness: as much due to chemicals as to the steam-roller-milling process. "The latest device for producing such absurdly white bread as the pampered taste of to-day likes to procure, is that of bleaching the flour by means of ozone, and nitrous acid. Can aught be more deleterious than this in the long run?"

With reference to "Stan-Myln" (Saxon, "Stone-Mill") flour, a firm of leading millers (at Kingston-on-Thames) draw attention to the fact that in the composition of stone-ground bread the wheat-germ itself is of a deep golden colour; and, as this is ground by the fraying action of the stones into countless minute particles which mingle with the starch of the flour, it must considerably modify the whiteness of the total product: (a paraphrase this in some sense, of the Scriptural query—"What man is there of you whom if his son ask bread, will he give him a stone?"). These manufacturers, stone millers, of sixty years standing, add: "We buy wheats of the finest quality only, for Stan-Myln flour, whilst paying scrupulous attention to their 'condition,' and blending." This may account for the absence of anything like a rancid flavour, such as has been observed in certain other breads, some of which are made from the germ obtained from roller mills, merely ground, and mixed with ordinary flour, and other material. "Up to the present we have not received a single complaint, as to any taint in our bread, such as would be caused by the presence of rancid germ-oil." "By our process we add nothing whatever to the flour; and 'Stan-Myln' bread is in every particular what one remembers fondly in boyhood,—the good old-fashioned, home-made bread of forty, or fifty years ago, when roller mills were unknown: except that this bread of ours is now made from a better average class of wheats, more carefully blended, than the miller of those days used." Personal recollections of our own certainly bear out the statement;

it being well remembered by us that baking-day,—a periodical little festival of childhood's time, and much reckoned on then, because of certain privileged Doughnuts, hot, sweet, and eagerly eaten,—did not recur more often than once a week at the outside; and that the batch of bread baked at such infrequent times continued to be appetising, and moist, and of nice flavour, to the last. Loving memories of the dear old wood-heated brick oven, immediately beyond the kitchen precincts, still dwell regretfully in our minds. In the "Stan-Myln" mills already noticed, the tough germ-seed escapes all risk of becoming flattened out, to the detriment of the flour; because contact with, and the friction of, the rough surfaces of the mill-stones reduces the germ to fine particles which are impalpably miscible with the flour. But in roller mills the result is far different, because the friction effected by two iron rollers revolving in opposite directions, is looser than that brought about by the close millstones; and thus the germ-seed becomes quickly liberated in the form of small discs, which escape altogether from the flour.

Lines—"To God."

"Bread for our service, bread for shew;
Meat for our meals; and fragments too:
He gives not poorly,—taking some
Between the finger and the thumb;
But for our glut, and for our store,
Fine flour press'd down, and running o'er."

"In former days," tells Dr. R. Hutchison, "when good flour was more expensive than now, adulterants were often added to bread; of which alum was one of the most harmful. Inferior flour will not form good dough because of too great a solubility of its proteids; but alum seems to unite with these proteids so that they become inert, the dough therefore retaining its toughness, and power of holding water. Sulphate of copper, and lime, will act in a like manner. Fortunately, however, these adulterations would seem to have become things of the past; and it is comforting to learn, on capable authority (Goodfellow), what may now be considered a certain fact, that the bread supplied to the people of England is practically pure." We may note that the crust of bread contains eight times as much soluble nutrient proteid as the crumb; also three times as much nitrogenous (muscle-building) matter, half as much again of starch (warmth-producing), and less than half as much water. A considerable portion of protein (a valuable constituent of wheat) is withheld in the coarser parts of the grain,—the bran, and pollard,—which, if left in the bread, would resist the action of the digestive juices, and defy digestion. But these valuable food-salts may be utilized by making "Bran-tea," which is specially beneficial for children affected with rickets. Such a "tea" may be readily brewed by putting one measure of ordinary coarse wheat-bran into three measures of the same size of fast-boiling water, and allowing it to simmer steadily for not less than thirty minutes. A small lump of cane-sugar, if added, will help to maintain the full boiling-point of the water. The liquor should be then strained through a sieve, and may be used as a tea; also in making stock for soup, or barley-water; as well as for boiling rice therein. Again, bran serves excellent purposes for outward use. Foot-baths prepared therewith are of capital service for relieving gouty limbs, as well as for affording comfort, and ease to tender feet. For which uses some bran should be put loosely in a large flannel bag (secured at its top), and completely covered by boiling water. The temperature of the bath must be kept as high as it can be borne.

In *Hard Times*, by Charles Dickens, 1854, a capital character, Mrs. Sparsit, who poses as a pattern of self-denial, but takes good care of Number One, in the privacy of her own (the Housekeeper's) room, is required by Mr. Bounderby, her master, to go as caretaker at Mr. B's Bank. She pleads, with a sigh—"I shall not be freed from the necessity of eating the bread of dependence!" (She might have said "the 'sweetbread,' seeing that this delicate article, in a savoury brown sauce, was her favourite supper.")

A writer of note in his day (long past;—1380), John Mirfield, advised "to take warm bread, a few morsels only, for prevailing against pestilential air, and against fetid morbific vapours. This is also good against the fetor of the sea ; and, if you have not warm fresh bread," wrote Mirfield, "da tostum":—use toast. It is remarkable with regard to this phrase " the fetor of the sea," that our present general notion that fresh lively breezes from the open sea are eminently salubrious, has not always prevailed. For example :—in an account of Northamptonshire, published in 1738,—the writer thus expresses himself: "The air of Northamptonshire is exceedingly pleasant, and wholesome ; the sea being so remote that this air is not infected with its (the sea's) noisome fumes."

Now-a-days we are grateful to modern science, with its precise methods and its sure conclusions, for telling us better than this. For, it is a well-ascertained fact that, whilst perhaps in crowded places on the coast bacteria may be abounding, especially of injurious sorts, yet when the open sea is reached, beyond the range of land breezes, most frequently no bacteria whatever are to be discovered in the air; for which essential reason a prolonged ocean voyage is to be emphatically commended for consumptive tuberculous patients; their strength being still equal to the undertaking.

In Queen Elizabeth's time the small wild Foxglove grew plentifully in dry ditches along Piccadilly (then known as a highroad to Reading). Dr. Wm. Salmon, in his *Family Dictionary*, 1696, wrote concerning this herb Foxglove: "For such as are in Hecktick Fevers, or Consumptions, accompanied with great heat, and dryness, the specifick which transcends all the medicines for a Consumption as here mentioned, and many others besides,—is the Herb Foxglove. The Decoction of this Herb, in water, or in Wine, or in half water and half wine, may be drunk as ordinary drink; and from the Juyce of the Herb, and Flowers, may be made a Rob, or Syrup, with Honey; which being taken, three spoonfuls at a time; first in the morning, fasting; secondly at ten in the morning; thirdly at four in the afternoon; and lastly on going to bed; will restore (where the patient is not altogether past cure) beyond all expectation. It cures a Phthisick, or Ulcer of the Lungs, when all the Medicines have failed, and the Sick is esteem'd past cure. It opens the Breast, and Lungs; frees them from tough Phlegm, and cleanses the Ulcer, and heals it, when all other Remedies are without effect. I have known it do wonders; and I speak from long experience. Persons in deep Consumptions, and given over by all physicians, have by the use of this Herb been strangely recovered, and so perfectly as to grow fat again. I commend it as a secret; and it ought to be kept as a treasure. These few lines as concerning this matter alone is worth ten times the price of the whole Book, were there nothing else in it besides, that one had occasion to make use of; I am very confident of this. The deplorable wasted Patients who have been long in tedious Consumptions, Phthises, and Hecticks, if they make use of it, will give me thanks for this notice; whilst they may have Reason enough to Curse even the memories of the Quacking Blood-suckers who, as they have drain'd them of a good part of their Estates, would, by a continuance under their hands (for all their Specious methods of cure) have fool'd them out of their Lives too."

Mirfield must have been a thinker, whose words of medical wisdom were well considered, and still deserve attention. "Gluttony," said he, "slays more than the sword! Foods are not to be mixed, but a meal of bread should be taken in the morning, and a meal of meat in the evening; and in this all doctors of faculty agree; but we English, from long habit hold the reverse." Yet he counsels every one to bear in mind the judicious lines :—

> "Si cena levis, vel cena brevis,
> Raro molesta;
> Magna nocet; Medicina docet ;—
> Res manifesta."

He advised Prelates, of sedentary pursuits, to have a rope in their study, hanging from the ceiling, and knotted at the end; on which they might take exercise; or to use weights in their hands (thus anticipating our modern dumb-bells) if not able to get outdoor activity.

As a further fact, somewhat relevant to the salt-water

topics just mentioned, it is recorded that the Sea-Hare, *Lepus marinus* was a remarkable creature known to the ancient Romans,—as we learn from Dioscorides, Galen, Pliny, and others. With this animal Titus was poisoned by Domitian. "*Is autem piscis humores quondam occultos habet mortiferos supra omnia venena quæ mare, terr que nascuntur; et Neronem hunc ipsum piscem epulis quandoque miscuisse tradunt adversus homines sibi inimicissimos.*"

It is also well worth knowing that no remedy is so efficacious, so simple, and so free from discomfort of application, in the treatment of warts, and corns, as sea-water. The plan for pursuing this treatment is, when at the sea-side, to bathe the feet in the sea twice a day, paddling in the water for from ten to fifteen minutes each time. Warts may be treated in the same manner; the hand, or hands, affected are to be placed in sea-water (made comfortably warm, if desired) twice daily, throughout at least ten minutes each time. For those persons who cannot get access to sea-water a solution of " sea salt " is to be advised, dissolving this (it must be of undoubted *marine* origin), in warm water, so measured as to raise it to the saline specific gravity of sea-water ; and using it twice a day, (likewise for corns,) until they are softened, and can be readily peeled off, as they most certainly may be at the end of a fortnight, if not sooner.

To resume about the Emerald : this is essentially a Silicate, consisting mainly of Silica, combined with Aluminium, and Glucinum, (or Beryllum,—a rare constituent). The Emerald, Beryl, and Aqua-marine are practically the same mineral (with differences of colour, and in other minor particulars). Pliny has told of an old Hebrew tradition that if a serpent fixes its eyes on an Emerald, it becomes blind. In the New Testament the Rainbow is said to be " like unto an Emerald " —(Revelation iv. 3): " And there was a rainbow round about the Throne, in sight like unto an Emerald."

An allied variety of Corundum is the Chrysoberyl, or Cat's-eye. This very brilliant Gem is of a yellowish colour; sometimes brownish yellow, and occasionally white; it possesses double refraction to a high degree, and acquires positive electricity by friction, retaining it for several subsequent hours. It contains Alumina, Glucina, with the Oxides, of both Lead, and Copper. Another Chalcedonic variety of Quartz has also been named " Cat's-eye "; but this is not the true stone. The true " Cat's-eye " (which is a rare variety of the Chrysoberyl) exhibits a remarkable play of light by reason of a peculiarity in its crystallisation. This ray of light is called " Line " by jewellers, and is most highly valued when reflected in the popular colours of clear apple-green, and dark olive. The Cat's-eye is the last jewel a Cingalee will part with. He believes it to be endowed with every virtue; and that its wearer is assured of good luck in all his doings. " The Stone," says an Indian traveller, " is indeed wonderfully beautiful, with its soft deep colour, and mysterious gleaming streak, ever shifting, like a restless spirit, from side to side as the stone is moved. No wonder that an imaginative people regard it with awe, and wonder, fully believing it to be the abode of Genii; wherefore they dedicate it to their gods."

The Emerald differs from Beryl in possessing a fine green colour; this being chemically attributed to the presence therein of chromium sesqui-oxide; furthermore it never presents the internal striæ which are so often seen in the Beryl. The Emerald is transparent, or translucent, and has a vitreous, rarely resinous, lustre. On friction it becomes electric. The Hebrew word *nophech* (rendered "Emerald" in the English version of the Scriptures) appears to have been actually the Carbuncle. In the East, previous to about the middle of the Fifteenth Century, the Emerald was subjected to cleavage, and was generally worn as a Jewel, in slices. The finest Emeralds are obtained from Muzo, in Columbia. Pliny tells that this Stone was highly valued by the ancients. Various virtues were formerly ascribed to the Gem. It was said to be good for the eyes, also to colour water green, on which account it was worn as a seal Ring; to assist women in child-birth; and to drive away evil spirits. The Easterns still credit it with Talismanic, and medicinal properties. This gem has been very successfully imitated by manufacturers of paste-Stones; the colouring matter used being oxide of chromium. What is termed the Oriental Emerald is in reality a green variety of Corundum,—an exceedingly rare Gem.

Dr. W. Rowland, 1669, described the Emerald, "Smaragdus," as "a clear transparent Gem; very beautiful, and the most brittle of all Gems. It stops (being drunk) all Fluxes whatsoever, chiefly the Dysentery, whether they come from a sharp humor, or venome; and it cures venomous Bitings. For a Dose—six, eight, or ten grains are given. Among Amulets it is chiefly commended against the Epilepsie; it stops bleeding if held in the mouth; it cures all bleedings, and dysenteries; it expels fears, and the Tertian Ague, if hung about the neck. There is a 'Prepared Smaragd; and a Tincture of Smaragd.'" Messrs. Lemery and

Tournefort, 1712, advise that both Eastern, and Western Emeralds "are proper to stop the Flux of the Belly, and Hæmorrhages; also to sweeten too acrid humors, being finely powdered, and taken inwardly—the dose from six to thirty grains."

When of a pale bluish-green colour the Emerald is *Aqua-marine*. This pale green of Aqua-marine is due to a small proportion of oxide of iron. In modern times M. Caillard, the persevering mineralogist, has rediscovered the Peruvian Emerald Mines, after their remaining unexplored by the foot of man for several ages. The Arabs entertain to this day the same superstitious fears with regard to the said mines that the ancients did. They cautioned M. Caillard strongly against sleeping near caverns, which were the abode of demons, who would resent the intrusion. The famous Emerald mines of Mount Zebarah were first worked by the engineers of the Ptolemies. The name Emerald is from the French—"Esmeraulde; which comes from the Greek, Smaragdus." Queen Alexandra owns a "parure" of Emeralds worth a King's ransom. Princess Charles of Denmark has one hundred Emeralds, of large size, and first quality; these forming a flexible waist-belt. Square Emeralds are a present craze. Mrs. George Keppel owns a priceless square Emerald, which she wears as a pendant.

In the *Magick of Kiram, King of Persia, and of Harpocration*, 1685,—containing "the magical and medicinal virtues of Stones, Herbs, Fishes, Beasts, and Birds,"—a work much sought after by the learned, but seen by few, and said to be in the Vatican, at Rome, "concerning Smaragdus,—a green Precious Stone," it stands written—"Engrave thereupon the Bird Harpe;

and under its feet a Sea Lamprey ; and wear the Stone against disturbance, and dreams, and stupidity. It causes Rest to Lunaticks, and to them that are troubled with the Cholick ; and it is better if the Fat of the Sea-Lamprey be put underneath; for such is Divine." The ancients were never tired of looking at their rings when garnished with this Jewel, because of its being such a strengthener of the eyes. Rabbins declare that the pleasure derived from viewing an Emerald is due to the refreshing influence exercised by the green colour, this Stone being the nearest resemblance to the luxuriant verdure of the fields, and trees. Isidorus, Bishop of Seville, supposed that it even gives a green colour to the surrounding air. Some persons further tell that engravers, and workers in Precious Stones, place Emeralds before them, to rest their eyesight upon whilst engraving minute objects. Certain lapidaries assert that the Siberian Emerald, which surpasses the others in value because of its great hardness, and freedom from defects, originates in Copper mines, where Verdigris is formed.

Boetius, *De Natura Gemmarum*, says of the Emerald : " It discovers false witnesses by suffering alteration when meeting with such persons." Formerly it was supposed that the colouring matter of the Emerald is the oxide of chrome; but the quantity of chromic Acid obtainable by analysis is so small as to be inappreciable ; it is therefore supposed that the exquisite tint of this Gem (being a Carburet of Hydrogen) is similar to that termed " Chlorophylle," which constitutes the green colouring matter in the leaves of plants. It is possible that this organic colouring matter may be derived from decomposition of the animals whose remains are now fossilised in the rock which forms the matrix of the Gem. This rock is a Limestone, slightly bituminous, often black, with white veins, whilst containing Ammonites, and other shells. The Emperor Nero—as is well known—observed the feats of gladiators through an eyeglass of Emerald. Hence the name of the Gem is sometimes "Neromanus." This Stone was also used during the Middle Ages for adorning Church Cups, and Chalices. Likewise one of the chief ornaments of the Crown of Charlemagne was a lustrous Emerald. But so rarely has a perfect Emerald been found that "An Emerald without a flaw" has passed into a proverb. The Greeks sometimes called the Emerald " Prasinus," on account of its colour resembling the greenness of Leeks. Pliny tells that a sculptured marble Lion, with Emerald Eyes, was placed on the tomb of King Hermias in the Island of Cyprus, near the fisheries. Such was the extraordinary brilliancy of these Emeralds, and so far out at sea did they shine, that the frightened fish swam to a great distance off. The fishermen, having ascertained the cause of the scarcity of their supply, abstracted the Emeralds, replacing them by other Stones, and thus induced the fish to return. An old treatise on Jewels tells that if a serpent, or snake, should fix his eyes on the lustre of Emeralds, he would straightway become blind.

For two centuries past the only country known to yield Emeralds has been Peru. The belief that demons, or wicked spirits guard the treasures contained in the Emerald mines is as strong at the present day among the Peruvian Indians as it was in the time of Pliny, or as it is now with the Arabs of Mount Zebarah.

The Beryl, or Aqua-marine (in the Hebrew "Belur," signifying "Crystal,"), and the Emerald are of the same chemical composition, whilst differing only in colour: the former (Beryl) is of a light blue, or sea-green hue. The Chryso-Beryl—"Cat's-eye"—owes its colour chiefly to iron, as a ferrous oxide. In the symbolical necklace of Vishnu the green Gem was held to represent the Earth, as a magnetic centre of human passions. Chemically the Emerald contains more glucina than the Beryl; and chemists find that the greater the quantity of glucina the greener is the Crystal. Some magnificent specimens of Beryl are met-with in Siberia; it is also discovered in Scotland. This stone is used largely in Birmingham, for imitation jewellery, and for ornamental adjuncts to metal work. Beads of Aqua-marine have been found in Egyptian Mummy-pits; furthermore the Greeks employed Beryl for intaglios more than two thousand years ago. Pliny mentions the Stone as "the Gem green as the Sea,"—*qui viriditatem puri maris imitatur*,—and hence, its name "Aqua-marine." In the *Magick of Kiram*, Beryl (Berils) is called—Panzoon, or "All Life." One may read therein thus—"Take a Beril Stone, and engrave a Crow upon it; and under its feet a Crab; wear it as you will; for Joy, and Exultation, and Acquisition, and Union, and Conjugal Love; and it will make the Bearer cheerful, and Rich; and it is as excellent as anything for lascivious, and Conjugal Love." "A Berill," says Aubrey, in his *Miscellanies*, "is a kind of Cristal that has a weak tincture of red. In this stone magicians see visions. There are certain formulas of prayer to be used before they make the inspection, which they term a 'call.' James Harrington told me that the Earl of Denbigh, then Ambassador at Venice, did tell him that one did show him three several times in a glass things past, and to come." The Beryl as a Jewel was mounted by the Romans for "cylindri," or ear-drops; cut into six-sided prisms. The Greeks employed Emeralds for "intaglio" work more than two thousand years ago. The grandest intaglio extant of the Roman period is carved upon an Aqua-marine of extraordinary magnitude, more than two inches square;—the Bust of Julia Titi—signed by the artist, "Euodus Epoiei;"—which Stone for nearly a thousand years had formed the knosp of a Golden Reliquary, being set with its convex-back uppermost, and regarded as an invaluable Emerald, in the Abbey of Saint Denys.

There are extant, in the British Museum, two Cameo-Portraits (Sixteenth Century) of Queen Elizabeth; —of French workmanship,—one exceedingly graceful, cut in a Turquoise; and another, very handsome, cut in Nicolo. But of the Precious Stones used for such artistic ornamental purposes the Emerald seems to have been the most esteemed. The Greeks were the Cameo cutters "par excellence." Their taste for engraved Gems arose perhaps from Pompey, in the first century, B.C. For the Emerald an immense veneration is entertained by the Easterns to this day; they believing that it imparts courage to the wearer, and averts infectious disease. Scriptural mention is made of the Emerald thus, (Ezekiel, chapter xxvii.): "Syria was thy merchant by reason of the multitude of wares of thy making: they occupied thy fairs with emeralds, purple, and broidered work, fine linen, agate, and coral."

The origin of the word "Emerald" is said to be a Sanskrit term signifying "green." By the ancients (who dedicated this stone to Mercury) it was deemed good for the sight : and was therefore worn in a seal ring. It was further taken for various diseases, when ground down into a powder,—the dose of which was six grains.

The Roman Emperor Claudius—(done to death A.D. 64—at first by drugged mushrooms, and then by a poisoned feather),—being fully persuaded as to the virtues exercised on him physically by the practice, was accustomed to " clothe himself in Emeralds, and Sardonyx."

A story is given to the following effect, in the *Oriental Memoirs* of Forbes : On a certain moonlight night an observer was watching a swarm of fire-flies within an Indian grove. After hovering for a while, illuminated by the moonbeams, one special fly, more brilliant than the rest, alighted on the grass, and remained there. The observer, thinking its permanency in that spot remarkable, went up to it so as to learn the probable cause, and he found there, not a fire-fly, but a shining Emerald ; of which he possessed himself, and afterwards wore it in a ring.

The famous " San Graal," of King Arthur's time, (and respecting which Tennyson has discoursed in noble, grand verse, *Idylls of the King*, (" Flos Regum Arthurus," 1862), was represented as a miraculous Chalice, made of a single precious Emerald, which was endowed from heaven with the power of preserving chastity, prolonging life, and performing other pious wonders. This Chalice was believed to have been brought directly from the hands of God by angels ; and to have been the actual Cup from which Christ drank at the Last Supper :—

" The Cup, the Cup itself, from which our Lord
Drank at the last sad supper with His own.
This . . . . the good Saint
Arimathean Joseph, journeying, brought

> To Glastonbury, where the winter thorn
> Blossoms at Christmas, mindful of our Lord;
> And there awhile it bode; and if a man
> Could touch, or see it, he was healed at once,
> By faith, of all his ills.—But then the times
> Grew to such evil that the holy Cup
> Was caught away to Heaven, and disappear'd."

The falling of an Emerald from its setting has been held an ill omen to the wearer, even in modern times. When George III. was crowned, a large Emerald fell from his diadem; and America was lost to England during his reign. De Boot, 1636, gives a method for extracting from Emeralds their colouring matter, which when taken internally proves so efficacious.

Of the Emerald, wrote Leonardus, 1565, " Its greenness is so intense that it is not only not dulled when put under any light, or the beams of the Sun, but is superior to all force; and stains the encircling Air with its greenness." De Boot alleged of this Precious Stone: "It will preserve the chastity of women; or will betray the violation thereof by straightway bursting into fragments."

Mr. King, in his *Natural History of Precious Stones, and Gems*, Cambridge, 1865, tells concerning the Cingalese (people of Ceylon). that they anxiously seek after the thick bottoms of our ordinary flint glass wine-bottles; out of which they cut very fine " Emeralds," which they dispose-of at high prices to the " Steamboat Gentlemans ! " After a like fashion the " Brighton Emeralds," so largely purchased by visitors to that popular sea-side resort, are similarly got from bottles thrown purposely into the sea by lapidaries there; which bottles (or rather their bottom ends) become by the attrition of the shingle, speedily converted into the form of natural pebbles.

"So, at last I bought this trinket,
  And—(how much I love to think it!)
She admired it, with a pretty little speech;
  Though I bought it of a pedlar,
  Brown, and wizened as a medlar,
Who was hawking odds and ends about the beach.

  But I managed,—very nearly—
  To believe that I was dearly
Loved by somebody, who (blushing like a peach)
  Seemed to like it; saying 'wear it
  For my sake; and I declare it
Seldom strikes me that I bought it on the beach.

  And, I'm ever, ever, seeing
  My imaginary being;—
And I'd rather that my marrow-bones should bleach
  In the winds than that a cruel
  Fate should snatch from me the jewel
Which I bought for one and sixpence, on the beach."

Verses, and Fly Leaves, C. S. Calverley, 1885.

Around Stockholm there are several suburban resorts where sea-bathing, and water-drinking go on (when the weather is warm, and favourable). At one of these resorts a visitor observed a large sign-board, at a gateway, reading thus—" Dam Bad Haus." This notice gave him quite a shock; it appeared so recklessly profane! until, presently, he discovered its innocent, common-place meaning to be "Ladies' Bath House."

As to water drinking, Dr. Wiley, U.S. Bureau of Chemistry, concluded a paper in the *Journal of the American Medical Association* the other day with a doggrel, as follows—

"Full many a man, both young and old,
  Has gone to his sarcophagus
  By pouring water icy cold
  Adown his hot œsophagus."

"As to the action externally of Mineral waters applied over the skin surface," writes Dr. Burney Yeo, on *The Therapeutics of Mineral Springs*, 1904, "the idea of absorption of mineral substances through the skin has been negatived by repeated experimental observation. It is therefore incorrect to suppose that the outward action of Mineral waters can be in any way dependent on the absorption of their constituents through the skin; for, it has been proved that the sound, and healthy human skin is not permeable to water, or to the fixed substances dissolved in it; even after prolonged immersion. Nevertheless it is asserted by some authorities that the skin has been found permeable to water, and watery solutions, when applied thereto in fine spray (at an elevated temperature); and it is suggested that the force with which this spray is thrown upon, and against the skin, serves to influence such absorption. Moreover, it may be borne in mind that volatile, or gaseous constituents of mineral baths can be absorbed through the respiratory organs; indeed, too, it seems probable from experimental observation, that the skin itself is permeable to certain volatile, and gaseous constituents of baths; as, for instance, carbonic acid gas, and sulphuretted hydrogen."

Some writers have said that the Emerald should be worn on a Friday for good luck, because dedicated to Venus, the Goddess of that week-day. But a mistaken notion underlies this practice, considering that the Scandinavian Venus, Freya, is here signified, the wife of Odin, and a woman of bad character. Nevertheless, to regard Friday as of ill omen for then undertaking anything of importance, is only a relic of an old Puritan superstition. It is simply a fortuitous circumstance that various untoward events have occurred on a Friday. Charles Dickens always chose this day of the week for any business which he particularly wanted to prosper. Palmists tell us that the Mount of Venus is situated about the ball of the thumb; and that persons who have this ball well developed find Friday to be for them the luckiest day of the week.

In the *Schoole of Salerne*, 1624, it was ordered: "Use eyther a Chalcedonium, or a sweet Pommander, or some like Precious Stone to be worne in a Ring on the little finger of the left hand; have in your rings, eyther a Smaragd (Emerald), a Sapphire, or a Draconites (Dragon-Stone), which you shall beare for an ornament; hold sometime in your mouth eyther a Hyacinth, or a Crystall, or a Granat, or pure Gold, or Silver, (or else sometimes pure Sugar-Candy). For, Aristotle doth affirm, and so doth Albertus Magnus, that a Smaragd worne about the necke, is good against the Falling Sickness; for surely the vertue of an Herbe is great, but much more the vertue of a Precious Stone, which is very likely that they are endued with occult, and hidden vertues." (The Dragon-Stone here advised—the Draconius of Albertus Magnus, 1230—was taken from the head of a Dragon as he lay panting; the virtue of the Precious Stone being lost if it remained for any time in the head after the death of the dragon. It was reputed to absorb all poisons, especially that of serpents. It renders its possessor bold, and invincible. Philostratus (*De Vitâ Apollonii*) tells how these wonderful dragons were captured—"by the exhibition of golden letters, and a scarlet robe; for, these monsters had an eye for rich colouring, as our modern ladies have for a scarlet coat.")

To the Chalcedonyx—as here commended—it was said that Milo, of Crotona, was indebted for the increase of his wonderful strength, always wearing it when about to undertake one of his feats. But he must have forgotten to employ this talisman when he tried his last exploit.

The Carnelian (Sardius), called of old "Odem," i.e., of red hue, is a pale red variety of Chalcedony; its colouring matter is a hydrated oxide of iron. It was considered among the Hebrews, and Arabs, to be an important preventive of illness; the former people ascribed to it the virtue of preserving life from the dangers of the Plague; the latter people—even now—according to Niebuhr, continue to employ it as an efficient agent for arresting a flux of blood. "It is a Gem," wrote Schroder, 1669, "half transparent, like the water wherein flesh is washed; or like bloody flesh; hence it is called Carneolus, or Cornelian, from 'caro'—genitive 'carnis,'—flesh. They are not of one colour; some are red; some only a little bloody; others are yellowish red." "The Babylonian Cornelians are best; the Indian, and Arabian are not despicable; nor the European." As for their virtues—"the pouder of them is good to drink against all fluxes; carried about it makes cheerful minds, expels fear, makes courage, destroys, and prevents fascinations, and defends the body against all poysons; it stops blood by a peculiar property; and, bound to the Belly, keeps up the Birth."

THE RUBY.

THE flaming blood-red Ruby, the "Live-coal" of the Greeks, the Anthrax, which (under its name of Carbuncle) was among the twelve gems making up the sacred Ephod of the Hebrews, is one of the most magnificent of all Gems. It is of a phosphoric nature, and when set in the full rays of the sun, or exposed to a great amount of heat, it gives out a radiance such as will account for the Eastern exaggeration, telling that, according to the Talmud, Abraham, when keeping his numerous wives shut up in an iron city, in order to give them light, set a bowl of Rubies in its midst, which filled all the air with lustre.

There are various kinds of Rubies :- the Spinel, or scarlet-red, the best form of true Ruby; the Balas, or rose-red; the Rubicelle, or orange-red; the Almandine, or violet-red; the Chlorospinel, or green-red; and the Pleonaste, or black; there is also a Cat's-eye, or opalescent Ruby, found in Burmah. A belief is held by the Burmese that Rubies ripen in colour gradually, whilst maturing in the earth,—like fruit upon a sunny wall.

This Gem (the Ruby) like all the nobler precious stones, has been thought to give warning of poison, whilst refusing to endure its presence. It grew dark, and cloudy if any evil was about to befall its wearer; but it banished sadness, and many forms of sin, and vice. Rubies were formerly believed to be male, and female; Pliny saying that "the males were more vigorous, and acrid, the females more languishing." The chemical composition of the Ruby is seventy-five per cent of alumina, seventeen of magnesia, four of peroxide of iron, with a fraction of silica, and of other minor elements. But the Gem consists chiefly of alumina, and magnesia.

The Oriental Topaz, and the Ruby, are the same generic stones, but of different colours. Yet the value of the Ruby surpasses that of the Topaz a hundred-fold, provided it has the proper precise pigeon-coloured, blood-red hue, whilst brilliant, and is free from flaw, or defect. The Ruby as a Gem is likewise of more value than the Diamond. In the Book of Proverbs ("the words of King Lemuel: the prophecy that his mother taught him") a virtuous woman is described as "of price far above Rubies."

"How the heart of her husband doth safely trust in her always;
How all the days of her life she will do him good, and not evil;
How she seeketh the wool, and the flax, and worketh with gladness;
How she layeth her hand to the spindle, and holdeth the distaff;
How she is not afraid of the snow for herself, or her household;
Knowing her household are clothed with the scarlet cloth of her weaving."

Both a Ruby, and a Sapphire, of the same size as a Diamond, would respectively be worth considerably more. The Ruby was formerly set with the blue part of a peacock's feather beneath it, instead of foil. The Ruby, Sapphire, and Oriental Topaz are properly Corundums: which name is of Indian origin, as derived from the Sanskrit "korund," applied to opaque massive Gems, generally of a dull colour. The first, and most important variety of Corundum is the Ruby, or Red Sapphire: this being the most valuable of all Gems when of large size, of good colour, and free from flaw. The Corundums, which vary in colour, and optical properties, are identical in composition, consisting principally of crystallised Alumina (the oxide of the metal Aluminium). The Ruby is coloured by traces of other metallic oxides, chrome, etc, but it does not contain silica, and its lustre is vitreous. The colour of the Ruby varies from the lightest rose tint to the deepest carmine. If of too dark, or too light a shade, the stones are not esteemed. The most valuable tint is that particular shade called by jewellers "Pigeon's blood," which is a pure deep, rich red, without any admixture of blue, or yellow. According to Pliny the Ethiopians had a way of increasing the splendour of Rubies by laying them for fourteen days in vinegar, which increased their lustre for a time, but made them afterwards softer, and more brittle. The rare occurrence of specimens of the desired vivid "pigeon's blood" red colour, when of any size, causes their value to increase in a proportion even greater than that of the Diamond. A Ruby of one carat weight is worth from fourteen to twenty pounds sterling. Mr. Streeter asserts that a Ruby of perfect colour, and weighing five carats, is worth at the present day ten times as much as a Diamond of equal weight; one of four carats weight is worth from four hundred to four hundred and fifty pounds. The magical properties formerly ascribed to Rubies were that they made amulets against poison, plague, evil thoughts, and wicked spirits, keeping the wearer in health, and cheering his mind. If he, or the stone's donor, were in danger, it would become black, or obscure, and would not resume its pristine colour until the peril had passed away. All, or nearly all, the fine Rubies which are met-with in collections are believed to have come from Burmah; the Ruby mines of which district have been long known, but the stones found there are almost always small, and seldom free from defects. One of the King of Burmah's titles is "Lord of the Rubies." When a particularly large, and fine stone is found, the usual custom is to send out a procession of grandees, with soldiers, and elephants, to meet it. The Ruby (or, Red Sapphire) is susceptible of electricity by friction, and retains it for a considerable time.

The true Ruby—a variety of crystallised Aluminium—is a Corundum, of red, or reddish colour. All Corundums contain more than half their weight of the metal Aluminium. Hebrew legends tell that the "blushing" red Ruby became the symbolical representative of Reuben, who brought such a blush upon himself by irreverent conduct towards his father. The name Ruby is derived from the Latin adjective "rubus"—red. Formerly it was alleged that the Ruby, when bruised in water, relieved infirmities of the eyes, and helped disordered livers. If the four corners of a house, garden, or vineyard, were touched with one of these precious stones, they would be preserved from lightning, tempests, and worms. It also dispersed infectious airs; and, when worn, it could not possibly be concealed, as its lustre would show itself beneath the thickest clothes.

According to Dr. Jno. Schroder, 1669: "You may try the goodness of the Rubine by the mouth, and tongue; for the coldest, and hardest are the best. They grow in a stoney matrix; of a rose colour, and at first are white, then by degrees growing ripe, turn red. As to their vertues: it resists poyson, resists sadness, restrains lust, drives away frightful dreams, clears the mind, keeps the body safe, and, if a mischance be at hand, it signifies this by turning of a darker colour."

It is more than probable that the specially pronounced sparkling red hue of the Ruby serves to exercise occult chemical, and psychical magnetic actions on any sensitive wearer of this stone. Properties of the same nature, but more crudely developed, are familiar in the practice of Photography, where the important fact is turned to essential uses that, whilst the violet rays of light blacken Silver-Chloride most readily, the red rays of light will not blacken it at all. Again in Chemistry, if such a substance as gum guaiacum is converted to a green colour by violet rays of light, its proper primitive colour can be restored by red rays. It is therefore fair to infer that the brilliant red of the Ruby is potential for subtle physical effects, whether beneficial, or the reverse.

On exposure to a high temperature the Ruby becomes green; but after cooling it regains its original colour, this behaviour showing the presence of Chromium. The simplest test of a true Ruby is its hardness, which is great; the sharp edge of a Corundum crystal will readily scratch either a Spinel, or a Garnet; but it has no effect on a Ruby.

The largest Ruby known in Europe is said to be a stone in size that of a hen's egg (small), which was presented by Gustavus Third to the Empress of Russia, whilst he visited St. Petersburg. When Peter the Great, Czar of Russia, came to England, 1697, (working as a shipwright in the Dockyard at Deptford), he paid a visit to King William the III., whom he had met before at the Hague; and in taking final leave of whom Peter fumbled for some minutes in his waistcoat pocket, presently drawing out therefrom a small parcel wrapped in a shabby scrap of dirty brown paper. This he pressed into the hand of King William; it was a Ruby worth ten thousand pounds. The Czar next went from England to Vienna. He had previously learnt ship-building in the Dockyards of Holland, where he was awarded a Certificate of Efficiency in all handicrafts connected with that business, by the head of the said dockyards. Peter's curiosity was insatiable; he was a man of singular magnetic powers, and endowments: possessing, moreover, a wonderful way of assimilating all the good materials about him. When in London he occupied, with his attendants, a big house in York Buildings.

The large historic Ruby, which is set in the Maltese Cross fronting the Imperial State Crown of England, is really only a Spinel. By means of the Oxide of Chromium an excellent imitation of the true Ruby colour can be obtained; and a paste (of which to compose the counterfeit stone) may be produced, almost as hard as rock crystal, by using for its manufacture silicate of alumina.

In the *Ambulance Hand-book*, by Dr. Beatson, Glasgow, 1895, a famous poem appeared anonymously, being quoted, it was said, "from the *Morning Post* of seventy years ago." Every effort was made, even to the extent of vainly offering fifty guineas, to discover the author. All that ever transpired was that this poem, writ out in a fair clerkly hand, was found in the museum of the Royal College of Surgeons, Lincoln's Inn, being placed there near a skeleton, of which the form, and bleached colour were signally fine. One stanza of these "Lines to a Skeleton" runs thus (bearing reference to its distinguished-looking bony hands) :—

> "Say, did these fingers delve the mine;
> Or, with its envied Rubies shine?
> To hew the rock, and wear the Gem
> Can little now avail to them:
> But if the path of truth they sought,
> Or comfort to the mourner brought,
> These hands a richer meed shall claim
> Then all that wait on wealth, or fame."

Rubies are found to become affected in their colour if exposed for any length of time to a strong light. Experiments have been made on two stones, each of equal strength of colouring to start with. One was exposed to continuous daylight; whilst the other was enclosed in a sealed box from which all light was carefully excluded. The stone kept in daylight had lost a distinguishable amount of colour after a few years when compared with the other stone which had been kept perpetually in darkness; and thereby the former stone had lost some of its value.

The **Balas Ruby,** or **Spinel,** is of a fine, lively, red colour, but has a common tint intermixed, which renders it far less brilliant than the true Ruby, or Red Sapphire. In chemical composition the Spinel contains one molecule of alumina, and one of magnesia; or, in one hundred parts,—of alumina seventy-two, and of magnesia twenty-eight. This stone does not exhibit electricity, either by friction, or by heat. During the Middle Ages the same supernatural powers were attributed thereto as to the true Ruby. Elianus, an ancient author, who wrote a *Natural History of Animals*, relates that a Stork once presented a woman named Heraclis with one of these stones, the bird thus showing its gratitude for her kindness to it in curing a broken leg. The colour of a Spinel will generally become deeper, and intensified if it is carefully heated. "The Balas," said Boetius, *De Natura Gemmarum*, "restrains passion and fiery wrath, and is a preservative from lightning." As already stated, the true Ruby—a red variety of Corundum—is of great rarity and value; whilst the Spinel, an aluminate of magnesium, is inferior in hardness, and much less esteemed as a Gem. The test of a perfect Ruby is its exact agreement in colour with the fresh blood of a pigeon, dropped upon the same sheet of paper immediately next the stone.

The **Tourmaline**—which sometimes goes by the name

of Brazilian Ruby—is a distinct Gem, seldom chosen for jewelry, but useful for optical purposes. Of the several varieties, the only one occasionally employed is that of a dark, olive-green tint. It is discovered also red, and pink, as "rubeolite"; blue, as indiolite; white, brown, and black. The red Tourmaline is that found in Ceylon, and in Siberia, which is known in commerce as the "Brazilian Ruby"; for which stone it is sometimes sold in mistake. The green, and blue varieties of Tourmaline are got from the Brazils, being occasionally called the Brazilian Emerald, and Sapphire. Chemically each of the Tourmalines contains silica, alumina, magnesia, oxide of iron, boracic acid, some soda, and some fluorine. By taking into consideration the physical, and the drug actions of these chemical elements, on the body, and mind, when administered therapeutically, we may form some conclusions about such influences for good, or evil, as the stones now under notice are likely to exercise on sensitive subjects, when worn as jewels, or otherwise externally applied. The said drug actions have already been considered here, of these several constituents; except as regards Magnesia, Fluorine, Boracic acid, Potash, and Soda.

Magnesia is the basic oxide of magnesium, which mineral, in one form or another, is universally disseminated throughout the whole of the earth's crust. Traces of it are, moreover, to be found in the ashes of all plants, and it is present furthermore in almost all Natural Waters. As familiar medicaments, carbonate of magnesia, and sulphate of magnesia (Epsom Salts), are well known to everyone. The chloride of magnesium corresponds pretty closely with chloride of sodium (common salt), and it has been authoritatively supposed that the salutary effects of sea-bathing may be partly due to the large proportion of chloride of magnesium contained in the water. Acting thus it would obviate scrofulous troubles of the skin; whilst possibly, indeed probably, affecting the system at large beneficially in the same respect. The hypothesis that by wearing, or otherwise applying, externally to the surface of the body, a magnesium-containing jewel (the infinitesimal quantity of this constituent being favourable rather than otherwise to its general effect on the health) need not be by any means thought untenable. Dr. Guernsey has shown that magnesia in its simple form, when much attenuated with inert sugar of milk, is of excellent advantage to children troubled with disturbed action of the bowels, wherefrom the " motions resemble the green of a frogpond."

Meerschaum, the light, soft, porous material used for pipes in which to smoke the choicer tobaccos, is a hydrated silicate of magnesium. Meerschaum (or Seafroth), when freshly dug, has almost the consistence of wax. The Turks spread this on bread, and eat it as a medicine. In Turkey, and in Germany, Meerschaum pipes which have been used are more valued than those newly made, by reason of the colouring which they have then acquired. The Soap-stone, or Steatite, is similarly eaten by the inhabitants of New Caledonia, when slightly baked, or when mixed with rice.

Fluorine (which is a special constituent of the Topaz,— occurring likewise in the Tourmaline), being derived from Fluor Spar,—in German—feld (field),—spah (spar),— is, with regard to the human body, a constant constituent of the teeth, and the bones; also it has been detected in the ashes of milk, and of blood. The mineral fluor spar is the "blue John" of Derbyshire-earths; and the "kann" of Cornish miners. It phosphoresces when exposed to light, and exhibits electrical phenomena.

Flourine forms with hydrogen, both in nature, and in the chemical laboratory, hydrofluoric acid, the use of which, through its power of acting on glass for etching purposes, has been in vogue since the year 1670. Most kinds of clay are composed of decayed feld-spar. Various physical effects on the body as wrought by medicinal uses of hydrofluoric acid, when diluted to a degree almost infinitesimal, have been faithfully, and reliably recorded. Similar effects may be reasonably expected to attend, in some measure, at any rate, the personal wearing of jewels which by analysis are known to contain fluorine as a constituent. By the hydrofluoric acid, given as described, varicose veins about the limbs have shrunk to half their size, fresh hair has grown on a bald head, whitlows on the fingers have been blighted, and a chronic soreness inside the nostrils has been cured. After smelling the strong acid a sense was felt in the brain as if on the verge of being struck with apoplexy. M. Maumene has been led by observations, and experiments, to conclude that the main cause of goitre is a presence of fluorides to excess in the drinking-water; these being particularly abundant in the water of goitrous districts.

Borax (whereof boracic acid is a product) has been found in certain mineral waters; as in those of Ischia, Thibet, and Persia. Pliny has described this substance under the name of "Chrysocolla," which is thought to be identical with our biborate of soda. The term "Baurach," from which our word "Borax" is derived, first occurs in Arabian writings. Native boracic acid got from mineral sources, and saturated by the chemist with soda, forms the medicinal " Borax " which doctors use commonly now-a-days. Some of this being dissolved in water, (and sweetened with honey,) makes a gargle which is curative of ulcerated sore throat, and mouth. When swallowed, borax produces its constitutional effects without being absorbed into the system; seeing that it can be detected passing unchanged out of the body in the excretions. Powdered Borax, when mixed with unsalted lard, is found to allay the pain produced by inflamed piles. Seeing that doses given medicinally of one-tenth of a grain of our Borax will cure the " thrush " of infants, as rapidly as an application of the same Borax, powdered, and mixed with honey, made directly to the sore surfaces inside the mouth, it may be readily believed that the action of the mineral here is dynamic rather than medicinal; and would equally follow a personal employment as an ornament, of this, or that, Precious Stone known to possess Borax as one of its constituents.

Quaintly enough, M. Pomet, in his *History of Druggs*, quoting Tournefort (1712) remarks, " The Ancients were not out when they said there was a ' greenish natural borace,' of the colour of a leek; any more than was Agricola, who rightly enough observes that he had seen a fossil nitre, solid and hard, like a stone, of which the Venetian Borace is made. But the same Author is very much mistaken when he says that then no borace was in use other than the factitious, or artificial, made of the urine of boys, (who drank wine,) of brass rust, and sometimes nitre, beaten together in a bell-metal mortar to the consistence of an oyntment; which is far from truth, since the borace he means is

only the fat borace refin'd, and shot into crystals."
" The refin'd borace ought to be prefer'd in medicine ; it is incisive, and penetrating." " They also use it externally to consume the excrescences of flesh ; 'tis of some profit likewise, since 'tis an ingredient of the unguent: citrinum."

This said " Unguent," according to directions given in the *Pharmacopœia Londinensis*, by Dr. Wm. Salmon (1690), " was to be prepared with fresh hog's lard, the outward rind of citrons bruised, crystal shells of the limpet, white alabaster, white Venetian borax, and beaten up, with suet of goat, or deer, being made into an oyntment according to art." " It was intended to take away deformities of the skin, as scabs, pimples, breakings-out : some say it will dispel freckles ; but that I question much." The chief modern use of borax is by jewellers and goldsmiths, for facilitating their practice of soldering gold, and silver.

Free *Potash* goes by the medicinal name of " Causticum." It is the active principle to which quick-lime and the caustic alkalies owe their causticity. This bears also the name " Æerstoff," which is our " hydrated causticum," or potassium. " It has been well ascertained," writes a competent author, " of late years that potash exerts a poisonous action quite distinct from that of any alkali ; which may be especially seen by the way potash, when harmfully employed paralyses the spinal cord and the heart." Dr. Meyhoffer says that for any overstrained exercise of the vocal apparatus, such as public singers, and speakers are liable to incur, " a specific remedy is at hand in kali causticum (the mineral potassium), which often in a single dose, infinitesimally attenuated, will remove any functional exhaustion of the vocal cords, and their regulating structures." As our pages show, several of the Precious Stones used for personal jewelry contain potassium as a leading constituent; which are, therefore, to be commended for curative wear under the conditions of physical infirmities thus indicated.

It should be always remembered, not only in the requirements under our present consideration, but likewise in general, with regard to jewel wearing, and jewel-uses externally, when having remedial purposes in view, that such jewels must be so set that the bottom facets of the several stones shall come into immediate unintercepted contact with the skin of the hand, or other part upon which each of such Precious Stones is worn, or applied.

Sodium (Natron, or Natrum);—a Carbonate of Soda; is found as a crystal, or in the form of an efflorescent powder, in several parts of the world, being at the same time a constituent of certain mineral waters, which are thereby made alkaline. It may be procured by the chemist from barilla, from kelp, or from sulphate of soda. Barilla is an ash usually obtained by the combustion of plants belonging to the chenopods, (or goose-foot Order), whilst kelp is procured by the combustion of plants belonging to the Order *Algaceæ* (sea-weeds). By digesting kelp in a small quantity of water, and filtering, and evaporating the solution, crystals of carbonate of soda may be procured. It has been imagined by mediciners that, as soda is contained in the tissues of animals more abundantly than potash, it should prove a more appropriate remedial agent within the body than potash. But experience seems to have proved the reverse: to account for which fact Sir George Blane has assumed that soda becomes applied to the general purposes of the internal body before it reaches the kidneys; and that, therefore, it fails to give relief against stone, and calculous troubles, by coming to act as an antacid solvent within the bladder, or kidneys. Nevertheless, a general conclusion has been arrived-at among writers on drug-actions that soda salts, unlike those of potash, have but little specific action on the human system. Carbonate of soda is manufactured at the present time almost entirely from common salt (chloride of sodium).

It may prove of advantage to state here (incidentally) that as an article of food lentils (of the red Egyptian sort) are rich in soda. They also contain a percentage (infinitesimal in quantity, but nevertheless appreciable, and of potential blood-making virtue) of iron; to which metal, indeed, they owe their ruddy colour. These lentils are highly nutritious, and, being almost sulphurless, do not provoke flatulence. But it is far from wise in most cases of adult life to try and live almost exclusively on any such leguminous foods, whilst rejecting all animal sustenance.

Dr. Haig, the well-known apostle of anti-gout diet, which he ordains as mainly vegetable, says, "It is necessary to know something about percentages, and values, so as not to replace meat (which has twenty per cent of albumin) by cabbages, and potatoes (which contain only from one to two per cent). This is where so many vegetarians make a mistake." "The fact is, that in some respects vegetarians suffer more than meat-eaters from uric acid poisoning, seeing that beans, peas, lentils, and peanuts, contain twice as much of the poison as meat. The natives of India are much affected by uric acid diseases, owing to the quantity of 'dahl' (lentils) which they eat. Other natives who abstain from 'dahl' are almost entirely free from uric acid ailments." One simple homely method by which any one can readily test the quality of his, or her circulation, so as to gain some reliable idea of the blood (as to its freedom, or the reverse, from uric acid in excess; and as to its activity of current), is to press the point of one finger on the back of the opposite hand, and to notice the rapidity with which the resultant white, bloodless spot thus produced recovers its redness after removing the finger. In a perfectly healthy condition it should do so in three seconds.

Common Salt is chemically a combination of Soda with Hydrochloric Acid; a Chloride of Sodium. As table salt, the article designated "Cerebos Salt" (irrespective of such commercial claims as it has to advance) is preferable for ordinary use, because of its special features, which serve important dietetic ends. Certain alimentary phosphates are blended with the common salt, whereby the deliquescent chloride is converted into a dry phosphate, and thus the salt preserves its fine dry powdery state; at the same time it is nutritively improved. If it should be noted that Cerebos Salt, when put into water makes it somewhat turbid, the reason for this is because of the (salutary) phosphates combining with the natural chlorides of the salt.

In the famous Salt Mines of Austria (which have been worked for the last six hundred years) the beds of salt are so thick that they have been excavated into houses, chapels, and other ornamental forms; and the Mines, when illuminated, are regarded as one of the sights of Europe.

Reverting to the subject of Rubies—the Tourmaline was first brought to Europe from Ceylon by the Dutch, "who gave it," says Harry Emanuel (1867), "the name of 'Aschentrekker,' from its sometimes attracting, and sometimes repelling, hot ashes when these were laid near it for any length of time." This Tourmaline will not only attract ashes from burning coals, but will also repel them again, in an amusing way: for, as soon as a small quantity of warm ashes leap upon it, and appear as if they were endeavouring to writhe themselves by force into the stone, they, in a little time, spring from it again, as if about to make a new attempt. Its possessed quality of acquiring magnetic powers, and becoming electrically "polar" by means of heat, readily distinguishes the Tourmaline from any other gem. Otherwise this is considered by some to be a Chrysolite when yellow, and a Sapphire when blue; being sold under such, and other spurious names. The crystals of Tourmaline are occasionally parti-coloured; frequently, those found in Elba are red at one end, yellow in the middle, and black, or brown, at the other end. These stones, when heated, or rubbed, acquire a different degree of electricity at each end respectively. And, if broken whilst thus electrically affected, their fragments, like artificial magnets, present opposite poles. The lapidary, when cutting Tourmaline for optical uses, has to remember that it is only transparent in one direction, parallel with the axis of the crystal; otherwise it will appear opaque on looking through it. The powers of polarising light which the Tourmaline exhibits make it of particular optical use. These powers are so special that when the Stone is cut into slices it can be employed in the polariscope for analysing the optical properties of other minerals. The two extremities of the Tourmaline crystal frequently terminate in a different manner; which occurrence is quite rare in other crystals. All mineral members of the Tourmaline group contain Fluorine, and water: some are further in possession of Boracic acid. The "currant-red" Tourmaline, of India, and Ceylon, is "Rubelite."

THE ROCK OF RUBIES; AND THE QUARRY OF PEARLS.

"Some asked me where the Rubies grew;
And nothing I did say,
But with my finger pointed to
The lips of Julia.
Some ask'd how Pearls do grow, and where?
Then spake I to my girl—
To "part her lips"; and show'd them there
The quarrelets of Pearl."

Herrick.

A recent triumph of modern constructive chemistry is the making of Rubies (out of genuine Ruby dust) from the real Rubies which come too small from the mine for any purposes of the jeweller; as well as from the chips, and dust produced when the actual Rubies are cut. Some clever chemists of to-day have perfected a process by which these genuine tiny mites may be fused, and recut; when they flash with a fire, and a brilliancy found to equal those of the natural gem. The only difference between the natural stones, and these reconstructed stones (being cut), requires a microscope to discern it. When viewed through that instrument the reconstructed stone shows a wavy line instead of the straight cleavage line of nature. In all other respects the two stones are identically the same;

of the same specific gravity; the same hardness; and each similarly "dichroic," that is, showing, when looked at through the dichroscope, two colours: maroon, and cochineal.

"A fine natural Ruby varies from five pounds to thirty pounds per carat, in price; while these reconstructed Rubies can be sold, cut, at from twenty-five to thirty shillings per carat."

From this Precious Stone Herrick has deduced,—in his Lines to Dianeme; (Hesperides)—an exquisite moral;

> "Sweet, be not proud of those two eyes,
> Which, starlike, sparkle in their skies;
> Be not you proud of that rich haire
> Which wantons with the lovesick aire;
> Since that red Rubie which you weare,
> Sunk from the tip of your soft eare,
> Will last to be a precious stone
> When all your world of beautie's gone."

GARNETS.

CHEMICALLY allied to the Ruby, as being similarly composed of the Silicates of Alumina, Lime, Iron, and Manganese, comes the family of Garnets. First there is the Precious, or Noble Garnet, of a deep, clear, poppy-red, being called also Almandine, like the violet-red Ruby, and being got from Ceylon, and Greenland. Then there is the common Garnet, with a dash of tawny in the red, and less transparent than the above; also the Grossularia, like a gooseberry, being of a dirty yellow-green, and coming from Siberia. There is, too, the Cinnamon Stone, of a light Cinnamon colour; and the Melanite, or black Garnet, again the Ouvarovite, or green, very like an Emerald; and the Oriental Garnet, found in Pegu, of an orange-red, drawing towards a hyacinthine yellow. Garnets can be melted into a black enamel, and they vary in size from a grain of sand to an apple; the Tourmalines, red, green, and yellow, being of this family. The distinctive title thereof—" Garnet "—is derived from the Latin name—*Granatum*—a Pomegranate; (or, as Lydgate calls it, the " Garnet-Appile ") on account of the resemblance which the granular varieties of the Garnet bear to the seeds of that fruit. Garnets occur in crystals; also in pebbles, and grains (as in alluvial deposits); and again massive, with a coarse granular structure. They vary from transparency to being almost opaque, also being sometimes red, red-brown, or black, in colour. Less frequently they are white, yellow, pink, or green. They are brittle; and more or less fusible, the least fusible form being the lime-iron Garnets. The element Yttrium has been found in Garnets. Three principal forms of Garnets are recognized; according (says the *Encyclopædia Britannica*) to their " sesqui-oxide basic components," viz., Alumina, Iron, and Chrome. These are further classed into numerous subordinate groups; as containing percentages of lime, chromium, iron, manganese, and magnesia." The Syrian, or Oriental Garnets vary in colour from a deep red to a violet-purple. The Garnet was much used as a jewel in ancient times. Antique intaglios on Garnet are usually recognizable by their fragmentary condition, as due to their brittleness, and by a softness of colour which time has imparted, and which defies imitation even by the ablest artists.

According to Pliny the large dull-coloured " Carbunculus of India " (a Garnet), used to be hollowed out into vessels which would hold as much as a pint. About

Cornwall the Garnet may be met with ; chiefly in greenstone. Dr. Rowland and M. Pomet—*History of Druggs*, 1669—tell about "Granates," "they dry, and cure palpitation of the heart; resist melancholy; stop spitting of blood ; dissolve tartar in the body ; and when hung about the neck are vulgarly believed to exercise these same virtues." "There are divers sorts of Gems that are of the colour of fire, as a Granate, a Hyacinth, etc.; therefore they call them ' Carbuncles,' from fire-coals."

The term **Carbuncle** is applied indiscriminately when Garnets are cut *en cabochon*; or, (to use the old English expression)—" tallow-topped " ; cut, not in facets, but with a flat, or hollow base, and a smooth convex top. The old writers of the Middle Ages ascribe virtues to Carbuncles similar to those which they attached to the Ruby.

"Bareketh" (or "flashing stone") was the Hebrew name for the Carbuncle ; this being derived from " barak,"—lightning ; it was a Stone in the breastplate of the High Priest. Eastern Legends assert that a Carbuncle was suspended by Noah, in the Ark, to diffuse light. Carbuncles of superior brilliancy are termed "males," those of a duller aspect are known as "females." When placed in a dark room the Carbuncle presents a rose colour ; but if exposed to the open daylight it glows like a burning coal ; being held against the sun it has the lustre of a flame. By reason of the deep red colour exhibited by most Carbuncles it is necessary for the lapidary to cut them *en cabochon* ; especially when the Stones are of any considerable size, so as to display their rich hues by the light passing through a comparatively thin stratum of the mineral. The Carbunculus of Pliny seems to have included all the deep-red coloured stones which were used for Jewelry and Gems, in his day; comprising the Ruby, and the Spinel, as well as the various kinds of Garnet. In the setting of Carbuncles a Ruby-like glow is frequently communicated to the Stones by a backing of coloured metallic foil which modifies their hue. This practice was similarly employed in former Roman times;—"tanta est in illis occasio arte subditis per quæ translucere cogantur." The finest Carbuncles come from Ceylon. Milton gives his Serpent eyes of Carbuncle: "His head crested aloft, and Carbuncle his eyes." Epiphanius has said about the Carbuncle: When worn it is impossible to conceal this Gem; for, notwithstanding with whatever clothes it may be covered, its lustre shows itself outside its envelope; whence it is called "the Carbuncle."

Lychnites: the Lamp Stone—Greek, *nuktalopos*—another name for the Carbuncle, was said, if hung round the neck, to give the power of seeing in the dark. It was further reputed to cure fluxions of the eyes if tied in a linen cloth upon the forehead. Thus wrote Psellus, *De Lapidibus*.

Similarly with regard to the Rock-Crystal (a form of Quartz) as a burning Glass; Pliny saith: "I find it asserted by Physicians that when any part of the body requires to be cauterized it cannot be better done than by means of a Crystal-ball held up against the Sun's rays." Crystals were employed thus by Surgeons, in old Roman days, who used the balls as lenses to burn out sores.

Exposure to sunlight has a curious effect on some Gems; Garnets, for instance, lose much of their colour in the course of time if they are worn continually by day.

Among Granites, the **Hyacinth** (Jacinth; or Zircon) occurs as a Gem, which is sometimes used even in modern jewelry. It varies in colour from red to yellow, brown, green, grey, and white. In chemical composition it consists chiefly of Zircon (66 per cent), with silica (33 per cent), and a trace of iron-peroxide. When the Hyacinth is of a smoky-white colour it is called a Jargoon. In the eighteenth century this stone was supposed to be an inferior diamond. The word " Zircon " is from the Arabic, " Zerk." What medicinal properties Zircon can exercise—external, or internal—has not yet been ascertained. A doubt exists as to whether or not this stone was the true Zircon of the ancients. By some it is thought to be the Lyncurion of Theophrastus; whilst the Hyacinth described by Pliny would appear to be the Amethyst, or the Sapphire, (having associated with it the blue " Fleur de Lys "). Anyhow, the Hyacinth was reputed in the Middle Ages to procure riches, honour, wisdom, and sleep. Furthermore, it would dispel evil spirits from the wearer. The roots of an allied Herb, likewise named " Jacinth," were used, 1696, " for the consolidation of green wounds." It was the " *Hyacinthus vaccinium* : or *Lilium purpureum*, "effectually helping the bloody flux and other Lasks." " Those persons," as M. Pomet directed, 1712, " who would have the Jacinth-stone for the confection that bears its name, must use no other than the milky Hyacinthus, being the true Oriental, and fit for medicinal use, it requiring no other preparation than to be ground to an impalpable powder."

The Hyacinth (Jacinth) of the Garnet family " strengthens the heart; is specifick against the Crampe, and Convulsion; it is counted, hung about the neck, for an Amulet against the Plague; or, if set in a Ring."

> "Sed quodcunque genus collo suspendere possis,
> Vel digito portes, terras securas obibis;
> Nec tibi pestiferæ regionis causa nocebit."

This Gem is of a yellow-red; and like the flame of Fire: "The Hyacinth that is us'd in Medicine," a soft milky Hyacinth, is a little stone, of the size, and figure of a moderate grain of salt; and of the colour of Milk; from whence it derives its name." The said Confection, made as it ought, is much prescribed because of its good qualities in fortifying the heart, and resisting of Poison." "The dearness of the Medicine, and the demand for it, is the reason that you have a thousand Sophisticators of it, who do it so grossly, and scandalously that they afford you no better than Honey, Bole, Myrrh, and some Leaf Copper, for this Confection; and sometimes they allow you a little Bastard Saffron; therefore, the best way is never to meddle with this except you have it from an honest, and reputable Dealer."

"The Jacinth," wrote Barrett, in his *Natural Magic*, 1801, "possesses virtues from the Sun against poisons, pestilences, and pestiferous vapours; likewise it renders the bearer pleasant, and acceptable; conduces also to gain money; being simply held in the mouth it wonderfully cheers the heart, and strengthens the mind." Again, "the Jacinth," wrote Boetius, *De Natura Gemmarum*, "if worn on the finger procures sleep; and brings honour, riches, wisdom." What a desirable Jewel for presentation to a wakeful sufferer, as a solace for the restless brain, (besides being a handsome finger ornament,) thereby securing for him benefit both of mind, and of body—

"The innocent Sleep;
Sleep that knits up the ravell'd sleave of care;
The death of each day's life; sore labour's bath,
Balm of hurt minds; great Nature's second course;
Chief nourisher in life's feast."

The manner in which babies are lulled off to sleep, by rocking in the arms, or in a cradle, is, so Dr. L. Robinson has shown, very remarkable as an instance of inheritance from arboreal, or monkey-like ancestors; because the rocking is a reminder of the to-and-fro swaying of branches; and such swaying would be the method of inducing sleep adopted by arboreal dwellers. It is singular to find that our nursery ditties embody a reference to matters arboreal in this instance, as if with a lingering tradition of ancestors who lived in trees. Thus the English mother, or nurse, in rocking her infant to sleep sings—

"Hush-a-by, baby; on the tree top
When the wind blows the cradle shall rock;
When the bough breaks the cradle will fall,
Down will come baby, cradle, and all."

"Another habit of children, which bears out this supposition,—and a destructive habit too,—is that of picking at anything loose, (any pieces of wall-paper especially), so as to tear it off. This habit is probably the survival of a monkey-practice of picking off the bark from trees, in order to search for insects. Any loose piece of bark indicates an insect refuge suggesting live prey; so that with the monkey an association is formed between loose bark and food. With the child this reason for the act has become lost; but the instinct to pick remains as a vestigial survival."

Certain Magical attributes were credited to Zircon in the Middle Ages; such as " procuring sleep, honour, and wisdom; besides driving away evil spirits." When clear, and without flaws, Zircon is one of the Precious Stones. Specimens thereof from Renfrew in Canada are remarkably fine; the colourless varieties are termed Jargoon. Zircon is the densest of the Precious Stones. It is found in the two Precious Stones, Jargoon, and Hyacinth.

The Hyacinth is indebted for its name to a supposed resemblance in colour to that flower, which Apollo is fabled to have raised from the blood of his favourite youth, Hyacinthus.

THE TOPAZ.

THE true Topaz (which differs from the Oriental Topaz,—really a Sapphire,—and from a Quartz Topaz) has its own peculiar and special attributes; being now known as the Chrysolite, or Peridot. It possesses a gift of inner radiance which can dispel darkness, just as the Carbuncle does. Formerly it was eagerly looked for by mariners when they had no daylight, or moon, to direct their course. Its name Chrysolite is derived from the Greek words, *kreusos*—gold; and *lithos*—a stone. Set in gold, and worn round the neck, or left arm, the Topaz was formerly believed to exercise a charm against all sorcery, and magic; it also had the power of dispelling night terrors, curing cowardice, calming anger, and madness; whilst being able to brighten the wit. This Stone was thought to give notice of poison by losing its colour. Its chemical composition is thirty-four of Silica; fifty-seven of Alumina; and seven of Fluoric acid, (fractions not being counted). The rose-red, and the pure white Topazes are those most esteemed. Brewster found—under microscopical inspection— fluid cavities, within the Topaz. The Oriental Topaz, (or Yellow Sapphire), which is of a soft Jonquil, or citron colour, shows sometimes bright, and golden; somewhiles as if full of gold, in fragments.

Next to the Oriental in hardness, and in richness of colour, comes the Brazilian, of a deep orange-yellow; or sometimes so limpid, and colourless as to be mistaken for diamonds, being then called "gouttes d'eau." Bohemian Topazes are hyacinthine, red, brown, or tawny,—sometimes of a dirty yellow-white; those from Saxony are hard, clear, and yellow; the native Topaz of Ceylon is a pale soft blue, this being called the "white, and water Sapphire." Furthermore, very fine green, and blue varieties are brought from Siberia, and Kamschatka.

Quite recently (1906), a Rock-Crystal hiberon—drinking vessel—(mounted with enamelled gold) was sold at Christie's, fetching the unprecedented price (for such a jewel) of sixteen thousand, two hundred, and seventy-five pounds sterling. Mr. Charles Wertheimer became, after a spirited competition, possessor of this cup; and at the same time the record-maker as to the highest auction price ever paid for a single object of art in an English saleroom. This wonderful vase, carved of Rock Crystal, is of Sixteenth Century Italian work; the body of the vessel roughly resembling a Monster, with the head forming a spout. It is about a foot high; and sixteen inches long.

To resume about the Topaz. This stone derives its name from the island Topazion, which was supposed to be situated in the Red Sea. There are the gold-coloured Topaz, and another, greenish-yellow of hue. This second species was called Chrysoprase, having a blend of golden, and leek, colours. The ancients supposed that the powers of the Topaz increased, and decreased, with with increase, and decrease of the moon. The true Topaz seldom occurs of a large size, without defects. It is not in vogue at the present day with jewellers, although fifty years ago it was fashionable enough. The stone is derived principally from the Brazils. It will become strongly electric by heat, friction, or pressure; retaining that condition, and remaining in it, for several hours. The Emperor Hadrian is reported to have possessed a seal-ring of Topaz, engraved with the lines—

> "Natura deficit;
> Fortuna moratur;
> Deus omnia cernit."

According to *The Honest Jeweller*—by a German writer of the seventeenth century—"when thrown into boiling water the Topaz at once deprives this of its heat."

The true, or Brazilian Topaz is one of the few precious stones which contain the element "fluorine." It may be regarded as a Silicate of Alumina,—wherein a part of the Oxygen of the Silica is replaced by the fluorine. The old Testament Topaz (Pit-doh) which formed a part of Aaron's Breast-plate, was probably a "peridot." Also the element "Vanadium" has been detected in the Brazilian Topaz. Powdered Topaz was formerly kept in apothecaries' shops, and sold as an antidote to madness. The Scotch Topaz is only a Yellow Quartz.

"The Topaz," writes M. Pomet, 1712, " needs no other preparation for medicine than to be ground with Rose-water on a Marble, in the same manner as Hyacinth, and other precious Stones." "The true Topaz of the ancients is a transparent Gem, of a diluted green colour that seems to have some yellowness, or a Gold colour in it, very glorious." "It is reported to be good against hæmorrhages, and all manner of fluxes of blood, as likewise to stop bleeding." This Topaz was afterwards called a Chrysolite; which name it still bears. The Topaz of the ancients was quite a different stone.

Some of the finest Topazes are almost colourless, and may be occasionally mistaken for Diamonds; but these stones are inferior in hardness, they lack "fire," and become electric when heated. Such colourless Topazes pass in England under the name of "minas novas." The coloured Topazes are usually either yellow, or blue; the yellow is liable to suffer bleaching by exposure to sunlight. In 1750 a Parisian jeweller discovered that the yellow Topaz of Brazil, when subjected to a moderate heat assumes a rose-pink colour; and it is now generally believed that all the pink Topazes occurring in jewelry owe their tint to some such artificial treatment. To effect this purpose now-a-days the stone is wrapped in German tinder, which is then ignited. The said "burnt Topaz" is known to jewellers as Brazilian Ruby. In like manner the blue Topaz passes under the name of Brazilian Sapphire; and the pale green as Aqua-marine; a name strictly applicable only to the sea-green Beryl. Occasionally the Topaz is found in Great Britain; but simply in small crystals unfit for jewelry. St. Michael's Mount, in Cornwall, has furnished specimens of such Topaz.

The **Malachite** Stone (a variety of Topaz) is an ore of copper, which presents in its finer varieties a beautiful green colour, thus leading to its use as an ornamental

Stone; also warranting the expectation of remedial action through its coppery dynamic influence, when worn (next the body) as a Jewel. Chemically the Malachite is a hydrated basic carbonate of copper. It usually occurs in stalactitic, or stalagmitic forms, containing—as a percentage of copper-oxide—seventy-two parts, carbonic di-oxide twenty parts, and water, eight parts. The colours of the internal structure of this stone, when it is fractured, are arranged in zones of light and dark tints, including various shades of apple-green, emerald-green, and verdigris-green. The name Malachite is given from the Greek word *malakee*, signifying the Mallow Plant; in allusion to the resemblance of the colour of the Mineral to that of Mallow leaves. This stone is believed to have been the "Smaragdus Medicus" of Pliny. For ornamental uses it is ground smooth with emery, and finally polished with Tripoli. Malachite, when ground to powder, is used as a pigment, which goes by the name of "pigment green" stone.

The Topaz, according to Leonardus, was first found on an island in the Red Sea always beclouded by fogs. Mariners continue to seek for it there when they have no guiding light; and from their making such search it originally took the name of "Topaz." "Blood flowing from a wound is stopped if this be bound over it; and it makes the bearer of it obtain the favour of Princes." The Topaz powdered, and taken in wine, was believed to cure asthmas, want of sleep, and divers other maladies.

The Emperor Maximilian, who, with a blow of his fist could knock out the teeth of a horse, and with one of his kicks break the animal's thigh, is said to have crushed Topazes to powder between his fingers.

Orpheus, as quoted by W. King, says concerning Agate, another of the numerous Quartz varieties: "If thou wearest a piece of the Tree-Agate on thy hand, the immortal gods shall be pleased with thee; if the same be tied to the horns of thy oxen, when ploughing, or round the plowman's sturdy arm, 'wheat-crowned' Ceres shall descend from heaven with full lap upon thy furrow."

"Of the stone which hight Agate" (saith the *Book of Saxon Leechdoms*, 1864) "it hath eight virtues for them who hath this stone with them; against thunder, sorcery, fiendish possession, venom, or poison, disease, the evils of strong drink, and outbreaks on the skin."

Agates embody minute particles of Iron in their structure; and thereto their varieties of colour are due. During the Middle Ages the Agate was considered hostile to poisons, and it was therefore made into drinking cups, and other such vessels. Or, another method for securing its protection was for the servants to touch all foods or cooking utensils with the Agate before serving provender therein. The Prophet Isaiah makes a laudatory allusion to this stone; "I will make thy windows of Agates."—

"Who comes in summer to this earth,
Owing to June his day of birth,
If wearing Agate on his hand,
May all the joys of life command."

"In shape no bigger than an Agate stone
On the forefinger of an Alderman."
Romeo and Juliet; Act I., Sc. 4.

THE AMETHYST.

The Amethyst (when "Oriental," a Sapphire) is one of the rarest of all gems : so rare, so beautiful, and capable of such transcendent polish, that many persons prefer it to a Diamond. But the true Amethyst is simply a crystal of Quartz, coloured with oxide of manganese, or peroxide of iron, whereto is due that rich purple colour of the grape which has crept like a drop of blood through all the veins of this crystal.

The Amethyst is the gem worn in the ring of the Catholic Bishops, being hence often called the "Bishop's Stone."

Because of its fabled origin as a Nymph beloved by Bacchus, but giving preference to Diana, and, therefore changed into a gem, the Amethyst has always been reputed to exhibit the most profound antipathy to drunkenness, and wine; wherefore the ancients used to drink out of cups studded with this gem, so that they might imbibe perhaps to excess, but never to intoxication. Again, the Amethyst was one of the twelve sacred gems worn on the Jewish breastplate; and was, as tradition has said, that particular gem which typified the tribe of Issachar. The finest Amethysts come from Ceylon, the Brazils, Silesia, and Murcia. The Brazilian stones are sometimes streaked violet and yellow, or violet and green. This Precious Stone is much used within the temples of Eastern countries. It is supposed to create an atmosphere of pious calm. Rosaries are made with beads of Amethyst, being finished with the figure of a deity for a pendant. As each bead is told, the devotee becomes more and more imbued with a sense of mental peace, and quietude. The stone is synonymous with chastity; and the Greeks held that wine drunk out of an Amethyst cup was powerless to intoxicate. Pliny, however, supposed the gem to get its name from the fact of its nearly, though not quite, approaching the colour of wine. Certain Amethysts, having a rosy hue shining through their purple, were called by the ancients—" Gems of Venus." The *Mirror of Stones* tells concerning Amethysts, " Their virtue is to drive away drunkenness; for, being bound on the navel, they restrain the vapour of the wine; and so dissolve the ebriety; they repress evil thoughts, and give a good understanding; they make a man vigilant, and expert in business; the barren they render fruitful by drinking a lotion of it; they expel poison; they preserve military men, and give them victory over their enemies; and prepare an easy capture of wild beasts, and birds."

The Indian Amethyst exceeds the other four varieties in colour, beauty, and price; it is of a purple hue, mixed with rosy, and violet tints. The Peruvians held a belief that if the names of the sun, and moon were engraved upon an Amethyst, and it was hung about a person's neck, together with a baboon's hair, or a swallow's feather; this would act as a spell against witchcraft.

In composition the Amethyst is made up chiefly of lime, magnesia, soda, and oxide of iron. It belongs to the vitreous order of quartz. The Oriental Amethyst—a Sapphire—is an entirely different Stone. The Amethyst is distinguished from common quartz by its purple colour (in every shade), and its transparent crystal. It was considered by the ancients " a Gem of Fire."

Such radiations of violet light as the Amethyst

eminently gives off, do really exercise, according to the pronouncement of modern science, salutary effects of a calmative nature upon those persons who come within their influence. Similarly, it has been found by experiment in lunatic asylums that a room hung with violet drapery has a soothing effect on insane patients, who are put to abide therein. Plants, again, which are purple in their blossom, and juices, exert sedative actions; for example, belladonna, henbane, foxglove, bitter-sweet, etc. The Amethyst is the Precious Stone associated with February, as its particular month; which month the Romans dedicated to Neptune, their water-god. It should further be worn specially on a Thursday, the day of Thor. In the eighteenth century the Amethyst was highly prized as a gem. Queen Charlotte possessed a necklace of perfectly-matched Stones, which was valued at two thousand pounds sterling. A modern French poet, making this precious stone the Amulet in a mystical Play, has feelingly styled it, *L'Etoile de l'amour, qui luit dans l'absence, et le deuil*. By candle-light the Amethyst loses a part of its beauty, being apt to appear of a blackish hue. In 1652 an Amethyst was worth as much as a Diamond of equal weight.

Marbodeus gives (Latiné) a line about this Stone:
"Hic facilis sculpi: contrarius ebrietati."
The Amethyst:—

"A lithos est' ametheustos ego d'o potas Dioneusos
Hee neephrein peisei; mee matheto metheuein."

"On wineless Gem I, toper Bacchus, reign;
Learn, Stone, to drink; or, teach me to abstain!"

This variety of quartz is told-of in the Revelation of Saint John the Divine as one of the precious stones in the wall of the Holy City. " The first foundation was Jasper; the second, Sapphire; the third, a Chalcedony; the fourth, an Emerald; the fifth, Sardonyx; the sixth, Sardius; the seventh, Chrysolite; the eighth, Beryl; the ninth, a Topaz; the tenth, a Chrysoprasus; the eleventh, a Jacinth; the twelfth, an Amethyst. And the twelve gates were twelve Pearls; every several gate was of one Pearl; and the street of the City was pure Gold, as it were transparent glass."—" Amethyst" in Heraldry is the purple in a nobleman's coat of arms.

Again, there is a pretty little blue spring flower (*Amythystea cærulea*) of Siberian origin, which grows, rarely, in our hedges

Richard Jefferies, always a close observer, when discoursing about the "winds of heaven" (in *Field and Hedgerow*,) says, " to the Amethyst in the deep ditch, the wind comes; it lifts the guilty head of the passionate Poppy, that has sinned in the sun for love."

The Amethyst is almost the only coloured stone which can be worn with mourning garb.

Inferentially it is fair to conclude with respect to the Amethyst that the violet rays, focussed from its own tutelary planet, serve to influence, as nerve tonics, the bodily system of its wearers; seeing that violet rays are now known by scientists to thus improve vitality; whilst yellow rays of light are concerned in promoting the decomposition of the carbon (carbon di-oxide) in the atmosphere, as involved in the growth of vegetation. By reason of its thus focussing the violet rays of light, (which are eminently calmative, and soothing,) the Amethyst has been supposed from the earliest times to subdue the passions; being specially an antidote to drunkenness, when habitually worn.

> "Hold up thy mirror to the sun,
>   And thou shalt need an eagle's gaze,
> So perfectly the polished stone
>   Gives back the glory of its rays."
>
> ("Turn it, and it shall paint as true
>   The soft green of the vernal earth;
> And each small flower, of bashful hue,
>   That closest hides its lowly birth.")
>
> *Keble (Christian Year).*

THE JASPER.

The Jasper, another variety of quartz—"Jashpeh,"—is a Precious Stone, which became known through its extensive use by artists in former times, for commemorative works, such as cameos, intaglios, etc.

The Greek name, Jaspis, signifies a ready yielding to the engraver's burine. According to Scriptural tradition the Jasper in the High Priest's Breastplate represented the tribe Benjamin. The yellow Jasper is found near the Bay of Smyrna, in Greece; also in various other places. A specimen of this Stone which may be seen in the British Museum, is thought to exhibit a likeness of the Poet Chaucer.

One "Onomakristos," five hundred years before the Christian era, has told of "the grass-green Jasper, which rejoiceth the eye of man, and is looked on with pleasure by the immortals."

Galen, amongst his other sage maxims, has advised that "if a Jasper be hung about the neck it will strengthen the stomach." Marbodeus (Marbœuf, Bishop of Rennes), who wrote a Latin Poem, *The Lapidarium* (1067–1081), described the Jasper Stone in the following verses, (fittingly translated):—

"Seven kinds, and ten of Jasper Stones reported are to be;
Of many colours this is knowne, wich noted is by me,
And said in manie places of the world for to be sene,
Where it is bred; but yet the best is thorough shining greene;
And that which prooved is to have it in more vertue plas't;
For being borne about of such as are of living chaste,
It drives awaie their ague fits, the dropsy thirsting dry,
And put unto a woman weake in travell which dooth lie,
It helps, assists, and comforts her in pangs when she dooth crie.
Againe, it is beleeved to be a safegarde franke and free,
To such as weare, and beare the same; and, if it hallowed be,
It makes the parties gratious, and mightie too, that have it,
And noysome fansies (as they write that ment not to deprave it)
It dooth displace out of the mind: the force thereof is stronger
In Silver, if the same be set;—and will endure the longer."

Again, to quote from *The Magik of Kiram, King* of *Persia*, (London, 1685), "Jaspis,"—Jasper,—is a known Stone. On a Jasper do you engrave a kite tearing a serpent; and under the stone put a stone taken out of the head of a kite, and enclose it; give it to wear in the Breste; for, it will draw away all harm of the stomach, and will create an appetite, to eat, and good digestion. For it has also other virtues; let it be worn only in the Breast." "The Jasper—Jaholum (*Pharmacopœia Londinensis*, 1696), is to be used as an Amulet against phantasms, and witchcraft; worn on the breast it helps the epilepsie, pain of the stomach, and colick. It is of the nature of the Bloodstone; for, it stops bleeding at the nose, and other fluxes of blood." "Being a very precious commodity," pronounced M. Pomet (1712), "it is very liable to be counterfeited in glass. Chuse such as are of a fine deep green, smooth, and shining, full of red spots, as if they were little drops of blood; and which can take no impression from the point of a needle drawn upon it, which is a sign that it is truly Jasper." "Ground fine upon porphyry the powder is astringent, proper to stop blood, and the scour of the guts."

Jasper is highly prized in China; the seal of the Emperor being made from it.

"The Jasper,"—Jaspis—quoth Isidorus (1612), "signifieth green; and such a green as doth illustriously shine forth with a very supreme viridity, or greenness of glory." *Cujus in argento vis fortior esse putatur*, saith Marbodus. Galen, always grave of thought, said, "the Green Jasper benefits a man's chest, and the mouth of his stomach, if tied over it." "Of this gem," quoth he, "I have had ample experience, having made a necklace of such stones, and hung it round the neck, descending so low that the stones might touch the mouth of the stomach; and they proved to be of no less service than if they had been engraved in the manner prescribed by King Nechepsos." De Boot likewise has testified that that in his own practice he has observed effects scarcely credible, from the application of the Green Jasper in cases of hæmorrhage; and he makes mention of the Jasper in general, "that a Gren Jasper engraved with the figure of a scorpion, when the sun was entering that sign, was a sure preservative against the formation of the stone in the bladder."

Galen is said to have always carried about with him one particular Jasper Stone, set in a Sigil. The figures represented thereon were a man with a bundle of herbs on his neck; this stone giving the power of distinguishing diseases, and stopping the flow of blood from any part.

Jasper (which is actually a coloured mixture of silica, and clay) owes its characteristic tints to peroxide of iron, being of a blood-red hue throughout the whole body of the stone. The brown Jasper is made so by the same oxide hydrated.

De Boot, the Judicious, tells thus concerning the

Jasper: "*Testari possum, qui aliis lapidibus, et gemmis tantas vires quantas vulgus solet,—non tribuo credibile vix. de Jaspidis viribus observasse. Nam, qui ancilla fluxu menstruorum ita laborasset per aliquot dies ut nullo modo sisti posset, Jaspidem rubram impolitam, et rudem, femori alligari jussi.*" "*Alius, in eadem domo, quum in pede vulneratus esset, nec sanguinis fluxus cohiberi posset, admoto lapide, extemplo impeditus fuit, licet vulnus non tegeretur.*" To these instances he adjoins a much more memorable example of a maid whom he cured at Prague, after she had been for "six years sick of a hemorrhage so vehement that there scarce ever passed a week in which she did not several times bleed; neither could she be relieved by any remedies, though she had long us'd them, till she was quite tired therewith. Wherefore our Author, setting them all aside, lent her a Jasper, of whose virtues in such cases he had made good trial, to hang about her neck: which when she did, the flux of blood presently ceased; and she afterwards for curiosity's sake, oftentimes laying aside the stone, and as often as she needed it applying it again, observed that whereas the flux of blood did not presently return upon the absence of the Jasper, but after divers weeks, yet upon the hanging it on again it would presently be stopped; so that she could not ascribe the relief to any thing but the stone; by which our Author tells us that at length she was quite cured. And speaking of the praises given by others to Green Jasper, speckled with Red, he concludes, "*Sed ego, quod multoties expertus sum refero.*"

"One passage there is," says again Robert Boyle, in his *Experimental Philosophie*, "which doth so notably confirm what we have deliver'd touching the greatest cures that may in divers cases be perform'd by *outward* applications that I must not here omit the mentioning of it; in the Epistle written out of Peru to the inquisitive Monardes, in these words—*In urbe Posto, ubi aliquot annos vixi, omnis generis morbos Indus quidam curabat solo cujusdam plantæ succo artubus, et parti affectæ illito. Ægros deinde stragulis egregie tegebat ad sudorum provocandum. Sudor e partibus illitis emanans merus sanguis erat, quem lineis pannis abstergebat, atque ita in curatione pergebat, donec satis sudasse putaret, optimis interea cibis eos alens. Eo remedio multi morbi deplorati curabantur; imo œgri juniores, et robustiores ab ejus usu fieri videbantur; sed, neque pretio, neque precibus, neque minis, unquam efficere potuimus ut eam plantam nobis demonstraret.*"

Paracelsus (Theophrastus 1650), laboured studiously to discover some means for prolonging life. Like Bacon, and Verulam, he maintained that the human body may be rejuvenated to a certain extent by a fresh supply of vitality; and it was his great aim to find the means by which such a supply could be obtained. As reasons for his belief, he argued thus, " Metals may be preserved from rust; and wood may be protected against rot. Blood may be preserved a long time if the air is excluded. Egyptian mummies have kept their form for centuries without undergoing putrefaction. Animals awaken from their winter sleep; and flies, having become torpid from cold, grow nimble again when they are warmed. (" Such a hot day was it ";— Dickens; in the dull, sunny little town favoured with a visit by Mrs. Jarley, and her renowned Waxworks; that " the very dogs were all asleep; and the flies. drunk with moist sugar, in the grocer's shop, forgot their wings, and briskness, and baked to death in dusty corners of the window.")—Therefore, if inanimate objects can be kept from destruction, why should there be no possibility of preserving the life-essence of animate forms. For this attempted purpose he prepared a remedy, which he styled *Primum Ens Melissæ;* this was made by dissolving pure Carbonate of Potass, and macerating in the liquid some fresh leaves of the Melissa Plant (Balm). Thereon some absolute alcohol was poured several times, in successive portions, so as to absorb the colouring matter; after which the liquor was collected, distilled, and evaporated to the thickness of a syrup. The second great secret of Paracelsus was his *Primum Ens Sanguinis,* which was prepared by mixing blood from the median vein of a healthy young person, and digesting it in a warm place with twice the quantity of what he termed 'alcahest.' After which the red fluid was to be separated from the sediment, filtered, and preserved. The aforesaid 'alcahest,' (his celebrated universal medicine,) was made with freshly prepared caustic lime, and absolute alcohol. These were distilled together ten times; the residue left in the retort was mixed with pure Carbonate of Potass, and dried. This was again distilled with alcohol. It was then placed in a dish, and set on fire; and the residue that remained was 'Alcahest.' "

Of **Quartz** there are other and beautiful crystals besides the Opal, the Amethyst, and the (false) Topaz, already described. First there are the transparent, or vitreous varieties, of which the type is **Rock-Crystal**, (or Ice-Crystal), in round smooth balls, the same as those (likewise of this Rock-Crystal) which the dandies of old Rome used to carry within their hands for cooling them during summer heat. These we cut nowadays into lenses, as specially valuable for spectacles, and which are known as "pebbles." The same Crystal is styled the Bohemian, or Scotch diamond; it has on occasions passed verily for an actual diamond.

About that purple, or blue violet Quartz, the *Amethyst*, a detailed notice has already been given. Then there is the **Bohemian, or Silesian Ruby,** a rose-Quartz, which fades in the light, and can only be restored to its original colour by being placed in the damp; again, the **Cairngorm**, a false topaz, this being of a light yellow, or citron colour; likewise some dozen other quartzes, of a minor sort, though including Rock-Crystal, spangled with gold, as found likewise in France; also the "**Chatoyant**" **Quartz,** or "**Cat's-eye**," which the Cingalese sometimes cut into the form of a monkey's face; and which, when fine, is very valuable.

There are further the Chalcedonic varieties of Quartz, including **Chrysoprase,** and the **Sard,** (one of the sacred twelve of the Ephod: deep brown, or blood-red of colour). This Sard "stanches blood, and secures its wearer against the bites of venomous serpents; it also serves to bind up.

The **Onyx,** again, is a Quartz which incites to quarrels, and contentions, and has been reputed to be of two sexes. Combinations thereof are the Onyx, banded black and white; the Sardonyx, banded white and flesh-red; and the Chalcedonyx, banded opaque and translucent. Each of these now mentioned has been specially appropriated for cameos, and engravings. The Fur Seal is said to swallow pebbles of Chalcedony, "with choice thereof, and relish."

Of the Jasper varieties of Quartz the most beautiful

is the **Bloodstone,** or Heliotrope; a green Jasper, spotted with red gouts. (In the Royal collection of France there is a medallion of Christ, cut in blood-stone, where these red spots are made to represent the drops of the Passion.) The term Heliotrope, from two Greek words which signify "sun-turning," is applied to this stone, because of a notion that when immersed in water it will change the sun's image into blood-red.

This Stone was said of old to make the wearer fortunate and rich; while Amulets of Jasper resisted fevers, and dropsy. Ancient warriors often carried an Amulet of Bloodstone, which was intended to stop bleeding when applied to a wound.

Concerning the *Lapis Sanguinarius*, or Blood Stone, found in New Spain, (with regard to which the Indians do most confidently believe that if the flesh of any bleeding part be touched with this Stone the bleeding will thereby be stanched), Menardes adds this memorable observation of his own, "*Vidimus nonnullos hæmorrhoidum fluxu afflictos remedium sensisse, annulos ex hoc lapide confectos in digito continue gestando; nec non et menstruum fluxum sisti.*" "The Vertue of this Stone is much above that of any other Gem, for it stops the flux of blood in any part." "We have seen some that were troubled with the flux of the Hæmorrhoides who found remedy by wearing Rings made of the Bloodstone continually on their Fingers."

That the principal Metals, in common with Minerals, (not only the Precious Stones, but likewise lesser minerals, such as Earth Salts, etc.), positively affect the bodily conditions, when applied externally, cannot be doubted. The modern helpful uses of Radium afford a remarkable illustration of this fact. Lieber, a well-known chemist of New York, has succeeded in dissolving Radium. Experiments have been made, in the Flower Hospital, with the solution thus produced, proving that it retains all the activity of pure Radium, and that it is assuredly curative of Cancer in some of its external forms. The solution is used in direct contact with the diseased part. Again, what are known as "rain cures" find many enthusiastic advocates of late; particularly in the States: (Texas, e.g.). All that is required of the patient is to stand in the open air, with the body bare of all clothing, and to let the falling rain pour thereon. For certain nervous disorders, of a strengthless type, and for chronic rheumatism, the treatment is almost infallible. "One good drenching shower of rain, followed by a brisk rubbing down, has likewise cured scores of cases of obstinate colds." This treatment is believed to have originated at Austin, where many persons have now become thoroughly convinced of the benefits conferred by rain baths. Since such a method of cure became popular numerous back-gardens at Austin are surrounded by high boarded fences, which serve to screen the citizens while pursuing the treatment; this being described as "not only invigorating, and an absolute nerve restorative, but also at the same time highly agreeable."

The virtues of rain water (thus outwardly applied to the skin surface) are exercised because of its containing, as chemists explain, air, carbonic acid, some traces of nitric acid, salts, and organic matter. To the carbonate of ammonia which is present they attribute the softness of rain-water. Carbonate of lime is another constituent. Brandes discovered various other substances therein, viz., chloride of sodium (common salt), chloride of magnesium, sulphate, and carbonate of magnesia, and sulphate of lime. The putrefaction to which rain-water is subject if kept stagnant shows that some organic matter is also present. It is not unreasonable to suppose that sea-bathing with marine water from the open ocean proves beneficial, and curative in a like manner, because certainly containing, as chemists now assure us, a measurable amount of dissolved gold. In 1872 Mr. Soustadt actually measured the quantity of gold in sea-water, and found that in the water of Ramsay Bay there was nearly a grain of the gold in a ton of the sea-water. A grain of gold is worth about twopence; and as there are about sixty thousand billion tons of water in the ocean, any one who could recover it all would have a nice little fortune of over five thousand million tons of gold.

Pliny relates that the sun could be viewed in a Blood-stone as in a mirror; and that solar eclipses became visible therein. Marbodus, (or Marbœuf, Bishop of Rennes), who wrote a Latin poem *The Lapidarium* (1067–1081), somewhat humorous in its tissue of marvels, charms, and talismans, connected with Precious Stones, has spoken of the Blood-stone under this its title, "Heliotrope":—

> "Ex re nomen habens est Heliotropia gemma,
> Quæ Solis radiis in aqua subjecta bacillo
> Sanguine reddit mutato lumine Solem,
> Eclipsemque novam terris effundere cogit."

"The Stone Heliotropium, green, like a Jasper, or Emerald, beset with red specks," saith Magus (or *The Celestial Intelligencer*, 1801), "makes the wearer constant, renowned, and famous, conducing to long life; there is likewise another wonderful property in this stone, which is, that it so dazzles the eyes of men, that it causes the bearer to be invisible: but then there must be applied to it the herb bearing the same name, viz., 'Heliotropium,' or the Sun-flower; and these kinds of virtues Albertus Magnus, and William of Paris, mention in their writings."

HELIOTROPIUM.

"Tot bona divino data sunt huic munera Gemmæ;
Cui tamen amplior his concessa potentia fertur;
Nam, si jungatur ejusdem nominis herbæ,
Carmine legitimo, verboque sacrata potenti,
Subtrahit humanis oculis quemcunque gerentem."

"To many a gift divine this Stone lays claim;
Surpassing which the power that makes its fame
Is,—when conjoined with Herb of title quaint,
Same as its own; whilst, spoken by a saint
Are incantations, holy, and a spell
Invoked,—with words the pious tongue can tell;
Of Gem, and Plant combined, the wearer then
Becomes invisible to eyes of men."

The **Bloodstone** is found abundantly in India, Bokhara, Siberia, and Tartary; likewise in the Island of Rum, in the Hebrides. There is a tradition that at the Crucifixion of our Saviour the sacred blood which followed the spear-thrust fell upon a dark green Jasper which was lying at the foot of the Cross; and from that circumstance sprang the Bloodstone variety of the Jasper. In the Middle Ages the red specks observable in this Stone were thought to represent the Blood of Christ; and the Stone was believed to exercise the same medicinal, and magical virtues as the Jasper proper. In a *Booke of the Thinges that are brought from the West Indies*, published in 1574, (and translated from the Spanish, 1780) we may read: "they doo bring from the New Spain a Stone of great virtue, called 'the Stone of the Blood.' This Bloodstone is a kind of Jasper, of divers colour, somewhat dark, full of sprinkles like to blood, these being of colour red: of which stones the Indians doth make certaine Hartes, both great and small; the use thereof, both there and here, is for all fluxes of blood, and of wounds. The stone must be wet in cold water; and the sick man must take him in his right hand, and from time to time wet him in cold water. In this sort the Indians doe use them. And as concerning the Indians they have it for certain that touching the same Stone in some part where the blood runneth, that it doth restrain; and in this they have great trust; for that the effect hath been seen." In *An Essay about the Origine, and Virtues of Gems*, the Honble. Robert Boyle, 1675, London, has written: " I know a Gentleman (a professed Scholar) who to the eye seems to be of a complexion extraordinary sanguine. This person was for a long time so troubled with excessive bleedings at the nose that, notwithstanding all the remedies that he could procure in an Academy of Physick present where he lived, he was divers times brought to Death's door; till at length, his case growing very famous, there was sent him by an antient Gentleman a Bloodstone—about the bigness of a Pigeon's egg,—with an assurance that it had done cures scarce credible, in his disease, by being worn about the Patient's neck. Upon the use of this Stone he quickly recovered his Health; and had long enjoyed it when I conversed with him; but yet when he left the Stone off for any considerable time his distemper would return. Furthermore, he had by the hands of a third person that liv'd not far distant, stop'd a hæmorrhage in a neighbouring gentlewoman whom the violence of the distemper kep't from knowing that anything had been apply'd to her, till a pretty while after the blood was stanched." " The virtues of (such) opaceous gems, and medicinal stones, may be accounted for in our hypothesis (which is this, that the main ingredients, whereof many such opaceous stones consist, were complete mineral bodies before they became stones ; some of these having been medicinal bodies ; or the like earths, abounding with metalline, or mineral juices." One such earth (as described by M. Pomet, *History of Druggs*, 1712) was the Hæmatitis, closely allied to the Bloodstone ; each containing red iron intermixed with their substance ; only this metal showing itself as red specks in the Bloodstone, but as fine " striæ " or needles, in the Hæmatitis earth. " 'Tis said," tells M. Pomet, " this mineral has a sovereign virtue to stop blood ; from which fact it derives its name." " The virtue of the Heliotrope (Bloodstone)," tells Leonardus, " is to procure safety, and long life to the possessor of it."

To quote relatively on this subject,—concerning Blood,—from our *Animal Simples*, 1890 : " Nowadays chemists prepare from the blood of healthy animals a ' residuum rubrum,' or ' dried residue ' : which contains all its active principles still in their integrity. This is given beneficially in those disorders which require blood-salts, in their organic combination, as existing in fresh, sound, animal blood. A desiccated blood-powder is made, which gives to water a magnificent red colour. It has been well tried at the Children's Hospital, in Paris, and has proved highly efficacious in cases where reconstituents were needed, such as iron, raw meat, and the animal phosphates. Monsieur le Bon reduced fresh bullock's blood by simple evaporation to a solid, which when powdered was readily soluble in water." Again, "Quite recently," (as shown in the *Lancet*, November 28th, 1896) "the value of healthy ox-blood, both arterial, and venous, against crippling rheumatic diseases of the joints, has been conclusively proved. It is given on the sure principle of containing all those various animal organic substances which serve to maintain the sum total of health." Furthermore, ox-blood is evaporated "in vacuo" by the manufacturing chemist, and its residuum supplied in condensed tabloids, as highly useful medicaments for the like essential purpose.

In the *Therapeutics* of Sidney Ringer (a Standard Work, 1897) it is enjoined: "in cases of bloodlessness, wasting, and prostration, the fresh blood of animals, such as fowls, when mixed with warm wine, or milk-punch, warm lemonade, or warm milk, or coffee, and taken immediately, before it coagulates, is found to prove highly useful. It relieves the prostration (as after flooding), restores the bodily heat, revives the circulation; acting better, and more promptly—it is said,—than transfusion of blood from vein to vein. The blood of two, or three, chickens should be taken thus in twenty-four hours."

Among civilised nations the pig is the only animal whose blood, as such, furnishes a distinct article of food. Being mixed with fat, (wherein the blood is deficient), and spices, the blend when packed within some yards of intestine, is made into black puddings, savoury, and restorative. In Suffolk these are eagerly raffled-for at Whitsuntide, by the yard. "A Whitsun' black pudden' be summat for a chap to look forra'd to," say the cottagers. It will be remembered that such a black pudding came bouncing down the chimney to Darby and Joan in the familiar old nursery tale. Dealing with this eminently plebeian subject, a writer in the *County Gentleman* tells how he ascertained that the real old-fashioned black pudding still obtains in many parts of the country; one such locality to wit being the remote Dorsetshire village in which he chanced to be sojourning. "It happened one day," says he, "that I entered the cottage of a poor woman at the identical moment when the manufacture of black puddings was proceeding; and, resisting the natural instinct to fly from the somewhat terrible scene, I sat down, and made myself acquainted with the process as conducted by my cottage friend. First, she lined the basins in which she proposed to boil the mixture, with strips of membranous fat (the caul) taken from the internal economy of the pig. In a large bowl stood the said mixture, from which these basins were to be filled, such mixture consisting mainly of the pure blood of the pig, to which she had added a little milk, a teacupful of bread-crumbs, and a seasoning of thyme, onions, (sage being also included, unless disliked), pepper, salt, and a dash of all-spice. The whole mass appeared to be in quite a liquid condition; and when a layer of fat had been put to float on the top, with a piece of clean paper over all, the whole basin was tied up in a cloth, and plunged into a great saucepan full of boiling water, whilst the spectator looked on in amazement, expecting to see the contents of each basin rapidly escape through the cloth, and mingle with the surrounding water. So rapid, however, was the process of coagulation that scarcely any appreciable quantity was lost; and I was told that the puddings would come forth with the consistency of batter puddings, at the end of the boiling. My informant added that many persons baked the puddings in a pie-dish; but she preferred her own plan."

"Without doubt," says the writer, "these puddings are very nourishing;" and, as the said cottager was living, with her father, upon the scanty income of six shillings and sixpence a week, whilst at a 'killing' the blood for the puddings could be had for the fetching, it is easy to understand why, in the nursery tale already alluded to, a 'yard of black pudding' came to be the first of the three wishes (fulfilment of which was promised by a kind fairy) which entered the minds of Darby and Joan on that memorable occasion.

In Suffolk, at Whitsuntide, the raffling for black puddings is the principal fun of the fair. The staking of sixpence by an agricultural labourer may perchance win for him a yard of this black pudding. The said concoction consists of oatmeal, chopped herbs, pearl barley, and lumps of pork fat, "as big as one's two thumbs," bits of onion, and an alarming indefinite ingredient of pig's blood, fresh from the slaughtered animal. "Oi tell ye there be a flavour about Whitsun pudden' oi never gets no time else."

A favourite method of carrying the pudding home is to string it round the neck, as "the luck of the raffle!" In Suffolk, likewise, the peasant is conservative of other traditions, and plays the game of "camp," just as this was played by the followers of Cæsar. He eats his Whitsun puddings with much the same Epicurean satisfaction as did his forefathers many centuries before him.

"I sometimes think that never blows so red
    The Rose as where some buried Cæsar bled."

November the 11th, (Martinmas,) was the great day, in good old times, for slaughtering cattle and pigs, to be salted down for a winter supply of meat. At Martinmas likewise the "gude wife" had her "puddings to prepare," long strings of home-made sausages, or hogs' puddings, black and white, which would keep for a considerable time, and were often dried, and hung up, with the hams, and bacon, the pickled pork, and the pigs' heads, the corned mutton, and "hung" beef (known as Martinmas beef), in the great open chimneys of the old-fashioned kitchens. Quaint Tusser tells thus (*Five Hundred Points of Husbandrie*) :—

"And Martinmass beefe doth beare goode tacke,
When country folks do dainties lacke."

In Germany there was a "Feast of Sausages" celebrated at this season with much merriment, when the new wines of the year were tasted for the first time. Schoolboys then went about singing of St. Martin, "Whom all the people worshippeth with roasted geese, and wine."

Akin to this topic of the Blood, are the Scriptural words of Agur, the son of Jakeh ; even the Prophecy (Book of Proverbs, cap. xxx. v. 33) : "Surely the churning of milk bringeth forth butter, and the wringing of the nose bringeth forth blood ; so the forcing of wrath bringeth forth strife." About butter, a passing note may be taken of the curious practice which obtains at Cambridge of selling butter by the yard. The dairymen there roll the butter so as to form a long stick weighing a pound ; which they sell in slices, as if it were a German sausage. In the Cambridge markets the butter merchants do not need to use either scales, or weights. By continued practice they are able to divide with a sharp knife the yard of butter into halves, quarters, or eighths, very exactly. Within the Colleges it is highly probable that, when prolix papers are read, and more or less complacently debated, the humorous lines of a minor poet are realized—

"When, ladling butter from alternate tubs,
Stubbs butters Freeman, Freeman butters Stubbs."

It was Jael, the wife of Heber the Kenite, who, basely treacherous to a sleeping guest, (but nevertheless strangely extolled by Deborah in Holy Scripture, when bursting forth into the grandest hymn of self-laudatory praise ever declaimed) " brought forth butter, ' tuban,' (narcotic, as then made from milk turned sour) in a lordly dish." This dish was of Damascus ware, inlaid with silver. The apology is that Sisera, by intruding himself within the inviolable sanctuary of Jael's inner tent, had incurred the fixed penalty of certain death. But this pretext cannot be easily reconciled with her unconditional request to him.—" Turn in, my lord : turn in to me : fear not ! (And when he had turned in unto her she covered him with a mantle.) "

From Butter to Cheese (whilst we are about it) is an easy transition :—

"The farmer's daughter hath soft brown hair
(Butter, and eggs, and a pound of cheese.)"

In former days Dr. Schroder wrote : " Cheese is seldom used in Physick ; some apply green cheese to the Liver, against heat of Feavers ; some eat old cheese to dissolve the Nodes in Gouts." In our modern day Thackeray declared " There is no delicacy in the world, such as Monsieur Francatelli, or Monsieur Soyer can produce, which I believe to be better than toasted cheese." A diet consisting mainly of good sound cheese (as regards albuminous foods, in place of meat, eggs, and fish) has come recently into vogue, because promulgated by Dr. Haig, the well-known authority on uric acid, and its prevention. He pronounces thus : " there is one animal food—namely milk, and its products, as Cheese—which develops little, or no uric acid." " Cheese contains more albumen than any other of the ordinary foods; it should be taken early in the meal, and well distributed through breadstuffs, or vegetables. It should be carefully masticated ; and, if the teeth are bad, it should be grated. Those persons who live on mixed foods rarely require to take more than one or two ounces of cheese in a day." " But even with such a careful, well-considered diet," says Dr. Haig, " some time must elapse before the evils results of the former system of living will have become entirely cleared away." He mentions as long as eighteen months, or two years, before the system will be quite free from this persistent uric acid, and its hurtful effects.

To make good Cheese it is essential that sweet new milk shall be used, not milk which by "turning,"—as in hot weather,—has become spontaneously curd, and whey. The new milk is to be curdled by adding Rennet, (got from the stomach of a calf)—a ferment which turns the milk-sugar into lactic acid, and this causes the casein (or clot) to separate itself from the whey. A junket is made after the same fashion.

Mr. Otto Hehner, the well-known analytical chemist, and food expert, says : " A proper admixture of soft ripe cheese and bread, with water, contains everything which a human being requires in the way of food. Weight for weight cheese is at least twice as nourishing as good meat; while it is far easier to take too much meat than it is to consume too much cheese." Naturally as age advances the allowance of both should be materially reduced.

The maxim of shrewd old George Cheyne is well worth practical pursuance by every man who is getting on in years : " Every wise man after fifty ought to begin to lessen the quantity of his aliment : and, if he would continue free of great, and dangerous, distempers, and preserve his senses, and faculties clear to the last, he ought every seven years to go on abating gradually, and sensibly ; and at last descend out of life as he ascended into it, even into the child's diet."

Good cheese made of whole milk consists of about one-third water, one-third fat, one-quarter casein, the remainder being salts, including highly useful phosphates. Soft cheeses, such as Camembert, Brie, and Port du Salut, are specially easy of digestion; because during the ripening of these cheeses a free formation occurs of "albumoses, and peptones," which are necessary products, (usually by early stages of digestion within the stomach), before the albuminous constituents become available for nourishing the system. But the most difficult cheeses to be attacked by the gastric juices for digestion are those made from wholly, or partly, skimmed milk. Among such are Dutch cheeses, the soft milk cheeses made in our Midland Counties, and sometimes Gruyère. With the exception of skim cheeses like these, it would be misleading to say that any one particular variety is more digestible, or more indigestible, than another. All depends on the state of ripeness.

"A raw, fresh cheese should be avoided ; or, if eaten, it should have the most thorough, and patient mastication." "All cheeses require the addition of bread, or of some other such farinaceous matter; because fat, and nitrogenous sustenance, (which constitute cheese) must be supplemented in the human diet by starchy, or sweet, nutriment, (carbohydrates).

Concerning this eminently national form of popular food Charles Dickens was an enthusiastic writer, thus: "Lastly, to crown all"—at the "Maypole," Chigwell: (*Barnaby Rudge*),—of which famous inn (built in the days of King Henry VIII) the bar was "the very snuggest, cosiest, and completest that ever the wit of man devised," "a stupendous Cheese displayed its huge bulk, as typical of the immense resources of the establishment, and its defiance to all visitors, to cut, and come again. Such amazing bottles, too, in old oaken pigeon-holes; such gleaming tankards dangling from pegs at about the same inclination as thirsty men would hold them to their lips; such sturdy little Dutch kegs ranged in rows on shelves; so many lemons hanging in separate nets, and forming a fragrant grove (of refreshing perfume), suggestive, together with goodly loaves of snowy sugar stowed away hard by,—of punch, idealized beyond all mortal knowledge; such closets, such presses, such drawers full of pipes, such places for putting away things, in hollow window-seats. All crammed to the throat with eatables, and drinkables, or savoury condiments."

Again, this famous old Maypole Inn, on a bitter wintry night, with a furious storm of keen north wind, and sharp dense sleet, and black darkness out of doors, is described as to its internal warmth, and wealth of hospitable resources, and glowing abundance of creature comforts, with inimitable force of pictured words, and rich descriptive colouring, by the master hand.

"Cheerily, though there were none abroad to see it, shone the Maypole light that evening. Blessings on the red, deep, ruby, glowing, crimson, old curtain of the window; blending into one rich stream of brightness, fire, and candle, meat, drink, and company, and gleaming like a jovial eye upon the bleak waste out of doors! Within—what carpet like its crunching sand; what music so merry as its crackling logs; what perfume like its kitchen's dainty breath; what weather so genial as its hearty warmth? Blessings on the old house; how sturdily it stood! How did the vexed wind chafe, and roar about its stalwart roof; how did it pant, and strive with its wide chimneys, which still poured forth from their hospitable throats great clouds of smoke, and puffed defiance in its face; how, above all, did it drive, and rattle at the casement, emulous to extinguish that cheerful glow, which would not be put down, and seemed the brighter for the conflict!

"The profusion too, the rich, and lavish bounty of that goodly tavern! It was not enough that one fire roared, and sparkled on its spacious hearth; in the tiles which paved, and compassed it, five hundred flickering fires burnt brightly also. It was not enough that one red curtain shut the wild night out, and shed its cheerful influence on the room. In every saucepan lid, and candlestick, and vessel of copper, brass, or tin, that hung upon the walls—were countless ruddy hangings, flashing, and gleaming, with every motion of the blaze, and offering—let the eye wander where it might —interminable vistas of the same rich colour. The old oak wainscoting, the beams, the chairs, the seats, reflected it in a deep dull glimmer. There were fires, and red curtains, in the very eyes of the drinkers, in their buttons, in their liquor, in the pipes they smoked!"

"Roquefort" cheese is a speciality made as a unique product, from sheep's milk. It is thus manufactured chiefly in Corsica; though one or two farmers in Lanarkshire produce the same speciality of "ewe-milk cheese." Certain other ingredients which are further employed for this "Roquefort" cheese, as prepared on the Continent, are kept more or less secret. The cheese is of a bluish-grey colour, and has a distinct flavour of its own, quite different from that of any other cheese. Butter for pastry is likewise had from sheep's milk, and is considered to be richer than that which is made with ordinary milk. This sheep's milk is drunk by some persons in the northern parts of Corsica. The "most digestible cheese in the world" is declared (and with good reason) to be Norwegian,—"mys-est." It is inexpensive, and delicious, having a certain sweetness of taste which is remarkable.

> "The farmer's daughter hath frank blue eyes;
> (Butter, and eggs, and a pound of cheese!)
> She hears the rooks caw in the windy skies;
> As she sits at her lattice, and shells the peas.
> (Butter, and eggs, and a pound of cheese!)
>
> Her sheep follow her, as their tails do them;
> (Butter, and eggs, and a pound of cheese!)
> And this song is considered a perfect gem;
> Whilst as to the meaning, it's what you please:
> (Butter, and eggs, and a pound of cheese!)"

A pretty simple game played by the unsophisticated children of the last century was for two or more girls to walk, or dance, up and down, turning, as they said—"Turn, cheeses, turn." (The said cheeses were made green with sage-leaves, and potato-tops.) Two girls together were "cheese, and cheese." Their refrain, as they spun merrily round, was:—

> "Green cheese, yellow laces;
> Up, and down the market-places;
> Turn, cheeses, turn!"

In happy fertile Devonshire (though Herrick thought it a sad, dull county,) until modern methods now serve to revolutionize butter-making, the famous cream (which was the surplus remaining after sufficient had been "clotted" for the day's use) was turned into butter by being beaten with the hand: in which way seven pounds of this delicious butter could be easily turned within the hour, being superior—so connoisseurs say—to what is made in the ordinary way by means of a churn. The famous "clotted cream" was originally manufactured in quite a primitive, and simple manner. As the rich milk came from the cow-shed it was placed in large, fairly deep tin pans, these being stood in outer pans containing water. The milk was then set over a slow fire, and left there for several hours. Gradually the cream would rise to the surface, thus becoming the "scalded," or "clotted," cream of familiar local commerce. But now—sad to say—all this is becoming changed for the worse: and only the smaller farmers still cling to the good old-fashioned method. On the larger farms the churn has been introduced, together with the up-to-date cream separator; so that the cream is mechanically separated from the milk, and is churned into butter. The lamentable result of which innovation is that no old-fashioned clotted cream can any longer be had in these leading farms; and the butter is only of the ordinary quality. Nor is it merely the would-be consumer of clotted cream who loses by the pursuance of this new method, but the calves that are reared on the "skim," or "separated" milk, have to be given, in addition thereto,—artificial foods; whereas the old-style "scalded milk" was far more nourishing, and proved quite sufficient as the sole diet (in their calf days) of the noted large well-grown Devon cattle.

> "For, O! it's the herrings, and the good brown beef,
>   And the cider, and the cream so white;
> O! they are the making of the jolly Devon lads,
>   For to play, and eke to fight."

Cheese-cakes are so called because of their being filled as to their pastry, with a soft curd (together with spice, butter, and egg). To Catherine de Medicis French people owe the introduction of such confectionery, (and, if malevolent rumour is to be credited, of half a dozen subtle poisons besides). Lady Morgan, indeed, insinuated that the Italian princess combined her skill, and craft, when sending as a present for our Queen Elizabeth, at her palace in Sheen, a large cheese-cake, cunningly poisoned. However, the "Bright Occidental Star," Elizabeth, survived Catherine de Medicis by more than ten years. Nevertheless there is most probably a measure of truth in the said report; it being not at all unlikely that Catherine did send Elizabeth a present of (innocent) cheese-cakes, which, being delicious were much relished by her Majesty, and by the ladies of her Court; insomuch that these acceptable cakes were imitated by the local pastrycooks at Richmond, where they survive to this day as the historic "Maids of Honour" associated with that place.

The Heliotrope is a precious stone, and is green, and sprinkled with red drops, and veins of the colour of blood. If it be put in water before the sunbeams, (a forecast of our modern burning-glass,) "it maketh the water sethe in the vessel that it is in, and resolveth it, as it were, into mist, and soon after it is resolved into rain-drops." "Also, it seemeth that this stone may do wonders; for, if it be put in a basin with clear water, it changeth the sunbeams by rebounding of the air, and seemeth to shadow them, and breedeth in the air red, and sanguine colours, as though the sun were in eclypse, and darkened. An herb of the same name (Heliotrope), with certain enchantments, doth beguile the sight of men that look thereon, and maketh a man that beareth it not to be seen."

The Sunflower (under its title—Heliotropium) with which the Bloodstone is here associated, is more commonly known botanically as Helianthus. Its large showy flowers, surmounting tall stalks, are popular ornaments, of brilliant yellow hue, in English cottage gardens, during the summer, and autumn. The central discs of the flaunting flowers are aggregations of black oily seeds, of which it is remarkable that an enormous quantity is consumed as food by the populace of Russian towns. These seeds, having an agreeable taste, are constantly chewed by that people. Their outer husks are detached by the teeth, and spat out. In days of public festivity the ground everywhere is covered with them as thickly as the streets of Paris are strewn with "confetti" during the Carnival. At every street corner a brisk trade is done in these seeds by old women, who sell them very cheaply. The kernels of the seeds contain helianthic acid; whilst the pith of the plant will yield a considerable percentage of carbonate of potash. The seeds thus embody a principle which is preventive of intermittent fever, and ague. About "Heliotropium" Marbodus has written, in melodious verse:—

"Sanguinis astringit fluxum; pellitque venena;
Nec falli poterit lapidem qui gesserit illum.
Et qui sanguineas maculas perhibetur habere,
Cerea cui facies—quia crebra—vilis habetur
Portanti manibus viresque ministrat Achates
Facundumque facit."

And again:—

"Naturæ lapis humanæ servire creatus
Stiptica cui virtus permulta probatur inesse;
Nam palpebrarum super illitus asperitatem,
Et visus hebetes, pulsâ caligine, sanat."

Both the Jasper, and the Bloodstone, are associated with the red rays of light, which are focussed thereupon, and which endow its wearers with a fiery, ardent disposition. Thus the Apostle Peter is supposed to have derived his significant name from the Jasper, which, through his nominal designation, holds supreme honour as the rock on which Christ said, "I will build My Church." Similarly the Jasper's Month of dedication is stormy, tempestuous March.

Quartz is the common name of Silicon; it being the Oxide of Silica; so hard a stone (Flint) that it will strike fire with steel, and will scratch glass. When Quartz is of a violet colour it is called Amethyst. The other kinds of Quartz are—as we already know—Cat's-Eye, Chrysoprase, Cairngorm, Agate, Carnelian, Chalcedony, and Jasper. Clear Quartz was at one time much used for vases, cups, and ornaments; but for such purposes it is now superseded by glass. This

Clear Quartz, or "Rock Crystal," contains forty-six per cent of Silicon, and fifty-three per cent of Oxygen. It is found in almost every part of the globe. Sometimes the Crystal embodies an admixture of Mica, Rutile, Tourmaline, Topaz, Asbestos, Bitumen, and certain other foreign matters; with the occasional presence of a greenish mineral—"Chlorite,"—a stone, or "pebble" used by opticians for making the lenses of spectacles, because of its superior hardness, and durability; in preference to glass, for its coolness, uncommon with most other precious stones. Formerly in this country the Crystal was powdered for medicinal use, being given, mixed with wine, in cases of dysentery; likewise pieces were held against the tongue for assuaging fever, and to slake thirst. Many of the red, green, and brown colours shown by members of the Quartz group are due to manganese, and oxides of iron. Traces of water, alumina, lime, and magnesia, also occur. Silex (Silicon) is never found free, but always united, either with oxygen, as "silica" (Rock Crystal), or with oxygen, and one or other of the metals, forming silicates of such metals. As a secret means of poisoning, the Hindus have a powdered glass, which they contrive unsuspectedly to mix with what the victim drinks, until a fatal intestinal irritation is set up.

"Glass was first found"—(Bartholomew Anglicus, *On the Properties of Things*—1250) "by Ptolomeida, in the cliff beside the river that is called Vellus, that springeth out of the foot of Mount Carmel, at which shipmen arrived." For, "upon the gravel of that river shipmen made fire of clods medlied with bright gravel; and thereof ran bright streams of new liquor that was the beginning of Glass." "But long time previous there was one that made glass pliant, which might be amended, and wrought with an hammer; and he brought a vial made of such glass before Tiberius, the Emperor, and threw it down on the ground, and it was not broken but bent, and folded. And he made it right, and amended it with an hammer. Then the Emperor commanded to smite off his head anon, lest that his craft were known. For, then gold should be no better than fen, and all other metal should be of little worth; for, in certain, if glass vessels were not brittle, they should be accounted of more value than vessels of gold."

"Crystal," so Saint Gregory, (his reason is true) has told, "may be gendered of water." "Water," saith he, "is of itself fleeting; but by strength of cold it is turned, and made stedfast Crystal. Men trowe that it is of snow, or ice, made hard in space of many years."

Robert Boyle (1672), "found the weight of Crystal to be, as relative to that of water, as more than two to one, which fact shows how groundlessly many writers make Crystal to be only ice extraordinarily hardened by long, and vehement cold; whereas ice is lighter than water, and therefore swims upon it. Moreover, Madagascar, and other countries in the Torrid zone abound with Crystal!"

In the palmy days of luxurious ancient Rome, when the Rock Crystal was generally supposed to be ice solidified during the course of long years, ladies carried Crystal balls in their hands, for cooling purposes, during summer weather.

"Et modo Pavonis caudæ flabella superbae;
Et manibus dura frigus habere pila."

"Now courts the breeze, with plumes of Peacocks fanned;
Now holds the flinty ball to cool her hand."

Under the Lower Empire Crystal Rings were worn for the like purpose; these were solid, being carved out of one single piece, which had its face engraved with some intaglio as a signet. Crystals are sometimes found with a cavity in their substance, containing a few drops of water, which moves about as the stone is turned.

> "Erstwhile the boy, pleased with its polish clear,
> With gentle finger twirl'd the icy sphere,
> He marked the drops pent in its stony hold,
> Spared by the rigour of the wintry cold;
> With thirsty lips the unmoisten'd ball he tries,
> And the loved draught with fruitless kisses plies."

By this epigram—one of Claudian's—an incontrovertible proof is afforded of the said former theory deducing the Crystal's slow formation from hardened, or solidified ice.

"The Crystal"—as stated in *Precious Stones: their History: Mystery*, (W. Jones, 1880)—"has been the most popular of all Oracles. The favourite stone was a Beryl, and the custom was to 'charge' the said stones; for which purpose set forms were used. Scott, in his *Discovery of Witchcraft*, gives the form for St. Helen; whose name was to be written on the Crystal with olive oil, beneath a Cross, likewise designed, and while the operator turned himself eastward. A child, born in wedlock, and perfectly innocent, was then to take the Crystal in his hands, and the operator, kneeling behind him, was to repeat a prayer to St. Helen, that whatsoever he wished might become evident in the stone. Finally, the Saint herself would appear in the Crystal, in an angelic form, and answer any question put to her." This proceeding was directed to be tried just at sunrise, and in fine clear weather. The famous Crystal of that prince of such magic— Doctor Dee—is still preserved in the Ashmolean Museum at Oxford; at which University he received some education. A Welshman by birth, he travelled throughout Europe, claiming to have discovered the "Elixir of Life," and the "Philosopher's Stone." He was a man of over-weening ambition, and delighted to hear himself styled, "Most Excellent." After journeying from one Court to another, where he is said to have performed wonderful feats with his Elixir, he returned to England, and settled at Mortlake, in which place Queen Elizabeth often visited him, to consult him on astrology; and he even ventured to predict her death. Dr. Dee was a prime favourite at Court in 1595, when the Queen made him Chancellor of St. Paul's, and Warden of Manchester. But eventually he died in great poverty.

Dr. John Dee, and Sir Edward Kelly were professed associates, the latter being the leading man in Alchemy. Dee writes, in one place: "This day Edward Kelly discovered the grand secret to me;—*sit nomen Domini benedictum.*" This was in allusion to the Philosopher's Stone, transmuting everything into gold. But the story went that these two had found a considerable quantity of gold in Glastonbury Abbey; with which they performed several of their most notable transmutations. Kelly, in particular, is reported to have given away rings of gold wire, to the tune of four thousand pounds, at the marriage of his servant-maid. And a piece cut out of a brass warming-pan, having been sent, by order of Queen Elizabeth, to Dee, and Kelly, when abroad, was returned of pure gold. Likewise

Dee could afford to make a present to the Landgrave of Hesse of twelve Hungarian horses.

The "**Art of Crystal Divination**" dates from ancient times. That particular Crystal which has ever found most favour for the purposes of Crystallomancy through the medium of Crystal-gazing, is the Beryl; a mineral (silicate of Beryllia) which crystallises in six-sided prisms, of which the sides are often striated longitudinally, but the terminating planes are usually smooth. Aquamarine, and the Emerald are varieties of this Beryl. Its chemical composition is as follows: silica, sixty-eight per cent; alumina, seventeen per cent; with glucina, and red oxide of iron. The Crystal-gazers of the fifth century were known as "Specularii," and were established in Ireland. The colours of the Beryl range from blue, through honey-yellow, to actual transparency; the latter colour resulting from the presence of peroxide of iron, whilst the green, and various shades of blue, represent the effect of protoxide of iron, in varying quantities. The favourite shade of this Crystal, as used by ancient seers, was that of the pale water-green Beryl, or delicate aquamarine; this water-green being astrologically considered as a colour especially under the influence of the moon, an orb exerting very great magnetic influence. It is alleged by supporters of the Crystal-gazing doctrines in the present day, that "when we reflect that the Beryl, Emerald, Sapphire, Adamantine Spar, etc., all contain 'oxide of iron,' a substance presenting the strongest affinity for magnetism; and when we also remember the strict injunctions of the ancient Occultists to utilise the Crystal only during the increase of the Moon," the idea naturally suggests itself that the connecting link between the Crystal and the unseen world is *Magnetism*, attracted to, or accumulated in, or around, the Crystal by the Iron infused throughout its constitution; and that the greater the increase of the Moon the greater consequently is the supply, and accumulation of the Lunar Magnetism in the Crystal. If this be so, the further question arises, "How does the gazer become placed '*en rapport*' with matters beyond his ordinary ken, or that of bystanders, through the medium of the Crystal globe?" The reply may be reasonably made that persons endowed with this self-asserted power possess a natural ability of concentrativeness, or fixing their isolated close attention on the accredited Crystal. With reference to this fixed attention, it was taught by the famous natural philosopher, Baron Reichenbach, (*Researches on Magnetism, etc.*, Germany, 1845) "that there streams from the human eyes an efflux of magnetism as projected from its reservoir in the lesser brain (cerebellum), when the gaze is fixed intently upon a given point." Again, Crystal-gazers claim that there exists within the Crystal the greatest possible influx of celestial, or terrestrial magnetism; perhaps of both.

Moreover, they hold it essential that there shall be a concentration of unalloyed magnetism occupying the body of the operator, by reason of purity of the amatory functions. Because of this indispensable condition the ancients enjoined as supremely important the engagement of ingenuous boys, and of chaste innocent young virgins, for Crystal-gazing, Clairvoyance, and other such occult efforts. Equally of moment for possession of such a power is purity of the blood. Therefore, food, digestion, sleep, and what drinks are taken, all must receive a proper degree of attention.

Seeing then that the condition of the blood at the time of experimenting with the Crystal is of such great importance, certain leading facts bearing directly upon this point may well be considered here. On an average there is contained one part by weight of iron in two hundred and thirty human blood corpuscles; and the total quantity of iron in the blood of a man who weighs one hundred and forty pounds, is about thirty-eight grains; while about one grain per day is on the average taken into the body with food. This iron forms the colouring matter of the " red " blood corpuscles.

The " white, or colourless," blood corpuscles, which are much fewer in number than the red in a healthy body, are diminished by fasting, and increased by eating; which fact is of serious interest in connection with the advisability of any prolonged abstinence from food prior to those magnetic experiments with the Crystal globe, such as were conducted by the Seers of the past. Two principal forms of iron are apparent in the blood; the " protoxide," or green ferrous salt; which is principally found in the venous, or dark blood; and the " peroxide," or red ferric oxide; found mostly in the arterial, or bright scarlet blood. Now, a compound of these two oxides constitutes what was formerly known as the " Loadstone " or black magnetic oxide of iron; and it is a remarkable fact that persons of dark, or very dark eyes, or very dark hair, eyes and skin, are the most magnetic; which darkness of hue is, it would seem, connected with a preponderance of the Protoxide of Iron in the blood, over the Peroxide, in the proportion of two to one; which happens to be a similar proportion to that existing in the Loadstone. Such persons are usually representative of a dominantly "bilious" tendency, or temperament; and we know that the amount of iron in the bile is important, this being present as a phosphate of iron. All which several facts point to the conclusion that a certain chemical balance between the ferric, and the oxygenic, (i.e., magnetic,) conditions of the blood, and the bile, is necessary towards developing the most perfect powers of concentration for Crystal-gazing, or Clairvoyance. John Melville, in his *Manual of Crystal-gazing*, 1897 (Nichols & Co.), has suggested that an infusion of the familiar English herb "Mugwort" (*Artemisia vulgaris*), the properties of which are antibilious; or of the herb Succory (*Cichorium intybus*), would, if taken occasionally during the moon's increase, constitute for the Crystal-gazer an aid towards the attainment by the experimenter's body of the best physical conditions. It is a relevant fact that both these plants are specially responsive to magnetic influence; their leaves, like the needle of the compass, invariably turning of themselves towards the north. Furthermore, besides being antibilious, these herbs act specifically upon the generative system, thus influencing beneficially the functions most closely allied to magnetic force. Furthermore, injunctions are given by the professed exponents of "Crystal-gazing" that the moon must be in her increase, i.e., going towards the full; (this should never be neglected; it is of the highest importance towards success!) The Crystal should be stood (enclosed in a frame of ivory, or of ebony,) upon the table; or, if simply held in the hand, its top end should lean away from the gazer, and should be held so that no reflections, or shadows appear therein. If stood on a table, the folds of a black silk handkerchief may be arranged about the Crystal so as to shut out such reflections. Persons of a magnetic temperament, being of the brunette type, dark eyed, brown skinned, and having dark hair, will charge the Crystal more quickly, (but not more effectually,) than those of the electric temperament, such as the blonde.

Persons of the male sex are not so readily developed into Seer-ship as the female; but they become superlatively powerful, and correct, when so developed. Among women, virgins see best; and next to them in order, widows. In all cases boys, before puberty, and girls, in their pucelage, make the quickest and sharpest seers: purity giving power in all magnetic, and occult experiments. There stands in *John Inglesant*, that very remarkable philosophical Romance, produced by Joseph Henry Shorthouse, in the year 1876, (the history of a soul-development, told with marvellous psychological, and literary power), a striking illustration of Crystal-gazing for the purpose of learning grave impending events.

Eustace Inglesant, brother to John, having strong reasons for supposing his life to be endangered through the vile machinations of an Italian desperado, who had gained the confidence of his sick, and superstitious wife; having moreover been secretly furnished with an admonitory horoscope of his own life, determines, together with John, to consult a famous astrologer, at Lambeth Marsh, as to the validity, or the mendacity of this warning horoscope. Accordingly, late on a certain afternoon, they " took a wherry at the Temple Stairs, and were ferried over to Lambeth Marsh, a wide extent of level ground between Southwark and the Bishop's (of London) Palace, on which ground a few straggling houses had been built. The evening was dark, and foggy, so that it was almost impossible to see more than a yard or two before them; and they would probably have experienced great difficulty in finding the wizard's house had not a boy with a lantern met them a few paces from the river, who was the wizard's own boy, thoughtfully despatched to find his clients, and guide them to his house. The boy brought them into a long low room, with very little furniture in it, a small table at the upper end, and a large chair behind it; also three or four high-backed chairs placed along the wall. On the floor, in the middle of the room, was drawn a large double circle; but there were no figures, or signs of any kind about it. On the table was a long thin rod. A lamp, which hung from the roof over the table, cast a faint light about the room, and a brazier of lighted coals stood in the chimney. The Astrologer was a fine-looking man, with a serious, and lofty expression of face, dressed in a black gown, with a square cap of a divine, and a fur hood, or tippet. Having thoughtfully perused the horoscope he acknowledged it to be very adverse in many of its aspects. He likewise informed the Inglesants that he had drawn out a scheme of the heavens for himself; in quite different ways, and by very different aspects; but much the same result had been arrived at likewise, by interpreting this scheme. Such being their unsatisfactory conclusions the Astrologer did not advise any further enquiry at his instance, but proposed that they should consult a consecrated Beryl, or Crystal,—a mode of enquiry far more high, and certain than astrology, this search into the Crystal being by the help of the blessed spirits, and open only to the pure from sin, and to men of piety, humility, and charity. As he said these words he produced from the folds of his gown a large Crystal, or polished stone, set in a circle of gold, supported by a silver stand. Round the circle were engraved the names of angels. He placed this upon the table, and continued thus: 'We must pray to God that He will vouchsafe us some insight into this precious stone, for, it is a solemn and serious matter upon which we are about to engage; second only to that of communication with the angelical creatures themselves; which, indeed, is vouchsafed to none, but only to those of the greatest piety, to which we may not aspire. Therefore let us kneel down, and pray humbly to God.'

"They all knelt, and the adept, commencing with the Prayer Book Collect for the Festival of Saint Michael, recited several other prayers, all for extreme, and spotless purity of life. He then rose, the two others continuing on their knees, and struck a small bell; upon which, the boy whom they had before seen entered the room by a concealed door in the wainscot. He was a pretty boy, with a fair, and clean skin, and was dressed in a surplice similar to those worn by choristers. He took up a position by the Crystal, and waited his master's orders. 'I have said,' continued the adept, ' that these visions can be seen only by the pure, and by those who, by long, and intense looking into the spiritual world, have at last penetrated somewhat into its gloom. I have found these mostly to be plain, and simple people, of an earnest faith; country people, grave-diggers, and those employed to shroud the dead, and who are accustomed to think much upon objects connected with death. This boy is the child of the Sexton of Lambeth Church, who is himself a godly man. Let us pray to God.' Upon this he knelt down again, and remained for some time engaged in silent prayer. He then rose, and directed the boy to look into the Crystal, saying, ' One of these gentlemen desires news of his wife.' The boy looked intently into the Crystal for some moments, and then said, speaking in a low and measured voice, ' I see a great room in which there is a bed, with rich hangings; pendent from the ceiling is a silver lamp. A tall, dark man, with long hair, and a dagger in his belt, is bending over the bed, with a cup in his hand.' ' It is my wife's room,' said Eustace, in a whisper, ' and it is, no doubt, the Italian; he is tall, and dark.' The boy continued to look for some time into the Crystal, but said nothing; then he turned to his master, and said, ' I can see nothing; some one more near to this gentleman must look! This other gentleman,' he said suddenly, and turning to John Inglesant, ' if he looks he will be able to see.' The Astrologer started: ' Ah!' he said; ' Why do you say that, boy?' ' I can tell who will see aught in the Crystal, and who will not,' replied the boy. The Astrologer seemed surprised, and sceptical, but he made a sign to John Inglesant to rise from his knees, and to take his place by the Crystal. He did so, and looked steadily into it for some seconds, then he shook his head. ' I can see nothing,' he said. ' Nothing?' asked the boy, ' can you see nothing?' ' No; I see only clouds and mist.' ' You have been engaged,' said the boy, ' in something that was not good; something that was not true; and it has dimmed the Crystal sight. Look steadily, and, if it is as I think, that your motive was not false, you will see more.' Inglesant looked again, and in a moment or two gave a start, saying, ' The mist is breaking; I see—, I see—, a large room, with a chimney of carved stone, and a high window at the end; in the window, and on the carved stone is the same coat of arms, many times repeated; three running greyhounds proper, on a field vert.' ' I know the room,' said Eustace, ' it is the Inn parlour of Mintern ; not six miles from Oulton.' ' Do you see aught else ? ' said the adept. Inglesant gave a long look; then he stepped back, and gazed at the Astrologer, and from him to his brother, with a faltering, and ashy look. ' I see a man's figure lie before the hearth; and the hearth-stone is stained, as if with blood. Eustace, it is either you or I.' 'Look again,' said the adept, eagerly, ' look again ! ' ' I will look no more,' said Inglesant, fiercely; ' this is the work of a fiend, to lure men to madness, and despair.' As he spake, a blast of wind, sudden and strong, swept through the room; the lamp burnt dimly; the fire in the brazier went out; a deathly coldness filled the apartment, whilst the floor, and the walls seemed to shake. A loud whisper, or muffled cry, was heard to fill the air; and a terrible awe struck at the hearts of the young men. Seizing the rod from the table the adept assumed a commanding attitude, waving the rod to and fro in the air. Gradually the wind ceased, the dread coldness abated, and the fire burned again, of its own accord."

Later on in the story we learn that this predicted ghastly episode became actually realized. Eustace, and his brother, travelling on to Oulton, were heedless enough to take Mintern in their way. One of their horses cast a shoe, thus causing delay, and separation of the brothers on the road. Eustace went on forward, whilst John Inglesant was detained behind, filled with strange, and awesome forebodings. Eventually he reached the inn at Mintern; and was told by the host that his brother and a foreign gentleman were upstairs in the parlour; he had thought they were having some words a while ago, but they were quiet now. John Inglesant told the host to follow him up the two flights of oak stairs; at top of which they entered the room over the hall, and porch. It was a large and narrow room, and was seemingly empty. Opposite them, in the high window, and on the great carved chimney to the right, running greyhounds coursed each other, as it seemed to Inglesant, round the room. A long table hid the hearth as they came in. With a faint certainty, Inglesant, as if mechanically, walked round it towards the fire, the others with him, where they stopped, sudden and still. On the white hearthstone—his hair and clothes steeped in blood—lay Eustace Inglesant, the Italian's stiletto in his heart. It should be remembered that Eustace Inglesant, having detected the base pretensions, and criminal villainy of this wily Italian, was an object to him of hatred, and of immediate danger in his crafty path.

In a previous chapter of this powerful Romance,— veritable in its main incidents,—we learn that the "malade imaginaire" Quakeress, wife of Eustace Inglesant, becoming daily more and more eccentric, and crotchety about her health, straightway adopted every new remedy, and every fresh religious notion which was brought before her. She "filled her house with quacks, (of whom Van Helmont was chief), mountebanks, astrologers, and so-called physicians,—a fine collection of 'beaux' esprits!" Dr. More, the Platonist, a scholar, and a gentleman, but an enthusiast, though he was staying in the house all one summer, did not see the sick lady more than once or twice. She urged him for months to search all over Europe for an Eagle's Stone, which she said was of great use in such diseases as hers; but when Eustace, her husband, found her one, at great labour, and expense, she sent him back word that it was not one; for some of her quacks were able to decipher it at once, and declared it to be a German stone, such as are commonly sold in London, at five shillings apiece. By some such cabalistic stones as these the sprites in the time of our grandsires used to preserve the fruits from hail, and storm. There is similarly a Salamander stone. The Eagle-stone is one made after a cabalistic art, and under certain stars, and engraved with the sign of an Eagle. "The virtue of these stones could be proved," Eustace went on laughingly to say, "throughout all arts and sciences, as divinity, philosophy, astrology, physiognomy, divination of dreams, painting, sculpture, music, and what not." This Aetites is a yellow clay Ironstone exercising sanative virtues, and thought to reflect mystic powers from Saturn, its patron Planet. Epiphanius, writing—1565.—"De duodecim Gemmis in veste Aaronis," told concerning the Eagle-Stone: "In the interior of Scythia there is a valley inaccessible to man, down which slaughtered lambs are thrown. The small stones at the bottom of the Valley adhere to these pieces of flesh, and Eagles, when they carry away the flesh to their nests, carry the stones with it. It has been believed that without these stones Eagles cannot hatch their eggs."

Such then, was the mystic art of Crystal-gazing as practised by certain earnest, and devout, though ecstatic, believers, about the time of our Charles I. After being allowed to slumber, as a well-nigh extinct creed, from then throughout a couple of centuries, this practical method of prying into the secrets of the future is again of late finding its advocates, whether as a pious proceeding of telepathic character, or as a fashionable fad, within the last fifteen, or twenty years. The Crystals, in which it is claimed that under certain closely studied conditions the future may be read, are spheres of rock Crystal varying from four to eight inches in diameter, whilst polished by cunning, and careful hands into the lustrousness of a brilliant. The preparation of some of these Crystal spheres occupies many years of skilled work; and their prices place them beyond the reach of all but very wealthy possessors. The most valuable Crystal in the world is said to belong to Miss Helen Gould, the daughter of Jay Gould. It is a unique specimen of the polisher's art; is two feet in circumference, and cost three thousand pounds sterling. This lustrous Oracle is mounted on a black pedestal, and is religiously shrined within a special sacred chamber. Again, a famous Crystal, uncanny of character, is the property of Dr. J. B. Street, a well-known apostle of the occult, in New York. Dr. Street guards his treasure with the most jealous care, and will on no account allow it to be desecrated by human touch. The slightest approach of an inquisitive finger clouds its purity of lustre for hours, and draws a curtain over the mysteries it might reveal. This same famous Crystal was for centuries the Oracle in a Japanese Temple; and many startling events have been foreshadowed by it. When the Oracle is now to be consulted it is placed on a pedestal, covered with a black cloth, immediately beneath a powerful electric light. At some distance above it, between the Crystal and the light, is suspended a bell-shaped reflector, of highly polished glass, to which is attached an insulated wire, ending in a finger-piece. This is held in the hand by the person who would consult the Oracle; when, by looking steadily into the Crystal, the future is indicated (if proper conditions have been conscientiously obeyed) by a panorama which portrays coming events.

It is not generally known, or remembered, that during, or soon after, the Commonwealth times, Crystal-gazing found so many advocates that it was avowedly employed as a means for detecting minor offences and crimes; insomuch that King James I.—"the wisest fool in Christendom"—passed laws making this Crystal-gazing a serious, and punishable offence. As to some scientific explanation of the visions which seem to be often indisputably produced under the (hypnotised?) gaze of an honest Crystal-reader (at the instance, and suggestion of an enquirer whose subjected mind is already intent on the matters to be revealed, though probably without his being sensibly aware of this), such visions are quite explicable on the said ground of hypnotism, and telepathy. The theory which now finds acceptance by the scientific world is that the human mind is dual in its nature; the upper (or "objective") mind being the medium by which we reason, and conduct the ordinary business of our daily life; while the lower (or "subjective") mind is the storehouse of memory, wherein every circumstance of life, from the first dawn of reason, is carefully chronicled, and remembered, though altogether forgotten most probably by the objective mind. Then, the subjective mind of one individual is capable of sending messages to the subjective mind of another, without the objective mind of either being aware of the fact. Such messages are known as intuitions. It is further possible for the subjective mind of one person to be read, and interpreted, by another subjective mind, when a state of passivity, or hypnosis, is induced in the objective mind of one, or of the other, or of both. This state is induced, consciously or unconsciously, by all Crystal-gazers, or other honest readers of fate, or fortune. Meanwhile the reader remains perfectly quiet, and stares at the Crystal, or at leaves in a teacup, or at a pack of cards spread out on a table, as the case may be. At such times the readers, or gazers, are able to recall mentally the events of the past, to give names, and descriptions of the living, or of the dead; all the particulars of which are chronicled in the subjective minds of the consulting enquirer, though he, or she, remains quite unconscious of this fact. It is likewise this "subjective" mind which flashes the whole panorama of his, or her life upon the mental mirror of a drowning, or a dying person.

Coming back, then, to what Dr. Pierre Janet has told us, from painstaking observation as made at the Salpetrière under Professor Charcot, we learn from him all the available facts which have been ascertained by scientists concerning the pursuit of Crystal-gazing. He found that the faculty of such telepathic "reading" is but seldom met with among persons in sound bodily, and mental health; it being indeed a neurosis, or morbid condition of the emotional nervous system, to which only abnormally sensitive, (or hysterical) persons are subject. The hallucinations perceived, and described, have for their subject-matter only those things which are within the conscious, or the unconscious memory of the gazer; and any anxious enquirer is as little likely to gain from them any hint of facts which lie outside the gazer's knowledge as to learn the future from the incoherent, stammering utterances of a drunken person.

When Crystal was used formerly for the engraving thereupon of intaglios, and cameos, the artist could sometimes conceal any flaws, or defects in the stone, amongst the strokes of his work; but when the Crystal was to be formed into cups or vases, this could not be done; and for such a purpose only the purest pieces, of a complete integrity, could be employed.

The remarkable effects which follow contact with certain Crystals upon persons of specially sensitive nervous temperament, have been most carefully investigated, and accurately recorded (as we have already told) by the famous Professor Karl Baron von Reichenbach, in his *Researches on Magnetism, Electricity, etc., in Relation to the Vital Force*. This erudite book was translated, at the express desire of the author, by Dr. Wm. Gregory, Professor of Chemistry in the University of Edinburgh, 1856. Reichenbach, by his conclusive experiments, established the indisputable fact that a "polar" force resides in Crystals which they possess in common with Magnets. But this polar force, while exercising a peculiar action on animal nerves, both in the healthy and in the diseased subject, is not identical with the magnetic force.

Summarising the results of his patient scientific enquiries into this occult question, Von Reichenbach has laid it down as a positive maxim that every Crystal exerts a specific action on animal nerves; this being remarkably powerful in highly sensitive, or cataleptic persons. The said force is most powerful at the opposite ends of a Crystal; it is therefore "polar." Luminosity is sent out from these poles, being visible in the dark to persons with sensitive sight. In certain diseases this force displays an adhesiveness of contact towards the human hand, resembling that of iron to a magnet. The said force is therefore a part of the influences of a magnet, which may be separated therefrom, and isolated. Reichenbach found that a Rock Crystal, or a fine Crystal of Sugar-candy, when laid on the hand of a sensitive patient, instantly excited involuntary contraction, causing the hand to become clenched, and to grasp the Crystal with a very strong spasm. "Here therefore has been discovered a peculiar power in single Crystals; a fundamental force which had hitherto remained unobserved." For this new, and specific force Reichenbach suggested the short name "Odylle," which conveniently groups, and describes the phenomena exercised, and produced. Sensitive persons placed in the sphere of action of bodies diffusing Odylle, only feel comfortable when, to the polar parts of their own frame, the oppositively-named poles of the said bodies are brought near. If poles named alike be brought in approximation together, then unpleasant sensations—soon amounting to illness—are the result. One anatomical site of this remarkable power is the mouth, with the tongue, (which are negative), giving on contact of the Crystal therewith, a sense of coolness.

Sensitive subjects feel everything most distinctly with the lips; especially the odyllic influence of the bodies thus examined. Conversely, therefore, the mouth in healthy persons is a point by means of which all objects may be charged with odylle,—even more strongly than by the hands. And, hence we obtain a not altogether uninteresting explanation of the true nature, and significance of a kiss. The lips are a focus of odyllic force, and "the mouth being negative, the kiss with the lips seeks to establish an equilibrium." By a parity of reasoning the curious action of tickling may be explained. As a puzzled querist asks, in *The British Apollo*, if the Editor can inform him, so far as to give him a reason "why I, that am so very ticklish, cannot tickle myself?" "And what power," says Robt. Boyle, "the Passions have to alter, and determine the course of the blood may appear yet more manifestly in modest, and bashful persons, especially women; when, merely upon the remembrance, or thought, of an unchaste, or indecent thing, mention'd before them, the motion of the blood will be so determined as to passe suddenly, and plentifully enough into the cheeks, (and sometimes other parts), making them immediately wear that livery of vertue (as an old philosopher styl'd it) which we call a blush." "In the animal economy, on-coming night, sleep, and hunger, depress, or diminish the odyllic force; whilst taking food, daylight, and the active waking state, increase, and intensify it."

All Precious Stones when cut with smooth surfaces, and intently gazed upon, are able to produce somnambulism in the same degree as the Crystal, likewise to induce visions (in the same way as hypnotism may be induced by fixing the eyes intently for a time on any shining object near at hand); the Diamond will thus deprive the Loadstone of its virtue; and is, therefore, the most powerful of all stones to promote spiritual ecstasy.

As concerning the mystic powers associated of old with the Rock Crystal, among the MSS. belonging to Jno. Guthrie, Esqre., of Guthry, Scotland, was a tiny duodecimo volume, in a parchment cover, and in writing of the seventeenth century, filled with prayers, and conjurations for revealing of secrets, and exorcising evil spirits. There are many diagrams, and drawings of figures to be used in these processes; some of them with reference to lunar, and stellar observations. Among much curious matter we find, *An Experiment to be seen with a Christal Stone.* " Take a Christall Stone, or Glasse, most clear, without a craise ; and wrape about it a pece of Harte's lether, saying, ' In the name of the Holy Trinity, and of the hey (sic) Deity! Amen!' Then holde the Christalle in the beam when the sun is most bright, and at the hottest of the day; and say these conjurations subscribed; and by and by you shall see the spirite peradventer appeiring himself. Then say to him, ' I conjure Thee, Spirit, by the vertue of all things aforesaid that thou departe out of the Christalle, and bringe with thee thy fellowes in any honest and decente forme, apparelled, some in blew, and some in yealowe. For som tyme he cometh alone, hiding his hede, sometim in a cloke, some tyme in a gowne ;—then commande him, or them, if you worke for thefte, to goe out of the Christall, and that they com againe, brynging or representing the forme, or shape of the thef, or theves, and thyngs stoln, or which shall be stoln,—' et fiat!' And he will brynge with him the theves, and will shew thee with hys finger, and their names, if thou wilt. Alsoe thou maiest aske, and be certified of Treasure, hid under the ground, how thou maiest have it, when it was laid there; and soe you may be certified of parents, frindes, or enemyes, being far, or near, or distant, or what other thing you will require."

To the Rock Crystal was ascribed by an early writer the power of producing the Sacred Fire used in the Eleusinian Mysteries; this fire being supposed to be most grateful to the Gods. For which the Rock Crystal was to be laid upon chips of wood in the sun; when first smoke, and then flame was produced. It would seem probable that this tradition simply arose from the use of glass, or Crystal Lenses (burning-glasses). The Priests in those days were well acquainted with the use of many scientific instruments, whilst carefully concealing the same from the vulgar.

Dr. Jno. Schroder, in his *Chymical Dispensatory*, "written in Latin," 1669, tells concerning the Crystal: "Some do hold Crystal in the sunbeams, and then burn the skin therewith, as with a cautery, or burning-glass." "As for its vertues, it is astringent, good against dysenteries, diarrhœa, cholick, increaseth milk, and breaking stone in the whole body, and is good in the gout."

Respecting the study of Crystallography as a whole, Nicolaus Steno, a Dane, from Copenhagen, in 1669, wrote a treatise, *De Solido intra Solidum Naturaliter Contento*, wherein the wondrous Rock Crystal with its special terminal points, led him to introduce some new notions, and terms, into this science. He saw that evidently these Crystals grew; and not from within themselves, but from without, by the addition of new layers of minute particles carried to the Crystals by a fluid, and laid down specially at the ends, as shown by the fine striæ which are never wanting on the middle planes. Furthermore, his rejecting the notion of extreme cold as the *causa efficiens* (in producing the Crystal), for the adopted thought of something similar to magnetic power, was a suggestive idea; and not less so his conclusion that therefore the Crystals were not formed only at the first beginning of things, but that they continue to grow, even to the present day.

The signification of the word Crystal is (from the Greek—*krustallos*) ice, or frozen water. All Crystals depend closely on their different geometric characters, and optic properties, for the various relations they bear to heat, magnetism, and electricity. These relations must have much to do with their physical effects on our bodies when the said Crystals are worn as Jewels, or otherwise applied externally.

Likewise, again, our sense of smell, as to its practical utility for meeting bodily needs, is comparatively unexplained. It certainly keeps guard over the air we breathe, lest it should invade our lungs with noxious fumes; also it serves to detect malodorous indications of impure, or putrid foods which would do us harm; but beyond these negative functions the sense of smell does not seem to exercise vitally important duties for us, as do the other indispensable senses of sight, hearing, touch, and taste. Perfumes are actually useless to us towards maintaining the economy of our daily life in active operation. Indeed, when too violent, or too lasting, they positively injure. " This uselessness," says a recent able journalist, " deserves our close consideration; it seems to hold behind it some fair secret." " Our scent is the only purely luxurious sense which nature has granted." "Is it an apparatus which is developing? or one that is wasting away? a somnolent, or an awakening faculty? Everything leads us to think it is becoming evolved on the same lines as our advancing civilization. The ancients interested themselves almost exclusively in the coarser the heavier, the unrefined, solid (so to speak) smells; as those of musk, benzoin, incense, whilst the fragrance of flowers has received but sparse mention in Greek, and Latin poetry, or in Hebrew literature."

Botanists of late have claimed the perfumes of flowers as spontaneously acquired to serve chiefly for attracting insects, so as to fertilise the flowers which they consecutively visit. But difficulties arise about granting this hypothesis; thus, many of the sweetest-scented flowers do not admit of cross-fertilisation by insects; again, because insects seek rather the pollen, and the nectar, (which are odourless), than obey the attraction of floral scents; they besiege in crowds the flowers of the maple, and the hazel-tree, whilst disregarding flowers of delicious perfume, such as the rose, the carnation, etc.

There are, therefore, strong reasons for making this sense of smell a further study; of questioning it, and cultivating its possibilities. Who can foreknow the surprises it keeps in store for us if brought to equal the perfection of our sight,—as it does in the dog,—which lives as much by the nose as by the eyes?

We have here a world almost unexplored as yet. This mysterious sense, which seems almost foreign to our organism, becomes, perhaps, when more carefully considered, that which enters into it most intimately. Is not the air around us our most absolutely indispensable element? and is not our sense of smell just the one sense that is able to perceive its parts, and significations? "Perfumes, which are the jewels of that life-giving air, do not adorn it without good cause. It were not astounding if this endowment, which we fail to understand, should be found to correspond with something very profound, and very essential; and rather with something that is not yet within our ken, than with something which has ceased to be. Hardly does it so much as suspect, even with the aid of the imagination, the profound, and harmonious effluvia which evidently envelop the great spectacles of the atmosphere, and the light. As we are already able to distinguish in a measure those of the rain, and the twilight, why should we not ere long succeed in recognizing, and fixing, the scent of snow, of ice, of morning dew, of the first fruits of the dawn, of the twinkling of the stars? for, everything must have its perfume, (though inconceivable as yet), in space; even a moonbeam, a ripple of water, a hovering cloud, an azure smile of the sky."

Since our boyhood's days that dear old sweetest of scents, Lavender-water, has gone much out of public favour. Its conservative principles as to stoutly maintaining the delightful old-fashioned English name, have caused it to fall much into the background. Frenchified, and other foreign titles, bestowed upon dubiously mixed perfumes, (with no little addition of certain coaltar products thereto,) are much more in vogue with the fair sex to-day. The good old musical cry of "Lavender, Sweet Lavender! who'll buy my sweet Lavender?" is no longer heard about the London streets, from the melodious lips of an honest-faced country lass, in clean print dress, and appropriate sun-bonnet. One is told, indeed, of "Mitcham Lavender," the truth being nevertheless that at Mitcham not a sprig of the fragrant herb is now grown. Some few lavender fields are yet to be found beyond Carshalton, and round about Wallington; where likewise the humbler Peppermint gets a certain sparse cultivation. As regards the Lavender-cutters of former days, they are now nearly all old men. But quaint notions still possess their minds concerning the scented spikes of their traffic; thus, that a spray worn inside the hat will commonly cure a headache; and, again, as to Lavender-water, "it be the finest drink there is,"—"to take a sup of it afore coming to work in the morning does a mort o' good!" In former days a pint of Lavender-oil (to produce from two to three pints of which oil a wagon-load of the spikes would be needed) was worth about seven pounds sterling; but it will not fetch nearly as much now. The distinctive title of "Lavender water, as simply thus, is a misnomer in these times. The fragrant scent sold as such is a compound of the essential oil of Lavender, with rectified spirit of wine, rosemary, jessamine, bergamot, attar of roses, orange-flowers, and musk. For this scent each manufacturing chemist has his own particular formula. Lavender-tea made from the sprigs is an excellent restorative. An old English rhyming verse tells of:—

"Rosemary green,
And lavender blue;
Thyme and sweet marjoram,
Hyssop, and rue."

"Peace Pillows" are now made for promoting "sweet slumber," such as is to be enjoyed in the fragrant noiseless recesses of a great forest. The soft stuffing of these pillows is impregnated with balsamic wood oils, the exhalations from which,—mainly those of Lavender, —as given off under the bodily warmth of the patient, being volatile, induce sound, and refreshing sleep. Any dreams associated therewith are invariably pleasant, and agreeable.

As stated elsewhere, it is a remarkable fact that, under the influence of strong, highly fragrant Lavender-water (which, being spirituous, is very volatile) even wild beasts, when captive (as in zoological gardens) may be made docile, and tractable.

Orange-flower water was evidently formerly in favour as a perfume. During Queen Elizabeth's reign Oranges were known as Portingales.

Respecting oranges, the amusing chapter on "Shop Windows," in Leigh Hunt's *Essays*, is well worth reading. His famous reply to a lady at whose house he was dining is also worthy to be remembered. "Don't you ever venture on an orange, Mr. Hunt?" she enquired solicitously at dessert. "I should be delighted to do so, my dear Madam," was his grave reply, "but I'm so afraid I should tumble off." For the smell of an apple the famous Schiller had a remarkable passion. He used to cut an apple into quarters, and keep these in the drawer of his writing-table.

Evidently our comparatively unsophisticated grandparents, in the heyday of their farmhouse pleasures of table, and field, were fully alive to the attractions of aromatic flavours, fragrant odours, and sweet-smelling perfumes. Simple-minded readers of their Bible, they bore in mind the "Proverbs of Solomon, which the men of Hezekiah, King of Judah, copied out," and amongst which it is declared: "Ointment and perfume rejoice the heart; so doth the sweetness of a man's friend by hearty counsel." Maeterlinck has said respecting flowers, " They yield up their soul in perfume."

Similarly in certain other respects, with regard to flowers, whether worn about the person, or carried in the hand, an interchange of positive sympathies, or antipathies, is a recognized fact. Thus a bouquet, or a button-hole, of rare blossoms, when worn by some persons will retain its freshness even for two or three days; whilst when appropriated by others in precisely the same way they will wither, and fade in the same number of hours. And these remarkable phenomena manifestly are not dependent on such mere physical conditions as stoutness, or leanness, activity of perspiration, use of baths, or other such common causes. Individual immaterial emanations underlie these indisputable results, or effects.

Now-a-days the scents favoured by fashionable society are much more varied, elaborate, and costly, than of old. Several leading ladies of fashion adopt a perfume, and make it their own, jealously guarding the secret of both its name, and its maker, from their friends. This recent custom took its origin from the marvellous secret toilet-water used by Queen " Carmen Sylva," of Roumania, who for years past has employed a scent prepared, and distilled, for her by women who are sworn to silence concerning their work, and who, according to local report, gather the flowers, and express the perfume intended for the Queen's use, in the recesses of a lonely wood, under the protection of a guard of soldiers.

A very favourite scent in Society circles is " violet pot pourri," made by sprinkling layers of fresh violets with salt, and essence of violets ; the combination being delightfully fragrant : though, indeed, Shakespeare, in his far-seeing wisdom, has told us that:—

"To gild refined gold; to paint the lily;
To throw a perfume on the violet;
To seek the beauteous eye of heaven to garnish;
Is wasteful, and ridiculous excess!"

Resuming our main present contention as to the indisputable influences exercised subtly on the subjective mind by its material surroundings, a cognate notion about the mental energies pervading space, and attaching themselves to objects upon which they are particularly centred, is now advanced; and this offers to explain telepathy, ghosts, and other such occult mysteries. Dr. Bernard Hollander teaches that such brain-energies, emanating from sensitive subjects, and pervading the atmosphere about them, underlie such (hitherto) supposed præter-natural) phenomena. Thus, assuming a person to be the victim of a murderous attack, his mind-energy during this fatal attack will be strained to its utmost, and projected with such force as to cling about the room, or place, in which the dastardly deed was done. If then some other equally sensitive person, with his mind not pre-occupied intently by other thoughts, should pass through that room, or place, his, or her, brain might receive such a stimulus as to produce some more or less defined image of the murdered man, apparently real, though ghostly. On the same theory, by holding an object (whether belonging to the dead, or to the living,) whereon intense thought has been by force of circumstances bestowed beforehand by its previous owner; or if occupying a chamber inhabited previously by some predecessor, while having his mind fixed attentively thereupon, a sensitive person may have visions of, and be able to describe, the said predecessor. So, in a perfectly dark room, if metallic objects are rubbed by a sensitive subject, under impressive suggestion, these objects will acquire a distinctly visible responsive luminosity, shed from, and around them, through the personal influence of the rubber.

When Mr. Micawber extols the attractions, graces, and virtues of Agnes Wickfield to David Copperfield, Dickens interposes a kindred personal reflection of his own, though attributed here to Copperfield: "We have all some experience of a feeling that comes over us occasionally, of what we are saying, and doing, having been said, and done, before, in a remote time,—of our having been surrounded, dim ages ago, by the same faces, objects, and circumstances; of our knowing perfectly what will be said next, as if we suddenly remembered it. I never had this mysterious impression more strongly in my life than before he (Micawber) uttered the words now recorded."

"Any book (if it be one of those which *are* books) put before us at different periods of life will unfold to us new meanings,—wheels within wheels,—delicate springs of purpose, to which, at the last reading, we were stone-blind; gems which perhaps the author ignorantly cut, and polished."—Charles Lamb, *Dream Children*.

Again, about spirituous Scents, and Perfumes, these undoubtedly serve to affect the brain, not only by their special odours, but also by the volatile spirituous fumes acting on the nervous centres through the nose. We know further that any ardent spirit taken as drink tends to stupefy rather than to stimulate the brain. It is true that just at first after alcohol is taken the intellectual activity is temporarily increased, because the blood-vessels of the brain are dilated ; so that this seat of thought, and of mental perceptions, is for a brief time flushed with blood, and vivified beyond its wont. But presently such intellectual activity becomes overpowered by the stupefying narcotic effects of the alcohol, as intoxicating, to a degree more or less intense. When treating about this topic, Dr. Robert Hutchison has related (in his *Food and Dietetics*, 1902), that "Thackeray is said to have remarked he got some of his best thoughts ' when driving home from dining out,—with his skin full of wine.' " "We need not doubt it;" adds Dr. Hutchison, "for the statement embodies a physiological truth. It *was* his skin which was full of wine, since alcohol dilates the surface blood-vessels, and along with them the vessels of the brain also. But, by the time Thackeray got home one may expect that the narcotising effects of the alcohol would have begun to assert themselves, and the brilliant thoughts would have fled."

Concerning the efficacy of alcohol towards maintaining the physical stamina during health, or recuperating it during illness, some remarkable views, supported by positive facts, have been lately adduced by Dr. Josiah Oldfield, who is a thoroughly qualified physician ; also D.C.L. Oxford, and has been for many years in medical charge of the Lady Margaret Fruitarian Hospital, at Bromley, Kent. He writes : "There is a point on which temperance people will probably misunderstand me, but I am bound to say it;—I look upon the liquor of grain as one of the most important causes of the stamina of the English people ; that is to say, the ' beer ' of old England. But, to my mind it is not the alcohol in the beer, but it is the mineral salts which are obtained from the barley, wherein consist the merits of this beverage. There are two things which I consider very valuable in promoting the growth of the English race ; one has been the beer, the other has been the old English dish of 'furmenty,' made from barley, (or, more commonly, wheat). I especially want to emphasize the fact that the beer originally drunk was much more of the nature of barley-tea than is the beer of to-day. Anyone who has been to the old farmhouse breweries will know what I mean when I speak of sweet wort, which is really malt tea. It is composed of malt barley put to stew, and soaked in large quantities ; and the liquor of which, on being drawn off, is really strong sweet beer. In my opinion herein was the essential value of the early beer, or, as it really was, malt tea. I fully believe in this form of beer. I think that the alcohol of beer is an injurious addition, 'to make it keep.' This malt tea contains, moreover, a substantial amount of nerve-food ; we use it in our hospital to a considerable extent." Dr. Oldfield goes on to say : " Our further experience here has been distinctly that the right use of fruit, and vegetable juices, is of the utmost importance, for improving the quality of the blood corpuscles in the body. I have come to look upon flesh food as a positive stimulant, and therefore needed only as such ; in the same way, and with the same object as alcohol, under exceptional circumstances of prostration, or of failing vitality. On the other hand, a certain number of fruits, and vegetables, are specially feeding, and therefore essentially nutritious. I put raisins as the first of all foods that I know of. They are far superior to grapes, because the sugar has been thoroughly matured, and ripened, and transformed ready for digestion; and because only the healthiest, and best grapes can be dried for raisins. In addition to raisins another valuable food is 'raisin syrup;' not the so-called 'raisin wine,' but what is styled in India 'Draksherash,' which is an Indian non-alcoholic wine, made of raisins, with a few spices. After raisins come apples, and pears, and their juices, in the form of sweet cyder, and sweet perry; both practically non-alcoholic; Then of the vegetables my experience has been that carrots are the best of all to use, and to eat raw, whilst at the same time grated, not chopped. Of the other vegetable foods the watercress is likewise beneficial."

The proper way to cook vegetables, if you want to retain their curative value, is to keep, and serve therewith the water in which they are cooked; or to steam them without water.

"But, Betsey Prig"—said the redoubtable Mrs. Gamp, when relegating her duties as night nurse (the gross, vulgar, ignorant humbug!) to her partner in selfishness, Betsey Prig—for day service, (save the mark!): "But, Betsey Prig"—speaking with great feeling—"try the cowcumbers, God bless you!" Her own instructions for supper refreshment on arrival, had run thus: "I think, young woman,—to the assistant chambermaid, in a tone expressive of weakness,—"that I could pick a little bit of pickled salmon, with a nice little sprig of fennel, and a sprinkling of white pepper. I takes new bread, my dear, with just a little pat of fresh butter, and a mossel of cheese. In case there should be such a thing as a cowcumber in the 'ouse, will you be so good as to bring it, for I'm rather partial to 'em, and they does a world of good in a sick room." "If they draws the Brighton Tipper here,

I takes *that* ale at night, my love; it bein' considered wakeful by the doctors." "And, whatever you do, young woman, don't bring more than a shillingsworth of gin and water, warm, when I rings the bell a second time; for, that is always my allowance, and I never takes a drop beyond." A tray was brought, with everything upon it, even to the cucumber. "The extent to which Mrs. Gamp" (vulgar old sensualist) "availed herself of the vinegar, and supped up that refreshing fluid with the blade of her knife can scarcely be expressed in narrative."

When Mrs. Gamp entertained Betsey Prig to supper in her bedroom at Poll Sweedlepipes, (as again inimitably related by Dickens), she arranged the tea-board, "even unto the setting forth of two pounds of Newcastle salmon, intensely pickled. Her preparations comprehended a delicate new loaf, a plate of fresh butter, a basin of fine white sugar, and other arrangements on the same scale. Even the snuff with which she now refreshed herself was so choice in quality that she took a second pinch."

"That Betsey Prig expected pickled salmon was obvious; since her first words, after looking at the table, were, 'I know'd she wouldn't have a cowcumber.' Looking steadfastly at her friend, Mrs. Prig put her hand into her pocket, and with an air of surly triumph drew forth either the oldest of lettuces, or the youngest of cabbages, but, at any rate, a green vegetable of an expansive nature, and of such magnificent proportions that she was obliged to shut it up like an umbrella, before she could pull it out. She also produced a handful of mustard and cress, a trifle of the herb called dandelion, three bunches of radishes, an onion rather larger than an average turnip, three substantial slices of beetroot, and a short prong, or antler, of celery; the whole of this garden-stuff having been publicly exhibited but a short time before as a twopenny salad, and purchased by Mrs. Prig, on condition that the vendor should get it all into her pocket." "Which feat had been happily accomplished, in High Holborn, to the breathless interest of a hackney coach stand." "She did not even smile; but returning her pocket into its accustomed sphere, merely recommended that these productions of nature should be sliced up, for immediate consumption, in plenty of vinegar."

"'And don't go a-dropping none of your snuff in it,' said Mrs. Prig; 'in gruel, barley-water, apple-tea, mutton-broth, and that, it don't signify; it stimulates a patient. But I don't relish it myself.' 'Why, Betsey Prig,' cried Mrs. Gamp, 'how *can* you talk so?' 'Why, ain't your patients, wotever their diseases is, always a-sneezin' their wery heads off, along of your snuff?' said Mrs. Prig. 'And wot if they are?' said Mrs. Gamp. 'Nothing if they are,' said Mrs. Prig. 'But don't deny it, Sairah'! 'Who deniges of it?' Mrs. Gamp enquired. Mrs. Prig returned no answer."

Again: "Mr. Richard Swiveller's apartments" (*Old Curiosity Shop*) "were in the neighbourhood of Drury Lane; and had the advantage of being over a tobacconist's shop; so that he was able to procure a refreshing sneeze at any time by merely stepping out on the staircase; and was saved the trouble, and expense of maintaining a snuff-box."

"A very important point is that the vegetables themselves for curative purposes must be healthy. In America, where they have so much virgin soil, the conditions are different; but here in England I look upon vegetables with a considerable amount of suspicion, because they are so often grown upon sewage farms, and as rapidly as possible, with the object of getting the maximum of weight in the minimum of time. All the quick-growing vegetables, especially cabbage, and rhubarb, are regarded by me as dangerous food; not that they contain disease themselves, but that their tissues are overladen with incompletely transformed fertilizing matter, and, therefore, they do not provide a completely organized pabulum for the human organs to feed upon."

The Paris working-man never drinks tea, and very rarely beer; but if he be a sober man he drinks his litre, or litre and a half,—that is to say, about two pints,—of red wine every day, and possibly a *petit verre*, or two, of horrible cheap cognac, or of marc, a colourless liqueur made from shelled barley. He also drinks absinthe sometimes, when he can afford it, but this is not often the case, for even the cheap kind costs twopence, or, twopence-halfpenny, a glass.

As a rule the Paris workman takes his midday luncheon with him; and it consists of a huge chunk of bread, some cold vegetables,—which he heats up himself, or can get heated for him at the place he buys his wine,—and cheese, which contains a great deal of nourishment at a small price. Dessert in these meals,—" red handkerchief luncheons," as they are usually called,—consists of a tablet or two of gritty chocolate.

Certain it is that a light breakfast has much to do with capability, and energy for work throughout the morning. As a remarkable instance of this fact, Mr. Absolom, who played Cricket for Cambridge from 1866 to 1869, is credited with having breakfasted, prior to a

University Match, on a quart of beer, and a pint of gooseberries.

Bananas as another excellent fruit, are seldom eaten native before the skin is discoloured, and the pulp of so soft a consistence that it can be scooped out with a spoon. An old volume, entitled, *The Glasse of Time in the First Age, Divinely Handled by Thomas Peyton* (1620), contains, (eighty-first stanza), these lines respecting the banana :—

> " A cucumber much like it is in shew,
> Of pleasing taste, and sweet delightful hue;
> If with a knife the fruit in two you reeve,
> A perfect cross you shall therein perceive."

" But, in order to see this clearly, it is necessary to cut the banana fruit when it first begins to ripen; or, if ripe, immediately after it is taken from the plant."

" Concerning fruit," Sydney Smith, when writing about the Scotch people (1802) said, "Their temper will stand anything but an attack on their climate; they would even have you believe they can ripen fruit there; and, to be candid, I must own that in remarkably warm summers I have tasted peaches that made most excellent pickles; whilst it is on record that at the siege of Perth, on one occasion, the ammunition falling short, their nectarines made admirable cannon-balls."

Frumenty, as commended by Dr. Oldfield, as well as " Flummery," is made from wheaten flour, each being an old-fashioned food, much favoured by our rustic forefathers. The former consisted of milled wheat boiled in milk; for the latter a " recipe " is given by Dr. Salmon (1696). " This, in the Western parts of England is made of wheat flower, which is held to be the most heatening, and strengthening. To prepare this, take half a peck of wheat bran; let it soak in cold water three or four days; then strain out the milky water of it, and boil to a jelly; then season it with sugar, rose, and orange-flower water, and let it stand till it is cold and jellied again; then eat it, with white, or Rhenish wine, or cream, or milk, or ale." In some farm-houses, "flummery" made from the husks of oats, and known as "sowens," was eaten on New Year's Day, between two and three o'clock in the morning, the said mess containing for the finders, a thimble, a button, and a ring; whilst some money was often put into it for luck.

In *David Copperfield*, Mrs. Micawber, who "never would desert Mr. Micawber," writes to tell Trotwood, in sad heroics, how secret and reserved Mr. M. has become (as lawyer's clerk to the designing Uriah Heep). "His life," she laments, "is a mystery to the partner of his joys, and sorrows. Beyond knowing that it is passed from morning till night at the office, I now know less of it than I do of the 'man in the South,' connected with whose 'mouth' the thoughtless children repeat a nursery rhyme respecting 'Cold Plum Porridge.'

> "Mr. East made a feast;
> Mr. North laid the cloth;
> Mr. West did his best;
> Mr. South burnt his mouth,
> Eating cold plum-porridge."

When, and where garden vegetables are scarce for the time being, certain wayside vegetables are not to be despised for the rustic table. Bracken shoots serve capitally as a substitute for asparagus. Only the young tops, whilst they are still more or less curled up, should be gathered, as the fully-opened fronds are too tough, and stringy.

These should be cooked just like spinach, but require rather longer boiling,—from one to one and a half hours,—and are then to be chopped fine, and flavoured with meat-stock and a few cloves, in the usual manner; after which they should be heated up again, and served. If the shoots are cut below the ground as soon as their tips appear, they may also be treated like asparagus.

Furthermore, the stalks of the greater Burdock (*Arctium lappa*), if stripped of their rind whilst they are still tender, as well as the young shoots, and stems of Solomon's seal (*Convallaria polygonatum*), will fulfil the same purpose quite as admirably. Again, mock "asparagus soup" made from the roots of the yellow Goat's-beard (*Tragopogon*) leaves nothing better to be desired. In the *Avis au Peuple* of Dr. Tissot (1766), printed at Lyons, many such curious remedies are set forth, "particularly for those persons who are at a distance from regular physicians." As regards the vegetable kingdom, thoughtful mother Nature has taken evident pains to denote by outward visible signs the inward spiritual graces possessed, so to speak, by many of her remedial productions. "But," as Dr. Schroder said (1668), "for the finding out of occult qualities, these may be first conjectured by the likeness, and then confirmed by experience.

"For example: plants that represent some parts of man, these are wholesome. Plants which in their colour represent the humour in a man, do agree with the same, by increasing it. Plants that seem to represent a diseased habit, do cure the same; so barren things make men barren; so again plants that agree only among themselves, or with any part of an animal, according to its form."

The decay of ripe fruit arises almost invariably from bruises and wounds on its surface, when germs develop rapidly, and feed on the sugar, etc., liberated from the contused tissue. Experiments made in the laboratory at Kew have proved that such rotting, and fermentation of ripe fruit are due to fungi, and bacteria, on the outside. If these living organisms are destroyed, the fruit will remain perfectly sound for a considerable length of time. In Germany, a method of preserving fruit commonly practised is that of drying the pulp, and making it up into the form of tablets, ; these keep well, and can always be reduced to a compôte by boiling. The finest pastes are manufactured there from apricots, mirabelles, and quinces ; after which come apples, pears, plums, cherries, and bilberries.

About " Precious (Cherry) Stones," C. S. Calverley has told humorously, *Fly Leaves* (1885) :—

" My Cherry Stones, I prize them ; no tongue can tell how much ;
Each lady caller eyes them, and madly longs to touch ;
At eve I take them down, and look upon them ; and I cry,
Recalling how my Prince—' partook '—(sweet word !)—of Cherry pie.
" And when His Future Majesty withdrew to take the air,
Waiving our natural shyness, we swoop'd upon his chair !
Policemen at our garments clutched ; we mocked their feeble powers ;
And soon the treasures that had touched exalted lips were ours."

A story appropriate to cherry-stones is told about Gounod. One of his lady worshippers while visiting him saw a cherry-stone on the mantelpiece. This she surreptitiously secured as a precious personal association with Gounod. She had the stone polished, and set in a brooch ; which she afterwards showed triumphantly to the famous composer. He looked at it, admired it, and then calmly told her he never ate cherries; and that the stone had probably been casually left on the mantelpiece by his valet de chambre.

"Cherries, and strawberries are commended for fevers; vinegar, put on red-hot shovels, to keep rooms cool; and tobacco for drowning persons." How this last-named remedy was to be applied is noteworthy: "A tobacco-pipe was filled, and covered over the bowl with a piece of perforated paper ('as we blow the juice out sometimes'). Then, one pipe was put down the mouth, and another up the fundament. Next you 'blow with all your might; and in a moment the dying person revives.'" This rude proceeding was manifestly a forecast, but ordained without sufficient intelligence, of our modern "artificial respiration," according to the more scientific, and, therefore, more successful, "Sylvester" method, practised by the Humane Society, etc.

The stupor and fumes of heavy tobacco-smoking may be dispelled by eating watercresses; whilst to take them for supper, with bread-and-butter, certainly promotes sleep.

According to Zenophon, Cyrus, King of Persia, was brought up on a diet of bread, and cresses, until he was fifteen years old; then honey, and raisins were added. In *The Old Curiosity Shop*, Daniel Quilp, the spiteful, vindictive dwarf, a warped, in body and mind, domestic tyrant, "suffered himself to be led by his meek little, patient wife, and by Mrs. Jiniwin, his rebellious, but subdued, mother-in-law ('too much afraid of him to utter a single word') with extraordinary politeness to the breakfast-table. Here he ate hard eggs, shell and all; devoured gigantic prawns, with the heads

16

and tails on; chewed tobacco, and watercresses at the same time, and with extraordinary greediness; drank boiling tea without winking; bit his fork and spoon till they bent again; and, in short, performed so many horrifying, and uncommon acts that the women were nearly frightened out of their wits, and began to doubt if he was really a human creature."

Talking of a Dwarf—" How's the Giant ?" said Short (Codlin and Short,—the Punch and Judy men,—at the " Jolly Sandboys," amid a company of strollers gathered there, prior to the morrow's races); " when they sat smoking round the taproom fire." " Rather weak upon his legs," replied Mr. Vuffin; " I begin to be afraid he's going at the knees!" " That's a bad look-out," said Short; " What becomes of the old giants ?" " They're usually kept in carawans, to wait upon the dwarfs," said Mr. Vuffin; " Why, I remembers the time when with old Maunders (as had three and twenty wans), at his cottage in Spa Fields, in the winter-time, after the season was over, eight male and female Dwarfs were a-setting down to dinner every day, who was waited-on by eight old giants, in green coats, red smalls, blue cotton stockings, and high-lows; and there was one Dwarf, who had grown elderly, and wicious, who, whenever his giant wasn't quick enough to please him, used to stick pins in his legs, not being able to reach up any higher." " What about the Dwarfs when *they* get old ?" enquired the landlord. " The older a Dwarf is the better worth he is," returned Mr. Vuffin; " a grey-headed Dwarf, well wrinkled, is beyond all suspicion. But a giant, weak in the legs, and not standing upright; keep him in the carawan, but *never show him.*"

" My Lord St. Albans (Francis Bacon, 1600) said that Nature did never put her precious jewels into a garret, four stories high ; and therefore that exceeding tall men have ever empty heads."

The garden Currant, though a very favourite fruit, is risky as food, because containing several small stones, hard, and not soluble when in the stomach. One, or other of them may lodge mischievously within the appendix (an ominous possession nowadays). It is true, that after generations of its cultivation the domestic Currant had been made seedless ; but it has been allowed to lapse back into its pristine harmful possessions. Of course, the juices strained from the seeds, and tough skins, are available, (whilst refreshingly wholesome,) for culinary purposes. Practical gardeners have now succeeded in likewise producing the pipless orange ; and, quite recently, the pipless apple.

Charles Lamb (*Elia's Essays*) has immortalised (for his hospitality) one of his neighbours, " Dr. Anderson, an agreeable old gentleman who gives hot legs of mutton, and Grape pies, at his sylvan lodge, at Isleworth."

As a dietetic substitute for fermented malt liquors, embodying all the actual nutriment thereof, several of our leading manufacturing chemists prepare malt extracts nowadays, which are concentrated, for more handy medicinal uses towards the same beneficial ends. Professor Fothergill, in his *Manual of Dietetics*, says, " A malt extract is a lovely food ; and, when a stomach is in active revolt, a teaspoonful of good malt extract every hour is an aliment which neither offends by its bulk, nor disagrees by its qualities."

The late Professor Menchikoff (who mainly originated our modern discoveries as to the all-important action of "toxins") has taught that the chief ferments in malt are "diastase," "peptase," and "lipase." They play a most important part in rendering harmless many noxious products which are apt to form within the human intestines, and to poison the blood. Besides yeast ferments, (these being prepared also in tablet form, each tablet corresponding to a teaspoonful of fresh yeast), those of champagne (as "Oenase,") and of cyder ("Cidrase,") are now prepared by the Chemist. They prove eminently useful against the rheumatism of uric acid in excess, by their destructive action on harmful micro-organisms within the intestines, and in the blood. These tablets can be readily taken when the beverages which they represent disagree.

Porson, the famous Greek scholar, who drank whatever form of alcoholic beverage come in his way, is said to have declared that the spirit from a friend's lamp was one of the most comforting liquors he had met with. The remains of Lord Nelson were placed in spirit (of some sort) for preservation during their transit home; but they arrived (as is well known) in a dry state, the preservative liquor having been imbibed (it is assumed) on the passage. The drinking of methylated spirit seems to be prevalent at the present time among the poorer classes in the Isle of Man.

In that clever, thoughtful story, *The Countess Eve* (Shorthouse, 1898), we read, "The little Viscount entered the supper room with two large dusty bottles in his hands. 'Wine,' said he, 'is a wonderful thing! I have read a book written by an English doctor to that King of theirs whose head they cut off, wherein this doctor, partly out of his own mind, also out of Van Helmont, and Paracelsus, tells strange things about strifes, and histories that go on within the nature of wine until the perfect spirit is born, and is purified, and escapes, and triumphs over gorgons, and demons, and becomes immortal, and the giver of immortality.' "

As a case in point, prosaic, and matter-of-fact, but none the less appropriate, Harrison Weir, the well-known depicter of animal life, was so desperately ill some years ago that the doctor in attendance told Mrs. Weir her husband could not live through the night. When the doctor had gone, the artist asked for some port wine. This was given him; he drank more than half a tumblerful, and felt all the better for it; soon after this he drank another like quantity, and fell asleep. On waking he finished the bottle. When the doctor came next morning he found the patient, not dead, as he had expected, but sitting up in the bedroom. Harrison Weir, who lived some years subsequently, always attributed his recovery to that bottle of port. Though Dr. Samuel Johnson, who was by no means a total abstainer, declared, "A man may choose whether he will have abstemiousness, and knowledge; or claret, and ignorance."

"What a pity it is," says Mr. Bagshot in his recent *Comments*, (full of original shrewdness), "that overeating is not followed by the same visibly scandalous consequences as over-drinking! There would be more thin people in the world, and less gluttony; but scarcely anyone would be sober at the end of a London dinnerparty"! "Again," he goes on to say, "it is ultimately the most disagreeable fact in nature that living things live on each other. In this respect man is divided from the brutes by the cook. There may be pleasures unrealized by man in the sense of smell, but I am devoutly thankful that the sight of a flock of sheep in a field does not appeal to my appetite as it apparently does to my dog's. Imagine a pastoral landscape, with cattle in it, pervaded by an odour of roast beef!"

"The expression, 'dumb animal,' is meaningless. There are hardly any 'dumb animals'; but the horse, to his great misfortune, is one of them. Who would dare to whip a horse if he cried out like a dog? Imagine the uproar in London, or Paris, or Naples, which would speedily arise under such a rash proceeding!"

About Plums: the School of Salerne pronounced:—

"Plums cool, and loosen belly very kindly;—
No way offend, but to the health are friendly."

In Somerset, associated with this familiar fruit, since Henry VIII's time, has been Mells Park, which has belonged to the Horner family for nearly five hundred years. Their forebears were renowned as sturdy English Parliamentarians in the Civil War. The most interesting fact in the family history is their descent from "little Jack Horner," whose name is familiar to every English-speaking child. Jack Horner was steward of the temporalities of the great Abbey of Glastonbury at the time of the dissolution of the Monasteries; and, like many of his contemporaries, put his finger into the pie, and pulled out for himself a plum in the shape of a good slice of fat monastic land.

"Parvus Ioannes sacratum, et dulce comedit
Artocreas, simplexque legens sibi pollice prunum,
Aiebat placide—" Puerorum en optimus ipse.'

The plum, in his case, took the shape of the title deeds of the Manor of Mells; and the Horners have commemorated their good fortune by always naming the eldest son in the family John. The said nursery rhyme used to be immensely popular among the people of Somerset.

Talking of the traditional pie into which little Jack Horner thrust his inquisitive pollex, Cornwall is deservedly sung about as the county of pasties, and cream; this latter luxury being indeed an article of daily sustenance with a majority of the people. Working girls take cream at their midday meal instead of drinking beer, or other alcoholic beverage. And the cream-eaters are popularly known to be good-tempered, as well as capital workers. In the farmhouses cream is brought to table at every meal. Then, during the fruit season, pasties and cream become united in a happy union. But the pasty is much more than a summer indulgence. It forms a solid, substantial, standing food with Cornish folk all the year round. The real veritable pasty is to be known by its pointed ends, its cable-twist, and its crust of tender brown, unwrinkled, and unbroken. Every Cornish maiden worth her salt can make a pasty. "It may be her only accomplishment; but this she *can* do deftly, deliciously, and beyond imitation." Well may one say, "a pasty, with its cable-twist perfect from end to end, is a work of art to look at." A Cornishman seldom travels without a pasty in his bag; the working man has one in his pocket. No knife and fork are needed for discussing the meal; which may be eaten without constraint whilst standing, sitting, or walking. It is to be noted (*vide Meals Medicinal*), that "The pasty, or turn-over, a Cornish device, originated in a need by the miners of some portable form of food which they might carry with them to the mines for their dinner, and might eat without incurring harm by handling the same with coppery fingers. Hence, arose the miners' pasty, which is commonly slipped by them into a small cotton bag with a string run in at the top, so that the contents may be eaten from out of the bag whilst held in the miner's hand, and turned back as the pasty diminishes.

THE OPAL.

Loveliest of all the crystals of quartz, or silica, is the beautiful starry *Opal*, the most bewitching, most mysterious of all gems! This is "Pederos," the child of love,—so named from the Greek word, boyish, pure, and innocent.

"Opalus,—the opal," as was said in the *Mirror of Stones*, translated 1750, "is a stone wonderful to behold; being composed of many, and divers colours of shining gems, as of the carbuncle, amethyst, emerald, and many others; with a variety equally glittering, and admirable to discern. It is found only in India, and is not bigger than a large filbert." How highly it was valued by the ancients we are informed by Pliny, in his 37th Book, who says it was estimated at twenty thousand sesterces, which sum signifies something more than two hundred pounds sterling. Its virtue prevails against all diseases of the eyes; it sharpens, and strengthens the sight. To credit this Precious Gem with such numerous virtues cannot be improper, since it partakes of the nature, and colour of so many stones.

The name "Opalus" was supposed to be another form of "Ophthalmius,—eye-stone"; whence sprang these notions of its ophthalmic virtues. Marbodus (1740) tells that the Opal was believed to confer the gift of invisibility on its wearer. Wonderful powers were ascribed to the Opal by our ancestors. One of which superstitions Sir Walter Scott has availed himself of in the episode concerning the Baroness Hermione, of Arnheim, in his *Anne of Gierstein*, when the Opal worn by that lady, whereon a drop of holy water chanced to rest, straightway shot out a brilliant spark, like a falling light, and then forthwith became lustreless, and void of colour as a common pebble. Strange to say, after the brilliant novelist's fiction was published, a belief that Opals are unlucky obtained such currency that these gems went quickly out of fashion. But lately they have come again into favour; and now promise to regain, (as they have always merited), high estimation; and this the more especially since they are the only Precious stones which defy imitation. And, in fact, so far was the Opal from being considered unlucky in the Middle Ages that it was believed to possess unitedly the special virtues of every gem with the distinctive colour whereof it was emblazoned. Petrus Artensis, *tempore* Henry IV., said, "The various colours in the Opal tend greatly to the delectation of the sight." But in modern times if a Russian of either sex, or of any rank, should happen to see an Opal among goods submitted to purchase, he, or she, will buy nothing more on that day, because the Opal is, in the judgment of subjects of the Czar, an embodiment of the evil eye. It is likely that the same superstition will be found to similarly obtain in other countries.

As a mineral the Opal is a natural form of hydrated silica, which has apparently hardened from a gelatinous state; and during consolidation it has undergone contraction unequally, in different directions. For which reason, though amorphous, it behaves in polarised light like a doubly refracting body occurring in a "porodine" condition. The most Precious, or "Noble" Opal is the best variety; it emits rays of light like the sun, being filled, as it were, with spangles of divers brilliant colours. When thus richly spangled it is further named the "Harlequin" Opal, on account of its resemblance to the motley tints of the harlequin's dress. Then there are the so-called "common" Opal, the "Semi-" (or half) Opal, the "Hydrophane," or Mexican Opal, and, finally, the "Wood" Opal, or opalised wood, of which huge masses are met with in Hungary, Tasmania, and other parts; whole trees being found occasionally converted into the ligneous structure called "Wood Opal." The "Hydrophane" Opal forfeits its colour and beauty when exposed to water, then becoming translucently dull; by which cause it happened that the stone told of by Sir Walter Scott lost its lustrous colour when accidentally sprinkled with holy water. The Spanish Royal Family has an unlucky opal, which has been the death of five princes, and princesses, and is now hung round the neck of "The Virgin of Almudena."

In the "Harlequin" Opal the various rainbow tints are flashed forth from small horizontal vitreous flakes, forming a kind of polychromatic mosaic; while in the other kinds of Opal the colours are disposed in broad bands, or in irregular patches of comparatively large area. The tints vary with the angle at which the light is incident, and with the relative position between the stone, and the observer; so that by moving the Opal a brilliant succession of flashes can be obtained. The colours are not due to any material pigment in the mineral, but are optical effects,— the iridescence being a case of the well-known colours of thin plates in layers.

The Opal is displayed to best advantage when cut *en cabochon*, or with a convex surface.

Pliny tells that the rich Roman Senator Nonius was proscribed by Mark Antony for the sake of a magnificent Opal which he possessed, (valued at two millions of sesterces, or sixteen thousand, and eight hundred pounds); a stone as large as a hazel nut, but which he refused to sell.

The so-called Black Opals consist of the matrix (penetrated in all directions by veins, and spots,) of Opal forming a mixture known sometimes as " Soot of Opal." But certain stones sold as Black Opal have manifestly been modified in colour by staining, or by heat. The American Opal is generally less fiery, and less milky in appearance than the Hungarian Stone.

Of late years some very brilliant opals have been sent into the market from Queensland. The Harlequin, and Noble Opals have the same chemical composition, i.e., ninety per cent of silica, and ten per cent of water.

Next in value ranks the Fire Opal, or Girasol, with bright hyacinthine, yellow, or fire-red reflections. Again, there is the rare dark Opal, black, with a sullen red-hot glow in its inner heart, which would put the burning Carbuncle to shame. Likewise the " Prime d'Opal," or Opal Seeds, with points brilliantly coloured, set in a sober matrix, and beautiful exceedingly when in large masses.

Other minor kinds are the deep brown ferruginous Opal, the waxen Green, and the Jaspery; also the Garnet-red, the rich Topaz-yellow, and the violet blue; all these being forms and phases of that grand crystal of common flint, the "Precious," or "Noble" Opal, the " Child of love." This " Precious," or " Noble," Opal is one of the most beautiful gems known : when held between the eye and the light it appears of a pale, milky, reddish hue, but when seen by reflected light it displays all the colours of the rainbow, in flakes, or flashes, or specks ; in fact, all the colours of the most beautiful gems are here united in one. " There is," according to the *Pharmacopœia Londinensis* (1696), " a false Opal, called the Pseudopalum, or Oculum Cati, (Cat's-Eye), and by Isidore " Ophthalmius," the Eye-stone ; but it is less glorious than the true Opal."

Pantherus est alius Lapis, ex Opalorum genere qui, a Pardalio (the Leopard), *seu Panthera* (Panther), *animal variegato colore, nominatur*; for, so saith Macer, *Pantheram patet esse feram diversicolorem.* " The stone is reported to have as many virtues as it has colours : but what they are authors are something silent about."

Opals are very brittle. Their lustre is, as Mr. Harry Emanuel testifies, always much more brilliant on a warm day. A dealer in Precious Stones, being aware of this peculiarity, invariably holds an Opal in his hand for a little while before showing it, thereby imparting warmth to the gem.

" The Opal," says an old writer, " is a precious stone which hath in it the bright fiery flame of the Carbuncle, the fine refulgent purple of an Amethyst, and a whole sea of the Emerald's green glory ; and every one of them shining with an incredible mixture, and exquisite pleasure." Another writer declares that the delicate colouring, and tenderness of the Opal remind him ever of a loving, and beautiful child.

Chemically the Opal is a hydrous form of silica.

The only Opal Mines are those of Hungary. These stones are also found in the Island of Sumatra, and in the East Indies. The Hydrophanous Opal, or *Oculus Mundi*, is so named because of an internal luminous spot which changes its position according to the direction in which this stone is held towards the light. The phenomenon of such stones becoming transparent in water is thought to be occasioned by that fluid soaking through their whole substance, in the same manner as the transparency of paper is occasioned by immersing it in oil. When taken from the water these stones, as they dry, become again opaque. Care should be observed not to immerse them in any but pure water, and to take them out therefrom as soon as they have acquired their full transparency; otherwise the pores will shortly become filled with earthy particles; when the stones will cease to exhibit this peculiar property, and will always afterwards remain opaque.

(Reverting for a moment to the Rock Crystal, it is interesting to know that a specially choice, valuable Crystal casket, which the late Queen Victoria possessed, was dedicated by her to enshrining the small Bible which General Gordon carried invariably with him through all his campaigns, and which was found still in his precious keeping at the time of his devoted death.)

The Hæmatitis already referred to, or "Lapis Sanguineus," is a hard, solid, heavy stone comprising particles of iron, disposed like needles, it being of a reddish-brown colour, and becoming red as blood according as it is reduced to powder. It "is brought from many places, there not being any iron mines wherein it is not found." "The best, and most esteem'd is that from Spain." "Chuse such as is of a brownish-red, weighty, solid, and smooth; it is astringent, and is called Hæmatitis from the Greek word 'aima,'—'blood,'. because, being powdered it is of the colour of blood, and stops bleeding." In the present day of advanced science, especially as regards the powerful effects produced (curatively, under proper guidance) by newly-discovered elements, Radium, and the X-rays, to wit, when externally applied, to this, or that part of the body, we may reasonably entertain notions of those benefits which have hitherto been ridiculed as merely superstitious being actually realized; when, for instance, a Bloodstone, or Hæmatitis, is applied, and worn, for the arrest of bleeding, whether this issues from within, or from without the body. And similarly with equal cogency may we adopt this scientific revelation of our surprising modern times to Precious Stones, Gems, and metals, when worn or externally used, after the several fashions already discussed in these pages. Each of such jewels, and each of such metals, has been shown to contain definite chemical constituents, determined by accurate, and reliable analysis. Each, therefore, may, without any absurd, or weak-minded credulity, be reckoned for chemical reasons a likely therapeutic agent when wisely employed; each likewise as probably mischievous if used rashly, or in excess. Quoth Sir William Huggins, most appropriately to the views we now advocate, in a speech at the annual dinner of the Royal Society, November 30th, 1906 : " Surrounded as we are by the deadly uniformities of conventional life, and deafened by the wrangling of parties, and of sects, have we not felt, as a freer air, even as a breath of fresh life, the wholly new conceptions of some aspects of energy, and of matter, which have been opened out before us through the recent remarkable discoveries of Becquerel, and of the Curies ? "

After the same lofty strain spoke Sir Fridtjof Nansen, and quite as convincingly, at the same dinner, to the following effect: "We know that it was not long ago that the element Radium was discovered; and this has opened before us an entirely new world of knowledge which even our boldest imaginations could not have pictured."

Bearing in mind these utterances, so pregnant with far-seeing wisdom, by foremost scientists speaking from conviction, we are justified in applying the same to our present argument that Precious Stones and the nobler metals are capable of exercising salutary, (or the reverse,) physical effects when worn as jewels, or when otherwise applied, next the skin, with remedial purposes in view. One most important fact can no longer be gainsaid, that nature prefers to demonstrate her highest, and most potential results as brought about by infinitesimal actions rather than by gross methods. Looking back to well nigh a century ago we may learn that a prophetic anticipation of such knowledge was entertained by a Master of Medicine, (who thereby became the founder of a distinct school,) as regards the latent and subtle effects of drug-medicines reduced to infinitesimal proportions; whether by repeated triturations, or by long-continued "succussion" of liquid medicaments, or by dilution carried up to a point of numerous centesimal degrees. Through the refined subdivisions thus adopted, remarkable developments of medicinal power were indisputably obtained, "even such inert bodies as the metals becoming actively pathogenetic, (i.e., symptom-producing) and curative"; whilst various insoluble minerals, such as flint (silicon), lime, alum, and common salt, were thus made to exhibit curative virtues of a potential sort hitherto latent, and altogether unsuspected.

The avowed object of this advanced pharmacy was so to prepare each substance that the whole of its capabilities for cure should be determined, and helpfully applied, within, or without the body. Diseases were regarded by the Master as dynamic derangements of our vital, (in a sense spiritual) principle, and therefore amenable to the ultimate (spiritual) potencies which exist innate within the innermost nature of medicaments. He maintained, (and with much experimental show of reason) that all such medicaments become, for curative purposes, more powerful as they are rendered more attenuated. Unhesitatingly adopting which view, (strengthened, and confirmed to-day by the fresh researches, and discoveries of modern science,) we contend that valid grounds warrant us in believing that Precious Stones, and the more noble Metals, bring to bear (by their innate highly subtilised principles) on the persons of their wearers positive physical results, in close, and immediate accordance with the component medicinal constituents which they have been proved by analysis to include within their substance. Each Precious Stone, and each Noble Metal, as adduced forward in these our pages, is shown to possess this, or that constituent element, of a medicinal sort, however refined; and for each of the same on this account are physical effects on the body, and mind of their employer, claimed. Furthermore, it is not to be doubted, (as our direct evidence makes certain,) that outward uses of such Precious Stones, and Noble Metals serve to effect sensible, and trustworthy beneficial ends on both body, and mind, when judiciously, and learnedly ordered.

Towards the close of his painstaking and steadily progressive career the aforesaid Master—in the last edition of his leading work, 1833—gave the most expressive evidence of his belief in the virtue of attenuations, by saying that he could scarcely name one disease which during the past year he, and his assistants, had not treated with the most happy results, solely by means of "olfaction," (or the practice of smelling the highly subtilized medicinal substances); and he added that a patient, even when destitute of the sense of smell, may expect an equally perfect action, and cure, from the medicine, through the act of olfaction, or smelling thereat; but only one such medicine may be used (in this way) at a time. As a striking illustration of such exquisitively refined, yet absolutely sure potency for cure, which external means, mineral or metal, when correctly chosen serve to exert, we would refer our readers to the instance of the Bloodstone, as given fully at a following page. Well authenticated cases will be found related of severe chronic bleedings becoming arrested solely by the patient's outward use of such a stone; and remaining arrested (in one instance) only so long as this stone was retained in wear. The *raison d'être* for these curative effects may be sufficiently accounted for by the recognisable presence within the substance of the Bloodstone of Iron Oxide, in red specks, or streaks; this Iron being of longstanding repute with doctors as an active, and effective astringent of bleedings. And similarly with respect to the Mineral Silica, (Flint),—which proves quite insoluble, as hitherto supposed, and medicinally inert,—this substance, under skilful trituration, has been converted into a most useful medicament for cures. When applied to a "simple," but obstinately chronic ulcer, let us say on the leg, it will promote speedy, and persistent healing. Moreover, its triturations with sugar of milk (as an inert diluent) to quite a remote attenuation, when administered internally is found to influence the general nutrition of the body most effectually. One of its main virtues is displayed in its power over "suppuration," the formative process of purulent matter from a wound, an abscess, or a sore. "When such a morbid process has become unhappily established," writes Dr. Richard Hughes, 1876, "and by its excess, or long duration, is causing mischief, the effect of infinitesimal doses of this Silica in checking it is simply magical." —(The juice of the common Marigold (*Succus calendulæ*) is likewise a marvellous healer of cuts and wounds; particularly if there is the slightest sign of pus (matter) forming. The late Dr. Helmuth wrote in his well-known surgical manual: "Pus cannot live in the presence of Calendula.")

We have instanced the recently discovered metal—Radium—as showing how potentially this agent, (and by fair inference other cognate Metals, and Minerals) can affect the human body, and influence its functions, when applied externally, on, or immediately adjacent to, this, or that portion of the skin-surface. Several remarkable further phenomena have been conclusively noted with regard to this metal. Thus, a tube of Radium wrapped in black paper will light up a Diamond placed in proximity thereto. Again, any investiture of cloth around Radium becomes rotted by the action of the emanations therefrom. Moreover, the Radium rays are found to destroy the vitality of seeds; so that mustard and cress seeds, if exposed for a considerable time to the action of Radium rays, will refuse to germinate. When directed against the skin of a living rabbit for some short space of time, the rays have been found to produce a reaction, followed by a marked increase in the growth of fur about that part. Nevertheless, it appears to be essential that during these effects (indeed, most probably causative thereof,) access of the metal to the open air shall be maintained; in order that the oxidising power of the air (ionised) may be brought to bear on the affected area which is being (so to speak) radiumised. Which being so, we may legitimately suppose that the kindred occult, but none the less actual, effects which potential Precious Stones, and the Nobler Metals, may be relied upon for exerting, will be materially enhanced by their applications being made directly to the part whilst bare of covering, and exposed to the air. Of course these imperative conditions are already provided for when the said remedial agents are worn as Jewels on the hands, or as ornaments around the unclothed neck. Sir Oliver Lodge inclines to the belief that Radium, for remedial uses, in the hands of doctors, will replace almost every other source of therapeutic rays. Curiously enough an old record of the seventeenth century tells about certain pills—"Pilulæ Radii Solis extractæ," (Pills made by the Solar Rays,)—which became as widely famous then as the well-known Morrison Pills later on. The inventor of the "Ray Pills" was one Lionel Lockyer, who lies buried in the Church of St. Saviour's, Southwark, (now a Cathedral). The Epitaph over Lockyer's tomb runs thus:

"His virtues, and his pills are so well known
That envy can't confine them under stone;
This verse, tho' lost, his pill embalms him safe
To future times without an epitaph."

It is a marvellous fact—judging by the limited experience which has thus far been possible—that the metamorphosing activities of Radium-rays seem to be inexhaustible by time, or use. They appear to emit a something which is almost, if not altogether, identical with vitality, as distinct from any such physical manifestations as heat, light, and electricity. How, and why the effects are produced, no scientist, or physician can yet say. The influence at work seems almost akin to the "Iodic" force which was so much discussed in the first half of the nineteenth century. But its efficacy is strictly practical, and objective; not depending on mental suggestion in the least degree. The "Radio-activity," as it is termed, is understood to signify an occult property shown by the class of newly-recognised substances, of which Uranium, Thorium, and Radium are the best known examples; each of which spontaneously emanates a special type of radiations. Very remarkable are the colouring effects of the (Becquerel) rays upon Diamonds; which Precious Stones, when "off colour," may be converted again by these rays into stones of the finest water. The much-prized blue tint can be thus imparted, and other similar wonders wrought. Furthermore, true Diamonds can be recognised by means of these rays. If going into a dark room, provided with a small quantity of Radium-bromide, and bringing this near a Diamond ornament, the Stone will at once glow with a bluish light. If the ornament includes other stones, such as Rubies, these will appear quite black. A ring consisting of Diamonds, and Rubies alternately, shows this very effectively. The Diamonds shine out brilliantly, while the spaces between them filled by Rubies are dark. Imitation Diamonds do not act thus, (i.e., fluoresce); in which simple way real Diamonds can be distinguished from false ones without any expert knowledge whatever.

For effecting medico-surgical cures (as of superficial cancer, and allied serious diseases of the skin,) the Radium is applied within a tube to the afflicted anatomical part; when, after repeated use therof, it is found that curative degeneration of the diseased tissues takes place; and healing action becomes presently developed. For "moles," and "port-wine" marks, a similar application of the Radium proves effective to cure. The Radium is contained in a disc of wood covered with mica, about a quarter of an inch in diameter. The patient holds it to the affected spot for fifteen, or twenty minutes at each sitting.

As the latest pronouncement on this subject of Radio-activity, M. Gustave le Bon has shown convincingly that this is a general phenomenon, and not solely the property of certain exceptional substances. He stoutly affirms that all matter is of itself producing energy, chiefly intra-atomic energy. He first discovered, and established the fact that light falling upon bodies produces radiations which are capable of passing through material substances. The original source of Radio-activity is now believed to be the sun; this Radio-activity being known to consist largely of a stream of rapidly moving particles, charged, either positively, or negatively, with electricity. Anyhow, the main conclusions thus arrived at by leading scientists lend much additional force to the arguments we are making bold to advance in favour of positive influences for good, or harm, exercised on their wearers, and users, by Precious Stones, and the Nobler Metals.

Of the Hæmatitis, (akin to the Bloodstone,) Marbodus tells :—.

> "Naturæ lapis humanæ servire creatus
> Stiptica cui virtus permulta probatur inesse:
> Nam palpebrarum super illitus asperitatem
> Et visus hebetes, pulsâ caligine, sanat."

Professor Elmer Gates, of the Laboratory of Psychology at Washington, has just concluded a remarkable series of experiments illustrative of the physical processes induced even by right and wrong thinking. He has reduced anger, jealousy, love, grief, and anxiety to chemical formulæ. According to this Professor, every change of the mental state of an individual is expressed in the secretions of the body. Treated with the same chemical reagent, the perspiration of an angry man shows one colour, that of a man in grief another, and so on through a long list of emotions.

After condensing the volatile constituents of the breath of his subjects, the Professor obtained a brownish sediment from anger, a grey sediment from sorrow, and a pink sediment from remorse. Of the brownish substance the Professor administered doses to men, and animals. In every case it produced nervous excitability, or irritability.

In his experiments with thought conditioned by jealousy, he obtained another substance from the breath, which he injected into the veins of a guinea-pig. The pig died in a very few minutes. After concluding from his various experiments that hate is accompanied by the greatest expenditure of vital energy, Professor Gates affirms that this passion precipitates several chemical products. Enough of these would be deposited during one hour of intense hate, according to him, to cause the death of perhaps fourscore persons, as these ptomaines are the deadliest poisons known to science.

Resuming our consideration of the Jasper varieties, these are many, and charming: red, yellow, green, and variegated, often offering strange accidental combinations to the artist; the most remarkable of all, perhaps, being in the profile of Louis XVI—with a blood-red crescent streak right across the throat. Furthermore, there are the Feldspars; the Chrysolite; the Chymophane, very lovely, but not much used; the Chrysoberyl; Jet, which is only a variety of coal; and Coral, which is only carbonate of lime built up as the house, and home of a small polypus. This Coral we shall discuss more at length in future pages. Likewise as to Amber, which appertains to the same group of Quartzes, formerly Amber was believed to be the tears of some defunct sea-bird, or exudations from the heated earth, or honey from the mountains of Ajan, melted by the sun, and congealed by the sea; notions, which whilst fanciful, and poetic, are now quite discredited, Amber being accepted as an honest resin, light, electric, and attractive of hue. Other belongings to the same group (of Jaspers) are the Malachite, a bright green carbonate of copper, with soft green velvet-green veinings, in the richest play of line and marking; whilst another such member is the Lapis-Lazuli, composed of alumina, silica, and sulphur; making as a pigment the painter's heaven of ultra-marine.

THE TURQUOISE.

Finally, as belonging to the same group, notice directs itself to the Turquoise; waxen blue, and so eminently sympathetic as to grow pale when its wearer is sick, or sorry; and similarly to straightway lose all its beauty if bought, and not bestowed as a gift. Turquoises are valuable; and, being so, are often imitated; their main composition consisting of phosphoric acid, and protoxide of iron; (though chemists differ as to the more absolute composition); which being understood, clever rogues tinge the teeth of fossil animals with phosphate of iron, professing to sell a grand set of turquoise ornaments, and taking for the same a fraudulent price, at the cost to themselves only of cheap old ivory. Artificial Turquoises may be readily distinguished from the real by acids, and fire; the one discharging all the colour, the other burning up the supposed Gem outright, leaving a nasty odour of burnt bone, as the only result of a bad bargain.

Additionally, respecting the Turquoise, the finest variety of this beautiful blue, (or bluish-green) mineral, so highly valued as an ornamental Gem, occurs in Persia; from which territory the Stone first came to Europe, by way of Turkey; thus getting to be named "Tuschesa" by the Venetians who imported it; and by the French, "Turquoise." It is chemically a hydrated phosphate of Aluminium, associated with a variable proportion of hydrated phosphate of Copper; to which latter constituent it owes much of its colour. The green tints of certain varieties appear to be further due to admixture with salts of iron. A fine blue Turquoise analysed by Professor A. H. Church, yielded alumina, 40·19; phosphorus pentoxide 32·86; water 19·34; cupric oxide 5·27; ferrous oxide 2·21; and manganous oxide 0·36.

The most valued tint of the Turquoise is a delicate

blue, inclining slightly to green. In many specimens the green becomes more pronounced with age. This mineral has never been found crystallised, but occurs as veins, nodules, stalactite masses, and incrustations. It takes a fair polish, and exhibits a feeble lustre. The Lapidary usually cuts it *en cabochon*, or with a low convex surface. In the East it is frequently engraved with Persian, and Arabic inscriptions, generally copied from the Koran; the incised characters being in many cases gilt. Such objects are worn as amulets. The Turquoise has always been associated with curious superstitions; the most common being the notion (already alluded to) that it changes its colour with variations in the state of its owner's health; or even in sympathy with the affections, and the characteristic physical influences of its wearer. That personal health determines the brilliancy, and beauty of jewels worn next the person of sensitively gifted persons, is a recognised fact. Mediæval writers were fully aware of this phenomenon. Thus, concerning the Turquoise, De Boot (1636) has related how it grew paler as its owner sickened, lost its colour entirely at his death, but recovered it when placed upon the finger of a new, and healthy possessor. Again, "Whoever," says Van Helmont (1620), " wears a Turquoise, so that it, or its gold-setting touches the skin, may fall from any height; and the stone attracts to itself the whole force of the blow, so that it cracks, and the person is safe." This particular virtue, however, at the present prosaic matter-of-fact time we altogether dispute, and should decline to put it to the test. Van Helmont, who was highly intelligent, believed in the Archaus, the soul of man after Eden, as the first cause of all diseases.

"The Turquoise," taught De Boot, "strengthened the eyes, and cheered the soul of the wearer; it saved him from suffering a fall, by cracking itself instead; it grew pale as the wearer sickened, lost its colour entirely on his death, but recovered it when placed on the finger of a new, and healthy possessor." "Suspended by a string, and within a glass, it would tell the hour by the exact number of strokes against the sides thereof." This is a hard gem, of no transparency, but full of beauty, its colour is sky blue, out of a green, in which may be supposed a little milkish infusion. A clear sky, free from all clouds, will most excellently discover the beauty of a true Turquoise.

As an instance of bodily response in colour, and texture, to the bodily health, we may adduce that of the late literary celebrity, David Christie Murray; a man of remarkable personal gifts, who was justly proud of his flowing locks, (covered, as they commonly were, with a Tennyson hat). He was vain of his hair, which was a mane of silk, and was moreover his health-barometer. A sharp attack of neuralgia, (whereto he was quite a martyr,) would leave this hair bleached for the time. But as his strength improved, the whiteness of his locks would give place to something like their golden hue of youth again. He was a fine, picturesque figure, even in his old age; and he knew it.

Concerning baldness, it is now confidently alleged (by Dr. Parker, of Detroit) that this, when premature, is almost invariably consequent on inadequate chest-breathing; whereby a poisonous substance becomes developed in the lungs, which circulates in the blood. The roots of the hair on the head become poisoned by this contamination of the blood, and baldness is the result. To practise deep chest-breathing daily, and perseveringly, is the remedy. Within six weeks new hair begins to make its appearance. "Craniums, says Dr. Parker, "that had been bald for twenty years have developed new hair after a certain amount of deep chest-breathing." He has studied this hypothesis for several years, thus treating baldness successfully; and experimenting similarly on animals, with the like results.

The Turquoise came originally from Nishabour, in Persia, but was imported by the Turkey merchants, and thus obtained its name. As regards this stone, there are always in the market a number of inferior stones, and of imitations. One of the most common is to be found—as already stated—in Mammoth teeth, derived from Siberia, and which, when coloured with iron phosphate, are known as fossil Turquoises; they have one advantage, in never losing the colour once imparted to them. A method has likewise been discovered of dyeing Chalcedony, "by which art the varied shades of the more valuable Turquoises are produced." It is believed that the production of fictitious Turquoises from Chalcedony is freely practised in Egypt; so that, evidently, a purchaser of Turquoise should act with no little circumspection. Among the Turks persons of rank almost constantly wear the Turquoise in some part of their dress, as a ring-stone, or to adorn the handle of a stiletto. Turquoise stones are imported into England from Russia, stuck, with pitch, upon the ends of straws; because, if mixed together in parcels, the purchaser would not be able, in turning them over, to observe their colour, and ascertain their value.

Magic lore has always averred that certain precious

stones are strongly susceptible to the personality of those persons who wear them; some stones being deemed lucky, and others malevolent. A stone must, therefore, be actually treated with affection, regarded as a sentient being, if its colour, and lustre are to be maintained, or improved. For instance, the Turquoise is thought to be wonderfully sensitive in this way. It will grow pale when its owner is sick, will entirely lose colour when the wearer dies, and will, as already told, recover this gradually when placed on the finger of a new and healthy person, the colour deepening every day. But if the Turquoise turns green upon any individual, such person ought not to wear this stone; otherwise misfortune will surely eventuate, since the Turquoise, under such conditions, is malevolent. By the Germans the Turquoise is used as a love-token; and is presented by a lover to his betrothed. Its colour is believed to remain permanent as long as the lover's affection lasts. Furthermore, the Turquoise is credited in Germany with a beneficial virtue for strengthening the eyes.

The Turquoise of commerce comes from Nishabour, in Khorasan, Persia, in a clayey state; being now frequently known as "callaite." If kept free from contact with acids, musk, camphor, or other scents, this stone will retain its pristine hue for many years; but turning at last to a green, or white. The Shah of Persia is thought to jealously retain all the finest Turquoises in his own possession.

During the reign of James VI of Scotland, 1622, enumerated among the valuables left by George, Earl Marischal, is "ane jasper stane for steming of bluid." A belief in the medicinable virtues of precious stones was not uncommon in those times. Even to this day a superstitious reverence clings around the Turquoise in Russia; the creed being that, if given by a loving hand, the stone carries with it happiness, and good fortune; whilst it will pale in colour if anything evil threatens the giver.

A Turquoise is too uniform in colour for having readily lent itself to the cutting of cameos; though twelve of the stones thus treated came into the market a century back, each being engraved in relief with a figure of one of the twelve Cæsars.

It lies within our personal knowledge and ability, concerning the Turquoise as being manifestly influenced by the physical condition of individuals who wear this precious stone, (such persons being of a sensitive temperament,) to bear witness of the fact in one remarkable instance. It concerns a lady of remarkable personal endowments, as to a shapely, well-developed form, beauty, of face and figure, vivacity of disposition, highly born, being moreover, the daughter of a man famous in the literary world. This lady, of Irish extraction, which makes her abound with wit and good humour, is most popular in society; where she frequently appears as the wearer of magnificent Turquoise jewelry, varied in its number of exquisitely brilliant sets. On being congratulated for possessing such a wealth of rare Turquoises she at once explains that they do not belong to herself; but that her friends who severally own these valuable gems, on finding their Turquoises exhibit loss of lustre, and splendour, forthwith lend them to the good-natured lady, whose virtues, and special endowments have been told of. They beg her to wear the stones for a while, immediately about her person, so that these may recover their pristine lustre, and sparkling beauty;—a restoration which always becomes effected under such salutary conditions. Taking this, and collateral instances of the same convincing character, and veracity, into thoughtful consideration, it is fair to conclude that a gem which has lost its splendour, and sheen, its brilliancy of lustre, and its whole beauty as a jewel, through being worn by a person out of health, or spirits, must have parted with some of its best natural gifts for the benefit of such a sufferer, especially; if found to regain these its natural virtues when worn afresh by some kindly Samaritan, who is enjoying full vigour of mind, and body, under the best possible physical circumstances, and conditions.

About the Turquoise wrote Leonardus: " There is an opinion that it is useful to horsemen; and that so long as the rider has it with him, his horse will never tire him, and will preserve him unhurt from any accident. It is further said to defend him that carries it from outward, and evil casualties."

Mediæval writers ascribe other marvellous virtues to the Turquoise; a list of which is given by De Boot (1636). " Whoever wears a Turquoise so that it, or its gold-setting, touches the skin,"—*vel, non perinde est,*—" may fall from any height, and the stone then attracts to itself the whole force of the blow, so that itself cracks, and the person is safe;"—though the Marquis of Villena had a fool who, when asked by a knight " What are the properties of the Turquoise?" replied, " Why! if you have a Turquoise about you, and should fall from the top of a tower, and be dashed to pieces, the stone would not break." The author of the *Orphic Poem on Stones* mentions one in the possession of Helenus which not only gave utterance to Oracular responses, but was even perceived to breathe!

Two or three centuries ago no gentleman thought his hand properly adorned unless he wore a fine Turquoise. The sympathetic property of the Turquoise as manifested by a change of colour corresponding to the health or welfare of its owner, is alluded to by more than one English poet. In Ben Jonson's play the flatterers of Sejanus recite :—

> "Observe him, as his watch observes his clock;
> And true as Turquoise in the dear lord's ring,
> Look well, or ill with him."

Again Donne says :—

> "As a compassionate Turquoise that doth tell
> By looking pale the wearer is not well."

Genuine Turquoise stones vary from pale blue to green, and white; but all except the azure are worthless. The only Turquoise mines in the world which deserve the name, are all on the south face of a hill, (or small mountain,) a thousand feet in height. Women, indolent men, and children, are chiefly employed in obtaining the precious stones. What these persons have to do is merely to dig up two or three feet of the soft soil, and to sift it. If one of the men when unobserved discovers a good stone he will swallow it. A couple of overseers carefully watch to prevent this, but, (says the report of a visitor to the mines) "their diabolical appearance impressed me with the conviction that turquoises formed their chief articles of diet."

In one of its earlier stages a Turquoise is a sort of soft cream-coloured chalk, which is said to possess medicinal properties, and which the people eat, with apparent zest. The original form of a Turquoise is roughly kidney-shaped. Any flaws, specks, or other defects on the stones are commonly covered by means of inscriptions in gold cunningly engraved upon them. These inscriptions are generally love mottoes, such as "*Naznin*,"—"Darling;" "*Fidyat shavam*;"—"Yours, body and soul": or sometimes a verse of the Koran will be inscribed. These engraved Turquoises are usually sold (in Meshed) glued on to the ends of pieces of stick, around which red paper has been neatly wrapped, to set them off. The slightest tinge of green in a Turquoise renders it practically of no value. It should be noted by purchasers that dampness will often temporarily revive the colour of a faded Turquoise. No one in Meshed would think of buying a stone of any reputed value without keeping it by him moist for a few days.

It was ordained by God, through Moses, that the Ephod of the Jewish High Priest should be "all of Blue." The sacred Hebraic colours (still retained) are "blue," that of heaven and truth; "purple," that of royalty; and "red," that of sacrificial blood. The significance and bodily influences, widely attached to various colours, when characterizing clothing, and personal ornaments, are very remarkable. William Blake, who has been credited with a special artistic insight into sacred mysteries, argued for pink as the colour of angels; this hue denoting pure happiness. Plain white expresses calm, unbiassed judgment. Thus Bacon appeals to the "white light of reason." But none the less is there a strong belief in the unluckiness of white as a colour, particularly among the peasant class of Staffordshire. Probably this dislike has actually originated from the difficulty of keeping the garments clean in that black, smoky, manufacturing district. But, quite independent of any such notion is the historical fact that when our English King, Charles I was crowned in white, a general superstitious uneasiness was felt throughout the country. Having resolved to adopt this Coronation dress, he did it completely, even to his shoes, and hat. Why he preferred such attire to purple, which every English sovereign before him had worn on the same occasion, is not known. "To him that overcometh," saith a Scriptural promise, "will I give to eat of the hidden manna, and will give him a white stone." The Chinese, as is notorious, favour yellow as a colour. But amongst the Spaniards yellow figured largely as connected with the Inquisition, and with the proceedings of the hateful "Auto-da-fés."

The treble string of the guitar used to be called yellow, and actually was so tinted, because, as the explanation went, it represented bile. Yellow, or yellow with green, is the colour which has long been assigned to jesters all over Europe. Even so late as in Ford's time a murderer was arrayed in a yellow baize gown for the execution. Judas Iscariot always wears yellow in primitive Passion play which Spanish, and Portuguese sailors perform about our docks at Eastertide. A doctor of Penzance told lately in one of the Journals how a young man known to him defied prejudice the other day, and walked recklessly from Newquay to Bodmin whilst wearing a yellow neck-tie, out of bravado. Rheumatic fever seized him that same night.

It has been long noted how certain persons are so constituted that they associate music with colours. In 1864 Benjamin Lumley, director of Her Majesty's (Queen Victoria) Theatre, chatted about voice colours in his *Reminiscences*. Therein he gave a chart of vocal colours. Patti's voice was a drab, with touches of coral; Mario's was a beautiful violet; Sims Reeves' was a golden brown; and so on, with the voices of twenty other singers famous in their time. More recently again it has been stated that Melba's voice is "a high blue, splashed occasionally with purple;" and that the voice of Mr. Forbes Robertson is "violet speckled with green."

Charles Kingsley, writing to his wife from Chagford, in South Devon, September, 1849, (whither he had gone to rest, and for recruital of his health), addressed her thus :—

"Oh, rose is the colour of love, and youth;
And green is the colour of faith, and truth;
And brown is the fruitful clay.
The earth is fruitful, and faithful, and young;
And her bridal morn shall rise ere long;
And you shall know what the rocks, and the streams,
And the laughing greenwoods say."

According to Charles Dickens "such were the exquisite rural beauty, and the delightful charm of an English lane in the summer time, that even the heart of that sanctimonious humbug of a Pecksniff could be stirred thereby to something like a sense of happy innocence, and guileless joy." Poor old Martin Chuzzlewit who, because of his money, had been for years subject to the wiles, and snares of needy fortune-hunters, had at length in his dotage become the easy tool, and plaything of designing Pecksniff, the "good man" who, "with the happiness of this conviction painted on his face went forth upon his morning walk." "The summer weather in his bosom was reflected in the breast of nature. Through deep green vistas where the boughs arched overhead, and showed the sunlight flashing in the beautiful perspective; through dewy fern from which the startled hares leaped up, and fled at his approach; by mantled pools, and fallen trees, and down in hollow places, rustling among last year's leaves, whose scent woke memories of the past, the placid Pecksniff strolled. By meadow gates, and hedges fragrant with wild roses; and by thatched-roofed cottages, whose inmates humbly bow'd before him, as a man both good, and wise, the worthy Pecksniff walked, in tranquil meditation. The bee passed onward, humming of the work he had to do; the idle gnats, for ever going round and round in one contracting, and expanding ring, yet always going on as fast as he, danced merrily before him; the colour of the long grass came and went, as if the light clouds made it timid as they floated through the distant air. The birds,—so many Pecksniff consciences,—sang gaily upon every branch; and Mr. Pecksniff paid *his* homage to the day, carolling as he went so sweetly, and with so much innocence, that he only wanted feathers and wings to be a bird."

BLUE BELL TIME.

"The grass in the wood was green;
　　To-day it has all turned blue.
Had any one told me—even a queen—
　　I could not have thought it true.

I wonder if I'm awake.
　　Those trees never used to grow,
Bathing their feet in a deep blue lake.
　　I can't make it out, you know.

I always thought of the sky
　　High lifted over my ead:
So please can you tell me the reason why
　　It's under my feet instead?

> But the bellmen of Elfin Town
>   Ring out a delicate chime :
> The world has not turned upside down;
>   It is only—Bluebell Time."

REQUIESCAT.

> " Strew on her roses, roses,
>   And never a spray of yew.
> In quiet she reposes:
>   Ah! would that I did too."
>
> *Roses.* (*Matthew Arnold.*)

Reverting to the Chrysolite, this was said of old to "cool boiling water, and assuage wrath." The stone is named Peridot when of a deep olive-green; "Olivine" when of a deep yellowish-green; and "Chrysolite" when of a lighter, or greenish-yellow colour. Its most ancient title was Tharshish; and from its "signature" it was judged to be of a solary nature.

Imitation Turquoises are now made with the same chemical composition as the natural stone. So as to discriminate between these, if a splinter of the stone to be tested is heated in a platinum capsule, the true Turquoise will be reduced to a brownish-black powder, with a decrepitating sound; but the false Turquoise does not thus decrepitate; it fuses to a glass, or is reduced to a frit.

By way of **summarizing** the set of arguments, and considerations, now advanced, so as to determine what fundamental constituents, of a character calculated to affect the bodily welfare, each Precious Stone individually possesses, the entire system of such stones can be first broadly classified; through doing which the distinctive salutary, or noxious components of the several Precious Stones in each class will be more readily understood.

On the whole, therefore, Precious Stones may be arranged in three classes, as determined, each by its main basic chemical elements; these elements being more or less medicinal, as we shall categorically, and succinctly endeavour to show.

The said three classes are :—

1. The Carbon Class.
2. The Alumina Class.
3. The Silicon Class.

To the First Class, or Group, which is characterised by Carbon, as a common base, only one Precious Stone belongs, viz., the Diamond, which consists of pure carbon, sublimated, and crystallised to the acme of excellence.

Class, or Group the Second, includes all the Sapphires (properly so called), among which are the true Sapphire, the Oriental Ruby, the Oriental Emerald, the Oriental Topaz, and the Oriental Amethyst. All these are composed of pure alumina, coloured in different ways.

Class, or Group Three, includes the Opal, the Amethyst, and the Agates, (amongst which are the Cornelian, the Chalcedony, the Onyx, the Sardonyx, and the Bloodstone). These are all made up chiefly of silica.

Between the Alumina Class, and the Silica Class, are several kinds of stones which are composed partly of alumina, and partly of silica (united with some other substances). Among these are the true Emerald, and the true Topaz, which differ from the Oriental Emerald, and the Oriental Topaz. Other stones, such, for instance, as the Garnets, are made up of various substances, and are of minor value as Precious Stones. The Pearl, Coral, and Amber, also Malachite, the

Turquoise, and Lapis Lazuli, though used for Jewelry, are not really Precious Stones.

Regarding, therefore, these several Precious Stones, as being esteemed of leading importance, for the most favoured wear, and of highest value, we thus see that their chief basic principles, from a physical point of view, which are likely to influence for good, or for harm, the bodily condition of their wearers, and users, are Carbon, Alumina, and Silicon. Their minor constituents may be subsequently considered, in brief detail.

Carbon—vegetable charcoal, of which the Diamond is the sole, and supreme instance among Precious Stones,—is generally supposed by writers about medicinal agents to be an inert substance as a drug, or almost so. Certain physicians prescribe it in bulk, as finely-powdered charcoal, which shall act, perhaps, as checking fermentation, and absorbing foul gases within the digestive organs. But with this coarse view of the question we have no concern, or sympathy here.

Again, the element Alumina (or, oxide of alumina), though not recognized as an ordinary medicament of the Pharmacopœia, has been tested experimentally, and thoroughly, when triturated to a high degree of patiently-extended attenuation. Being thus scientifically utilised, alumina "seems to affect chiefly the sexual system, and the mucous membranes;"—several maladies of which latter organs have completely yielded under the influence of the mineral. Thus it has proved curative "in sensitiveness of the nose-lining membranes to cold; in chronic sore throat, with redness, and dryness thereof; in hacking cough from persistent irritability of the windpipe; in indigestion through deficient gastric juice; and in constipation from lack of intestinal secretion."

"The ailments for relief of which this alumina is particularly suitable are of a chronic character, especially when occurring in old persons, or in dry, and thin subjects." Under physical circumstances of such a nature the employment by outward wear, as Jewelry, (and in other well-devised ways), all the Sapphires should prove specially beneficial, as well as highly ornamental. Perhaps also under these bodily straits brief changes may be rung on the "true Emerald," and the "true Topaz," as compound gems of alumina, and silica.

Respecting Silica, (of which mineral element common flint is an oxide,) we have already had something explanatory to tell. Pure silica, (triturated to an infinitesimal degree of attenuation, and thus, as is alleged, potentially dynamised), or, flint, is shown to exercise medicinal properties, and to subserve curative uses which cannot be controverted. It would appear that such flint was employed as a medicine long ago; even by Theophrastus Paracelsus (translation, 1650), being praised by him, and his followers, as of virtue against stone in the kidney, or bladder; likewise in suppression of the milk during the nursing time of mothers. But the use of flint as a medicament became abandoned from that time until our more modern school, encouraged by the practical success attending the trituration of metals otherwise inert, applied the same process to insoluble, obdurate flint. It turns out that silica exercises a slow, steady action for good on the bodily nutrition when this is impaired, being better calculated to remedy organic changes, than to meet functional disorders which need a more immediate setting to rights. The Agates, the Amethyst, and the Opal are the jewels specially endowed with properties which serve to meet these physical requirements.

Being already at twenty-eight a surgeon much in advance of his times, though intolerably arrogant, Paracelsus travelled into Turkey, where he was made a captive for some while. On his return to his native country he assumed the title of "*utriusque medicinæ doctor*"; both physician and surgeon! He became appointed to the Chair of Medicine and Philosophy in the University of Basel. At his first lecture he ordered a brass vessel to be brought into the middle of the school; where, after he had cast in sulphur, and nitre, he proceeded to burn, in a very solemn manner, the books of Galen, and Avicenna, proclaiming that henceforth the physicians should all follow him; and no longer style themselves Galenists, but Paracelsists. "Know, Physicians," said he, "my cap has more learning in it than all your heads; my beard has more experience than all your academies." "The great fame, and success of this man," said Magus (1801), "have been attributed by many to his possessing a 'universal medicine.'" It is certain he was well acquainted with the use of opium; which the Galenists of those times rejected (as cold, in the fourth degree). Operinus relates that he made up certain little pills, of the colour, figure, and size, of mouse-turds, which were nothing but opium. These he always carried with him, and prescribed them in most diseases; particularly if attended with pain. "To be alone possessed of the use of so extraordinary, and noble a medicament as opium, was sufficient to make him famous." With regard to this drug, Lord Macartney has explained that the vulgar saying, "running a muck," owes its origin to the fact that the Malays, and the Japanese, when under an extraordinary dose of opium, become frantic, and rush about, stabbing the objects of their hate, whilst shouting as they run— " A mok! " " A mok ! " (" Kill ! " " Kill ! ")

Another grand remedy with Paracelsus was Turbith mineral, (the yellow subsulphate of mercury). In his early manhood he had mixed much with the miners of Hungary, and Germany; thus becoming acquainted with the virtues, and medicinal effects of various Minerals, and metals. He thereby learnt to employ mercury (likewise in small pills) frequently, with curative results. "His famous laudanum did such wonders," says Mr. Robt. Boyle (1670), " that Operinus himself hath this passage of it:—*De Laudano suo (in pilulis instar murium stercoris) ita gloriabatur ut non dubitarit affirmare ejus solis usu se e mortuis vivos reddere posse; idque aliquoties dum apud ipsum fui, re ipsa declaravit.*"

Reverting to Carbon; medical experimentalists of another school have indisputably brought about beneficial, and curative results by administering vegetable charcoal, carefully and patiently triturated, until the millionth of a grain, and no more, was the dose taken at stated intervals.

The charcoal used in this way has been made from wood, of the poplar, beech, or birch trees. Doses of the said remedy, given thus infinitesimally, will act dynamically rather than as if merely chemical, or roughly medicinal.

"One of the results," says a physician, whilst employing the highly-attenuated charcoal, "coincides singularly with its chemical action when given in bulk. I mean, its power over flatulence, whether existing alone, or associated with acidity, and heart-burn; it is my favourite remedy for this condition. I have seen the most distressing oppression, and troubled breathing through intestinal distension, (as recurring grievously after every meal), quite removed by its use." "Then there is a state of bodily strengthlessness for which the highly-triturated charcoal is likewise a specific remedy. The condition is apart from any feverishness, and is characterised by manifest evidences (such as blueness, and coldness, through defective circulation, and imperfect oxydation of the blood.") "When such a state exists, in affections of the aged, this carbon is a most effectual rallier." And under similar physical conditions we may plausibly believe that to wear one, or more diamonds, of fine water, in immediate proximity to the skin, whether in finger-rings, or, without any intervention of setting, over the site of this, or that vital organ, will secure like benefits to the patient.

Furthermore, on the same principle, the possession, and constant wear of exquisite diamonds may be relied upon for a salutary exercise of dynamic, or so to say, spiritual, virtues :—

"For, Spirits, when they please,
Can either sex assume, or both ; so soft,
And uncompounded is their essence pure ;
Not ty'd, or manacled with joint, or limb,
Nor founded on the brittle strength of bones,
Like cumbrous flesh ; but in what shape they choose,
Diluted, or condens'd, bright or obscure,
Can execute their airy purposes ;
And works of love, or enmity, fulfil."—*Milton.*

"The more jewels," thought, and said, Madame de Barrera (1860), "the more guardian spirits ; and, surely, very safe may be deemed the fair one whose form is encompassed by angels."

Theophrastus Bombastus Paracelsus (1493 to 1541),

"the Reformer of Medicine," "Luther Alter," has been given his truest conception of personal character in the noble poem of Browning—*Paracelsus*. He picked up his scientific knowledge (which was sound, and extensive) by any means rather than from books. "All reading," said he, "is a footstool to practice, and a mere feather-broom. He who meditates, discovers something." His only volume was Nature, whom he interrogated at first hand. He died at the age of forty-eight, having been attacked by certain physicians who were his jealous enemies, so that by reason of a fall, he sustained a fracture of the skull, which proved quickly fatal.

"The wondrous Paracelsus, life's dispenser;
Fate's commissary, idol of the schools, and courts."

Some innate virtue, or power, must have been presupposed even by primitive barbarous nations, who valued as articles of luxury precious stones (whilst as yet lacking lustre, and play of light, because still uncut); and gold, simply for its weight.

"The deep, and slow action of Silica makes it appropriate to chronic rather than acute maladies." M. Teste says, "It is especially suited to fat persons, of a temperament partly lymphatic, and partly sanguine." For scrofulous troubles of the joints, or bones, silica is an admirable remedy. And, curiously enough, silica has the unique virtue of controlling excessive perspiration of the feet; not an uncommon affliction.

Besides forming the basic constituent of those Precious Stones which we have particularized in this respect, silica is a constituent of several mineral waters; among others, those of Teplitz, and Gastein, where it exists in the proportion of three-fifths to three-tenths of a grain in the pound. In the American springs of Missisquoi, and Bethesda, it forms a much larger percentage; the former spring containing ·016000 parts in a thousand. And these waters can boast a great reputation in their own country for giving curative results against cancer, tumours, diabetes, and passage of albumin from the kidneys.

Flint is employed by many persons as a test for ascertaining the purity of silver coins. This is done by rubbing them on the flint, when, if the mark which they leave be not perfectly white, they are rejected as spurious.

It will not be out of place to make some mention here of a kindred mineral, the Jade, which, by its names, and its character, bears an implied medicinal, and remedial significance. This Jade is of a mineral species known as "Nephrite," from the Greek word *nephros*—the kidney; being so named from its reputed efficacy in disorders of the kidneys. It is a compact variety of hornblende, consisting of a silicate of magnesium, and calcium, having been known formerly as the "kidney-stone."

In past times the conquerors of Mexico and Peru were acquainted with the character of this mineral substance, Jade; which they named, in Spanish, *Aspiedrade Hijada*, or "Stone of the loins."

Jade is but seldom employed for jewelry in this country; but throughout the whole of Asia it is a favourite stone. The colour varies from a creamy white to a dark green. It cannot be actually polished, because "the superficies always sweats with fat, as if anointed with oil." Mysius said, "It expels the stone, and the gravel, being tied to the arm." Schroder likewise has commended it against the stone, and to expel gravel; "the which it cures being tied to the arm, or hip, or worn in bracelets about the neck." It was first mentioned by Monardes, 1565.

Its virtues are mainly dependent on radiations from the silica, alumina, magnesia, and iron (a trace), which enter into the composition of the stone.

The said mineral is a native silicate of calcium, and magnesium. It never exhibits crystalline form, nor cleavage; and, whilst not hard of structure, is remarkably tough. Its colour is subject to great diversity; some varieties of the stone presenting almost every shade of green, whilst others are yellowish, grey, or even white. By the Chinese, who know this mineral as the "Yu-stone," it is often elaborately carved. New Zealand is one of the famous localities for Jade; the natives there work it into amulets, (and axe-heads), with much labour. It is known by the Maoris as "Green-stone." The original American Jade was "Spleen-stone," another significant term denoting curative powers as possessed by this mineral. By the Maories, "Hei Tiki" Jade, of dark olive-green colour, arded as a luck-bringing stone, and is cut into rous shapes for small ornaments to be worn about erson. Some of these charms, and trinkets are of it, grotesque design. They have found their way is country, and are now displayed for sale in the -windows of several London jewellers.

e Ancients classified the different varieties of Jade vn to them under seventy-seven headings; but for nineral itself they had no distinct generic name. cording to the famous Philosopher Khivan Ghung, wrote in the seventh century B.C., the contempla- of a piece of Jade opens to the eyes of a true Chinaman a whole history of poetic visions. In it he sees reflected nine of the highest attainments of humanity. In its glossy smoothness he recognizes the emblem of Benevolence; in its bright polish he sees Knowledge emblematized; in its unbending firmness, Righteousness; in its modest harmlessness, Virtuous action; in its rarity, and spotlessness, Purity; in its imperishableness, Endurance; in the way in which it exposes its every flaw, Ingenuousness; in the fact that, though of surpassing beauty, it passes from hand to hand without becoming sullied, Moral conduct; and in the circumstance that when struck it gives forth a note which floats sharply and distinctly to a distance, Music.

"It is this," adds the Philosopher, "which makes men esteem the Jade as most precious, and leads them to regard it as a diviner of judgments, and as a charm of happy omen." Other philosophers have pronounced this mysterious mineral the very essence of heaven, and earth.

So much for Jade, which has become known especially because of the supposition that a piece of it when suspended to the neck will dissolve calculous stones in the kidneys, or bladder. It is a crypto-crystalline variety of hornblende; having been originally termed the "Spleen-stone."

As a deliberate conclusion, therefore, from this series of facts (in some measure theoretical; in other respects confirmed by practical experience), we commend to persons whose health, and comfort are interfered with by either of the infirmities, or liabilities which have been now enumerated, to favour the Opal, the Amethyst, and Agates (comprising the Carnelian, the Chalcedony, the

Onyx, the Sardonyx, and the Bloodstone) for personal wear, of a continued sort, and for other such outward uses next the skin as may be found feasible, convenient, and pleasant. In these cases also a variation of the jewelry chosen for wear may be sometimes made to the compound gems (of both silica, and alumina), to wit,—the true Emerald, and the true Topaz.

And we would by no means overlook the additional virtues, and properties ascribed of old, to, or assumed later on for, the Precious Stones as considered by us, whether traditionally, or speculatively, in the body of this our book. The probabilities may be fairly taken for granted that grounds, more or less valid, and trustworthy, warrant a belief in the premises adduced, as well as in the practices empirically commended. Quoting again Mr. Boyle's *Experimental Philosophie* (1675), he bids us " not prætermit among the proofs of the efficacy of appended remedies those memorable examples which are deliver'd by the judicious Boetius de Boot, 1630, concerning the virtues of that sort of remedies."

" The employment of Precious Stones for medicinal purposes," wrote De Boot, " originated from an Arabian belief which held that they are the mystic residence of spirits." They were first worn as amulets; then gradually came to be given internally.

A certain stone (of Laurentian gneiss) greenish-yellow of hue, is found in the Island of Iona, one of the Hebrides, on the Western Coast of Scotland, where Columba founded his first monastery, 563 A.D. To amulets made from this kind of stone is attributed, even now, a power of protecting their wearers from all danger by drowning. Small crosses, finger-rings, breastpins, and brooches, are prepared therefrom for personal adornment, with this salutary view, and are for disposal to tourists who visit the Island.

CORALS.

CORALS, though beyond the actual pale of Precious Stones, are nevertheless to be in some sort regarded as jewelry. Scientifically they are "calcareous aggregated skeletons of defunct coralligenous zoophytes."

Each single polype has inhabited one of the diminutive cells which are now massed together on a common earthy base. By continued growth, and aggregation, great banks of Coral become formed, which are known as Coral reefs. "These are confined to seas in which the temperature of the water during the winter does not sink, on an average, to below 68° or 66° Fahr."

The most important Coral fisheries extend along the coasts of Tunis, Algeria, and Morocco. Red Coral is also obtained in the vicinity of Naples, and on the coasts of Corsica, Catalonia, and Provence. A condition very essential to the welfare of living Coral polypes is an abundant supply of pure, and properly aerated seawater. The Red, or Precious Coral (*Corallium rubrum*) is, and has been from remote times, very highly prized for jewelry, personal adornment, and for decorative purposes. Furthermore, it exercises distinct, and very beneficial medicinal properties. Of old, too, it was highly esteemed in India as a substance endowed with occult sacred virtues.

The Gauls, as Pliny relates, were in the habit of using coloured Coral for ornamenting their weapons of war, and their helmets. Among the Romans branches of

Coral were hung about the necks of children to preserve them from danger, or to cure some of their ailments.

Even at the present day, in Italy, Coral is worn as a protection from the evil eye ; and by females as a cure for sterility. In colour the Red Coral varies, through all shades of red, from a deep crimson to a delicate rose pink, or flesh-colour, fine tints of which are rare, and highly prized. Sometimes also Coral is obtained of a milk-white hue. While the price of the finest tints of rose-pink may range from eighty pounds to one hundred and twenty pounds an ounce, ordinary red-coloured small pieces sell for about two pounds the ounce ; and the diminutive fragments called " collette," as used for children's necklaces, cost about five shillings an ounce. In China large spheres of good-coloured Coral command high prices, being in great requisition there for the Button of Office worn by a Mandarin.

" By means of certain acids," says M. Pomet, " the Japanese make a tincture of Red Coral, which is afterwards reduced to a so-called syrup ; this being reckoned an admirable cordial, and useful to purifie, and cleanse the mass of blood." " There is likewise a magistery, and salt made of this substance; but the most common way of using it is when reduced to an impalpable powder, by levigating it upon a marble, with rose-water, etc." Oddly enough, Mr. Tournefort (1712), generally a correct authority, and translated by M. Pomet for the French King,— has erroneously described Coral as " a plant that grows at the bottom of the sea ; it has neither leaf, flower, nor seed ; nevertheless, it sticks to the rocks in the nature of a root, and is cover'd with a bark, that is adorn'd with pores like stars, which descend to the bottom." " It is undoubtedly increased by its seed, which is the opinion countenanc'd by all those that rank Coral amongst the number of plants."

Again, Dr. John Schroder (1660) has written: "Coral is a shrub, growing under the sea-water." He adds, as to its "Vertues." "All Coral dryes, cools, binds; strengthens the heart chiefly, then the stomach, and liver; purifies the blood; makes men merry, (but the Black Coral makes them melancholy); it stops all fluxes of the belly, and womb; it prevents epilepsies in children, if you give ten grains to a new-born child (before it takes anything else) in the mother's milk; it is outwardly good against ulcers, and fills them with flesh; it helps to extenuate scars, to stop weeping eyes, and to refresh the sight, put into collyria. The dose to give is from twenty grains to one drachm. The tincture of coral is of great force as against convulsions."

The solid, compact part of the animal Coral, or polydom, in the case of Red Coral, is mainly carbonate of lime, with small quantities of carbonate of magnesium, oxide of iron, and organic matters; the exact nature of the red colouring matter remaining unknown. The insects, polypes, which produce Coral, resemble eight-pointed stars, notched on each point, with a mouth in the centre. The earthy skeleton further contains fluorides of calcium, and magnesium, phosphate of lime, alumina, and a small quantity of silica.

Among the ancient Greeks Coral was thought to "baffle witchcraft," counteract poisons, protect from tempests, and robbers, and, mixed in powder with seed-corn, (rather a costly agricultural agent!), to secure growing crops from thunderstorms, blight, caterpillars, and locusts.

One of the Greek names for Coral was Gorgeia, from

the tradition that blood dripped from the Head of Medea, which Perseus had deposited on some branches near the sea-shore; which blood, becoming hard, was taken by the Sea Nymphs, and planted in the sea.

Formerly Coral was thought to deepen in colour when worn by a man, and to become paler when used thus by a woman.

Dr. Salmon (1696) ordered, "To prepare Coral": "Take such a quantity as you think convenient; make it into a fine powder, by grinding it upon a porphyry; or in an iron mortar; drop on it by degrees a little rose-water; and form it into balls for use." "After this same manner, crabs' eyes, pearl, oister shells, and precious stones, are prepared to make up cordials compounded of them, and other suitable materials, for the strengthening the heart, in fevers, and such-like violent diseases, and to restore the decays of nature."

From our *Animal Simples* (1890) we make—without apology—some few final quotations about Coral, which seem to us well worthy of repetition here. "Red Coral, powdered, when given experimentally in somewhat large doses, has been found to excite a violent spasmodic cough, with suffocating irritation of the windpipe. Acting on which knowledge, and being mindful that much reduced doses of a violent medicament will commonly act in precisely an opposite way, (proving curative to symptoms of incidental illness similar to those which a larger toxic quantity of such medicament has been proved to induce), M. Teste, and others have found the diluted powder of Coral almost a specific for curing whooping-cough, and the spurious croup of young children." Furthermore, "'For a chronic convulsive cough,' says M. Teste, 'it is like water thrown upon fire.' This false croup coming on distressingly at night owes its origin to some irritation, reflected most commonly from teething, as then in progress; so that it is a piece of true wisdom (combined with sponsorial affection) to give as a christening present to a baby a finger-length of Red Coral, mounted in silver, with tinkling bells, and a welcome whistle; in anticipation of this tooth-cutting time, and its attendant physical risks. The said bells, which may be supposed an adjunct to the toy for delighting the child, were originally designed in miniature to frighten away evil spirits; just as church bells are employed, (or were primarily), with the same object in view. Rabbi Benoni in the fourteenth century, said to be one of the most profound alchemists of his time, pronounced the axiom that, " the Red Coral is a cure for indigestion if worn constantly about the person."

Armand de Villeneuve asserts that ten grains of Coral given to an infant in its mother's milk, provided this be its first food, will effectually preserve it from epileptic, or any other fits, throughout life. Byron wrote, " So children cutting teeth receive a Coral."

Dear, fascinating old Izaak Walton, in his *Compleat Angler*, makes Maudlin say, to the fishers, " with a merry heart ":—

> " A belt of straw, and ivy buds,
> With Coral Clasps, and Amber Studs;
> And if these pleasures may thee move,
> Come, live with me, and be my love! "

" To sweeten the blood, and cure acidity, take Coral, the largest and reddest you can get," teaches Boyle, *Collection of Remedies*. " Reduce it by grinding on a marble stone to an impalpable powder, of which, made without acids, give the patient once, or twice a day, as needs shall require, a large dose, ordinarily about sixty grains at a time, mixed in a dessertspoonful of water, or milk; and let him long continue the use of this."

About Italy, especially in the neighbourhood of Naples, charms of Red Coral in the shape of a partly-closed hand, or pieces of the Coral in form like a tiny carrot, (evidently phallic), are worn, for the purpose of protecting the possessors from being bewitched by the *mal occhio* (evil eye).

"The shining Coral," says Dr. Schroder, "according to Paracelsus, makes an amulet against fear, and frights, fascinations, incantations, poysons, epilepsies, melancholy, devil's assaults, and thunder."

"The White Coral hung about the neck to touch the breast, stops abdominal colic, and dispels the pain thereof."

Thus also Marbodus tells about the Coral: *Collo suspensus pellit de ventre dolorem.*

Sir John Harrington, in his *School of Salerne* (1624), has enjoined to "Alwaies in your hands use either Corall, or Yellow Amber, or some like Precious Stone, to be worn in a ring upon the little finger of the left hand; for, in stones, as also in herbes, there is great efficacie, and vertue; but they are not altogether perceived by us; for surely the vertue of an herbe is great, but much more the vertue of a Precious Stone, which is very likely they are endued with occult, and hidden vertues."

"Coral," says the *Jewel Home of Art and Nature,* "hath some special sympathy with nature; for the best Coral being worn about the neck will turn pale, and wan, if the party that wears it is sick; and will come to its former colour again as they recover health.

"I know," saith Magus (1801) " how to compose Coral amulets which, if suspended even by a thread shall, (God assisting), prevent all harms and accidents of violence, from fire, or water, and help them to withstand all their diseases."

In the *Three Ladies of London* (1584) we read, " You may say, Jet will take up a straw; Amber will make one fat; Coral will look pale when you be sick; and Crystal will stanch blood."

THE PEARL.

THE PEARL is well said to be the purest, and loveliest of all gems. Its supposed origin was long a mystery; the general modern belief concerning this question is that some foreign body within the shell of the oyster, (this being almost invariably the Pearl's habitat), acts as an irritant to the mollusc, which therefore proceeds to coat over, for self-protection, the invading offender with successive layers of nacreous matter.

At one time Pearls were believed to be the production of celestial dew; at another time to be oyster eggs. But, proceeding on the theory advanced above, Linnæus induced the Government of Sweden to give him £450, with permission to teaze mechanically the fresh-water mussel, (a pearl-bearing mollusc), within its shell, at his will. He did this; and produced pearls; but they proved far dearer than customary pearls obtained in the natural way from the oyster.

Pearls do not naturally appear until the oyster's fourth year; and when examined after being procured, they are found to be chemically nothing but carbonate of lime, and gelatine. These substances, arranged in successive concentric layers, like those of an onion, form the whole volume of the peerless Pearl. The finest Pearls come from Bahrein, (Persian Gulf), from whence the best are sent to Europe; and the smaller pearls to China, where they are sold by weight, for medicinal purposes. When the oysters are brought to land, at the Pearl Fisheries, (of which the most famous are at Ceylon), they are all thrown into a mass together, and left there for several days to decay, so that the gems may be more easily detached. But if left too long in what presently becomes a foul, putrid mass, the pearls grow yellow, and lose their purity of sheen, and colour.

When detached from the shells they are shaken through sieves of successive fineness, those sieves which have the largest interstices keeping back only the largest pearls; and so on through the whole quantity of ten sizes down to the small grains known as seed-pearls, which, if not very valuable, are yet very pretty, if well-wrought. When a lot of the oysters, heaped together, had become "matured," (as Mr. Somers Somerset has told from personal observation, 1907), it was taken away in sacks to a spot some distance apart from all dwelling-houses; a large tub was procured, and partly filled with water; and the putrefying contents of one sack were emptied into it. To describe the appalling stench which immediately arose is an impossible task; a stink quite overwhelming, and absolutely unendurable! In a moment the surface of the water was covered with thousands of maggots, struggling wildly to escape out of the tub. These were drained off, and fresh water was poured in; while the shells were picked out from beneath the water, tapped together so as to shake out any pearls which might have chanced to adhere within them, and then thrown away. The putrid molluscs now remained in a mass under the water; and this was kneaded by the men, (who must not, without permission, remove their hands from the tub during the operation). Every few minutes a man, churning the filthy mixture, would come upon a pearl, and would hand it over. This continued until the whole mass of material had been broken up, when it was removed in cloths, and left in the sun to dry. Even when such drying had taken place the smell was horrible; and among these unsavoury remains it was necessary to search for the smaller pearls which had escaped notice during the washing. The quantity thus discovered was quite extraordinary; and, though the majority of these secondhand pearls proved small, or misshapen, yet a few good pearls appeared amongst them. "I do not think that after a few days at the fishery it is possible ever to regard these beautiful jewels with the same admiration as before." "One remembers, when looking at their wonderful refinement, and splendour, the ghastly corruption in which they are discovered." "One remembers, also, that they are but a disease, a kind of tumour, epidemic in certain places: and, though the pearl itself shines bright, and clear, among the filth in which it is first seen, one does not forget how many days must pass before the fœtid odour of putrid flesh finally leaves it clean, and pure, and fit to be agreeably worn."

Pearls are made round, and polished, only by pearl-dust; the best of these gems being pear-shaped, like the famous jewel which Cleopatra, Queen of Old Egypt, recklessly proud, and prodigal, is said to have drunk in a royal draught of vinegar thus rendered priceless.

Pearls are subject to a strange malady, which disease

is communicable from one pearl to another. Not infrequently all the pearls in a casket are attacked thereby, and thus become reduced in a short time to dust.

As regards the classic story of Cleopatra swallowing recklessly for a wager one of her immensely valuable Pearl ear-rings, dissolved in vinegar, competent medical authorities assert that no acid which the human stomach could endure is capable of entirely dissolving a pearl, even after prolonged maceration therein. Barbot, on trying the experiment, found that the outer layer was reduced to a jelly, whilst that beneath was not at all affected. No doubt the wily Queen swallowed the pearl whole, in some potation more pleasant than vinegar; feeling secure of its recovery within a short time, undamaged. And she invented the fiction of its instantaneous, and complete dissolution, (which rested entirely on her own testimony), in order to win the wager.

Concerning the Pearl—*Unio*—Marbodus says :—

"Auget opus idem sese reverenter habentes;
Omnibus in causis dans persuasoria verba."

Archbishop Trench has described with poetic sweetness the fanciful formation of a Pearl by natural means :—

"A dewdrop, falling on the wild sea-wave,
Exclaimed, with fear, 'I perish in this grave';
But, in a shell received, that drop of dew
Unto a Pearl of marvel'ous beauty grew,
And, happy now, the grace did magnify
Which thrust it forth—as it had feared—to die;
Until again, 'I perish quite,' it said,
Torn by rude divers from its ocean bed;—
Oh, unbelieving! so it came to gleam
Chief Jewel in a Monarch's diadem."

The Pearl "of purest ray serene" (poetically), is practically, according to the *National Druggist*, a prosaic substance, the product of morbid functional derangement affecting the kidneys of the pearl oyster, or mussel. Chemical analysis shows this gem to be a compound of phosphate, and carbonate of lime, mixed with an organic substance called conchyoline. These materials are deposited in concentric layers, the nucleus, or centre of which is almost invariably a foreign substance: a grain of sand, an atom of shell, an animal parasite, or one of many other diminutive molecules, occupying the point of concentration within the pearly matter around it, and making eventually a concretion; which is expelled by the kidney wherein it has become formed. It escapes almost invariably into the closely neighbouring genital gland. Thus the highly-prized, and lovely gem is " nothing more nor less than a urinary calculus; whilst its parent. the famous, and aristocratic pearl oyster, is actually a poor, unhappy, gravelly mollusc.

Pearls should never be wrapped in jewellers' wool, but should be kept in magnesia, or in common hair-powder, and never suffered to become damp. British Pearls are obtained from the mussel, not from the oyster. Pearls are sometimes coloured black, and pink, and roseate, and bluish-grey, and pale yellow; but neither of these is equal in value, nor in beauty, to the true, or typical Pearl; the symbol of purity, chastity, and all feminine virtues. Moreover, pearls are religious emblems, as well as ornaments of favourite, and fashionable wear. In the " New Jerusalem " each of the twelve doors was one entire pearl; likewise a Pearl was one of the sacred gems of the priestly Ephod. Furthermore, in the Hindu mythology Pearls play almost as important a part as flowers; none of the gods, or goddesses, being depicted without a profuse embellishment of these gems, together with others more rightfully called Precious Stones. Of late Pearls have become very popular among English ladies who lead the fashions.

When absolutely without flaw, or blemish, these gems are, relatively speaking, as valuable as Diamonds, or Rubies. In determining their worth experts look first at the colour. Pearls should appear as if covered with a glistening skin, either pure white, or of an ivory white, faintly tinged with pink.

Round Pearls, or those shaped like the pear, are held equally in repute ; but any spots, excrescences, clefts, dots, shadows, or other such marks, are considered to be blemishes ; and detract from the value of the precious stones. For a single Pearl, of what may be called standard quality, and of perfectly spherical form, the price can scarcely be stated with exactness. Such a Pearl is worth, perhaps ninety pounds, if it weighs one carat; four times as much if it weighs two carats ; and eight times as much if it weighs four carats. Button Pearls, which have one side convex, and the other flat, are less valuable than round pearls ; but pear-shaped Pearls often fetch a still higher price. The majority of Pearls used in jewelry are half Pearls, i.e., Pearls sawn in half.

Seed Pearls are perforated by careful drilling. The Pearls which were set of old in antique Roman ornaments have rarely survived entire to the present day. Sometimes the place of such Pearls in their setting has come to be represented by a small brownish residue. Sometimes again the reduced form of each Pearl is still to be seen, deprived of much of its lustre by the long-continued action of water charged with carbonic, and vegetable solvent acids from the earth.

The substance of the solitary Pearl is identical with

the "mother-of-Pearl," or nacreous material which lines the interior of the shell. It consists of that form of carbonate of lime which is known as "aragonite," being harder, and heavier than "calcite," the other, and commoner kind. Pearls are secreted by the mantle of the mollusc in the same way as that by which the shell is formed. It may be asked, "How does the detached Pearl first come into being?" Its occurrence is the outcome of irritation to the mantle caused by the intrusion of some foreign body: which foreign body is frequently a minute parasitic animal (a *Cestode* larva).

The Chinese take advantage of such action, introducing for their purpose some such a foreign body within the bivalve shells of a fresh-water mussel (*Dipsas plicata*). They keep the mussels in a tank, and insert between the shell and the body of the mollusc rounded bits of mother-of-pearl, or little metal images of Buddha. In either case the object introduced becomes slowly coated, and cemented to the shell. A specimen of this may be seen in the Shell Gallery of the Natural History Museum, at Kensington.

"Pearls," wrote Leonardus (London, 1750), "have physical virtues exceeding the commodiousness of Ornament: being boil'd in meat they cure the Quartan Ague; bruised, and given with milk, they heal putrid Ulcers; and, being so taken, wonderfully clear the voice. If mixed with Sugar they yield help in Pestilential Fevers; and they render him who carries them chaste."

The "oneirocritics," or interpreters of dreams, were wont to draw their interpretations from Pearls. Among the medicines given to Charles VI. of France, for trying to restore his reason, a decoction of Pearls with distilled water was administered.

Margaritæ significant lacrymarum flumen;—" Pearls portend a torrent of tears,"—declared Astrampsychus. Pearls have for ages been thus significant of tears. A few nights before the assassination of Henry IX. of France, his Queen dreamed that all the jewels in her crown were changed into Pearls; which, she was told, betokened tears.

The " Majoon," in which there is a large quantity of Pearls, is much sought-after by Asiatics as a restorative. (But Diamonds are never used by them medicinally, being considered too hard for absorption.)

A Rabbinical story tells that Abraham, on approaching Egypt, concealed his wife Sarah in a locked chest, so that no one might see her surpassing beauty. On arriving at the place for paying custom he was asked for the dues, which he at once said he would pay. " Carriest thou garments ? " asked the tax-collector ; and Abraham without demur offered for such, (as well as for gold, and other valuables specified questioningly by the same official), their required duty. " Surely then it must be pearls thou bearest with thee ? " said the collector at last; to which Abraham replied, " I will pay for pearls." Seeing that they could name nothing of value for which Abraham was not willing to pay custom, the officers said, " Then it must be that thou openest the box, and let us see what is therein." So they opened the box ; and the whole land of Egypt was illumined by the lustre of Sarah's beauty, far exceeding even that of pearls.

At Cleopatra's famous banquet Cæsar quaffed costly wines from large cups made of such rare Gems :—

" Gemmæque capaces
Excepere merum."

The famous feat of Cleopatra in swallowing a Pearl of fabulous price is recorded to have been tried somewhat before by Clodius, a son of Æsopus, the player, who, having discovered that dissolved Pearls possess the most exquisite flavour, did not keep his knowledge to himself, but gave a Pearl apiece to each of his guests to swallow. In former times powdered Pearls were considered invaluable for stomach complaints.

The occult medicinal virtues of Pearls were highly esteemed in the early ages. "Rich honesty," saith Touchstone, in Shakespeare's *As you Like it*, "swells like a miser, Sir, in a poor house; as your Pearl in a foul oyster." The chemical composition of the Pearl is entirely carbonate of lime, and organic matter. It is readily affected by acids, and by fœtid gases; furthermore it calcines on exposure to heat. Throughout China, Pearls are used medicinally; a belief existing among Orientals that these gems possess great virtues in syncopes, fluxes of blood, and other such exhausting losses. In Bengal at one time virgins wore Pearls on their arms as a preservative of virtue.

Dr. Schroder, "that most famous, and faithful chymist," wrote (in Latin), 1669, concerning Pearls, "They are round stones found in some shell-fish, produced of the same peristoma by which the shells are made. They are an excellent cordial, that strengthens the balsam of life, resists poison, pestilence, and putrefaction, and clears the spirits; and they are so famous that men in the greatest agonies are refreshed thereby." Paracelsus (translated, 1650) attributed much virtue to the salt of Pearl; "for," said he, "though the process of making this be simple, yet, believe my experience, the Pearls therein have a wonderful operation; not from art, but from nature; the vertue is in the grosse substance, and cannot work but like a dead body; but, its resolution being made, the body thereof is revived." "The salt of Pearl is made by dissolving it in vinegar, or juyce of barberries, or limons, and inspissating after filtration until the salt remains, and then washing." "The Pearls need no poudering, for they dissolve whole, or without digestion, in distilled vinegar." "As to Pearls," wrote Pomet, 1712, "all the Eastern countries are much of our minds in choosing them white. For, I have always made it my observation that they love the whitest Pearl, the whitest Diamonds, the whitest bread, and the fairest women." "All Pearl is esteemed cordial, proper against infection, recruiting, and restoring lost spirits; but their chief virtue is to destroy, and kill the acids, as other alcalies do, and likewise to correct the acrimony of the stomach." "Pearl is also good against a canine appetite, a flux of the belly, and the hemorrhage. The dose is from six or ten grains to a dram." "Ladies of quality use the fine-ground powder of seed Pearls to give a lustre and beauty to the face. They make use thereof likewise with acids, etc., in a magistery, and a salt, to which they attribute large virtues; besides other imaginary preparations, as 'the arcanum of Pearl,' the flowers, spirits, essences, tinctures, and the like; to pick fools' pockets; but the best and only useful preparation of it is the powder, well levigated." "Then, as to the Mother of Pearl, this is to be got from great greenish oyster shells that are rough and uneven on the outside, and of a white, inclining to be a little greenish, within. These shells serve for several sorts of fine works; a great many people preserve, and grind them into powder;

after which they form them into troches, and sell 'em for prepared Pearl. When ground to powder on a porphyry this Mother of Pearl is used by women amongst their pomatum, for a fucus, to beautify the face."

Said Sairey Gamp, (the Monthly Nurse, for all time), an authority about the Skin, by virtue of her function: " Now aint we rich in beauty this here joyful arternoon! I'm sure," (dropping at the same time several curtseys to Ruth Pinch, and smilingly shaking her head frequently), " and often have I said to Mrs. Harris, ' Oh! Mrs. Harris, Ma'am, your countenance is quite a angel's — which, but for pimples it would be!' 'No, Sairey Gamp,' says she, 'Harris had it done afore marriage, at ten and six; and wore it faithful next his heart till the colour run, when the money was declined to be give back, and no arrangement could be come to. But he never said it was a angel's, Sairey, wotever he might have thought.'"

The pigment known as "Pearl white" is an oxide of the metal Bismuth; this powder is sometimes made use of by ladies as a cosmetic for the skin, but it turns black when assailed by any sulphur-containing fumes; and such ladies as thus mentioned, after bathing in the Harrogate waters have come from the bath tawny-coloured of complexion.

A Pearl of the first water should possess a perfect "skin," and a fine "orient"; being of a clear, almost white, translucent colour; with a subdued iridescent sheen.

The largest known Pearl is one, of irregular shape, to be seen at the South Kensington Museum, in the collection of Mr. Beresford Hope. This magnificent

Pearl weighs three ounces, has a circumference of four and a half inches; and is surmounted by an enamelled, and jewelled gold crown.

River Pearls are produced by the fresh-water mussels inhabiting the mountain streams of temperate climates, in the northern hemisphere,—Scotland, Wales, Ireland, Saxony, Bohemia, Bavaria, Lapland, and Canada. The Pearls of Britain, as known in former times, are mentioned by Tacitus, and by Pliny. A breast-plate studded with British Pearls was dedicated by Julius Cæsar to Venus Genitrix.

Dr. Schroder, (as we have related in our *Animal Simples*: 1890), declares that these gems cure heart-burnings beyond other medicines, and are the chief of all cordial medicaments; "the crude powder," says he, "is, in my opinion, much beyond the salt of magistery."

"In the salt, or magistery of Pearls," wrote Dr. Fuller—"Body of prescripts": 1710, "though vinegar is ordered by the London College as a dissolvent, yet we know by experience that juyce of limons, or spirit of sulphur, dissolves them much better and easier." Their first Pharmacopœia was written in Latin, (1696), being dedicated to Gault Charleton, M.D., President of the College of Physicians. It was further styled *Bateana*, and included the *Arcana Goddardiana* of Jonathan Goddard, M.D.

Imitation Pearls are small spheres blown on tubes of slightly opalescent glass, and coated internally with a preparation made from the silvery scales of the bleak, roach, and similar small fish; this preparation being known as "Essence d'Orient." The little opalescent globe first receives, while still soft, a few very slight dents; then a coating of the pearly film, mixed with some isinglass, is introduced, by being blown, whilst hot, into each bead through a small glass tube; after which, when the essence is dry, the beads are filled with melted wax, this giving them weight, and making them less liable to become broken.

While dining with a friend at a Hamburg restaurant not long ago, a lady found in an oyster served at table a Pearl, appraised at one hundred and fifty pounds. The proprietor claimed this valuable "treasure trove;" and the question to whom it rightly belonged was brought before a Court of Law; when the decision was given against the restaurant proprietor, the judge holding that by purchasing the oysters the guest became entitled to anything found in them.

Pearls require very special treatment, and particular care, if they are to look pure, and to show a proper lustre. The reason why they appear dull, and colourless on some persons, whilst regaining their sheen and brightness with others, is mainly due to the effect produced by the constitutional condition of the wearer, it being a well-known fact that Pearls never show to advantage with weakly persons. As a rule they are said to exhibit a double amount of brilliancy when worn next the skin. They should never be kept locked up, where the rays of the sun cannot reach them; since any continued deprivation of light, and air, has a deadening, and bleaching effect on them, which frequently needs years of special treatment to counteract. A Pearl necklace of historical interest from the collection of M. Thiers is now in the Louvre Museum at Paris, which is rapidly forfeiting its original value of twenty thousand pounds. This necklace has not been worn for many years, and the Pearls are losing their lustre: in a word, they are dying. When not in use a necklace of Pearls ought never to be put away in a velvet-lined case, or laid in cotton-wool; but it should be rolled up in soft fine linen, or in a silk handkerchief, or chamois leather. No grease, or oil should ever be permitted to approach them, as anything of this nature not only deprives the Pearl of its lustre, but further corrodes its polished surface. Sea-water is said to restore "sick," or dulled Pearls to their original freshness; and many an historic chain, or chaplet, has been revived at intervals in the course of its existence by being submerged (in a perforated case) at the bottom of a deep rock-pool, the secret of which as to its whereabouts being revealed to only a few trustworthy persons. It is said that experts have been known to employ a baking process for Pearls which have become much damaged by an unsuitable climate, or long neglect. The necklace, or clasp, is enclosed in a lump of dough, made with barley-meal, the loaf being then baked in the usual way. Nothing so effectively preserves the shimmer, and brightness of a healthy Pearl as confinement in a tin box filled with clean dry sawdust.

Not long since (February, 1906) Herr Karcsay, a remarkable Hungarian gipsy violinist, astonished the London public by his wonderful rendering of real Hungarian Music; which, said the violinist,—is "like old Tokay wine: it possesses the character of the ancient folk-songs; the vague aspirations of a thousand years of conflict and trouble, sparkling in its melodies." Two peculiar instruments hitherto unknown in this country, were introduced at the several recitals; one, the symbal, or symbaloni, as usually played by gipsies and resembling a xylophone; the other a tarogato, or combined flute and horn. When playing, Herr Karcsay always wears a mysterious ring on one of his fingers. It is very large, being made of copper, gold, and silver, with a flat Pearl in the centre, surrounded by Bohemian garnets, and rubies. About this he refuses to say a word except that it is a sacred jewel which has played an important part in his life. He shuddered at the idea of playing without it. Herr Karcsay, his ring, and his violin, the "Andreas Guarnerius," are absolutely inseparable. Only recently he was offered a thousand pounds for his violin; which he unhesitatingly refused. He has played the violin ever since he was six years old. Though incapable of reading a single note of music, he possesses a natural knowledge of harmony, and can render almost any tune by ear.

Told, in a wealth of words particularly akin to our present topic, is a "menu" of jewel dishes given by Ben Jonson in *The Alchymist* (1610), and including a cure for epilepsy:—

> "My meat shall all come in; in Indian shells;
> Dishes of Agate, set in Gold, and studded
> With Emeralds, Sapphires, Hyacinths, and Rubies;
> The tongues of Carps, Dormice, and Camels' heels,
> Boiled in the Spirit of Sol, and dissolv'd Pearl;
> —Apicius' diet 'gainst the Epilepsy!
> And I will eat these broths with spoons of Amber,
> Headed with Diamonds, and Carbuncles."

In the autumn of 1800 the noted Sydney Smith established himself, together with Mrs. Smith, at No. 46, George Street, Edinburgh, when the latter "sold her Pearl necklace for five hundred pounds, buying linen, and plate, with the proceeds."

Pearls were chosen by Christ: (Matthew xiii. 46) as typically precious enough to be compared to the kingdom of heaven. Again, our Saviour warned His disciples, "Give not that which is holy unto the dogs, neither cast ye your pearls before swine." The instinct of Christian consciousness has usually interpreted Pearls here as referring to the "words of divine revelation." And this would be in strict accord with Oriental usage. The Arabian verb for Poetry is to "string Pearls," and thus a poem is called a string of Pearls, or "the precious Pearl."

Pink Pearls are found in the conch—or shell—which is mostly a product of the West Indies, and Panama. These are valued more highly than the white Pearls.

The word "Pearl" occurs in many Teutonic dialects, but the Italian form "perla" suggests an affinity with the Greek "beryllos." If this be so, then beryl, and Pearl are different versions of the same word.

At Christie's (April 17th, 1907) among the jewels which were on sale, as having belonged to the late Mrs. Lewis-Hill, there was put up to auction a magnificent necklace, composed of forty-five large graduated Pearls. Bids for this, opening at a thousand pounds, rose rapidly in their amount, until when the hammer fell, Mr. Well (of London) was declared the purchaser at the big figure of sixteen thousand, and seven hundred pound.

"Gems," wrote Madame de Barrera, 1860, "are never, in one sense of the term, 'secondhand.' Their value, on the contrary, is frequently increased by their antiquity; whilst their primitive lustre, and beauty remain undiminished." There is something sad to a reflecting mind in perusing the catalogue of a great jewel sale, whereat the names of former owners are appended to the several articles, so as to enhance their value. When acquainted with the history of some such former illustrious owners, we look, with pathetic interest on gems which have survived so many griefs, fears, hopes, and joys; but still retaining, in most instances their sheen, and their brilliancy as luminously as of yore.

"Pearls," as Mr. Harry Emanuel asserts, 1847, "are frequently imitated with marvellous skill, but it will be seen that false Pearls are much lighter in weight than real ones; that generally the former are brittle, (although some are made solid, of fish-scale, and do not break so easily), and the holes, which in the real Pearl are drilled very small, and have a sharp edge, in the false are larger, and have a blunt edge."

In the Pearl-oyster (*Meleagrina margaritifera*), and the Pearl-Mussel, about one shell in four is found to contain a Pearl. A Pearl of particular purity, from the river Conway, in North Wales, was presented to the Queen of Charles II. by Sir Robt. Wynne; and is now in the Crown of our King, Edward VII.

> "Full many a Gem of purest ray serene
> The dark unfathom'd caves of Ocean bear;
> Full many a flower is born to blush unseen,
> And waste its sweetness on the desert air."

AGATES.

AGATES are of the Quartz family of Precious Stones. They comprise Chalcedony (the Carnelian sort, red, or brownish—muddy), its colouring matter being a hydrated oxide of iron; Mocha stones, which are grey; Moss-Agates, exhibiting arborisations of oxide of iron; the Bloodstone; Plasma, which is grass-green; and Chrysoprase, apple-green, by reason of its oxide of nickel; this last stone is found in Silesia. Agates are got largely from Uruguay, and sent from thence to Oberstein, near Mayence, where the cutting, and polishing of such silicious stones forms almost the sole industry of the locality. Coming from South America, these Stones are known in the trade as "Brazilian Agates." Likewise Agates are commonly obtained from Germany; also from Scotland, as Scotch Pebbles. The name "Agate" is derived, according to Theophrastus, from the river "Achates," in Sicily, (now called Drillo), from whence these stones were first brought. The Hyacinth (Jacinth), and the Amethyst, are varieties of Quartz, in common with the other Agates. The Rabbins translated "Shebo," their name for an Agate, as "Hyacinth." Again, the "Cat's-eye" is another Chalcedonic variety of Quartz; though the true "Cat's-eye" (Chrysoberyl) is often called "Chrysolite Cat's-eye," being actually a much more beautiful gem. The "Cat's-eye" has obtained its name from possessing a peculiar opalescent lustre, partly resinous, and partly vitreous, which shows best when the stone is cut "*en cabochon*" Then, if held towards the light, it seems to resemble the contracted pupil of a cat's eye; this singular effect being caused by fibres of "amanthoid asbestos" running parallel across the stone, which is generally translucent, sometimes quite transparent, and very easily broken. It is a compound of Alumina and glucina, with varying proportions of oxide of iron. The Agate was formerly in great request among the Romans, because of its reputed medicinal, and talismanic properties. When powdered, and mixed with water, it was said to counteract the venom of serpents. Pliny quotes the Magii as teaching in Persia that storms might be averted by burning Agates. The Tree-Agate of former times—light green in colour, whilst mottled with yellow, (our Jasper)—was supposed to make sure of fertile crops if it were tied about the ploughman's arm, or attached to the horns of the oxen ploughing the fields. An esteem for the virtues of the Agate came down to the days of our Queen Elizabeth, who received from no less eminent a person than Archbishop Parker, the gift of an Agate, with an inscription on parchment detailing its miraculous properties.

Agates for the most part are made up of Silica; and their several colours come from particles of iron mixed therewith, in different ways. To be seen in the British Museum is a very remarkable Agate from Egypt, which shows on both sides a likeness of the Poet Chaucer.

THE ONYX.

THE Precious Stone "Onyx," is actually an Amethyst. Its original name was "Achlamah." There are five varieties of the Onyx; the first, "Finger-nail Stone," which is white, resembling the human nail at its root, where a white crescentic lunula is to be seen; for which reason it has received its (Greek) name; this variety is not marked by any stripes. The second sort is a white stone striped with red; the third is white striped with black; the fourth is all black, without stripes; and the fifth—the most valuable Onyx—is black, with white stripes. Mediæval writers sought to find a Scriptural basis for superstitions then current by connecting "Achlamah"—Onxy—with the verb "chalam"—to dream; and asserting that therefore this precious stone occasioned to its possessor, or wearer, a multiplicity of bewildering dreams. When one of the layers consists of the brown chalcedony known as "Sard," the stone is termed a Sardonyx, which Sardonyx is supposed to have derived its name from ancient Sardis; or from the Greek word "Sarx" —flesh; because of its colour somewhat resembling raw flesh. This beautiful stone is marked with layers of white and rich orange brown.

Concerning the Sardonyx, it was told in the *Magick of Kiram, King of Persia*, 1686: "Upon the Onochytes (Sardonyx),"—a stone known to all—"engrave a Quail; and under its feet a Sea Tench; and when you are willing not to be seen, put a little of the concoction under the stone in the hollow of the ring, and wear the ring; and no man shall see you, if you do anything in the house; no; not if you should take anything away that is in the house."

"For pastime illusion dissolve the eyes of the Quail or of the Sea Tench with a little water in a glass vessel for seven dayes; then add a little oyl, put a small quantity of this in the candle, or only anoint a rag, and set light to it among the company; and they will look upon themselves like devils on fire, so that every one will run his way."

The Onyx was further supposed in former times to create strife, to cause melancholy, and to be a cure for epilepsy. Soaking in sugar, or honey, followed by treatment with strong sulphuric acid, will bring out black and white bands in the naturally grey Onyx.

India has for ages yielded the finest Onyxes. The true Indian stones are found as pebbles,—associated with Moss-agate, Jasper, and other such siliceous minerals—in river-gravels. According to the authorised version of the Old Testament an Onyx formed the eleventh stone in the breast-plate of the High Priest. But "it is more probable," says the *Encyclopædia Britannica*, "that the said stone was a Beryl." The chief ornamental use of the Onyx is for making "Camei," and "Intagli." The Onyx, consisting as it does of layers of variegated chalcedony, arranged in bands, is one of the Agates.

Concerning the Onyx, Marbodus puts it (*Latiné*)

"Et collo suspensus Onyx, digitove ligatus,
Insomnes lemures, et tristia corda repellit."

The ancient Greeks said about this stone, that Cupid, with the sharp point of his arrow, cut the nails of the sleeping Venus; clippings from which fell into the Indus; being celestial they sank, and became metamorphosed into the Onyx. About the Sardonyx, Marbodus also tells :—

"Hic solus lapidum caelam convellere nescit;
Hic humilem, caestumque facit, multumque pudicum."

During the Middle Ages the Onyx bore a most unfavourable character. Thus, Marbodus asserts that a wearer of this stone was exposed to the assaults of demons, and to ugly visions by night; besides being plagued with quarrels, and law-suits by day. The only efficacious preventive was to wear also a "Sard" stone, which would completely neutralise the mischievous influence of the Onyx. The Sard,—or "Oriental Carnelian,"("Sardius;" not the Sardonyx) was reputed to be of virtue for curing tumours; and for healing all wounds not made by iron. It was esteemed of old as a styptic; particularly the flesh-coloured stone. De Leet,

1647, testified from his own experience as to its power to stop bleeding from the nose. At that time rings were cut entirely out of the Sard stone,—to be worn with this same purpose in view. Such rings are still made and worn in Italy; the said benefit of arresting bleeding from the nose being their reputed object.

Resuming our notice of the Onyx, as to the Cameos formerly designed thereupon, the darker shades were usually left to form the ground, whilst the lighter shades were cut into figures. Onyxes, and Agates may readily be stained to almost any colour by artificial means. For black, the stone is first boiled in honey; (and then in sulphuric acid, which carbonises the grape-sugar). Only the porous parts of the stone absorb the sugar, so that the carbonisation greatly heightens the contrast between the white and black layers of the stone. The Nicolo variety of Onyx has a deep brown ground, overlaid by a layer of bluish-white. Honey is likewise employed for giving increased transparency to other gems, if steeped in it for a time. Pliny relates that all gems are brightened if boiled in honey (*Mellis decoctu nitescunt*), especially in the honey of Corsica, which was noted for its acridity. But all other acids are detrimental to precious stones.

Speaking of honey, we call to mind the circumstance that in Tudor times honey was poured over the meat at table in good houses. Furthermore, an amazing quantity of sweets was eaten at dessert; for discussing which refection the guests adjourned to another room; or to the garden if it were summer-time; indeed, at that date sugar was eaten with almost everything; so that the teeth of most persons were black.

Lemprière relates that Polycrates (of classical times),

the tyrant of Samos, had such a continued run of good fortune, and became so powerful, with an enormous fleet of ships, that his ally felt some alarms, and advised him to propitiate adverse fates by relinquishing some of his most favourite objects. Accordingly Polycrates threw into the sea a beautiful seal (made, as we learn, from a Sardonyx stone), the most valuable of his jewels. This voluntary sacrifice of so precious a stone afflicted him for some time; but a few days after, he received as a present a large fish, from the belly of which the jewel was recovered.

From primitive times, even down to the present day, the Fakirs of India have worn, and still wear, rosaries made of Onyx beads. "This wonderful property is said to be in the Onyx," according to Leonardus, 1750, " that being applied to a weak eye, it enters thereinto of its own accord, as if it were a sensible thing, and goes round it without any trouble; and if it finds anything within that is noxious, it drives it out; and tempers the hurtful, and contrary humours."

THE LOADSTONE.

"THE LOADSTONE," wrote Magus, in his *Occult Philosophy*, 1801, " possesses an eminent medicinal faculty against many violent, and implacable disorders."

Its name is a corruption of Lydius lapis—the stone of Lydia,—a guiding stone,—as the load-star, or leading star.

Helmont says that the back of the Loadstone, as it repulses iron, so it also removes gout, swellings, and rheum, which are of the nature, or quality, of iron. Likewise the wearing of the Loadstone eases, and prevents the cramp, with other such-like disorders, and pains.

THE LOADSTONE. 317

"Magnetes lapis," according to Marbodus, (eleventh century),

> "Conciliare potest uxoribus ipse maritos;
> Et, vice conversa, nuptas revocare maritis."

Though not esteemed for personal wear as an ornamental gem, or for being set as a jewel, nevertheless the Loadstone, (or Lode-stone) can exercise so many undoubted virtues that it well merits attentive consideration in these pages. "You would be surprised," says Mr. Henson, the Regent Street mineralogist, (well known in London), "at the uses people make of Loadstones now-a-days. One gentleman with whom I am acquainted never goes to sleep without a loadstone in his hand; another keeps one on a little shelf at the head of his bed; he says he sleeps the better for it; and he is thinking of placing another at his feet. Yet a third gentleman carries one always about in his pocket, near his person; he tells me that when out walking he finds a difference of distance through its aid, of a mile an hour. "This piece which you see here I am purposing to grind flat for a lady, who will use it (as known by her from past experience to be most helpful) for applying upon her face when suffering from neuralgia."

It must be conceded that Helmont (quoted above) was given to many fanciful, and superstitious notions. For instance, whilst extolling (in this very same chapter) the numerous, and varied virtues of magnetism, he adds, quaintly enough, "If anyone happens to committ a nuisance at thy door, and thou will't prevent that beastly trick in future, take the poker, red-hot, and put it into the excrement; and, by magnetism, his posteriors shall become much scorched, and inflamed." Again, "if women, weaning their infants, shall milk out their milk upon hot burning coals, the breast soon dries." Respecting the same Loadstone, Dr. John Schroder wrote, 1669, " It is (as Galen saith) of vertue like the Bloodstone; binds, and stops blood; being burn't it purgeth gross Melancholick humours; but is seldom used." "Some make a plaister of burn't Loadstone, and wax; and commend it highly for the gout."

It was Mr. Richard Swiveller who, on discovering that Sophy Wackles was lost to him for ever, took to playing the flute, as a good, sound, dismal occupation. The particular air (on one specially mournful occasion) was " Away with Melancholy,"—a composition which, when it is played very slowly on the flute, in bed, with the disadvantage of being discoursed by a gentleman but imperfectly acquainted with the instrument, who repeats one note a great many times before he can find the next, has not a lively effect. It was not until he had exhausted his subjects of gloomy meditation, and had nearly maddened the people of the house, also at both next doors, and over the way, that he shut up the music-book, extinguished the candle, and, finding himself greatly relieved, and lightened in mind, turned round, and fell asleep."

In Monsieur Pomet's *Compleat History of Druggs*, 1712, he has discoursed somewhat at large about the Loadstone, saying that " when attracting iron very forcibly it is called a generous or noble stone ; the way of keeping it is in a dry place, wrapped in a scarlet cloth ; or, rather for preserving its vertue, to hang it up by its equator, with a cat's gut, so that it may have its free tendency to the south. It is said that this stone, taken inwardly, intoxicates, and renders stupid ; and that its antidote or counter-poison, is gold, or Emeral'd stone." Wrote

Mr. Boyle (the Honble. Robert, 1662), "those great transactions which make such a noise in the world, and establish monerchies, or ruine empires, reach not so many persons with their influence as do the theories of physiology. To manifest this truth we need but consider what changes in the face of things have been made by two discoveries, trivial enough ; the one being but of the inclination of the needle, touched by the Loadstone, to point toward the pole ; the other being but a casual discovery of the supposed antipathy between saltpetre and brimstone. For, without the knowledge of the former, those vast regions of America, and all the treasures of gold, silver, and precious stones, and much more precious simples they send us, would have probably continued undetected. And the latter, giving an occasional rise to the invention of gunpowder, has quite alter'd the condition of martial affairs over the world, both by sea and land."

The magnetic iron, of which the Loadstone consists, includes twenty-five per cent of the ferric protoxide.

"The Loadstone," said Leonardus, 1502, "being carried about one cures the cramp, and the gout ; likewise it reconciles wives to their husbands, and husbands to their wives." "It makes a man gracious, and persuasive, and elegant in his conversation." "Garlick binds up its virtue. We can give no reason for this, since philosophers are ignorant of any. Some call it the sacred stone, because of the virtues which the Great Creator has given to it." Granting it to be true that Garlick exercises some potential action on the Loadstone, this argues that far from being altogether inanimate, the stone is subject to volatile vegetable exhalations ; and it is fair to infer that, " pari passu," the stone can in its turn exercise certain influences, for good, or ill, on any person wearing it, or otherwise being within its sphere of radiating activity.

M. Pomet, *Compleat History of Druggs*, 1768, gives it as his opinion that the Loadstone, which can make the filings of iron move upon a plate by only passing the stone along underneath, without touching it, may very well serve for any medicinal purpose, and for the Emplastrum divinum, which is its chief use therein." Thus, "they make the Loadstone an ingredient in the composition of plaisters applicable to wounds that are made with a sword, where they think that some pieces may be left behind; for they believe that the Loadstone which is in the plaister, attracts, and draws the iron out of the wound; tho' all the virtue in the Loadstone could never produce this effect; for, first of all, being powder'd finely, as it ought to be, it loses all its force of attraction; and, secondly, being mix'd in the plaister, tho' its virtue should remain, it would not have power to act, being confin'd by the viscidity of the gums, and rosins." "All Loadstones are astringent, and stop blood, outwardly apply'd."

Magnetic iron is supposed to have been originally found near the town of Magnesia, in Lydia:—

"Quem Magneta vocant, patrio de nomine Graii,
Magnetum quia fit patriis in finibus ortus."

Plato says that most persons called it in his day the "Heraclean Stone." The early Greeks, and Romans, knew not only that the Loadstone will attract iron; but also that it endues iron, if in contact with itself, with its own peculiar property. They also had an idea that, under certain circumstances, this magnetic attraction might be replaced by magnetic repulsion.

"Fit quoque ut a lapide hoc Ferri natura recedat
Interdum, fugere, atque sequi, consueta vicissim."

These peoples further held that the magnet is effective in the cure of disease; that it affects the brain, causing melancholy; that it serves as a love philtre; that it may be used in testing the chastity of a woman; that it loses its power when rubbed with garlic, but recovers it when treated with goat's blood; and that it will not attract iron when in the presence of a Diamond; all of which notions were eagerly adopted by the wonder-working adherents of the Middle Ages.

Into the scientific phenomena of magnetic action on the needle in the mariner's compass, causing the same to point approximately north and south, at its opposite ends, we do not feel called upon to enter in these pages. As is commonly known, these opposite ends of the magnetised needle are called "poles." The first accounts of the compass in Europe go back to the twelfth century.

Marbodus has told curiously about the Loadstone, that if its powder be strewn secretly upon live embers, this proceeding will compel all the inmates to quit the house; panic struck, and thus allowing robbers free access into it unmolested.

When the Prophet Ezekiel was ordered (by the divine "appearance of fire," of the colour of amber; from a throne "having the appearance of a sapphire stone), to eat a roll, as given him; and to "go, speak unto the house of Israel," he was bidden to fear them not, because his face was made strong against their faces; "as an Adamant, harder than flint have I made thy forehead."

The Adamant, (supposed by some early writers to

signify the Diamond,) is more lately known to denote the Loadstone, or Magnet. "If an Adamant," told Bartholomew Anglicus, 1250, (*On the Properties of Things*), "be set by iron it suffereth not the iron to come to the magnet, but it draweth it by a manner of violence from the magnet, so that, though the magnet draweth iron to itself, the Adamant draweth it away from the magnet." "This is called a precious stone of reconciliation, and of love. For if a woman be away from her housebond, or trespasseth against him, by virtue of this stone, she is the sooner reconciled to have grace of her husband."

AMBER.

AMBER, "Succinum"—though neither a mineral, nor a gem, but actually a resin,—is nevertheless worked by the lapidary, and the jeweller, so as to serve for personal ornamentations, and for utilitarian purposes akin to the same object. Moreover, Amber is eminently endowed with remedial virtues, and medicinal properties, so much so indeed as to unquestionably merit explicit present notice at our hands.

This familiar substance is a fossilised resin, (thought to be derived from an extinct species of pine), being found in irregular masses, without cleavage, and possessing a resinous waxy lustre, which varies in colour from transparent to opaque. Amber is composed chemically of carbon, hydrogen, oxygen, calcium, (i.e., lime), alumina, and silica (flint). It is found in abundance on the Prussian Coast of the Baltic, from Dantzic to Menel, also on the Coast of Denmark, in Sweden, Norway, Poland, Switzerland, and in France. It occurs likewise embedded in clay, on the coasts of Essex, Suffolk, and Norfolk.

In colour it varies from white, pale yellow, to a deep brownish-orange: it is very brittle, and yields to the knife. Pliny surmised the fact that Amber is of vegetable origin. The trees which are thought to have produced it originally were of the *Pinites succinifer* kind. This substance is much used to make mouthpieces for pipes; it being customary in the East to have the pipe lighted by a servant, and the Amber being esteemed as incapable of transmitting infection from such a source.

An oil of Amber, as well as succinic acid, is got from Amber by distillation; the residue serving for the manufacture of a black varnish. The designation "Amber" is probably derived from the Arabic "Anabaron" which denotes this resin, the Greek name being "Electron," (whence our term "Electricity" is obtained), from the property Amber exercises of attracting to itself small substances when it is subjected to friction. Another title once bestowed upon it was "Lyncurion," since it was supposed to be a deposit from the urine of the lynx, that of the male animal giving a deep, and that of the female a pale tint. Pliny records the medicinal use of Amber, and tells that necklaces made from the substance were formerly hung about the necks of young children to preserve them from the evil powers of witchcraft, and sorcery. The Shah of Persia possesses—to be worn around the neck— a cube of Amber reported to have fallen from heaven in the time of Mahomet, and which can thus make him invulnerable.

Tacitus describes the Amber-gatherers as a sacred nation, worshipping the mother of the Gods. In Copenhagen, as we learn from one of its famous professors, popular notions are current that Amber is a sovereign panacea for asthma, dropsy, toothache, and various other ailments. Another belief is that it will serve to drive away adders. Dr. W. Salmon has ordered, in his *Family Dictionary*, 1696: "For the falling sickness, take half a drachm of choice Amber, powder it very fine, and take it once a day in a quarter of a pint of white wine, for seven or eight days successively." And again, "for a falling fundament," "Take bits of Amber, and in a close-stool put them upon a chafing-dish of live charcoal, over which let the patient sit, and receive the fumes."

In such repute was Amber at Rome during Pliny's time that he sarcastically observed, "The price of a small figure made therefrom, however diminutive, exceeds that of a living, healthy slave." The substance was further used there for producing imitations of precious stones by artificial staining.

In England Amber has been found within the sandy deposits of the London clay, at Kensington.

This translucent resin often furnishes within its substance the appearance of enclosed foreign bodies, such as insects, leaves, twigs, etc., such insects being mostly of extinct species, as likewise the remnants of plants. The familiar term, "Flies in Amber," is proverbial for an incongruous mixture of natural objects. "Admire" says Claudian, "the magnificence of the tomb of a vile insect. No sovereign can boast one so splendid."

"Non potuit tumulo nobiliore mori."

Eastern folk entertain a feeling of veneration for Amber, because of its mystic virtues, this sentiment serving to enhance the value of Amber thereby.

Formerly Amber entered into the composition of "Eau de Luce," (now an obsolete preparation), being then in combination with alcohol, and ammonia.

In ordinary modern medicinal practice the oil of Amber (oleum succini) is given in small doses for hysterical affections; externally it is employed as a rubefacient (to stimulate redness and warmth of the skin-surface), as for the relief of bronchial troubles, and likewise of rheumatism; and further as an ingredient of "Roche's Embrocation," to be rubbed into the chest (back and front), specifically against whooping cough.

The Greeks had of old a tradition concerning the origin of Amber, that it arose from the tears which the Electrides shed on learning the death of their brother Phaeton; these sisters being then turned into Poplar trees, and continuing to pour forth perpetual tears into the River Eridamus, or Padus, which tears became congealed into the succinum (or Amber). Thus Ovid relates:—

> "Inde fluunt lacrymæ; stillataque sole rigescunt
> De ramis Electra novis, quæ lividus amnis
> Excipit, et muribus mittit gestanda Latinis."

In former Grecian times Amber, being ground up with honey, and rose-oil, was counted a specific for curing deafness; also, if mixed with Attic honey, it obviated dimness of sight.

At ordinary temperatures Amber has neither taste, nor odour. When burnt it emits a pleasant aromatic smell. More than probably this is the actual, (though unsuspected,) reason why the Eastern smokers regard their Amber mouthpieces as exercising disinfecting powers. Combustion takes place readily, producing a bright yellow flame, and leaving a black, carbonaceous residue. At 287° Fahr. Amber fuses, and becomes decomposed, yielding water, an empyreumatic oil, and succinic acid. Amber is soluble in alcohol. By chemical analysis it is shown to be rich in carbon; being therefore specially suitable for remedial wear against those ailments which are told about here as amenable to charcoal (carbon).

Yellow amber beads were formerly in fashion for necklaces, and other use as personal ornaments in this country. "Succinum is a bituminous juyce, or rosin," tells Dr. W. Rowland, 1669, "of the Earth, well digested; thence brought into the sea, and there chiefly concreted. Bound to the neck behind, it cures defluxions of the eyes, and hung about the neck keeps destillations from the throat. It is proper chiefly for the head, and womb."

"There are several sorts of Succinum, so-called officinally, as the white, yellow, and black; but the shops have only two sorts, the white, and the yellow. The yellow is best which is clear, and is sweetest when powdered, the black spotted is worst."

For a delicate person, liable to attacks of relaxed sore throat, to wear pretty constantly a necklace of somewhat large beads made from the transparent yellow Amber is found to be an admirably preventive measure. In playful allusion to which troublesome ailment Hood's title for a dummy book (amongst others, equally humorous, and clever, as supplied at Chatsworth to the Duke of Devonshire, in February, 1831) ran thus: *On Sore Throat; or The Migration of the Swallow.*

Hood's assistance had been asked for by the Duke towards constructing a door of sham books for the library staircase at Chatsworth, that he would give some inscriptions for the unreal folios, quartos, and duodecimos, to be thus simulated. Accordingly a series of some eighty facetious, and punning names was furnished with admirable readiness, and skill. The following are some of the best: *Percy Vere, in forty volumes. Lamb's Recollections of Suett. Tadpoles; or Tales out of my own Head. Autographia; or Man's Nature known by his Signature. Pygmalion, by Lord Bacon. John Knox, on Death's Door. Haughty-cultural remarks on London Pride. Voltaire; Volney; Volta; three Vols. Johnson's Contradictionary. Cursory Remarks on Swearing. Cook's Specimens of the Sandwich Tongue. Boyle on Steam. Life of Jack Ketch; with cuts of his own Execution.*

Nero fantastically called his Pompeia "Amber," she being a blonde, with auburn hair. On which account hair of such sort then became the fashion in Rome, some of it being ruthlessly taken from the heads of the German "female savages"; also the Roman ladies converted their black locks into red by steeping them in a strong alkali.

"Caustica Teutonicos accendit spuma capillos;
Captivâ poteris cultior esse comâ."

From the second Imperial epoch, down to the middle of the fourteenth century, Amber was carved into knives, and one-pronged forks, which the Princes, and great Church dignitaries used for cutting-up various kinds of fruits, and vegetables, especially the esculent fungi (mushrooms), and the like. There is an archaic Amber cup now in the museum at Brighton; this having been found originally in a barrow at Hove.

Amber, as already stated, is a fossil resin of vegetable

origin. Its chemical components are: A volatile oil, several resins, and succinic acid.

As to the electrical properties of precious stones, their power of attracting, or repelling smaller bodies, some of such stones are conductors, and others non-conductors of electricity; their properties (formerly either "vitreous," or "resinous") being positive, or negative.

The faculty of retaining electrical conditions when induced is very varied in all minerals. Some crystals will become electrical by pressure; for instance, Iceland Spar, to a very high degree. But much less so all the stones which come under the denomination of quartz: the topaz, amethyst, etc. The electricity which is produced in some of these bodies is known as "pyro-electricity," with which property the Indians have been long acquainted. It is not heat which causes the development of electricity, but the change of temperature. In certain stones two kinds of electricity are developed (by a decreasing temperature) at the opposite ends, or poles, respectively. By an increase of heat the positive pole becomes negative, and the negative, positive. The topaz continues to still affect the needle (with which it is placed in contact) after twenty-four hours; this property of the stone having been well known to the Greeks. Their name of Amber, "Electron," was conferred thereon because of its power of attracting small bodies by friction.

Again,—as concerning the Quartzes: with regard to the Onyx, it should be further stated that of old this was the "gem of Saturn:" but not as embodying metallic lead, of which that deity was held to be the symbol; rather because through the gloomy blackness of its main broad bands being supposed to induce mental heaviness, stupor, and despondency. (Such physical effects as these were known to be the toxic symptoms of chronic lead-poisoning.) Pope verifies this notion (in his *Dunciad*) :—

> "Then rose the seed of Chaos, and of Night,
> To blot out order, and extinguish light;
> —Of dull, and venal a new world to mould,
> And bring Saturnian days, of Lead;—"

So likewise Charles Lamb, (in Elia's Essay—"*Christ's Hospital*,") has described "Th—," (a Co-Grecian there,) as "a tall, dark, *Saturnine* youth, sparing of speech, with raven locks."

In reality the black colour of Onyx is due to minutely subdivided particles of Iron incorporated with the Silicon base : so that to wearers of this stone it should prove tonic, and exhilarating, instead of engendering lowness of spirits, or melancholy thoughts.

LAPIS LAZULI.

LAPIS LAZULI, a mineral of a fine blue colour, which is due to the constituent therein of sulphide of iron and sodium, was a favourite with the ancient Egyptians, as shown by the large number of Egyptian Ornaments in this material which have been preserved from the time of Pharaoh. This stone was the Greek Sapphire, "sprinkled with gold-dust," said Theophrastus ; because it frequently contains disseminated particles of iron pyrites, which by their colour and lustre might well be mistaken for gold. But the same description would be utterly inappropriate to any variety of our modern Sapphire.

Some kinds of Lapis Lazuli exhibit violet, green, or even red tints, or are altogether colourless. The mineral is always opaque, with only a slight translucency at the edges.

Lapis Lazuli "is an open stone like a saphire,"—William Rowland, Doctor of Physick, 1669,—"adorned with golden atoms, or flames, harder than the Armenian stone; it is called the Sky-coloured Stone, and is in vertue like the Armenian-Stone but weaker; it purgeth chiefly melancholy, cures quartans, apoplexies, epilepsies, diseases of the spleen, and many others from dementia." "It is worn about the neck for an amulet to drive away frights from children; it strengthens the sight, prevents faintings, and abortion, but it must be taken near the time of delivery lest it keep up the ohild." As an internal dose give one drachm, (i.e., sixty grains,) in powder.

M. Pomet, in his *History of Druggs*, 1712, tells respecting this Lapis Lazuli, or azure stone, "It is a heavy stone, of a sky blue; most frequently streaked with veins of copper, which the Antients, and some Moderns, believ'd to be gold. It is a silicate of alumina, calcium, and sodium; sulphur, too, being always recorded. The chief use to which it is put is for making the ultramarine, by being ground, calcined, and levigated in water. When it is burnt to make ultramarine, it will stink extreamly, having a sulphurous smell, which shows that it proceeds from copper, and not from gold." There are authors who attribute great virtues to this stone. "Lapis Lazuli prepar'd purges melancholy humours, fortifies the heart, and is used in the confection of Alkermes." This confection, of "Scarlet Grain,"—our Coccus Cacti,—Cochineal, was reckoned very cordial, and proper to comfort women in child-bed, giving half a dram of it, powdered, in an egg.

But a great many people advise it without the Cochineal, who believe that two grains thereof will answer the same purpose." "This 'grain,' (really an insect,) is one of the principal riches of the countries in which it grows, especially for the poor people throughout all Provence, and Languedoc, where the peasants gather, and sell it by the pound to the apothecaries, who from the pulp make a syrup they call Alkermes; and the remainder which is left in the sieve, or strainer, after it is cleansed, they sell again to the dyers."

One of the Palaces at St. Petersburg contains rooms lined with Lapis Lazuli. The names of this gem are derived from the Latin word *Lapis*, a stone, and the Persian word *Lazur*, blue. It is now said to be an established fact that by directing the rays of blue electric light on the eyes, while carefully excluding every other ray, a person can be thrown into a deep sleep, with complete insensibility, which is both harmless, and pleasant. This sleep lasts two or three minutes, and may be indefinitely repeated. It further appears that blue lights, combined with blue surroundings, of carpets, hangings, wall-paper, furniture, etc., in a room, are wonderfully exhilarating, and will do much for the relief of nervous disquietude.

The "Armenian Stone" (referred to as possessing the medicinal, and curative virtues which the Lapis Lazuli similarly claims), is "full of spots, green, sky-colour'd, and blackish, like Lapis Lazuli, with golden spots, and it differs not from it but in maturity, for both are discovered in the same mines. But Lapis Lazuli, which is the ripe, is found in gold mines, the Armenian in the silver mines. It dryes moderately, cleanseth with a little sharpness, and binding; taken inwardly it purgeth melancholy upwards, or downwards; but if you wash it twelve or fifteen times, it only purgeth downwards, and is good in madness, melancholy, epilepsie, etc. The dose in substance is from one drachm to eighty grains. Outwardly it is used for the eyes, likewise for soreness of the eyelids." This stone is called "Armenian" because it was first brought from Armenia; but now it is found in Germany.

Bartholomew Anglicus, 1250, foreshadowed Shakespeare in commending music "which hath holpen madmen to their wits." The brain, in mediæval times was regarded as the home of the senses exclusively. "If there be signs of frenzy, then men must soon be holpen, lest they perish." In the beginning of medicine he shall be let blood in a vein of the forehead, and be bled as much as will fill an egg-shell." This recalls to mind Juvenal's satirical advice respecting his friend about to marry, "O, Medici! mediam pertundite venam" —"Let the doctors bleed your head-vein."

THE MOONSTONE.

THE MOONSTONE, though not properly a gem, or precious stone, yet as possessing a certain value, likewise a certain mystic reputation, and being therefore adopted for personal wear, calls for some detailed notice in our pages. It is an opalescent variety of felspar (orthoclase), having a "chatoyante" (sparkling) reflection, like that of the "Cat's-eye," and is of a pearly-white colour. The best Moonstones are brought from Ceylon.

An opaque and green variety of the Moonstone, owning an admixture with copper, comes from Siberia, where it is called "amazon-stone," but this is very little known in England. Another name sometimes borne by the

Moonstone is that of the Ceylon Opal. Its crystals are seldom found of any large size. The Stones are cut *en cabochon* by the lapidary.

Magus (Francis Barrett, 1801), affirms the belief entertained of old, that this stone, Heliotropium, Moonstone, green, like a jasper, or emerald, and beset with red specks, makes the wearer constant, renowned, and famous, conducing also to long life; there is likewise another wonderful property in this stone, which is, that it so dazzles the eyes of men as to make its wearer invisible. But then there must be applied to it the herb bearing the same name, viz., Heliotropium, or the sun-flower; and these kinds of virtues Albertus Magnus, and William of Paris mention in their writings.

The "Moonstone," as popularised by Wilkie Collins, in his remarkable, wonder-stirring fiction of that name, was formerly an object of special veneration because of its reputed lunar attraction. Pliny described it as shining with a yellow lustre, from a colourless ground, and bearing an image of the moon. "Which image," he relates, "if the story be true, daily waxes, or wanes, according to the state of that luminary then obtaining. Marbodus likewise, in the eleventh century, termed the Moonstone "sacred." Concerning the lime which is present, (though only as a trace, and therefore all the more potential,) as a constituent of this, and some other such stones, Basil has said, "It fixeth the volatile spirit of minerals." Furthermore, "Washed lime," wrote Dr. Rowland, 1669, "dryes without nipping, and is therefore good against stubborn ulcers, and burns, and others that are not easily cured." "Formerly," tells Mr. Harry Emanuel, "the Moonstone was fashionable in this country, although now it is seldom seen."

The best Moonstones come principally from Ceylon. This stone is known also by the name of Ceylon Opal; it is a variety of felspar, or orthoclase, containing as its main chemical constituents silica (two-thirds per cent), alumina, and potash; therefore when remedially worn it is specially adapted by nature for persons to whom silica (flint) is likely to prove useful, as described here under that heading.

The Moonstone is, popularly speaking, so named because of the play of light which it exhibits. The scientific name of the mineral is "Adularia," from Adula, the summit of a Swiss mountain-peak, (St. Gothard).

The Moonstone, a romantic tale, ("tail out of his own head," as Tom Hood said of the tadpole), was told by Wilkie Collins, in 1868. It is founded—as stated in the original preface—in some important particulars, on the stories of two of the royal diamonds of Europe, "the magnificent stone which adorns the top of the Russian Imperial Sceptre, and which was once the eye of an Indian idol; and the famous Koh-i-noor, (which is also supposed to have been one of the sacred gems of India, and, further, to have been the subject of a prediction prophesying a succession of misfortunes to the persons who should divert it from its ancient uses)." Towards enhancing the interest, and importance of his story the author, allowably enough, supposes the Moonstone to have been a Diamond, which, as we now see, is not really the case. This famous "Yellow Diamond" (the moonstone), according to the earliest known traditions, had been set from time immemorial in the forehead of the four-handed god who typifies the moon. Partly from its colour, and partly from a superstition which represented it as feeling the influence of the deity whom it adorned, whilst growing, and lessening in lustre simultaneously with the waxing and waning of the moon, it first gained the name by which it continues to be known in India to this day, "The Moon-Stone."

Presently this Moon-god in the story escapes the rapacity of conquering Mohammedans, and, being preserved by three Brahmins, with the Moonstone still intact in his forehead, is transported to the city of Benares, and set up again for worship in a magnificent new shrine inlaid with precious stones, under a roof supported by pillars of gold. One age follows another, until eventually Aurungzebe, Emperor of the Moguls, plays havoc with the said shrine, allowing the Moonstone to be seized by an officer of rank in his army. Powerless to recover their lost treasure by open force, the three guardian priests follow in disguise, and watch it through innumerable strange adventures, and hair-breadth escapes.

Generations succeed each other. The soldier who had committed the sacrilege has perished miserably; the Moonstone (carrying its curse with it) has passed from one lawless Mohammedan hand to another; and still, through all chances and changes, the successors of the three guardian priests have kept their watch.

Time has rolled on to the last years of the eighteenth Christian century; then at length the "diamond" has fallen into the possession of Tippoo, Sultan of Seringapatam, who caused it to be placed as an ornament in the handle of a dagger, commanding that it should be kept among the choicest treasures of his armoury. Even then the three guardian priests, having won the Sultan's confidence by conforming, (or seeming to conform), to the Mussulman faith, have become three Officers of Tippoo's household, still maintaining in secret their jealous watch over the Moonstone. Thus the romance opens, and its highly interesting, most fascinating, and marvellous incidents, continue their course of action; until finally, having been rescued,—even from England, whither it has travelled as an ill-omened, malignant captive, in a marvellous manner,—Eastern magnetism assisting as an occult means,—the Moonstone reappears under the custody of three strange Hindoos, at a great religious ceremony in honour of the God of the Moon. This superstitious function is being held before thousands of thronging fanatical spectators, at night, on a hill, close to the sacred city of Somnauh, in the wild region of Kattiawar, in the north-west of India. At the weird, awesome ceremony, suddenly there appear three figures on the platform of a rock. They are the Brahmins, who have forfeited their caste in the service of their god. On that night the three men were to part company so as to receive their purification by pilgrimage at the command of the god. Never more were they to look on each other's faces.

Then the curtain between the trees was drawn aside, and the shrine was disclosed to view. "There, raised high on a throne, seated on his typical antelope, with his four arms stretching towards the four corners of the earth, there soared above all, dark, and awful in the mystic light of heaven, the God of the Moon. And there in the forehead of the deity, gleamed the 'Yellow Diamond;' whose splendour had shone last on its English possessor from the bosom of a woman's dress! Yes! after the lapse of eight centuries the Moonstone looks forth once more over the walls of the sacred city in which its story first began. How it has found its way back to its wild native land, by what accident, or by what crime, may be," concludes the author, "in your knowledge but is not in mine. You have lost sight of it in England, and (if I know anything of this strange, mystic people) you have lost sight of it for ever."—With queer, little, shrewd Miss Mowcher (in *David Copperfield*) the modern reader of this strange, eventful history may well feel inclined to exclaim, "Oh, my stars, and what's-their-names!" meaning—mock-modestly—"garters."

Felspar is "spar of the fields" (German). It is much used in making the noted Sèvres porcelain. The Moonstone, Adularia, is the purest kind of felspar that is known.

THE TOADSTONE.

SHAKESPEARE has told the world, in eloquent speech, that "the toad, ugly, and venomous, wears yet a precious jewel in his head." And long prior to his time some such a notion must have possessed the minds of our ancestors, who had firm belief in the many virtues of the "*Toadstone*." If swallowed it was a certain antidote to poison. Erasmus has described this stone as a "gem" to which no name had been given by the Greeks, or the Romans; but the French have named it after the toad. The figure of a toad shines through as if enclosed in the stone itself. Some authorities of repute, add, moreover, that if the stone be put into vinegar, "the toad will swim therein, and move its legs;" which account induces a belief that the said wonderful stone was in all probability a lump of amber, enclosing some large insect magnified thereby into the semblance of a toad. Lupton (Thomas, 1583,) gave instructions how to procure the toadstone. "You shall knowe whether the tode-stone be the righte, or perfect stone or not. Holde the stone, before a tode so that he may see it; and if it be a ryght, and true stone, the tode will leape towarde it, and make as though he would snatch it. He envieth so much that none should have that stone."

"The toad," as Magus conjectured (*Occult Philosophy*, 1801), "is an animal ordained of God, which, at the sight of man, from a natural quality seated in him called antipathy, conceives a great terror, or astonishment; hence it happens that a poison ariseth in the toad which kills the poison of terror in man."

Again, "so great is the fear of the toad, that if he is placed directly before thee, and thou dost behold him with an intent furious look, (so that he cannot avoid thee), for a quarter of an hour, he dies, being fascinated with terror, and astonishment." The author adds in a footnote, "I have tried this experiment upon the toad, and other reptiles of his nature, and was satisfied of the truth of this affirmation."

Even M. Pomet, chief druggist to the French King, 1712, has told, with some measure of credence, about the Toadstone—"Buffonites"—"It has been believed," says he, "that this stone was bred in the head of an old toad, whence it was voided by the mouth of that creature when put upon red cloth"; "but those who have made exact enquiries after it affirm that this stone is formed in the earth commonly of two sorts, the round, and the long. Men do set them, especially the round sort, in rings; but that is more for ornament than any virtue in them; for they are very uncertain in their effects, especially when it be supposed that they allay the inflammation occasion'd by the sting of bees, or other insects." "Some again do hang these stones about their neck against quartan fevers; but all these virtues are imaginary; for the toadstone hath nothing in it but an alkaline quality proper to absorb acids, and to stop looseness; but it is not in use."

Concerning a toad itself—"*Bufo*"—"*Rana venenata*," Wierus said (15th century) that "the powder of a dry'd toad, taken half a drachm for a dose, cures almost incurable dropsies, carrying away the water by urine." "The ashes of burnt toad, hung about the neck as an amulet, cures the wetting of the bed."

Another odd stone which obtained equal curative faith during the Middle Ages, and with no more trustworthy pretensions than the said Toadstone, was the "Bezoar," Bezuar, or Beza; as procured from the kidneys of a certain wild goat, or deer, of Arabia. It was implicitly believed that this Bezoar Stone gave protection against poison; and hence its name was derived—"Pad-gahr," "expelling poison."

In a certain Warrant of Indemnity for the delivery of Jewels to King James the First, mention occurs of "one great Bezar Stone, sett in gould, which is Queen Elizabethes": "one other large Bezar Stone, broken in peeces, delivered to our owne handes by the Lord Brooke."

As some warrant for the actual occurrence of these stones, it is to be held in mind that at times such stony concretions do become aggregated within the stomachs of herbivorous quadrupeds, being formed originally around some small indigestible nucleus which happens to have been taken into the stomach.

"The Occidental Bezar," as M. Pomet relates, "is brought from Peru, where it is found in some goats, harts, or those animals that produce the Bezar; and, as they are but rarely met withal in the belly of these animals, the consequence is that very few are brought into France. It has furthermore a very sweet smell, and is much stronger than the Oriental Bezar." "And because this Bezoar is very scarce, the Dutch, and other nations, make it, with a grey paste which they form into sound balls, of what size they please; and I can assure you that I have seen one of the bigness of a tenis ball, that was in the middle of a silver cup, (so fixed that it could not be remov'd), to the end that it might be infus'd in the liquor put into the cup, in order to give a flavour to it before they drink it." "There are those who have these stones hung in little gilt chains to put into any liquor, for the infusion; they keep 'em in little gold boxes."—as likewise set in medicinal rings.

Many such rings were collected by Cardinal Benedict Odescalchi, who became Pope Innocent XI., and died in 1688. The value of these rings depends rather on their rarity and on their historical associations than on the splendour of diamonds, and other precious stones; but the chief treasure is a pontifical ring, with large sapphire and reliquary, with coat-of-arms enamelled on the lid, formerly the property of Cardinal Antonelli. An eighteenth century poison ring has the hollow appropriately enclosed by a devil's head.

Concerning poison rings, Dr. Wynter Blyth, in a lecture delivered at the International Health Exhibition, July 15th, 1884, on "Old and Modern Poison Lore," said: "In the middle ages some poisons were reputed to have been administered by contact: and there are many stories of poisoned rings used for such a purpose. These rings were said to be poisoned on the interior. having a sharp point there, so that when a person grasped the hand wearing the ring, some of the poison was passed into his body. But I believe the statement to be altogether without foundation, because there is no kind of proof that the ancients had such a subtle poison as is here supposed. We have hardly got such a thing now, and I think it can scarcely have existed in the Middle Ages."

The ring has always been the favourite ornament of the human race, from the time of the prehistoric cave-dweller to the present day; from the plain bronze hoop of prehistoric man to the classic intaglio ring and the masterpieces of the Renaissance craftsmen. There are signet rings, papal rings, and memorial rings,—poison rings, and incantation rings,—symbolical rings, and ceremonial rings,—rings with Egyptian scarabs, Hebrew inscriptions, Koran texts, and reliquaries. There are rings oriental, and occidental, of gold, and of silver, of bronze, and of bone, of amber, and of terra-cotta.

THE EAGLE STONE.

OF Stones "less precious" which were at one time in favour for wear, as of supposed mystic properties, the Eagle Stone (no longer recognised by our leading jewellers) may be taken for a fair instance. "The *Eagle Stone* (Dr. J. Schroder, *Compleat Chymical Dispensatory*, 1669) "is so called because it is found in an eagle's nest, brought thither by an eagle, to help delivery." "An Eagle Stone hath another stone that rattles within it, (which is called Collimus)."

As for "its vertues," "it provokes the birth, if it be bound to a woman's thighs; but if to the arm, keeps it up. But you must remove it presently, after delivery, lest it draws the matrix towards it." "What we call the Eagle Stones," writes M. Pomet, "chief druggist to the present French king," 1712, "are certain Stones that are hollow in the middle, and contain in them a stony nut, or kernel, that makes a noise when we shake them. We commonly find but four sorts of them, that are indifferently called, in Latin *Lapis Ætites*, but the kernel, *Collimus*. They are found both in Germany, and in Portugal. It is now no longer believed that they are discovered in the eagle's nest." "Authors believe that reduc'd to powder, and mix'd in a cerate, it lessens the paroxysms, or fits of the epilepsy, if apply'd to the head." "'Tis also said that the marle, or clay, that is found in the hollow, is sudorifick, and will stop the flux of the belly." M. Lemery adds, "It is astringent, and proper to stop loosenesses, and hemorrhages, if taken inwardly. The kernel, which is softer than the stone, is more advantageous for all the same purposes."

"They are call'd Ætites, that signifies aquiline, or, of the eagle; because it was believ'd that the eagles furnished their nests with these stones to preserve their young." "Without which stones,—of two kinds; the male, and a female,—they bring not forth," said Dr. Salmon — *Pharmacopeia Londinensis* — 1696. Dioscorides (*De Materia Medica*) gives a strange account as to how the Eagle Stone was formerly employed to detect petty thefts. All the suspected persons being called together, flour was kneaded up in their presence, sprinkled with the powder of the stone; a certain incantation being repeated at the same time. The paste was then rounded into balls as large as eggs, and some thereof given to each of the persons, with a little drink; but the guilty one found it impossible to swallow a mouthful, and choked in the attempt.

The Eagle Stone—described as of a scarlet colour—rendered its owner amiable, sober, and rich; preserving him from adverse casualties. By an entry in the *Mercurius Rusticus* (1658) one learns that "Among other things valuable for rarity, and use, the rebels took from Mr. Bartlett, a Cock-eagle's Stone; for which thirty pieces had been offered by a physician."

Dr. Bargrave (1650) had purchased from an Armenian at Rome a Lapis Aquilaris, or Eagle Stone, of excellent qualities and use, which, by applying it to child-bearing women, would keep them from miscarriages. "It is so useful that my wife can scarce keep it at home; and therefore she hath sewed the strings to the knit in which the stone is, for the convenience of the tying of it to the patient on occasion; and hath a box, she hath, to put the purse, and stone in. It were fitt that either the Dean's, or Vice-Dean's wife, (if they were marry'd men,) should have this stone in their custody for the public good, as to neighbourhood; but that still they have a great care into whose hands it be committed, and that the midwives have a care of it, so that it be still the Cathedral Church's stone." This Dr. John Bargrave, Dean of Canterbury, was born in 1610, and bequeathed his museum to Christchurch, Canterbury, 1676.

Magus has said: "Amongst stones, those which resemble the rays of the sun by their golden sparklings (as does the glittering stone Ætites) prevent the falling sickness, and poisons, if worn on the finger."

We read that when Geoffrey, Sixteenth Abbot of St. Alban's, was completing the shrine of his patron Saint,—for which the treasury of the Church was utilised,—a precious stone was forthcoming so large that a man could not grasp it in his hands, the same being reputed to help women in child-birth : and therefore this stone was not made fast in the masonry of the shrine, because it might be of service to save women's lives. On it was carved an image as of one in rugged clothes, holding a spear in one hand, with a snake winding itself up it ; and in the other hand a boy bearing a buckler. At the feet of the image was an eagle, with wings expanded, and lifted up.

This "Cock-eagle's stone" of Mr. Bartlett brings to mind a ludicrously pathetic incident which occurred when our unfortunate monarch, poor George III. ("Farmer George," as people then styled him,) first showed indications of mental infirmity. The lamentably grotesque occasion was when he addressed the assembled Houses of Parliament as "My Lords, and turkey-cocks!" Manifestly his mind was already confusing kingly duties with the pastimes of his poultry yard. Parliament was straightway prorogued till November 1st, 1810; but the demented Sovereign was not then in a fit condition to perform any royal act. Under the circumstances Parliament met without being summoned by their king; so that it devolved upon the Speaker to take the Chair of Presidency on that memorable occasion.

"Among all fowls, in the eagle the virtue of sight is most mighty, and strong. And the sharpness of her sight is not rebounded again by clearness of the light of the sun, neither disperpled. There is one manner of eagle that is full sharp of sight; and she taketh her own birds in her claws, and maketh them to look even on the sun, and that ere their wings be full grown; and except they look stiffly, and stedfastly against the sun, she beateth them, and setteth them even before the sun. And if any eye of any of her birds watereth in looking on the sun, she slayeth him, as though he went out of kind, or else driveth him out of the nest, and despiseth him, and setteth not by him."

The Eagle Stone is a natural concretion, a variety of argillaceous oxide of iron.

The Imperial Eagle of ancient Rome,—symbol of its lofty power,— being on one memorable occasion threatened in the Capitol with stealthy assault by invasion, was saved by the timely cackling of geese, (birds the intelligence of which is much under-rated). After the same fashion (as a well-known fable relates), the lion, king of beasts, was rescued from the toils of the hunter, in which he had become entrapped, by the humble nibblings of a small mouse at the meshes of the hostile net, until a rift large enough to allow of escape had thus become helpfully made.

As to the domestic Goose, (in Latin, *anser*), a modern anecdote tells that when the Bursar of Worcester College, Oxford, 1850, was ruffled in temper by his futile endeavours at table to carve a very tough bird of this kind, he passed off his irritation by making a Latin joke—"'tis only a soft 'anser' that turneth away wrath."

Marbodus has said, in classical terms, about the Eagle Stone :—

"Incolumes pueros dat vivere, sive puellas,
   Atque caducorum (epileptica) fertur prohibere ruinas."

Again, a certain Stone—the Galactides, (known to the old Magii under various names,)—was credited with powers identical with those attributed to Aladdin's Lamp in the *Arabian Nights* tale. Ghosts could be called up thereby, to answer questions, and to confer benefits. It further possessed the faculty of re-uniting in love people who were at variance. A test of its genuineness was to smear one's body with honey, and then expose it to the flies: when, if the stone was true, the flies, and bees, kept off.

Other less precious stones,—now disused as such, and not of import for our present purpose, so as to merit any detailed notice here,—were the Amianthus (feathered alum); the Jew's Stone,—Lapis Judaicus;—and the Osteocolla,—bone-binder. Only one variety of Amianthus (Hornblende) is used in the arts; viz., Asbestos, so called by the ancient Greeks because believed to be "unquenchable" by flame; for which reason wicks were made of its long flexible fibres, towards maintaining the perpetual sacred fires of the temples. Napkins of Asbestos could be cleansed by being thrown into the fire; and Asbestos-cloth was used in the process of cremation, to keep the ashes of the body distinct from those of the fuel.

Cloth made of Asbestos (Amianthus), when greasy, or otherwise dirty, may be cleansed by throwing it into a bright fire. Thereby the stains are burnt out, whilst the cloth remains entire, being presently restored to a dazzling whiteness. Kircher, the German philosopher, had a lamp-wick made of asbestos, which burned for two years without injury, and was at last destroyed only by accident.

JET.

JET,—Gagates,—so-called from Gagas, a river of Lycia, in Asia Minor,—though not a precious stone, is an article of the jeweller's trade, being wrought into personal ornaments, buttons, toys, and other such matters. It is a solid, dry, black, inflammable, fossil substance, hard, capable of taking a high polish, and glossy in its fracture. This bitumen is found in beds of dry coal, chiefly in rocks of the Tertiary, and Secondary periods. Important Jet-veins exist near Whitby, Yorkshire.

Shakespeare, in his *Lover's Complaint*, says:—

" A thousand favours from a maund [basket] she drew,
Of amber, crystal, and of beaded Jet."

(At Yarmouth the name "maund" is now given to a basket containing five hundred herrings.) Tennyson again has told incidentally of this fossil's deep black colour, in *The Day-Dream*:—

" Year after year unto her feet
The maiden's jet-black hair has grown."

Jet, in former times, was considered, when powdered, and mixed with beeswax, a sovereign ointment for reducing tumours. Also, mingled with wine it was given for the relief of toothache. Seeing that Jet is actually wood-coal, (a form of " carbon,") its remedial uses correspond naturally with those which we have specified under that heading. It is much harder, blacker, and tougher than cannel coal.

Cardanus tells that the saints of old wore bracelets, and rosaries, made of this substance, for numbering their prayers. Here, in our day, Jet is chiefly used for mourning jewelry. It is polished with tripoli, and oil. During manufacture it must be frequently moistened with water, or, becoming heated by the friction, it will fly to pieces. Thus, as Isidore saith, "it is kindled by water, and quenched by oil." "Being worn it helps the nightmare. An oyl may be made from jet, like oyl of amber, but with a stronger fire. Put to the nose this is good for joynt-gouts, cramps, convulsions, and palsies." "Everyone knows," quoth Schroder, "that an oyl drawn from rock-coal ripens wounds, and softens tumours." Similarly, Jet, when burnt, gives off a dense pungent smoke, which, if insufflated by the nostrils, will exercise the like remedial effects.

In Prussia the amber-diggers call Jet "black amber." They manufacture it into various ornamental articles, and sell these to unwary persons, as "black amber," at a great price.

THE ADDER STONE.

WHAT was formerly known as the "Adder Stone" is reported to have come again recently into demand. It was not, and is not, a stone at all, but simply a glass ring, which was worn in old times, prior to the Roman occupation of this country, as an amulet, or charm; but without having any actual connection with the adder, or other snake, beyond a reputed efficacy for curing the bites thereof. Such rings are rare now-a-days as relics of former times; but one of the same is occasionally picked up in a South of England rural district. This curio is accepted by antiquarians as a proof that the ancient Britons knew something about the art of making glass. Certain round perforated stones, (thought to have served the purpose of spindle-wheels, are similarly found, and pass by the name of Adder Stones. But the genuine article—the "*Ovum Anguinum*,"—was superstitiously held to owe its production to a number of adders putting their heads together, and hissing until their foam became consolidated into beads; which beads, or stones, were considered to be powerful charms against disease, as used by the Druids,

> "And the potent Adder-Stone,
> Gendered 'fore th' autumnal moon;
> When, in undulating twine,
> The foaming snakes prolific join."—
> *Mason* ("*Caractacus*.")

The origin of a belief in the magic power of most precious stones has always been traced to Chaldæa. Pliny refers to a book on the subject which was written by Lachalios, of Babylon.

Byron (in *Heaven and Earth*) relates about Azazial, a Seraph who fell in love with Anab, a granddaughter of Cain, that when the flood came he carried her under his wing to some other planet. It was this angel who "first taught the nature, and uses of precious stones" to mankind; how their virtues find response in the human body, which they affect accordingly—"like the stars"—

> "Making our dim existence radiant with
> Soft lights which were not ours."

This Poem is "a mystery:" founded on the passage in Genesis: "And it came to pass that the Sons of God saw the daughters of man that they were fair: and they took them wives of all which they chose."

Dr. E. Clapton, (lately Physician to St. Thomas's Hospital), tells, in his *Life of Saint Luke*, (Churchill, 1902), that the "beloved physician" affixed to his writings the personal seal which distinguished him.

The special symbol, or device thereupon, was the impression of a bull, or ox; and this signet has remained attributed to St. Luke ever since. In the title-page of the Douai version of the New Testament, 1633, occur the lines :—

"Effigies vituli, Luca, tibi convenit; exstat
Zachariæ in scriptis mentio prima tuis."

When in Greece St. Luke visited the famous temple at Epidaurus, of Æsculapius, the fabled god of the healing art. The priests of this mythical god devoted themselves to occultism, and their remedies were mystic. The divinations which they practised consisted chiefly in putting precious stones, or crystals, in water, within divining cups; the medical priests interpreting the nature of the disease, and its infallible remedy, according to the relative position, brilliancy, and special properties which the said stones revealed. By the Greeks similar stones were worn as protective charms. Each precious stone was considered to act as a sovereign remedy against some particular disease: the Carbuncle, and Ruby against plague; the Diamond against insanity; the Chrysolite against delirium; the Amethyst against alcoholism; Coral against poisons; Jade against renal diseases; Amber against contagion; whilst Agates, with serpents engraved thereupon, were specially dedicated to Æsculapius, whereby stings of serpents, and scorpions were cured. Furthermore, in large white crystals the Æsculapian priests professed to see visions, and to read future events. It is certain that Saint Paul at that time could exercise marvellous personal curative powers; as shown by his casting out the "spirit of Python" from the Thyatiran damsel who had "brought her masters much gain by sooth-saying;" and by his afterwards restoring Eutychus to life at Troas.

"Judea," says a modern writer, "is now a reminiscence; but the great ideas of the Jewish people have penetrated the whole Western world. The business of the Greek has utterly vanished; his fortune was spent centuries ago; nobody cares what his occupation was; but his ideas, expressed in language or stone, are priceless possessions for all time.

Respecting the twelve precious stones in the Breastplate of the Jewish High-Priest, Dr. Clapton has convincingly shown (*The Precious Stones of the Bible; Descriptive and Symbolical*," 1899), that a purposeful, significant harmony was designed, between these twelve, and the twelve foundations of the Holy City, described by St. John, in his Book of Revelation. Also that an intimate connection holds good between the Tribes, and Apostles, whose names were associated with their corresponding precious stones. He has further exposed the unfortunate renderings about several Biblical stones, as changed in the revised version of the Old Testament. Thus, in the passage, "the price of wisdom is above rubies," the Revisers have put for "rubies," in the margin, "red coral," or "pearls;" which could not possibly be. Both Coral, and Pearls are products of marine carcases, and therefore would be abominations in the eyes of all true Hebrews. Again, for "windows of Agates," the phrase "pinnacles of rubies" has been substituted; which is meaningless. Likewise, in every instance, for "Carbuncle" the Revisers have put marginally, "or Emerald;" and for "Emerald," "or Carbuncle;" as if these stones could be thus interchangeable. So, too, (Exodus xxviii. *v*. 18) Diamond has against it the marginal note, " or Sardonyx ; " as different a stone as possible. Once more, against "Jacinth," " or Amber " has been needlessly put; whereas Amber is not a precious stone at all.

Being allied, in certain important respects, to herbs, and medicinal plants, Precious Stones have been aptly, and happily termed, " blossoms of the rocks," also, " the flowers of the caves, and torrent beds."

The herbalists of old knowingly selected their healing plants on the " doctrine of signatures," or, a distinct correspondence of features, and effects between the manifest attributes of the herb or plant, and the positive symptoms of the malady which it was found to cure. Similarly, according to the same doctrine, it may be told by the attributes of not a few precious stones, (such as their colour, shape, and lustre,) for what illness, or bodily ailment, each of such stones is innately calculated to benefit, and protect its owner, and wearer.

EPITOME.

CONCLUSIVELY about Precious Stones as considered remedially, we will now epitomize their several aptitudes, and their respective claims for selection to be worn against this, or that infirmity of body, or mind.

The *Diamond*, because of its pure carbon, (highly-subtilised " Charcoal,") is of excellent avail against a disposition to acid, flatulent indigestion. It is furthermore a heart-cordial ; and inspires courage. It rallies the strength in old age.

At the Ball given by Milly Fane, of Lutrell Court, ("Comin' thro' the Rye," Mrs. Reeves: Helen B. Mathers, 1875), we are told :—" Here come the Listers :— Lister *mère*—in a low (save the mark !) black velvet dress, with uncommonly fine Diamonds resting on her withered, brown, fleshless old collar-bones. I suppose Mahogany is a better foil to the precious stones than Alabaster; since it is so much more often seen."

(Quite recently a right loyal motion was made by General Botha in the Legislative Assembly at Johannesburg, for purchasing the Cullinan Diamond, so as to present it to our King; and this was carried (all but unanimously). The gift is made by the people of the Transvaal as a token of their loyalty, and as gratefully commemorating the grant of responsible government to the Colony. General Botha justly maintained that the splendid stone, being the most valuable Diamond ever discovered, is pre-eminently fitted to be the brightest jewel in the British crown. But, nevertheless, considerable speculation must arise as to what His Majesty may best do with this magnificent jewel. The great size of the diamond is at once its chief virtue, and its serious hindrance. Cut it into a number of small brilliants, and all special interest therein vanishes straightway. Leave it as it is, or fashion it into a single large brilliant, and it would remain too large, and heavy to be worn. In fact, the King's Crown is already of great weight—thirty-nine ounces, and five penny-weights,—no light burden for His Majesty's head, on State occasions. The Cullinan diamond would increase this weight by about three quarters of a pound avoirdupois, which is what the jewel would weigh after being cut for the purpose.)

All the *Sapphires* are commendable by reason of their innate alumina (which obviates bleedings, as from piles and fluxes; likewise any tendency to catarrhal troubles, with sore throat). The true Sapphire makes its wearer devout, and chaste. The genuine *Ruby* keeps the body safe, and averts danger.

Agates ; the *Amethyst ;* and the *Opal*, are endowed with particular attributes for the advantage of their wearers, because containing Silica (flint) infinitesimally potentialised. The Agates include *Carnelian* (good against fluxes), the *Chalcedony* (which imparts physical strength when habitually worn), the *Onyx* (which is cordial), the *Sardonyx* (of some repute for dispelling tumours), and the *Bloodstone* (about the established virtues of which we tell at large in the body of this our book). The *Amethyst* subdues inebriety, and makes temperate, whilst maintaining a condition of pious calm. The *Opal* has special gifts toward improving the eyes of its wearers, both as regards sight, and as to their general strength for use. The *Beryl*, (and the Cat's-eye), embodying with their silica an oxide of iron, are tonic for constant adornment therewith. Again, the *Turquoise*—which is likewise a silicate,—helps the general bodily nutrition ; giving at the same time an immunity from danger through falls, and other such casualties.

Because containing both alumina and silica, in combination, the true *Emerald*, and the *Topaz* can boast special qualifications for wear by certain individuals. The former (*Emerald*) promotes a functional activity of the liver, and of the bile-making organs, (whilst giving relief from dysentery). Moreover, this stone, of a superlatively green colour, is admirably protective to the eyes of its possessor. The true Topaz prevents hæmorrhages ; and dispels troubled dreams.

Stones which embody Magnesium, (there being certain traces thereof in the Sapphires,) are opposed to scrofula in its various forms ; this constituent of a Precious Stone will also correct for children the liability to loose stools, of a grass-green colour. Meerschaum—being a Silicate of magnesium—perhaps owes to this occult formation the universal favour in which it is held for their pipes by smokers of choice tobaccos.

The *Topaz*, and the *Tourmaline*, through their fluorides, serve to promote the health of the teeth, and of the bones. They impart proper contraction in size to varicose veins of the legs. And, yet again, they prevent baldness; also they make whitlows wither, and become painlessly resolved.

Amber, being electric, and a fossil earth, will resolve glandular swellings over which it is worn, and will protect against soreness of the throat.

The *Garnets* (including the brilliant crimson Carbuncle) resist melancholy, and inspire gladness of spirit. They at the same time will give quiet to a palpitating heart.

The *Lodestone*, by its magnetic virtues, is of admirable service for inducing healthful sleep.

Coral (already told about at some length) should be supplied for an ornamental appendage to children when cutting their teeth. It prevents convulsions at such a time. Likewise it will cut short the paroxysms of whooping cough.

Malachite, which contains copper, will exercise the virtues of that metal, when outwardly applied, defending from cholera, and colic.

The *Lapis Lazuli* aids for healing boils, and sores.

Pearls, which are essentially Lime, specially organised, prove remedial against the complaints, and infirmities which that mineral substance has been shown to cure, or to prevent. They are excellently cordial for their wearers. But Lime, whilst a normal constituent of the healthy body, may be absorbed by its tissues in excess, as in goitrous districts. Then the whole assimilative system of nutrition suffers grievously; much in the same manner as too habitual a use of chalybeate waters will make the drinkers thereof bloodless. It is precisely in such a condition of lime-surfeit that the wearing of *Pearls* proves eminently beneficial. Similarly against obstinate acid indigestion, with a distaste for all fatty foods, self-ornamentation with Pearls is effectually remedial.

Thus have we attempted to concisely render some guidance in the choice of Precious Stones for their respective remedial virtues, and powers, as confidently advocated in these pages.

METALS—THE NOBLER.

INTRODUCTION.

AMONG the *Secrets of Physick and Philosophy*, first written in the German tongue by the most learned Theophrastus Paracelsus,—(and now published, 1633, in English, by John Hester, of London)—the " Seconde booke contains the ordering, and preparing of all metalls, mineralls, allumes, saltes, and such like, for medicines, both inwardly and outwardly; and for other uses." "Therefore," says he, "Gentle Reader; peruse this booke with discretion; and then if thou seest it stand to thy mind, set thy hand to the plough, and be diligent in thy worke; so that thou mayest knowe the proofe, and feele the ready commoditie thereof; for, yee shall understand that there is no medicine in the world that can be found of so quicke operation as the mineralls are, if they bee truely prepared, and as I shall shew you hereafter. But, if they be not well prepared, they are very hurtfull, and are not to bee allowed. Therefore looke that ye prepare them as I shall shew you; and then you shall wonder at their working."

"Heere, in this Treatise wee will set foorth that which wee have seen, and wrought, and prooved, and are expert therein. And, although it be sprung out of the Art of Alchemie, yet it is not to that intent; for, it serveth not to transmute metalles, but it serveth to helpe those diseased both inwardly, and outwardly; who—of the common sort of chirurgions—are counted uncurable, and are also given over of the physitians. Those patients shall be holpen through the hidden mysteries, and heavenly secrets of this science. For, I am sure there is nothing better in all physick that ministereth eyther better, or readyer helpe to cure man's body, than this science of preparing METALLS with fire rightly. I say—rightly prepared;- not as the unskilful apoticaries have ordered them; or as the unlerned physitians have occupied them; for, the apoticary is no other than a servant in the kitchin (as I may terme him) and no master cooke; so long as he knoweth not these preparations which I will shew you.

"In like manner it is to be thought of the physitian that hath no skill in these preparations. For, wee have seen, and prooved divers times that the first vapour or smoake of any herbe, or spice is the best that there is therein; and yet our learned physitians commaund it to be boyled until halfe be consumed." Then note, if the best flie awaye in the boyling, what strength can the medicine have? Therefore I say that the physitian, without this arte of preparation, is little or nothing worthe, although they tak the patient's money. For, he goeth to worke blindly, with a blinde leader, which is the apoticary. But the physitian that is expert in this science, and doth prepare his medicines truely, he is to be praysed above all other. Therefore is the Arte of Alchymie worthy to be praysed: and the Alchymist to be praysed also. Therefore I will not speak against this, but hold it in great estimation to our intention; that is, the helpe of the sicke, and diseased persons, and to prepare the mineralles wherewith you may doe that which cannot be done with any other hearbs, or simples or spices. And herewith will we finish this Preface, and write of the names of the *Metalls* which are occupied in this Arte."

By the ancient writers each of the nobler metals was associated with its particular precious stone, and with its special planet. Thus, Gold was ascribed to the Diamond, and dedicated to the Sun; Silver was ascribed to the Crystal, and dedicated to the Moon; Copper to the Amethyst, and dedicated to Venus; Lead to the Turquoise, and dedicated to Saturn; Tin to the Carnelian, and dedicated to Jupiter; Quicksilver to the Loadstone, and dedicated to Mercury; Iron (an ordinary metal) to the Emerald, and dedicated to Mars.

In the Middle Ages a prevailing chemical theory about metals ran thus:—The metals were considered to be composed of Sulphur, and Mercury. These substances (themselves compounds) were reckoned elementary in the composition of metals. Sulphur represented their combustible aspect, and also that which gave them their solid form; while Mercury was that to which their weight, and powers of becoming fluid, were owing. This theory was due to two main facts. Most ores of metals, especially of copper, and lead, contain much sulphur, which can either be obtained pure from them, or be recognized by its smell when burning. This gave rise to the sulphur theory; while the presence of mercury was inferred doubtless from the resemblance of the more commonly molten metals, silver, tin, and lead, to quicksilver. So that the properties of each metal respectively were put down to the presence of these two substances.

A list of Seven Noble Metals is that which obtained in the most ancient times: Gold, Electrum (clearly an alloy of gold and silver), Silver, Copper, Tin, Lead, Iron.

The subject of Metallurgy is just now attracting to itself special scientific attention. At Sheffield, to wit, there is a school established for the particular study of this science. Its chief, Professor J. O. Arnold, has recently delivered a lecture at the same on the "Internal Architecture of Metals," January 25th, 1907. Speaking there about a metal rod, as used in the construction of a motor-car, he explained that the metal forming this bar consists of crystals; "upon the nature of which towards one another depend nearly all those metallic properties that are of such great practical importance for working purposes." And it is an undoubted fact that these aggregated crystals are liable to fatigue from too prolonged, or too arduous a strain; which so-called "fatigue" of metals is a generic term now used to explain all cases of fracture, such as may be thus understood. It bears likewise on "repose in the living animal, as in the not living metal, or mineral." For, "there is more than a superficial resemblance between so-called 'fatigue' in a metal, and the fatigue of an overwrought literary man;"—"only the metallurgical explanation would be expressed in vastly different terms from the physiological explanation."

GOLD.

"Among metals," (which are, according to Aristotle, "Meteorites"), "there is none fairer in sight than Gold; also, in virtue there is none so effectual as Gold." Plato saith it is more temperate, and pure than other metals. For, it hath virtue to comfort, and to cleanse superfluities when gathered in bodies. And, therefore, it helpeth against leprosy, and meselry. (Recently, when Miss Viola Tree was attacked with measles, Sir F. Burnand wrote amusingly to her father, " Very sorry to hear of Miss Viola's illness. However, measles is (are) one (or more) of those things that flesh is heir, and heiress to ; and I trust that the attack will not be severe, but run its normal course, and leave your daughter (as soon as possible) better than ever. It is a cowardly distemper, coming in the plural, and attacking a defenceless unit. The case, however, can never be singular." "Ours, being a large family, we had the measles divided among five children all at once, a measle apiece. This lightened the attack, but increased the doctor's bill."—" I doubt," said David Copperfield, "whether two young birds could have known less about keeping house than I, and my pretty Dora did. We had a servant, of course. Her name was Paragon. Her nature was represented to us, when we engaged her, as being but feebly expressed in that name. She was a woman in the prime of life; of a severe countenance; and subject (particularly in the arms) to a sort of perpetual measles!" "She had a cousin in the Life Guards, with such long legs that he looked like the afternoon shadow of somebody else."

Three parts of sulphur, and three of caustic potash,

dissolve one part of Gold when boiled with it in water. This is the process of Stahl, and is the one he supposed Moses was acquainted with when reducing the Golden Calf of the idolatrous Israelites to a fine powder, and making them drink thereof. But this notion of Stahl's is refuted by the words of the Scriptural text (Exodus xxxii. 20), "He took the calf which they had made, and burnt it in the fire, and ground it to powder, and strewed it upon the water, and made the children of Israel to drink of it." " Not the least intimation is here given" (says Professor Pepper, *Play Book of Metals*), " of the gold having been dissolved, chemically speaking, in water. After the form of the calf had been destroyed by melting in the fire, it was stamped, and ground, or, as the Arabic, and Syriac versions have it, filed, into a fine dust, and thrown into the river, of which the children of Israel would drink. Part of the finely-powdered gold would remain, notwithstanding its greater specific gravity, suspended for a time on the surface of the river; in which condition the gold might be swallowed, distastefully indeed, but harmlessly, together with the water, in the manner described. If actually the Israelites had drank the gold in a state of solution they must have thus imbibed a rank poison."

Gold is altogether insoluble in either of the mineral acids when used uncombined. Finely-divided gold may be boiled for any length of time in either nitric, hydrochloric, or sulphuric acid, and no solution of the metal will take place; but directly nitric and hydrochloric acids are mixed together (thus making " nitromuriatic " acid), then the gold, if immersed therein, will be attacked, and soon disappear; and then, if this solution is afterwards slowly evaporated, pure terchloride of gold is the result. The mixed acids thus described, when containing gold dissolved therein, make a compound known as "aqua regia."

The classical story of Jason and the Golden Fleece has been frequently suggested to be a fanciful romance in which is embodied an ancient rude method of collecting gold (when washed down with the stream adjacent to the telluric source of the metal) by means of sheep's fleeces. So that the "fleecing" of the King of Colchis probably signified the robbery from him of the gold collected in this way from the streams, and rivers of his country.

The quality of Gold is estimated by the number of carats of pure Gold in an ounce (troy); thus, pure Gold is of twenty-four carat; half pure Gold is of twelve carat only; but Gold is most commonly of nine carat. Each carat may be reckoned as of value 3s. 6d. Gold for coin consists of eleven parts of pure Gold, and one part of copper.

"Gold was called by the older chymists the Sun; because it was thought sympathetically to answer the Sun in the macrocosm (in a general sense); and the heart in the microcosm (as concerning man); and thus the character of the Sun and Gold became all one." "Gold is the king of metals, because it is chief of them. The Arabian Gold is held to be best; then the Hungarian; and then that of Rheine." "It is a great strengthener," according to Dr. Schroder, (*Chymical Dispensatory*, 1669,) "of the natural balsam, or heat; and is given as a cordial to strengthen in all diseases; it cleanseth the blood by discussing humours by sweat." "The antients put leaf-gold into many compositions; but I know not for what end but to feed the eye; for, its substance is too solid, and compact to be dissolved by our heat, and brought into act; nor is it available that some make the vertues, or spirits of Gold sympathising to those of the heart, and therefore give leaf-gold; for, by that same facility it may destroy the heart. And it may be apply'd outwardly in greater quantity, and with more profit, with little, or no inconvenience." Dr. W. Salmon tells (*Family Dictionary*, 1696) that the famous " Manus Christi " was made in his day with gold-leaf, rose-water, and sugar. ("A rose, besides its beauty, is a cure," sings George Herbert.)

With regard to the efficacy of Gold as a remedy in various diseases, Dr. Salmon was most vehement of classical utterance : "*Cujus virtutes infinitæ sunt; nec libro integro comprehendi possunt. Beatissimus est Medicus qui eo uti potest; ut honoris culmen acquiret, et oculos omnium, et linguas, laudes, et encomia, prædicantes, in se convertat.*"

The Muriate, or Chloride, of Gold has recently been employed, in very reduced quantities injected under the skin, for curing "lupus," a cancerous ulceration which eats away the skin of the face, with terrible disfigurement. The solution thus used for injection is exceedingly attenuated, to the degree of one per cent; and signal success has attended this plan of treatment in several cases.

Again, the Bromide of Gold, a combination of metallic Gold with bromine, has proved singularly useful for the relief, or even actual cure, of epilepsy.

Goubert, the French physician, found that the Bromide of Gold completely controlled epilepsy; some cases going for several years without any return of the complaint. The same remedy has likewise a marked curative effect upon chronic rheumatism. One prominent physician reports that since taking this remedy he has not suffered from rheumatism in the least ; a relief such as he had not experienced before for years. What chemists name the " Bibromide" of Gold is still more effectual for bringing about the cures now mentioned.

Late writers tell of highly gratifying results from the use of Gold Bromide in a variety of diseases; "notably in spinal troubles from thickening of the cord, and in locomotor ataxia." Once again, Gold is remarkably beneficial for restoration of the sexual functions.

But these preparations should only be employed internally under competent advice, and supervision ; the utmost care must be exercised in their preparation ; none but glass, and porcelain utensils being used. The said medicaments should not be allowed to come into contact with another metal at any time, either during their manufacture, or when dispensed.

Linné wrote concerning the metal Gold, " It is a *vis politica* ; a *usus œconomicus*." " Magpies, crows, and other thieving birds are attracted by its colour, and sheen."

When administered medicinally a soluble preparation of Gold (the Chloride) if given in quite small, fractional doses, stimulates the functions of the brain, and promotes improved digestion ; but in large doses the same salt of Gold is a violent poison. Geber extolled Gold as a " *materia lætificans, et in juventute corporis conservans.*"

Pliny, the elder, in the year 76, wrote : "*Aurum plurimis modis pollet in remediis ;—vulneratisque et infantibus applicatur ut mirus noceant quæ inferantur veneficia. Ex melle vero decoctum cum melantho, et illitum umbilico leviter, solvit alvum. Verrucas curavi eo." "Aurum"* (Gold), declared Glauber, 1657,) *"medicina est catholica in senibus, et juvenibus*—for both old, and young;—*quia est in eo virtus dominitiva.*" The Greek word *auron* is parent of the Latin *aurum*, and of the French *or*; but the more usual Greek name of the metal is now *kreusos*.

" Aurum (Gold)," said the famous Hahnemann, " has great remedial virtues, the place of which no other drug can supply." *Das Gold hat grosse, unersetzliche Arzneikraefte.*

Dr. J. C. Burnett published in 1879 a treatise on " *Gold, as a Remedy in Disease*," " notably in some forms of organic heart disease." Bearing reference to the quotation from Hahnemann given above, Dr. Burnett then said, in the Preface to his booklet, " Having myself used Gold in my practice for several years, I have come to regard it in the same light as Hahnemann." " I cannot do without it." " To my mind there are varieties of disease that Gold, and Gold only, will cure; and others that Gold, and Gold only, will alleviate to the full extent of the possible." " As a heart-remedy alone it claims the most earnest attention of every medical man." " In my practice I have used the Muriate of Gold a good deal; but I prefer the pure triturated metal "; " it being an incontrovertible fact that metallic Gold, though otherwise insoluble, may be so finely subdivided that it becomes operative upon the living tissues of the body, and thus acquires medicinal properties of the highest order." " The history of Gold," writes Dr. Burnett, " begins very early in the records of our race; it is the first metal discovered by man; and also the first metal mentioned in the Bible." The eleventh verse of the second chapter of Genesis reads, "The name of the first is Pison, that is it which compasseth the whole land of Havilah, where there is gold." Thus it is scripturally noticed even before Eve was created. "The first trituration of Gold (as has been already mentioned in these pages) was made by Moses from the golden calf of the idolatrous Israelites."

Dioscorides, and Avicenna employed Gold in the metallic state as a remedy. Paracelsus used it with sublimate as a universal panacea, calling this "*Calcinatio, et solutio solis*" ("Calcined, and dissolved sunlight.")

Gold was highly prized, and praised by the Alchemists of old; they being in a search (more or less scientific as at that day) for the philosopher's stone; so that it then became also the stock-in-trade of secret-mongers, and quacks of all kinds; the result being that eventually the medical profession abandoned the therapeutic use of this valuable metal altogether. At length, some generations later on, "Hahnemann," says Dr. Burnett, "gathered up the disjointed fragments of knowledge concerning Gold as a remedy, and welded them together, with the light of his law, thus giving fixity to the whole." The proof of this assertion lies in the fact that Gold has never ceased to be used by his followers as a means of cure, in cases judged appropriate, from his day to this; and that is well nigh for eighty years.

The ancient Alchemists had their "Powder of Gold," their "Tincture of Gold," their "True Potable Gold," their "Tincture of the Sun," their "Golden Tincture," etc., etc. "Furthermore," continues Dr. Burnett, "Gold deserves a very much higher place in the armamentarium of the physician than is accorded to it in general."

"For centuries Gold has been used with excellent effect in scrofula, heart-disease, skin diseases, dropsy, melancholia, and the morbus Gallicus, or syphilis." "But of course the metal must be first highly triturated, or else dissolved, in order to become remedial." As to the results of Gold, taken experimentally, and to a toxic extent, by persons in full health, triturated gold-leaf (*Aurum foliatum*) being used for this purpose, they have been plaintive depression of spirits, melancholy, and passionate irritability; or, in some instances, great hilarity, as just the opposite condition. Again, pustular eruptions have appeared on the face, with inflamed soreness inside the nostrils. Symptoms of asthma, with disturbance of the heart's action, were produced in some of the provers; difficult breathing, and a sensation of heavy weight beneath the breast-bone, being marked symptoms; precisely what occurs in " angina pectoris." It is certain that a whole series of Arabian physicians successively employed finely powdered Gold, beginning as far back as the eighth century.

It has been repeatedly found that dry, warm weather favours the curative action of Gold; whereas cold and wet weather has quite an opposite effect, even aggravating the symptoms for which the Gold is given. Moreover, the fact is well ascertained that the preparations of Gold will act beneficially sometimes for a long while after they have ceased to be given.

Pliny, who died in the year 79, described at large the use of Gold in medicine. His translators, Bostock, and Riley, tell that the external application of pure Gold will remove styes on the eyelids. A popular adoption of this teaching is in vogue to this day, as shown by the common practice of wetting a gold ring with fasting saliva, and then gently rubbing the ring thus moistened, (and probably superficially dissolved by the saliva), along the outside of the eyelid over the stye. Again, M. Varro assures us that Gold is a cure for warts.

Dr. Richard Hughes, in his noted *Pharmacodynamics*, has said concerning Gold, "It is an admirable remedy for constitutions broken down by the combined influence of syphilis and mercury. I once gave a poor fellow thus afflicted the trituration of gold (finely diluted with dry, powdered, inert sugar of milk). He came back to me in a week's time looking quite another man, and exclaimed, 'Surely you have given me the elixir of life!'"

As to the efficacy of Gold in melancholia, Hahnemann has said, and his followers have fully verified the dictum, "I have cured several cases of melancholy (similar to those produced by Gold in its provers), promptly, and permanently, with this metal; and the cases were of such persons as went about with the serious intention of committing suicide." For the whole treatment of any such a case Hahnemann needed only the nine-hundredth part of a grain of pure Gold (triturated into a powder, together with some inert substance, such as the powdered sugar of milk). Once more: Gold has shown itself to be a capital remedy in old age; not that it will make an old organism young; but, nevertheless, it will materially benefit the senility, thus, *pro tanto*, rejuvenate it.

For dental purposes Gold is used either cohesive, or not cohesive; in the latter case it is made solid within the hollow tooth-cavity by close compression. Gold-leaf is the form of the metal employed (*Aurum foliatum*). Seeing that Chloride of Gold is a soluble salt, and the assertion being made by some chemists that by combination with the saliva a soluble Sulphocyanide of the metallic Gold (when made the basis of false teeth within the mouth) is produced, the important question naturally presents itself, may not the constant chemical action thus going on from day to day, (together with absorption of its products by the mucous membrane within the mouth,) exercise a prejudicial effect insidiously on the health of sensitive persons, thus morbidly undermining the same, whilst the latent cause altogether escapes suspicion? Indisputably, too, there is almost a certainty that the table-salt eaten with food, (such table-salt being a compound of chlorine and sodium,) will act chemically on the metallic Gold of the teeth-setting, and will form in this way persistently a daily measure of injurious soluble Chloride of Gold during mastication of the meal.

Dentists likewise employ another metal—Zinc, the phosphate,—as a filling powder, for stopping cavities in carious teeth; the calcined oxide of Zinc, when pulverized, is mixed with crystals of, (or fluid) glacial phosphoric acid, so as to make a stuffing which presently hardens within the dental cavity, being applied along its floor.

It may be thought straining the point beyond probability, almost beyond possibility, to suppose that the Zinc in this minute quantity, and solid form, can slowly, in a subtle manner, undermine the health of any person within whose mouth, and subject to a minimum amount of continuous absorption, are teeth (one, or more) which have been thus stopped. And yet it has been experimentally ascertained that the Oxide of Zinc, taken in doses all but inappreciable, for some length of time uninterruptedly, "has a marked effect on the nervous centres, causing giddiness, sleeplessness, chronic itching of the skin, and muscular tremblings of the arms, and legs."

Thus also Wilmer testifies about Zinc " The action of extremely small doses, if their use is prolonged, may produce a general decay of strength, with prostration of the nutritive functions; the intellectual faculties become likewise impaired; the beats of the heart become slow and feeble; whilst the walking powers, and the general bodily endurance are enfeebled to a high degree." The phosphide of Zinc, given in doses of the seventy-second part of a grain, has been found to produce severe frontal stabbing headache. So, it would certainly seem that to have hollow teeth stopped with pure Gold-leaf, though more costly, is much the safer plan.

Concerning human saliva a remarkable statement made by Bartholomew Anglicus (*On the Properties of Things*, 1250), is on record : " The spittle of a man fasting hath, in a manner, strength of privy infection. For it grieveth and hurteth the blood of a beast, if it come into a bleeding wound, and is medlied with the blood. And that peradventure is, as saith Avicenna, by reason of rawness. And therefore it is that holy men tell that the spittle of a fasting man slayeth serpents, and adders; and is venom to venomous beasts, as saith Basil."

Whilst discoursing of false teeth, to make amends for the losses within the mouth caused by advancing age, we may mention the somewhat alarming theory (at least as regards men who are more than half a century old), which has lately been revived by Professor Osler; whose fixed notion is that after their sixtieth year men are practically useless to the State, and to the rest of the community. He reminds us that certain wise nations in former times ordained that by their laws "*sexagenarii*" (men past sixty) should be precipitated to destruction from a bridge. In Rome such men were styled "depontani." Anthony Trollope has written a charming novel, *The Fixed Period*, discussing the practical advantages in our modern life of returning to this usage; his leading idea therein being that of instituting a College into which at sixty, men should have to retire for a year of quiet meditation before being peacefully disposed of by chloroform.

But any such sweeping charge of incapacity as a general rule after the sixtieth birthday is founded upon error. With many a man, as Cicero tells, in his *De Senectute*, even if the body then shows signs of decay, the mind continues with unabated vigour, and strength. Furthermore, the physical longevity of comparative youthfulness varies much according to the innate vitality individually possessed. And in no small measure such a degree of longevity may be cultivated, and acquired.

Hermippus, an ancient Roman, had learnt this secret. Feeling that his years were beginning sensibly to tell, he cut himself clear from all companions coeval with himself, and associated only with young, active, healthy persons, taking part in their games, their pursuits, and their studies. Acting thus wisely, he lived to the age of one hundred and fifty-three years,—"*puerorum habitu relocillatus, et educatus.*"

A certain little book—now extremely scarce—was published in the time of Charles I., having been written by John Taylor; "*The Old, Old, Very Old Man;* or *The Long Life of Thomas Parr;* (of Winnington,

Alderbury Parish, Salop), born in the reign of Edward IV.; and now living in the Strand, aged one hundred and fifty-two years." The woodcuts in this small volume, occupying about two inches square, whilst having its particular page devoted to each, were hexagonal, and represent Parr's presentation to the King, his journey to London (very quaint); cheating his landlord, his visit to the Fair, etc., etc.

As to the ages which animals respectively attain in the ordinary course of their nature, only vague notions are commonly entertained. The facts are, that, given ordinary health, and luck, a dog will live to the age of fifteen years, a cat for a dozen, or more, but a rabbit only five years. Seven-and-twenty years are about the extreme of a horse's age; the cow, the ox, and the pig have their lives prolonged to some twenty-five years apiece; whilst the lion and the camel endure for forty years. The elephant, if left to himself, in peace, will exist for a century; and, yet more patriarchal, the tortoise can survive on throughout four centuries.

The Alchemical symbol—as derived from the Arabians —which signified Gold, was an outer linear ring, enclosing within its circumference, at its centre, a much smaller circle; and yet again within this smaller circle, a central small dark spot. It was Geber (or, rather, Abou Moussah Djafar, al Sofi) who is said to have first made the important discovery about "Aqua Regia," nitric, and sulphuric acids, and the metallic salts. The term "Alchemy" was originally adopted about the time of Geber; this being derived from the Arabic *tal*, "the," and *kema*, dark, or secret.

Dr. Samuel Johnson, the lexicographer, has asserted that the origin of the word "gibberish," as signifying that which is outlandish, and more or less rhapsodical nonsense, first arose from the name of Geber, because his works were written in such a very unintelligible style. As an illustration of this style we may quote a passage (bearing reference to the "philosopher's stone"; which was to turn everything it touched into Gold) :—" Thence we define our stone to be a generalising, or fruitful spirit, and living water, which we name Dry Water, by natural proportion cleansed, and united, with such union that its principles can never be separated one from another; to which two a third must be added for shortening the work, and that is one of the perfect bodies attenuated, or subtilised." Geber was well acquainted with the properties of Gold, and of other metals. He was succeeded in the year 1193, by the famous Albertus Magnus, who in his day made great efforts to discover the philosopher's stone, and the elixir vitæ.

Roger Bacon, another noted Alchemist, and Raymond Lully, were contemporaries of Albertus Magnus. The latter of these two is worthy of praise because he took Geber for his model, and, instead of pursuing the pretended arts of astrology, and necromancy, studied most diligently the nature, and properties of the metals. Roger Bacon firmly believed in the possibility of transmuting other metals into Gold. Many years subsequently our Henry VI. granted Letters Patent to several persons for investigating a universal medicine, and for performing the transmutation of certain baser metals into Gold, and Silver. These Letters Patent remained in full force until the year 1689, when the noted Robert Boyle obtained their repeal because the Act was supposed to operate to the discouragement of the melting, and refining of metals. Professor Pepper relates in his *Play Book of Metals*, 1877, that "At the time when Alchemy flourished as a thriving trade, nothing was more common than to find men in the garb of beggars who professed to be Alchemists. Such persons made their way unscrupulously through the towns, and villages, quietly duping many avaricious victims who were ashamed to complain openly of their losses. But with Pope Julian they met different consequences. This shrewd Pontiff, when canvassed by a fellow who undertook to make the Prelate's fortunes by metallic transmutation, if first supplied with a little ready money to go on with, presented the rogue with an empty purse, remarking that of course the possessor of the transmutation secret could easily fill this purse! Sometimes the charlatans would display a rusty iron nail, and a bottle of the wonderful elixir; then some cabalistic high-sounding words were solemnly pronounced, the nail was stirred in the elixir, and now Gold would flash on the eyes of the delighted, and credulous beholders. The nail was straightway handed round for inspection, and was found apparently changed into Gold where it had been immersed in the elixir. Of course it was urged that the small quantity of fluid remaining in the hands of the Alchemist had then parted with its power! But some more could be similarly made if only money were forthcoming to buy the necessary apparatus, and chemicals. When these funds were provided, the impostor decamped, taking with him his prepared nail, one half of it being iron, and the other half Gold, so that when the nail was stirred in the elixir (i.e., water), this innocent liquid served to remove the outer covering of paint, and the Gold appeared. One such a nail is still preserved in a cabinet of curiosities belonging to the Grand Duke of Tuscany. A monk presented a dagger of similar construction to Queen Elizabeth of England, the blade of which was half Gold, and half steel, the former having been alleged to be the product of transmutation. Coins, prepared in a like manner, one face being made of Gold, and the other of silver, were also shown to the credulous as proofs of the successful transmuting art.

By another such mode of conjuring (under the name of transmutation, but really by sleight of hand), Gold, or silver, covered with wax, was conveyed into the crucible, and disclosed when the heat had melted away the wax. Indeed, this is perhaps one of the oldest tricks ; and finds its parallel in the pious fraud of the good Spanish monk who produced an omelette in a frying-pan out of his staff for one of his hungry flock, having conveyed therein beforehand the materials usually employed for making that culinary delicacy.

The chief Alchemists who distinguished themselves in the sixteenth and seventeenth centuries were Auguretto, Cornelius Agrippa, and Paracelsus. The latter was a man of undoubted talent and abilities, but also of the most outrageous vanity, which displayed itself in empty boasts, and bombastic assertions. His true name was Hohenheim ; to which appellation were prefixed the baptismal names Aureolus Theophrastus Bombastes Paracelsus ! He affirmed that he had learnt the art of transmutation, and was also possessed of the elixir vitæ. And it is said that he died in consequence of drinking too freely of this last-named remedy, so as to stave off old age,—the said remedy turning out to be strong distilled alcohol! Last of the Alchemists came Dr. Dee, who was half crazed by his belief in this so-called art; as likewise in his Crystal, of a convex form, which he alleged had been presented to him by no less a person than the angel Uriel. Dr. Dee believed also in the possibility of communicating with the spirits of the invisible world, supposing that he had only by looking intently into his Crystal to behold those who had been long dead, and to converse with them. It is now known that this wondrous crystal was nothing more than a polished piece of cannel coal. In a catalogue of a well-remembered sale held by Mr. George Robins, 1842 (that of the effects of Horace Walpole, at Strawberry Hill) we find the following puff:—" One glance must be allowed at the little glass case in the corner, which is filled with curiosities. Here is the wondrous speculum of the renowned Dr. Dee,—the mirror which Kelly (another contemporary magician) did all his feats upon." The same is a highly polished piece of cannel coal, of a circular form, with a handle to it. It is a very mysterious-looking object, and worthy of being called " the devil's looking-glass."

As regards the planetary symbol of the sun, previously noticed here, it is to be said that the origin of such planetary symbols—applied to all the nobler metals—is wrapt in obscurity; what their primitive meaning signified is by no means clear. Obviously the moon—which denotes the metal silver,—was designated by the crescent, as a representation of herself. The alchemists of the sixteenth and seventeenth centuries, who were all more or less astrologers, thought out an explanation of these planetary metallic symbols, which briefly was this: Gold, as we have told, was represented by a circle, with a dot in the centre, *id est*, the character signifying the sun; the circle being always taken as the index of perfection and simplicity, because enclosing the greatest space under the least superficies; all straight lines drawn from its centre to the circumference being equal. Gold was betokened as the most simple metal, the most perfect, and the heaviest, because it includes the greatest quantity of matter under the least surface. The character for the Moon (signifying silver) was a half circle, because it is half Gold, as chemists agree, but that half lies hid. The character for Copper (Venus) denotes that the body is of Gold, joined with some corrosive menstruum. The explanation of the character for Lead was the same as for Tin, but inverted, with the corrosive passing through the middle. Neither of these two significations is clear. A skull—(*caput mortuum*)—was designed, and shown at the end of the metallic symbols; this "*caput mortuum*" meaning the residue of dregs left in the retort, or alembic, after distillation.

The Arabian physicians were in the habit of using Gold,—giving the metal itself in a fine powder—as a medicine, which proved highly curative in their hands. Far later, in 1811, Chretien revived in Paris the curative use of powdered metallic Gold; making public his *Observations sur un Nouveau Remède dans le Traitement des Maladies Vénériennes, et Lymphatiques*, wherein he communicated a number of cases illustrating the curative value of this medicine in syphilis, and scrofula. He stated that finely powdered Gold-leaf produces the same beneficial effect as the Chloride, or the Oxide, of the metal. The nasal action of the medicine has led to its successful use in raw soreness within the nostrils, with formation of crusts therein, attended with offensive smelling of putrid odours.

Hahnemann has stated that the most striking medicinal analogue of Gold as to its curative effects is Platinum, which is "to the female sex what Gold is to the male."

As we have told in our *Kitchen Physic*, "The pulp of tamarinds possesses naturally traces of Gold in its composition." This small quantity, though scarcely appreciable by chemical testing, may nevertheless exercise a very positive beneficial effect against those diseases in which, as we have seen, the metal administered in material doses acts specifically.

A century ago our grandsires quaffed "lemon-punch,"—in various forms,—copiously. One such form was that of "quack punch" (much of a favourite) made with gin, and flavoured with black currant whisky, whilst having two pods of sweet tamarinds added to each bowl. Again, likewise the cockle (*Cochlea*, a shell-fish), or "poor man's oyster," is supposed to possess Gold, though infinitesimally, in its composition, as derived from sea-water. It may therefore be taken as an acceptable esculent towards helping to cure the same aforesaid diseases for which tamarinds are to be commended. "These cockles," writes Yorke-Davies, (no mean authority), "are in their nature the most delicious, and the most digestible bivalve that the sea produces. Properly dressed, the cockle has only to be tasted to be appreciated. Like the oyster, if it is boiled it is spoiled. The proper way to cook a cockle is to put it in a saucepan without any water, except the water contained within the cockle-shell itself. It should come almost to the boil, and then the steam cooks the cockle thoroughly. As soon as the shell is open the cockle inside is fit to eat; and with a brisk fire this occurs in a very few minutes. If it is cooked beyond this stage, or boiled, it is simply, as is the case with the oyster, rendered hard and unpalatable." Like the oyster, too, it should be served with bread and butter.

In *Queen Mab* (Percy's *Reliques*) we read about :—

> "The brains of nightingales,
> With unctuous fat of snails,
> Between two Cockles stewed,
> Is meat that's easy chewed."

> "Quantum in luscinia latet cerebri,
> Et testudinum adeps inunctiorum,
> Cum binis Cochleis perinde coctus,
> Non est difficilis cibus molari."

But cockles rapidly take in the infective bacilli of typhoid fever when such are present in the sea-water which the bivalves are inhabiting. Speedily the number of these noxious organisms increases in a large measure, even though the cockles are removed, and put into fresh pure water, or are kept in clean sand for several days; insomuch that it would be still dangerous to take them as food.

As an historical instance of the faith which was formerly attached to the external use, and application of metallic Gold, may be quoted the ceremony which used to be conducted annually at Westminster, on Good Friday, of blessing cramp rings: which ceremony was carried out by the king himself. He went into the Chapel Royal on that day, accompanied only by his Almoner; and then, crawling on his knees to the crucifix, he there blessed bowlfuls of golden, and silver rings. These rings were afterwards distributed to be worn by persons afflicted with epilepsy, or rheumatism. The practice had its origin in a certain miracle-working ring which was given by a saintly pilgrim to Edward the Confessor, and which was kept in Westminster Abbey. Similarly it was believed during the first half of the nineteenth century that in various maladies the application of metallic plates to the soles of the feet brought about curative results, as also to carry metallic balls within the palms of the hands. Gold was reputed to increase the vitality; Silver to clear the brain; (and Sulphur to cure rheumatism).

As regards certain further facts about Gold—medicinally considered—than those which have come under our notice thus far in the present treatise, a repeated reference may be now permitted to several pertinent particulars which have been detailed previously in our *Animal Simples*. This metal was used curatively by the Chinese two thousand years before Christ. As a "good medicine to be employed by one that is in a consumption," there was ordered of old, 1650, "to be presently drunk with a cake, or two, of *Manus Christi*, made of Gold, (or Pearls),—asses' milk, concocted with rose-water, and hen eggs."

Plato declared, "The peelings of Gold taken in food, or drink, do preserve, and hinder breeding of leperhood; or this hideth it, and maketh it unknown."

In the *Rich Storehouse of Medicines*, 1650, is given, as a sovereign drink for any infected person: "Take a piece of fine Gold, or the leaves of pure beaten Gold, and put it into the juyce of lemmons, and let it lye therein for the space of twenty-four hours; then take the same juyce, and put to it powder of Angelica root; and then mingle them with white wine; and let the patient drink a good draught thereof. This is a most pretious drink; and it is greatly to be wondered at what help, and remedy some that have used this drink have had thereby; although it hath been supposed by many learned physicians that the sick persons were past all hope of remedy, yet, by God's providence, they have recovered again." The *New London Dispensatory* (1695) ordered Gold, or "Sol," in various forms; such as Thundering Gold; Sweating Gold; Potable Gold; Flowers of Gold; Salt of Gold; Transparent Glass of Gold; Faber's Tincture of Gold; and Dye of Gold. Evidently, therefore, much curative value, and remedial importance were attached to this leading metal at that time. Dr. Salmon, the compiler of this *Dispensatory* (above-named) added further "that superlative Gold, given in Canary Wine, will revive such as are senseless, and stupid; being excellent therefore for dull pupils; it takes away the malignity of cancers, causing their speedy healing." "It exceeds," saith Horstius, "all other secrets in strengthening the heart, and all other parts of the humane body which serve for the conservation of life; it keeps back old age, and renews the radical moisture." "It may be taken at any time in cinnamon-water, or broth, or milk." Shakespeare, after the same fashion, in modern times, has made Prince Henry (Henry IV.) speak of Gold as "preserving life, in medicine potable"; this is because of its supposed incorruptibility, which it will communicate to the body of him who takes it, or wears it next the person.

Chaucer had written, at an earlier date, respecting it:

"For, Gold in physic is a cordiall,
  Therefore he loved Gold in special."

A quaint Latin distich sums up the same matter with much force of epigram :—

"Pharmaca das ægroto ; Aurum tibi porrigit æger ;
 Tu morbum curas illius ; iste tuum."

Pious George Herbert sings reverently in his poem, *The Church*, that the true Elixir of Life is discovered when we see God in all things :—

"This is the famous Stone
That turneth all to Gold ;
For that which God doth touch, and own
Cannot for less be told.
A servant with this clause
Makes drudgerie divine ;
Who sweeps a room as for Thy laws,
Makes that, and th' action fine."

In substitution for the "Cramp" rings, under several occupiers of the throne, pieces of Gold were given to the applicants for the "Royal Touch"; a Gold coin perforated for suspension to the neck, being conferred on each. But William III. was far more sturdy-minded than to encourage this superstitious custom. On one occasion he laid a hand on an importunate supplicant, with the invocation, "God give you better health, and more sense!"

Nevertheless, under Queen Anne the ceremony was renewed. During her reign a Church of England Prayer-book contained a Form of Service. "At the Healing," the Queen laying hands on the infirm persons who knelt in her presence, then proceeded to put the Gold about their necks; the Chaplain turning to her Majesty and beseeching God's blessing on her work.

A belief in the possible efficacy of a royal curative "touch," (implicit faith in which is inspired by the circumstances, and surroundings,) may certainly claim authority from Scripture. Christ Himself, the supreme psychic teacher of human capabilities for healing, has warranted such a practical doctrine. "If ye have faith, as a grain of mustard-seed, nothing shall be impossible unto you." A striking instance of such healing, and a fair example of our Lord's utterances on this subject, stand recorded in Matthew ix. 28, 29, 30 : " And when He was come into the house, the blind men came to Him; and Jesus saith unto them, Believe ye that I am able to do this ? They said unto Him, Yea, Lord. Then He 'touched' their eyes, saying, According to your faith be it unto you. And their eyes were opened." Again : " And, behold, a woman, which was diseased with an issue of blood twelve years, came behind Him, and 'touched' the hem of His garment. For, she said within herself, If I may but 'touch' His garment, I shall be whole. But Jesus turned Him about; and when He saw her, He said, Daughter, be of good comfort; thy faith hath made thee whole. And the woman was made whole from that hour."

Native Gold always contains more or less silver; when the proportion reaches twenty per cent, this is called "Electrum." In the Calcite of New South Wales, finely-divided Gold is found, as " sponge-Gold "; " mustard-Gold "; and " paint-Gold."

Amulets of Gold were also highly esteemed of old. This precious metal was thought to strengthen the heart, drive away melancholy, and other bodily infirmities. Silver was supposed to exercise similar properties, but in a lesser degree. Amulet Rings were always worn on the third finger, which was called the "medicine finger," because through it the heart was held to be most susceptible to any such influence; *Quia in illo digito est quædam vena procedens usque ad cor.*" The Jews used the eleventh and twelfth verses of the 139th Psalm as an amulet to discover hidden thieves; it being supposed that through hearing these mystic words they would find themselves compelled to come forth into daylight. The modern burglar requires an amulet of a more forcible nature in these very practical days of the common law, and the police courts.

The greatest part of the Gold of commerce, commonly called Gold-dust, is obtained by washing the sands of rivers in South America, and Brazil.

Pure Gold is remarkable for its exceeding ductility, and malleability. A single grain of Gold may be extended into a leaf which will cover fifty-four and a quarter square inches, being not more than a millionth part of an inch in thickness. None of the acids except the nitromuriatic have any action upon Gold. "Aurum Potabile"—potable Gold—is an ethereal solution thereof, being an inert compound of Nitromuriate of Gold, with ether, and some essential oil. According to the French physicians, the best mode of medicinally exhibiting the salts of Gold,—for instance, the Chloride of Gold (and Soda),—is by means of friction on the gums; or rubbing this in externally where the skin is most thin.

Furthermore, if Gold, as Chaucer puts it, gives comfort to the heart, it likewise, according to Bartholomew Anglicus, 1250, gives wisdom and sense to the brain; for, "as some men ween, that the milt is cause of laughing, it is by this spleen we are moved to laugh, by the gall we are wrath, by the heart we are wise, by the brain we feel, and by the liver we love."

Incidentally here, Coral may receive a further passing notice because often considered to exercise powerful tonic effects on the brain. Marbodeus, in his writings, *De Lapidibus Pretiosis*, when telling of Coral as an admirable remedy against demoniacal possession, has said :—

"Fulmina, Typhones, Tempestatesque, repellit
A rate, vel tecto. . . . . . .
Umbras dæmoniacas, et Thessala Monstra repellit ;
Collo suspensus pellit de ventre dolorem."

Treating of laughter: this may sometimes be grim, ironical, and (as is the rule in melodramas) "that of a fiend." For, it seems that your fiends always laugh in syllables, and always in three syllables,—never more or less,—which is a remarkable property in such gentry, and one worthy of remembrance. Thus, "it has always been the same with me," said Dick Swiveller (when jilted by Sophy Wackles for Cheggs, the greengrocer, of Chelsea) "always;" taking from his pocket a small parcel of black crape, and applying himself to folding, and pinning the same upon his hat, after the manner of a hatband. "'Twas ever thus, from childhood's hour, I've seen my fondest hopes decay; I never loved a tree, or flower, but 'twas the first to fade away; I never nursed a dear Gazelle, to glad me with its soft black eye, but when it came to know me well, and love me, it was sure to marry a market-gardener." "And this," said Mr. Swiveller, "is life, I believe." "Oh, certainly! Why not!"—"I shall wear this emblem of woman's perfidy, in remembrance of her with whom I shall never again thread the windings of the mazy; whom I shall never more pledge in the rosy; who, during the remainder of my existence will murder the balmy. Ha! Ha! Ha!"

(Other details concerning the remedial uses of Coral when worn as a jewel have been already particularised.)

Bacon wrote (1600): "The pursuit of Alchemy is

at an end! Yet, surely to Alchemy this right is due; that it may be truly compared to the husbandman whereof Æsop makes the fable, that when he died told his sons that he had left unto them a great mass of Gold buried underground in his vineyard; but could not remember the particular spot in which it was hidden; who, when they had with spades turned up all the vineyard, Gold, indeed, they found none: but, by reason of their stirring, and digging the mould about the roots of their vines, they had a great vintage the year following. So, the painful search, and stir of alchemists to make Gold, hath brought to light a great number of good, and fruitful experiments, as well for the disclosing of Nature as the use of man's life."

From the earliest times, Gold, and a great greed for this metal, have served in text, fable, and verse, for preaching wisdom and warning.

Ancient Roman mythology tells the fable of Midas, King of Phrygia, who was opulent from infancy, when ants deposited their stored treasures in his mouth as a place of security for the same. Midas rescued Silenus from danger, and restored him to Bacchus, who rewarded Midas by permitting him to choose whatever recompense he pleased. Midas had the impudence, and avarice, to demand of the god that whatever he touched might be turned into Gold. His prayer was granted; but its supreme folly soon brought its penalty. And when the very meats which he attempted to eat became Gold in his mouth, he besought Bacchus to take back this ruthless power, which would speedily prove fatal to its possessor. He was therefore ordered to wash himself in the river Pactolus; the sands of which were fabled to have been turned into Gold by the touch of Midas.

Ultimately Apollo changed his ears into those of an ass; and he died from drinking hot blood from a bull because of troubled dreams.

Our own Saxon forefathers esteemed Gold as teaching honesty and integrity when rightly used. One of their wise sayings—old enough to be quoted by Chaucer, in *The Canterbury Tales*—declared that "Every honest miller hath a golden thumb." ("And yet he had a thomb of Gold parde.")

Shakespeare admonishes against "Saint-seducing Gold," yet praises the refined metal in terms unstinted, and familiar.

That Gold augments the salutary powers, and virtues, of gems to which it forms a setting, has long been an article of implicit belief by those writers who have discoursed thoughtfully about precious stones. The similar influence of silver mountings is not so strong.

Ecclesiastes, the Preacher, inculcated the precept to "Remember now thy Creator, in the days of thy youth, while the evil days come not," "Or ever the silver cord be loosed; or, the Golden bowl be broken; or, the pitcher be broken at the fountain; or, the wheel broken at the cistern."

A modern *Golden* Legend is that of Miss Kilmansegg, and her Golden Leg, as related at considerable length, and in the most charming verse; an inimitable medley of true poesy, wit, humour, pathos, and tenderness, by Thomas Hood (*Colburn's New Monthly Magazine*, 1840). Hood was then in comparatively humble lodgings at Camberwell; and sadly ill with blood-spitting.

"A Patriarch Kilmansegg had lived of yore, who was famed for his great wealth and possessions."—

> "Gold! and Gold! and Gold without end!
> He had Gold to lay by; and Gold to spend;
> Gold to give, and Gold to lend,
>   And reversions of Gold ' in futuro.'
> In wealth the family revell'd, and roll'd;
> Himself, and wife, and sons so bold!—
> And his daughters sang to their harps of Gold
>   ' O bella eta del' oro.' "

In a subsequent generation, Sir Jacob Kilmansegg comes to inherit the title, and wealth; to whom a daughter is born in due course, growing presently to womanhood, and saturated, as it were, with the precious metal.

> " She painted shells, and flowers, and Turks;
> But her great delight was in Fancy Works
>   That are done with Gold, or Gilding.
>
> Gold! still Gold! the bright, and the dead,
> With Golden beads, Gold lace, Gold thread,
> She work'd in Gold, as if for her bread;
>   The metal had so undermined her;
> Gold ran in her thoughts, and fill'd her brain;
> She was Golden-headed, as Peter's cane,
>   With which he walk'd behind her.
>
> When she took a ride in the Park,
> Equestrian lord, or pedestrian clerk
>   Was thrown into amorous fever,
> To see the Heiress—how well she sat,
> With her groom behind her, Bob, or Nat,
> In green, half smother'd with Gold, and a hat
>   With more Gold-lace than beaver."

But presently, she gets an ugly fall from her runaway horse, in the said Park.

> " 'Yes,' ' No,' ' Yes!' they are down at last:
> The Furies and Fates have found them!
> Down they go with sparkle and crash,
> Like a bark that's struck by the lightning flash.
> There's a shriek and a sob,
> —And the dense dark mob
>   Like a billow closes around them.

'She breathes.'—'She don't.'—
'She'll recover.'—'She won't.'—
'She's stirring! she's living! by Nemesis!'
—Gold! still Gold, on counter, and shelf!
Golden dishes as plenty as delf!
Miss Kilmansegg's coming again to herself,
    On an opulent Goldsmith's premises.

Gold! fine Gold, both yellow and red;
Beaten, and molten, polished, and dead.
The Gold is seen with profusion spread
    In all forms of its manufacture!
But what avails Gold to Miss Kilmansegg,
When the femoral bone of her dexter leg
    Has met with a compound fracture?

Gold may soothe Adversity's smart;
Nay! help to bind up a broken heart;
But to try it on any other part
    Were as certain a disappointment,
As if one should rub the dish, and plate,
Taken out of a Staffordshire crate,
(In the hope of a Golden service of State)
    With 'Singleton's Golden Ointment.'

The King's Physician who nursed the case
His verdict gave, with an awful face;
    And three others concurr'd to egg it.
That the patient, to give old Death the slip,
Like the Pope, instead of a personal trip,
    Must send her Leg as a Legate.

The limb was doom'd; it couldn't be saved.
And, like other people the patient behav'd,
Nay, bravely that cruel parting brav'd
    Which makes some persons to falter.
—But when it came to fitting the stump
With a proxy limb, then flatly, and plump,
    She spake in the spirit olden!
She swore an oath; or something as good,
    That the proxy limb should be *Golden.*

'Gold, Gold, Gold! Oh, let it be Gold!'
Asleep, or awake that tale she told;
    And when she grew delirious,
Her parents resolved to grant her wish;
If they melted down plate, and goblet, and dish;
    The case was becoming so serious."

Accordingly the leg is made, of solid gold ; and presently sets the fashion, becoming the talk of the town.

> " A foreign Count then comes ' incog,'
> Not under a cloud, but under a fog,
> In a Calais packet's cabin.
> To charm some lady, British-born,
> With his eyes as black as the fruit of the thorn,
> And his hooky nose, and his beard half shorn,
> Like a half-converted Rabbin."

Miss Kilmansegg gets entrapped, and marries the said "Count"; having a specially resplendent wedding, which is duly described, in the most gorgeous verse. Before long, the "Count's" true character becomes revealed as that of an impostor, a gambler, and a thorough miscreant. Eventually, during her troubled sleep, after months of discord, and unhappiness, she awakes in horror, and half-paralyzed with fear, sees

> " ' The Count,' as once at her foot he knel't,
> That foot which now he wanted to melt ;
> But hush ! 'twas a stir at her pillow she felt,
> And some object before her glister'd.
>
> 'Twas the Golden Leg ! She knew its gleam ;
> And up she started, and tried to scream ;
> But e'en the moment she started,
> Down came the limb, with a frightful smash ;
> And lost in the universal flash
> Which her eyeballs made at so mortal a crash,
> The spark call'd Vital departed !
>
> Gold, still Gold ! hard, yellow, and cold ;
> For Gold she had liv'd ; and she died for Gold,
> By a Golden weapon, not oaken.
> —In the morning they found her all alone,
> Stiff, and bloody, and cold as stone ;
> But her Leg, the Golden Leg, was gone,
> And the ' Golden Bowl ' was broken.
>
> *Moral.*
> Gold : Gold ; Gold ; Gold !
> Good, or bad ; a thousand fold !
> How widely its agencies vary !

> To save; to ruin; to curse; to bless;
> As even its minted coins express;
> Now stamp'd with the image of good Queen Bess,
>   And now of a Bloody Mary!"

The largest lump of Gold in the world was discovered by Mr. Richard Oates, who, together with his companion, John Deason, found the celebrated " Welcome Stranger " nugget, at Mohagul, Victoria, on February 5th, 1869. It contained 2,516 ounces of pure Gold; and was valued at £9,582. It rested upon stiff red clay, and was barely covered with earth; in fact, it was in the rut made by the puddlers' carts. It measured twenty-one inches in length; and ten inches in thickness. The lucky finders detached, and gave to their friends, a number of pieces of gold from the nugget before it got into the hands of the bank managers.

Of the Three Wise Men who brought precious gifts from the East as offerings at the Nativity of the Infant Christ, it was Balthazar who bore Gold; giving thenceforth to that superlative metal increased remedial virtues.

> " Jasper fert Myrrham; Thus Melchior; Balthazar Aurum;
> Hæc quicunque secum portat tria nomina Regum
> Solvitur in morbo, Domini pietate, caduco."

" For all manner of falling evils " (epilepsy), as is directed in *The Pathway to Health*, " take blood from the little finger of the sick man, and write therewith the above lines; to be thenceforth worn as an amulet round the neck; and it shall help the party so grieved."

In Southey's *Commonplace Book*, fourth series, is given an extract from Augustin St. John's *Journal in Normandy*, to the effect that " Branstome's uncle, Chastaigneraye, as soon as he was weaned, his father, by the advice of a great physician at Naples, had gold, steel, and iron, in powder, given him in whatever he ate, and drank, *pour le bien fortifier*, till he was twelve years old; and this answered so well that he could take a bull by the horns, and *l'arrester en sa furie*."

(In the same volume, p. 433, it is related, "The ancients say there was a stone found in Arcadia, of the colour of iron, which, if it were once heated red-hot, never grew cool again; they called it 'Apoyctos.'" Some such a "warming-stone" is used in Cornwall, and Yorkshire, to lay by the feet in bed, because of its property of retaining heat a long time.)

To the sacred mistletoe (*Loranthus*, or "All-Heal,") as found growing on the oak tree (*Quercus pubescens*), and called also "pren-awyr"—the air plant,—the ancient Druids attributed many curative medicinal virtues. But, in order to develop the same, it was indispensable that the Arch-Druid, habited in white, should ceremoniously mount the tree, and cut away the mistletoe with a GOLDEN sickle, receiving it in a purely white cloth.

Virgil has described a plant of like character, and of similar healing virtues, as the "golden bough" of the infernal regions. This he compares, in terms which speak for themselves, to the mistletoe aforesaid:—

"Fronde virere novo, quod non suo seminat arbos,
Et croceo fœtu teretes circumdare truncos."

Modern medicine has fully confirmed the therapeutic properties of the mistletoe; particularly when got from the oak. It has been thus used by itself; also when dried, and rubbed into powder, together with metallic gold, a combination which seems essential!

Its special powers against epilepsy have been dwelt upon the at some length in our *Herbal Simples*. Herrick, Devon Poet, of quaint, graceful, and pious old verse, has prayerfully hymned thereto the following pertinent lines :—

"Lord, I am like the Mistletoe,
Which has no root, and cannot grow,
Or prosper save by that same tree
It clings about ; so I by Thee !

What need I then to fear at all,
So long as I about Thee crawl ?
But if that tree should fall, and die,
Tumble shall heaven ; and down will I."

The "Robur"—Oak—was the sacred tree of the Druids ; whatever was found growing on it they regarded as sent from heaven ; particularly on the sixth day of the moon.

To the Mistletoe (*Viscum album*) when thus produced they assigned the name "Heal-All" (*Omnia sanantem*). The parasite was gathered with much pious ceremony. After certain sacrifices, and banquets had been duly prepared beneath the oak tree, two white bulls were brought, the horns of which were then for the first time bound. Presently the high priest, clothed with a white robe, ascended the tree ; then as he cut the mistletoe off with a *golden* sickle, it was caught below in a white mantle. Straightway the victims were then slain ; and prayers offered that God would bless the plant. Concocted as a draught, it was given against sterility : —*Conceptum fœminarum adjuvare, si omnino secum habeant ;*—also as an antidote to poisons. Pliny tells, that the said parasite was known as *hyphcar* in Arcadia. Here with us in England it grows most abundantly on apple trees. But the considerable quantity which is got for Christmastide is chiefly obtained from the apple orchards of Normandy.

Somewhat similarly (to compare the little with the great) is the annual ceremony conducted on Twelfth Night upon the stage of Drury Lane Theatre, in London. According to the terms of a bequest made by Robert Baddeley, 1794 (of one hundred pounds, three per cent consolidated Bank annuities, as the yearly interest thereof), cake and wine are provided for the actors, and actresses, then performing there on His Majesty's boards. The master of this fund stands at the head of a table on the stage, before a large iced cake, flanked with bottles of champagne. He takes " a special *knife* of finely-tempered steel, and, amidst a round of cheers, proceeds to cut the cake ; each member of the company being at the same time handed a paper bag, in which to take a share of the souvenir away. As to what remedial virtues are subsequently exercised here likewise by the metallic influence on those who thus become possessed of the steel-cut confection, and its traditional benison, deponent saith not.

Robert Baddeley was an Englishman who spent the early part of his life as a pastry-cook in Paris. On returning from the Continent he became an actor, and made a reputation at Drury Lane, as the representative of foreign footmen, Jews, and old men. He was the original "Moses," in *The School for Scandal*; and died on November 19th, 1794, having been taken suddenly ill, after dressing for that part.

Reverting to the Mistletoe, we may remind our readers that Drayton, in his *Polyolbion* (1612-1622) tells how,—

> "The fearless British Priests, under the agèd oak—
> Taking a milk-white bull, unstainèd with the yoke,
> Then with an axe of *Gold*, from that Jove-sacred tree,
> The Mistletoe cut down."

Sir George Colbatch, a physician in the reign of George I., published (1719) a *Dissertation Concerning Mistletoe*, commending it as a specific against epilepsy. A preparation of the berries was advised; but in earlier times merely a branch of the mistletoe was hung about the patient's neck. "The fruits," says Miss Pratt (*Flowering Plants of Great Britain*,) "look very beautiful when mingled with the red berries, and glossy leaves of the holly in the winter bouquet. But the plant is very properly excluded from the boughs which decorate the churches at that season; not, however, for the reason which that orthodox old antiquary, Brande, supposes, because of its heathenish associations; but because it is so often connected in rustic places with secular Christmas merriment that it might awaken remembrances scarcely favourable to religious thought, and devotion."

The ancient Britons manifestly set store on personal ornamentation with Gold, and Precious Stones. For instance, a primitive bracelet found at Colwall, in Herefordshire, during 1650, is thought to have been lost by Margadud, king of South Wales, in a battle fought with Athelstan, the Saxon. This relic, of Gold set with Jewels, was discovered by a poor man whilst digging a ditch round his cottage. A goldsmith of Gloucester gave the finder thirty-seven pounds for it; he sold it to a jeweller in London for two hundred and fifty pounds. The latter disposed of the Stones alone for fifteen hundred pounds.

The "guinea" as a coin of the Realm is now only a

conventional expression. It has come to merely signify the twenty-one shillings paid as an honorarium, or by way of a subscription, or what not. Originally this name was given to the piece as being coined from gold got from the coast of Guinea; it has represented at various times—20s., 30s., 22s., 21s. 6d. The coin was meant originally to be in value twenty shillings, and for the first forty-four years it stood at that sum.

As to modern articles of genuine Gold (twenty-two carat), every portion of each such article, e.g. every link of every chain, every boss of a belt, etc., has to be stamped at the Assay Office. The goldsmith never knows where the symbol which guarantees quality will be placed; so he sends up his goods in the rough, leaving the place of the mark to the stamper's whim, or caprice. Not until the goods have passed this test, and received the necessary *imprimatur*, can the final touches of the artist in metal be applied.

Herr von Bulow Bothkamp, a German savant, whose authority goes for much in Berlin, has lately declared that by means of a rod made of steel wire he can discover Gold at almost any subterranean depth; his previously proved successes in revealing subterranean waterways through divining-rods has been amazing. Dr. L. Weber, the eminent Professor of the University of Kiel, is now about to publish a pamphlet, entitled, *The Divining Rod; and the Art to Discover Water, and Gold.*

Works for extracting Gold from sea-water (by the "Snell" process, which is kept secret) have been erected not long since on Hayling Island, near Portsmouth; but an action at law arose because of their failure; Mr. Snell contending that the contract made with him was for establishing these Works at Malta, where the sea-water indisputably affords more gold than does the sea-water on the Hampshire coast. Justice Darling, before whom the action was tried, said this scheme brought to his mind the proposal discussed in *Gulliver's Voyage to Lilliput*, (written by Jonathan Swift, at sixty, 1726,) on the part of certain wiseacres, to "extract sunbeams from cucumbers."

It is alleged that a guinea's worth of Gold has been obtained from five hundred tons of sea-water.

Sea-water, when frozen to congelation, is found to reject nearly all its saline particles; wherefore, on being afterwards thawed, its ice yields water so fresh that it may be drunk without unpleasantness, or harm. Salt water may likewise be rendered wholesome, and palatable by distillation.

Sterling gold consists of an alloy of about twenty-two parts of gold with two parts of copper. The "New Standard" gold consists of gold in eighteen parts to six parts of copper. Each of these is stamped at Goldsmiths' Hall; the former with a lion, a leopard's head, (the mark of the Goldsmiths' Company), a letter denoting the year, the King's head, and the manufacturer's initials; the latter is stamped with the King's head, the letter for the year, a crown, the number 18, to designate its quality, and the manufacturer's initials. "Trinket gold" (which is unstamped) is much less pure than either of those named above; and the "pale gold" which is used by jewellers is an alloy of gold with silver. When gold is beaten into leaves certain animal membranes are used to lay between the very thin sheets of metal. Fine skins made for this purpose from the entrails of oxen are known by the name of "gold-beaters' skin."

"Sit, Jessica: Look how the floor of heaven
Is thick inlaid with patines of bright Gold:
—There's not the smallest orb which thou behold'st
But, in his motion, like an angel sings,
Still quiring to the young-ey'd cherubims:
Such harmony is in immortal souls:
But, whilst this muddy vesture of decay
Doth grossly close it in, we cannot hear it.—"
Merchant of Venice.

SILVER.

SILVER was symbolised by the moon in former times. Mines of this precious metal are worked in North, and South America; likewise in Mexico, and Peru. In China, Silver constitutes the chief portion of the currency. It occurs in Europe; also in France. Native Silver has been likewise met with in various parts of Cornwall. A saying has obtained belief that the ocean may contain a little of everything soluble in water; and it is curious to find from the experiments of foreign chemists that sea-water holds a determinable quantity of Silver in solution.

Various seaweeds (such as the *Fucus serratus*, and the *Fucus ceramoides*) contain an appreciable fractional amount of Silver. Some of this metal may likewise be discovered in the ashes of certain land plants. Silver is commonly found amalgamated with lead in its ore. Common salt (which is chemically chloride of sodium) when made to act upon metallic Silver forms Chloride of silver, a chemical salt highly sensitive to daylight, and thus used largely by photographers.

Silver is again readily dissolved by nitric acid, whether strong, or dilute. The chemical product is Nitrate of Silver, (known more familiarly as lunar caustic).

Some of this is the blackening basis of most marking

inks. As a valuable surgical remedy, thin Silver-leaf (*Argentum foliatum*) is used in Austria, and elsewhere on the Continent, for helping to promote the healing of indolent sores, by covering the same with a thin sheet of this Silver-leaf (sterilised), over fine gauze, also sterilised, and laid next the surface of the sore. Medicinally the nitrate of silver, administered in small continuous doses, has long been recognised as of special benefit against epilepsy; but in such cases, when the remedy has been given for any length of time, some of the metal becomes separated within the system from its accompanying chlorine, and deposited about the skin-surface of the body, staining this of a bronzed hue, particularly the parts which are exposed to sunlight. In fact, the skin-surface becomes as it were, in a certain measure, similar to a piece of what photographers style P.O.P.—" Printing-out-paper."

The Nitrate of Silver—lunar caustic—was extolled highly by Boerhaave, as a diuretic against dropsies. In modern practice it is prescribed, as a tonic, and antispasmodic, in Epilepsy, Saint Vitus' dance, and for Heart-pang (angina pectoris).

Also a solution of this salt is frequently resorted-to for the manufacture of those compounds which are employed for changing the colour of the hair. Some such preparations have been offered for sale under the mystic titles of Grecian Water, Essence of Tyre, etc. If applied recently to grey hair, any of these preparations renders the hair black after exposure to light; but the colour soon changes; the grey roots of the hair again appear, and the person presents a ludicrous appearance of having hair half grey and half black.

When administered medicinally in small doses, from

one-sixteenth to half a grain, in a pill made up of plain soft breadcrumb, Nitrate of Silver stimulates the heart, and the chief nervous centres as a tonic. Silver will become tarnished only in the presence of free sulphur, of sulphur gases, and of phosphorus.

The famous witty divine, Sydney Smith, married Miss Catherine Amelia Pybus, on July 2nd, 1800. His "total wealth then consisted of six small Silver teaspoons." These he flung into the bride's lap, saying, "There, Kate! You lucky girl! I give you *all* my fortune!"

Taking into consideration the solubility of Silver when converted into a chloride, as by the action upon it of common salt, it will be readily understood that for persons suffering from various neuralgic head troubles, and for whom the remedial action of metallic Silver commends itself, to bathe in the open sea, whilst wearing Silver ornaments (bangles, and the like) next the skin of the wrists, ankles, or waist (by a Silver belt), will probably be of essential service towards a cure. Or, in a minor, and more convenient way, at home, to immerse the hands, and wrists, with the Silver bangles, etc., thereon, in lukewarm water to which table salt has been added (making this about as salt as sea-water), for a quarter of an hour at a time, twice or thrice in the day. It is because of Silver thus chemically becoming a chloride on its surface when placed in immediate contact with common salt, that has led to the practice of lining our silver salt-cellars, and salt spoons with an inner gilt coating. Concerning the former receptacles our grandfathers and grandmothers made use of good old-fashioned salt-cellars furnished with an inner cellar of dark-blue glass. Finding them as an "antique" in curio shops, we are all of us familiarly acquainted with these primitive silver table equipments.

To be "born with a Silver spoon in the mouth" is proverbially a lucky thing for the babe. None the less is it of absolute certainty that to be constantly taking much of our food with Silver spoons, and retaining these for more or less time within the mouth, are practices likely to gradually entail some limited absorption into the system of certain soluble silver Salts ; the sulphocyanide, for instance, produced by the chemical action of the saliva on the metal. Moreover, we know that the absorbent vessels within the mouth, and cheeks are perpetually active for taking up all solutions which come in their way. Inasmuch, however, as metallic Silver, and its salts, are potentially destructive of bacteria, (swarms of which commonly infest the mouth, from decayed teeth, and serve by their noxious juices to poison the whole system), to anticipate such matters by a silver "coral" before dentition begins, and to keep up an acquaintance with the salutary metal throughout life by a lingering dalliance with the Silver spoon at this, or that meal, are likely thus much to prove preventive of many a septic illness. Chronic "rheumatism"—so-called—of the general system often depends on self-poisoning from carious teeth within the mouth.

The wearing of Silver ornaments next the skin, and toying with the Silver spoon whilst eating therewith, together with teeth-extraction, when needed, by a skilful dentist, should prove curative of this trouble.

In Aberdeenshire, rheumatism is known as "wins." Thus, respecting a certain worthy woman there, we have heard it said "Of nothing else did she complain, but her ' wins,' and want of goodness."

"I remember," writes Mr. Robert Boyle—*Experimental Philosophie*—"that the experienc'd chymist, Johannes Agricola, relates how 'he hath seen an earth digg'd at the Rheinstran, not far from Wester waldt, which was more inclinable to white than to yellow, and will dissolve silver better than other menstruums'; since, as he saith, 'The silver may thereby be easily made potable, and be prepar'd into a very useful medicine for the diseases of the head.'" "And, for my part," adds Mr. Boyle, "I do not much wonder at the efficacy of this, and other such earths, when I consider that divers of them are imbu'd, as well as dy'd, with mineral fumes; or tinctured with mineral juices, wherein minerals, or metals may lie, as the chymists speak,—*in solutis principiis*; in which form, having never endured the fire, many of their usefullest parts are more loose, and volatile; and divers of their vertues less lock'd up, and more disposed to be communicative of themselves, than they are wont to be in a more fixed or coagulated state, or when they have lost many of their finer parts by the violence of the fire."

Metallic Silver—*Argentum*—in the form of the finest silver leaf, (rubbed into a powder, together with dry, inert sugar of milk,) was administered medicinally by Hahnemann; and with indisputable benefit. Acting on the leading principle, which he specially advocated, of determining the diseases in which any drug substance would most probably prove remedial, by noting the several symptoms produced by that same drug substance when taken in toxic, or even poisonous quantities, Hahnemann found this metallic Silver curative for neuralgic pains in the principal joints; likewise against chronic hoarseness, and irritative congestion of the windpipe.

Again, "A word fitly spoken," says Solomon, in the Book of Proverbs, "is like apples of Gold in pictures of Silver." "Take away the dross from the Silver, and there shall come forth a vessel for the finer." Furthermore, a German maxim, quoted by Carlyle, tells, that whilst "Speech is Silver, silence is Gold."

By the Spaniards the metal Silver is called "Platta," being the best, and most perfect metal next to Gold. "It is white, hard, extensible, and very agreeable to the sight."

"Concerning the '*Lapis Infernalis*, or the Silver Caustick," wrote M. Pomet (1712), "this stone is much used by surgeons to burn, and consume dead and superfluous flesh; but special care must be taken not to touch the sound flesh, because the stone will not fail to burn it, and cause an extremity of pain, especially if the place be wet." "Silver is proper for those who have used too great a quantity of quicksilver, either from without, or taken inwardly; for, it binds, or amalgamates itself with this, in the body, and, depriving it of its weight, takes away its virtue." The metal Silver is alleged by several authors to be an infallible medicine for diseases of the head, and brain. The Astrologers, and the Alchymists called Silver "Luna," because they imagined this metal to be "of the same matter as the moon, and that it receives from that luminary continual nourishment." "It sympathizeth," wrote Dr. Schroder (1660), "with the moon in the macrocosm; and with the brain in the microcosm." "It is held as a special strengthener of the brain, to comfort the animal spirits, being good in all head diseases, epilepsies, apoplexyes, etc." "It hath been found out that the Silver spirit (Closs.) takes out the root of the epilepsie." "The magistery of Silver," tells Dr. Salmon (*Pharmacopeia*

Londinensis, 1668), "as made from a precipitate of the metal, is wondrous fair and white; which put thou into a glass bottle, and keep it close stop't for use." "It is chiefly designed for a fucus for the face, and skin, being the best of any yet known in the world. It heals, and dries up ulcers; the precipitate may be used either alone, by rubbing the skin with it, or else by mixing it with pomatum, or into an oyntment made with white virgin wax, and oyl."

Another experimentalist of the same school was led to give the metallic Silver in cases of womb cancer. In one instance he has reported as to the relief afforded by this remedy being so great that for a time a complete cure seemed about to be effected.

Again, there appears to be distinctive evidence that the metal Silver is antidotal to epilepsy. Professor Hempel has recorded a case of a sufferer from epilepsy for forty years gaining an accidental cure at last by inadvertently swallowing a Silver coin; which coin was not ejected from the man's stomach until after twenty months; it was then but little diminished in size.

Furthermore, Dr. Shipman, of Chicago, observing that workers in Silver become white-blooded, and chlorotic, because of their blood being insufficiently oxidated, was induced to give Silver, finely sub-divided, to these persons, knowing that Silver as a slow poison will induce just such an impaired state of the blood. Meantime, in consequence of this defect, carbon and nitrogen accumulate to excess in the blood. Dr. Richard Hughes, of Brighton, has adduced testimony to the same effect regarding the remedial value of medicinal Silver for correcting chlorosis, and defective oxidation of the blood-system generally.

Ulcerative soreness within the mouth, and throat, is another morbid condition which benefits curatively if metallic Silver is exhibited to the patient; and on the same guiding principle as already enunciated. Another physician of eminence, Dr. H. C. Wood, observed that in Silver-poisoning (argyria) convulsions became determined, and paralysis ensued. This fact bears again on the utility which Silver has vindicated to itself against the convulsive attacks of epilepsy, and as bearing out the same view, even when the Silver is worn externally over some part of the body, in lieu of being taken medicinally.

In confirmation of this fact may be quoted an old custom which obtained formerly in England of distributing the silver sacramental coins among epileptic sufferers in each particular parish, to be worn remedially about their persons. It will not be out of place to repeat here what we have told concerning this matter in our *Animal Simples* (1899), that " A ring made from a piece of Silver collected at the Communion in church, or from small Silver coins given by five bachelors, unknowingly to each other, or contributed by twelve young women, and worn constantly on one of the patient's fingers, was formerly believed to guard against epileptic attacks. In Norfolk, even at the present day, it is affirmed that a ring constructed from nine sixpences given freely by persons of the opposite sex to that of the sufferer is similarly efficacious.

Furthermore, notice has been already taken of the curative virtues exercised by the Chloride of Silver, this being a soluble salt. And, inasmuch as under certain conditions this said Chloride of Silver becomes formed when human saliva, common salt (chloride of sodium), and metallic Silver meet in combination, it may be reasonably supposed that sucking a Silver coin, together with some table-salt, daily by an epileptic person, is to be suggested as promising curative results. The Chloride of Silver in a soluble state will thus be absorbed into the blood through the lining membranes of the mouth; and some of the same will find its way into the stomach by being swallowed. As a metal Silver is sometimes discovered native and pure; but more often as mineralised with oxygen, sulphur, the carbonic, and muriatic acids.

The London Pharmacopeia (1695) ordered as medicinal preparations of Silver: potable Silver, a tincture, a spirit, and an essence; likewise Lunar Silver pills, and Silver crystals. "In giving of the Lunar pills, wrap them up in a wet wafer, the pap of an apple, or a stewed prune, because of their bitterness." "With this medicament," affirmed the learned Horstius, "I have perfectly cured beyond expectation old headaches of near twenty years' standing."

Silver "Apostle spoons" were fashionable from about 1500 to 1650. The selling value of twelve such, in good condition, is to-day about eighty pounds. At one time spoons were used in England for snuff-taking.

Silver forks must come in for a small share of suspicion about forming a harmful product by use in the mouth together with table-salt during mastication at a meal; though, as their tercentenary is just now being notified, they have been a long time about doing much chemical harm. Anyhow, they provide us for the moment with a delightful anecdote respecting a demure little girl whom Oliver Wendell Holmes saw near the refreshment table (at a children's party), looking longingly at the tempting sweets, and confectionery displayed thereon;

but not attempting to get any. "Why don't you help yourself to some cake, or a sandwich?" he asked. "Because I have not a fork," she replied. He smilingly said, "Yes, my dear! but, don't you know, fingers were made before forks?" When, much to his amusement, and surprise, she sagely replied, "Not my fingers."

Charles Dickens (always exercising a wonderful power of observing small details of his surroundings) when telling (in *David Copperfield*) of the solemn interview between Mr. Spenlow, Miss Murdstone, and David, in a coffee-house adjoining Doctors' Commons, says, they "found Miss Murdstone there, supported by a background of sideboard, on which were several inverted tumblers, sustaining lemons; and two of those extraordinary boxes, all corners, and flutings, for sticking Silver knives, and forks in, which—happily for mankind—are now obsolete."

On the sloping tops of these old-fashioned bits of "marqueterie" sideboard (Sheraton) furniture were painted central inlaid pictures of convoluted shells, in neutral tints of (time-worn) colouring. Such articles now take rank as antiques in the brokers' shops. It is a curious fact that the Conch shell in its occult relation to ancient Indian religious rites, merits enquiry. Thus, a Conch shell which has its spirals twisting to the right (instead of to the left, as usual), is thought to be worth its weight in gold. Some years ago a Conch of this description was offered for sale in Calcutta, with a reserve price of a lakh of rupees put upon it, which Conch was eventually bought in for the sum of four thousand pounds.

When simple-hearted, painstaking Traddles had

married "the dearest girl;" a curate's daughter; one of ten; down in Devonshire; "and had started for such small fry of legal practice as he could pick up, to start with;" (afterwards he rose to be a judge!)—"bless his soul! they were two of the happiest people! —"Then our pleasures! Dear me! they are inexpensive; but quite delightful!" "The streets of an evening abound in enjoyment for us. We look into the glittering windows of the jewellers' shops; and I show Sophy which of the diamond-eyed serpents, coiled up on white-satin rising grounds, I would give her, if I could afford it; and Sophy shows me which of the gold watches, that are capped, and jewelled, and engine-turned, and possessed of the horizontal lever escape-movement, and all sorts of things, she would buy for me if *she* could afford it; and we pick out the spoons and forks, fish-slices, butter-knives, and sugar-tongs, we should both prefer if we could both afford them; and really we go away as if we had got them."

Meantime, "there was a little room in the roof, a very nice room when you're up there; which Sophy papered herself, to surprise me; and that's our room at present. It's a capital little gipsy sort of place;" "there's quite a view from it!" "And, as to plate; Lord bless you, we haven't so much as a teaspoon." "Of course, we've something in the shape of teaspoons, because we stir our tea. But they're Britannia-metal."—(An alloy of antimony with tin.)

At Ham House, Petersham, the historical old mansion of Lord Dysart; and at Knole, in Kent; are Silver fire-irons, and dogs; whilst magnificently carved, Silver-framed mirrors are amongst the many treasures which are found at the former house. Horace Walpole visited it in 1775, and then complained of its " mixture of pomp and tatters." At that time exquisite velvet, and tapestry-hung beds, and Chinese silk embroideries, were to be seen, in rooms of which the floor was only plain deal; whilst Silver chandeliers, black with age, and tarnish, hung suspended in chambers where great cabinets full of priceless miniatures, and piles of Chelsea china, had been lying almost for centuries, undusted, and untouched. But now, during some years past, Ham House has been adequately kept up; and the Earl of Dysart takes great pride in his beautiful old country seat.

Is it in the least unreasonable to believe that the former possessors of these rare treasurers, particularly the old Silver belongings, have left behind them, as retained therein, attributes of mind, and body, which will actively revive under favourable conditions? Indeed, it is said already, as a matter of tradition, that visitants from the land of ghosts (perturbed spirits these, in all probability) have been recognised within the corridors, and chambers of Ham House. Thus likewise beneficent souls which are now enjoying the rest and perfect peace of Paradise, may be still diffusing from fondly-prized relics left behind them, some of the noble excellences, or the sterling simplicity of character, which distinguished these worthy ancestors on earth. Furthermore, is it not more than likely that the special store now set on old family plate, on tankards, coffee-pots, and the like, (which realise at the present time up to seven, or eight pounds an ounce,) may be actually dependent on some such an occult cause, unsuspected, but none the less actual, as that which we have suggested?

Antique Silver fabricated into articles of ornament,

or domestic use, during the times of James II., William III., Charles II., Queen Anne, (by famous artificers), fetch high prices at the present day; from three pounds to nine pounds per ounce.

Quite recently a Silver tankard, with cover,—time of Queen Elizabeth,—was sold by auction, for two thousand and three hundred pounds, i.e., at more than one hundred pounds per ounce. This tankard stands over seven inches high, being beautifully chased; and having three medallions round the barrel. Likewise an old French patch-box of the seventeenth century, less than three inches high, was sold at Christie's lately for two thousand, one hundred and fifty pounds. As a work of art it is probably peerless; and this enormous price, which works out at more than seven hundred and sixteen pounds an inch, is amply justified by an examination of the delicate gold mounting, and the superb rose Diamonds set into it. The actual box is formed of brown agate, and on the cover is seated a charming little enamelled figure.

Though Silver, as a metal, is harder than Gold, and therefore serving more usefully as coin of the realm, subject to rough usage; yet it has lent itself in one special instance to the gentler service of popular verse. Moreover, the said verse, familiar to us all from our nursery days, is indeed a delightful little allegory. But this fact is nevertheless known to but few children, young, or old, who have conned the lines by heart almost from their cradle.

"Sing a song of sixpence;
A pocket full of rye;
Four and twenty blackbirds
Baked in a pie.

When the pie was opened,
   The birds began to sing;
Wasn't it a dainty dish
   To set before the King?

The King was in his counting-house,
   Counting out his money;
The Queen was in her parlour,
   Eating bread, and honey.

The maid was in the garden,
   Hanging out the clothes;
Along flew a blackbird,
   And snapped off her nose."

"Sing a song of six hours;
   A clock-face full of Time;
Four and twenty black signs
   Round from prime to prime.

When the morning opens,
   The birds begin to sing;
Is it not a splendid sight,
   The sun-rise of the King?

From out his Eastern coffers
   He scatters golden beams,
Which wax in warmth, and glory,
   Till blaze of noon-tide gleams.

Anon, when shadows lengthen,
   The Moon-Queen leaves her bed;
Bees carry home their honey;
   The sheaves are stacked for bread.

Vesper, the Maid-Star, twinkles;
   Then hangs the sky with clouds;
Black night cuts short her twilight;
   And darkness all enshrouds.

Hence we should learn the lesson,
   To number so our days
That each may find his heart applied
   To Wisdom's worthy ways."

CARMEN SEX DENARIORUM.

"Incipe cui titulo 'Denarios'; incipe cantum!
　Huic tumulo loculo massa secalis inest;
Sex quater in patina merularum corpora crustum
　Queis superimpositum pista farina fuit;
Procubuere simul; sed quando ad aperta farina est,
　Concordes merulis insonnuere modi;
Mirum opus harmoniæ! nonne inter fercula posset
　Hæc vel regificæ lanx placuisse gulæ?

Rex erat in camera, numerans sibi pondera nummi,
　Pondera plebeio non numeranda viro;
Mel mandit, panemque, morans Regina culina;
　Dulcia plebeia non comedenda nuru;
Ad solem vestes siccans Ancilla per hortum
　Ibat, et expansas aere funis habet:
Quum merula affine descendens arbore, nasum
　Ancillæ insinuit, seque ibi constituit."

"(Ancill' in horticulo—hanging out the clothes,
Quum descendens corvix eripuit—her nose.")

Such were the innocent thoughts, and pastimes of our earlier days, with respect to this so-called " precious " metal, now coveted, and sought for, in a more sordid spirit. Alas!—

"The sports of childhood's roseate dawn
　Have passed from our hearts like the dew-gems from morn;
We have parted with marbles; we own not a ball,
　And are deaf to the hail of a 'whoop, and a call.'
But there's an old game that we all keep up,
　When we've drunk much deeper from life's mixed cup;
Youth may have vanished, and manhood come round,
　Yet how busy we are on 'Tom Tidler's ground';
　　Looking for gold and silver!"

Tom Tiddler's Ground (*All the Year Round*, Christmas Number, 1861, by Charles Dickens). "And why Tom Tiddler's ground?" asked the traveller. "Because he (Mr. Mopes, the hermit) scatters halfpence to tramps, and such like; and of course they pick 'em up; and this being done on his own land, (which it *is* his own

land, you observe, and were his family's before him);
why, it is but regarding his halfpence as 'gold and
silver,' whilst turning the ownership of the property
a bit round your finger; and there you have the name
of the children's game complete." "Mr. Mopes (the
said disreputable 'hermit'), by suffering everything
about him to go to ruin, and by dressing himself in a
blanket, and skewer, and by steeping himself in soot,
and grease, and other nastiness, had acquired great
renown in all that country-side."

But this mention of "Tom Tiddler's Ground," by
Dickens, certainly did not originate this oft-quoted
phrase. It is true that Mr. Mopes, the hermit in question,
was a real person, a slovenly, filthy tinker, (Lucas, by
name, at Redcoats Green, near Stevenage, in Hertford-
shire), who wallowed in a ruined hovel, without a pane
of glass in any window, and not owning a plank, or
beam, other than rotten. Nevertheless, long before
then, to play at "Tom Tiddler's ground," was a game
with which village lads were commonly familiar. Moreover, Dickens himself had made express allusion thereto
some twenty odd years previously, in *Nicholas Nickleby*,
(first published 1847). Mr. Mantalini, the lazy,
luxurious, gambling, dandified husband of Madame
Mantalini, (a fashionable dressmaker in London), had
gone to raise money from the usurious Ralph Nickleby
on certain securities filched from his wife's private desk.
She surprises him by likewise visiting Nickleby's office
at the same time, seeking protection from her husband's
disastrous extravagance. He—Mr. Mantalini—evinces
considerable discomposure, and hastily sweeps into his
pocket the cash just borrowed on the aforesaid securities.
"Oh, you *are* here," said Madame Mantalini, tossing

her head. "Yes, my life, and soul, I am," replied her husband, dropping on his knees, and pouncing with kitten-like playfulness upon a stray sovereign; "I am here, my soul's delight," "upon Tom Tiddler's ground, picking up the demnition gold, and silver." The title "Tiddler" was probably first used as signifying "Th'Idler" (the idler).

A specimen nugget of native Silver, weighing more than five hundredweight, is to be seen in the mineral collection at Copenhagen.

It has now become a recognised, and established fact, as demonstrated several years ago by Professor Charcot, before the assembled medical savants of Paris, at the Hôtel Salpetriére, 1877, that the nervous systems of all sensitive persons display either a sympathetic attraction, or an unmistakable physical repulsion, with respect to certain metals; even when the same are only externally applied; and this phenomenon occurs according to the particular idiosyncrasy of each of such individuals, for, or against, this, or that special metal. Similarly Paracelsus, of old, had a ring made from a variety of metallic substances; which ring he named "Electrum." If it were put on by a patient during the night when an epileptic attack was imminently threatened, or actually commencing, it would straightway stay the attack, or terminate the seizure.

Again, Cotta relates a "merrie historie" of some such an approved spell; this time for sore eyes. "It was for a long time worn as a jewell about many necks, never failing to do sovereign good when all other helps were helplesse. But no sight might dare to reade, or no hande to open it." At length, while a patient, wearing the same, slept, a curious mind ript open the mystical cover, and found inside only these disappointing Latin characters: *Diabolus tibi effodiat oculos; impleat foramina stercoribus.* "May the Devil dig out your eyes; and fill their sockets with turds."

F. Barrett, in his *Occult Philosophy*, 1801 (see our Introduction, page 10), says, " We have taught that our own spirit is the vehicle of celestial attraction, transferring celestial, and spiritual virtue into seals, amulets, rings, glasses, etc. Also we have not forgot to give the most clear and rational illustration of sympathy and antipathy; attraction and repulsion. We have likewise proved how cures are performed by virtue of sympathetic powers, and medicines, by seals, rings, and amulets, even at unlimited distances, which we have been witnesses of, and are daily confirmed in the true and certain belief of. We know how to communicate with any person, and to give him intimation of our purpose, at a hundred, or a thousand miles distance; but then a preparation is necessary, and the parties should have their appointed seasons, and hours for that purpose. Likewise both should be of the same firm constancy of mind, and a disciple, or brother in art."

Charcot's experiments concerning the varied effects of particular metals when applied externally over different portions of the skin-surface of persons who were highly sensitive as to their nervous system, indeed, in some cases positively hysterical, were conducted likewise by Dr. Burg.

He observed that as soon as small plates of metals have been brought into intimate contact with skin-regions which, through disease, had lost their capacity for touch, or sensation, those regions—previously pale, and flaccid—recovered their sensibility, whilst an increased afflux of blood became determined thereto. But Dr. Burg had to conclude that this incitement afresh of the skin-sensibility proved transitory, being lost again within a short time after removal of the metallic plate, or plates ; and, secondly, that in order to produce the effects of restored sensibility (even for a time), different metallic plates, according to individualities, must be applied ; a particular metal for each particular individuality. The correctness of this series of experiments was confirmed by a Commission of medical savants in Paris ; it being thus demonstrated that by the contact of different metals with living organic tissue, such as the skin, currents of contact electricity are incited, which for a longer, or shorter time serve to restore to the paralysed nerve-fibres their functional faculty. In other words, so as to bring about the desired restoration of skin-sensibility in a cutaneous region which had lost the same, a metallic plate had to be applied, which for one person would consist of copper, for a second person of zinc, for a third person of iron, for a fourth person of gold, silver, or platinum, etc. When applied over the skin-surface of a part where the contact sensitiveness was impaired, (as is commonly the case during hysteria, and similar nervous derangements,) a metallic plate of the approved metal (if Gold, two or three sovereigns being used, tied together, and kept in touch with the skin,) will cause the part, in from a few seconds to fifteen, or twenty minutes, to feel numbed, whilst its skin-surface turns red. If the metal be now taken away, the restored sensibility is retained for one or two days ; but if the metal is allowed to remain on, then, strangely enough, the insensibility of skin soon returns, even more intensely than before.

Quite remarkably too, at the same time the power of distinguishing colours with the eye on the same side of the body becomes perverted; thus the proper colours of objects disappear in a mathematical series, first violet, then red, then green, then yellow; and blue is the last to disappear. But if a piece of the same metal (as best suited to the individual patient), let us say, of gold, is applied over the temple, on the same side, then a proper perception of colours is restored, and in the same order as it became lost.

Professor Charcot, having succeeded thus far with his patient, proceeded to add internal metallo-therapy, or metallic curing; if the beneficial metal was gold, he gave ten drops (in a spoonful or two of distilled water) of a solution of gold (with sodium as a solvent) before each meal; if the patient had proved sensitive rather to copper, then the oxide of copper in powder, was given; or the natural mineral water of St. Chrystan, which contains copper; if the sensitiveness improved under zinc, then small doses of its sulphate were administered; or if iron was the favouring metal, one of its soluble salts was similiarly given.

And not only were hysterical, or otherwise too highly emotional sufferers benefited by these means, but also any partial paralysis of sensation about the head, or face, with, or without impairment of vision on one side, was equally amenable to the said treatment.

In such cases the metallo-therapy by iron seemed to prove most successful. Some rare cases were found not to prove sensitive to any known metal.

As to such subtle influences of certain metals on sensitive subjects, some scientific discoveries made quite recently seem to bear thereupon very suggestively.

Herr Gruhn has by patient labour, and experiment arrived at the conclusion that "all bodies give out emanations, each of them possessing an emanation of its own." Dr. Gustave Le Bon has detected an ionising emanation in all metals, it having been suggested two years previously by Professor Thomson that every substance possesses a characteristic radiation in proportion to its density. Herr Gruhn notices the motive forces in metallic rods, as affected by the weather. And it has been shown by Professor Rutherford that emanations supposed to belong naturally to substances other than the acknowledged radio-active substances, radium, thorium, actinium, and polonium, have been gained by these substances through exposure to the atmosphere, which always contains a certain amount of radium. "It seems reasonable therefore to suppose," says a leading scientist of to-day, "that Herr Gruhn has done much towards proving the existence of a new force, one, moreover, which is specially exercised in the case of this, or that metal." "Although at present there may be no positive means of detecting the characteristic radiations thus referred to, it is not at all improbable that the day is at hand when apparatus will be devised of sufficient delicacy, and of such a type as to detect them." "When this shall be done, the problem, moreover, of the 'divining-rod' will be solved, since the familiar electroscope has been the 'divining-rod' of radio-activity." Lord Kelvin said as long ago as in 1892, that "for the happy individual whose destiny it is to conclusively unravel the hitherto bewildering enigma of the divining rod, his reward will be the honour of fixing an added laurel on the crown of applied science by the capture of another of Nature's secret forces." These words certainly suggest that if it were found that the mysteries of the "divining rod" have a scientific explanation, this same explanation will be one which concerns metals fundamentally.

PLATINUM.

The metal Platinum, obtained from native Platina, though but seldom used by the jeweller, possesses a just claim to our attentive consideration because of its special curative virtues. It was first eliminated as a distinct metal by the famous chemist, Dr. W. H. Wollaston, in 1805.

Platinum has the highest specific gravity of all metals. Spongy platinum, and platinum black, are its two chemical forms. As a curious, and interesting proceeding, if a platinum wire, turned in a spiral form, is placed over the flame of a spirit-lamp, whilst lighted, and the lamp be then extinguished, the wire will continue to glow after the flame is blown out. And if the lamp be then fed with eau de Cologne, or tincture of benzoin, and a small glass tube be inserted in the wick, carrying a platinum wire, (which is supporting a ball of mixed platinum, or clay), then the lamp will continue to distil delightful odours into the room until the spirit is exhausted. The metal Platinum taken experimentally in material quantities by provers for ascertaining its medicinal effects, when pushed to a degree of almost poisonous toxication, has brought about a tendency to sensific paralysis, with marked mental depression; also torpor of the intestinal canal, with chronic constipation; and again a premature monthly flux with women. It is found by practitioners of medicine that each of these ill conditions will yield successfully to the wearing of small platinum plates applied immediately next the skin of the forearms for a week, or longer; as likewise to taking a very finely reduced measure of the metal (rubbed up for this purpose, with dry inert sugar of milk), in small doses, regularly repeated twice, or three times daily, as long as needed.

COPPER.

COPPER can scarcely be termed a "noble" metal; nevertheless it exercises important medicinal effects of a curative sort, and therefore it merits discussion at our hands in the present treatise. Its name, Copper, is derived from the Isle of Cyprus, where "it was first gotten in great plenty," as "Æs Cyprium, the Brass of Cyprus." This metal was named "Venus" of old by the Alchemist, not on account of any remarkable metallic attractiveness, but in consequence, says Webster, who wrote a *History of Metals*, of its easy union with other metals, and the change which ensues in its nature. Thus, bronze is a mixture of Copper, tin, and zinc.

"*Æs, sive Cuprum, sive Venus*, that is, Copper," saith Lemery, 1712, "done into English," "is a beautiful metal, shining of a reddish colour, easie to rust, abounding in Vitriol. When the same Copper has been twice, or thrice melted it becomes more pure and ductile, and you have a red Copper more beautiful than the common. It is a metal of good use in physick, and is said to strengthen the generative functions in men, and women. Thin plates of Copper infus'd all night in lime-water only, make the same an admirable collyrium for to wash the eyes with, against mists, clouds, films, pearls, suffusions, etc." "This metal," tells Dr. Rowland, 1669, (who translated Hippocrates, Bartholinus, and others,) " is called Copper, or Venus, because it sympathizeth with Venus in the Macrocosm, and with the generative parts in the Microcosm." " Some say no metal is wholesomer." " The verdigreese mundifies (cleanses) wounds excellently, (and is in the plaister Oppodeldoch)."

Verdigris with lard makes an ointment which is very useful to be applied for cleansing foul ulcers, and for checking the growth of "proud flesh," (fungous excrescences). It is sometimes taken inadvertently through harmful solution in wine, or vinegar. Sugar, and syrups have been considered the best antidotes to poisonous Copper; but these would seem only to act as emollients after the poison has been expelled from the stomach. Really, albumen, or the white of egg, given freely, in copious draughts of water, is the most effectual counter-poison for all the salts of Copper.

The "precious stone" Malachite is a green carbonate of Copper. What is called "compact Malachite" is sometimes used as a green pigment; it bears a fine polish. Chalcopyrite is the most important of Copper ores.

The Greek, and Roman sculptors executed fine works of art in porphyry, granite, and other hard materials, by means of their Copper instruments. There is no doubt that their axes, and other ancient tools were almost as sharp as our steel surgical instruments. This great hardness of the ancient copper instruments induced historians to believe that these ancestors possessed a particular secret for tempering Copper, and converting it into steel. Such axes, and other instruments of Copper have been discovered in the tombs of the ancient Peruvians, and in those of the early Mexicans. They were so hard that the sculptors of those countries executed therewith large works in the hardest greenstone, and basaltic porphyry; their jewellers cut, and pierced the emerald, and other precious stones, by using at the same time a metal tool, and a siliceous powder. It is stated that Copper mines have been worked in Anglesea from a very remote period, and that the Romans were acquainted with the Hamlet Mine, near Holyhead. The metal Copper when obtained in a pure state has a remarkable red colour. The smell of Copper is very peculiar.

Verdigris, or the subacetate of Copper, is prepared by covering Copper plates with the husks of grapes, after their juice has been squeezed out. Fermentation takes place, and the Copper becomes oxidised; then by further treatment with distilled vinegar the Subacetate of Copper, or Verdigris, is formed. This is obtained in crystals of a deep bluish-green colour. When powdered, and mixed with Cinnamon, its taste very much resembles the odour thereof.

This metal may be beaten out into very thin leaves; when alloyed with zinc it forms the metal leaf called "Dutch Metal," which is extensively used for the ornamentation of toys, and of certain kinds of gingerbread.

Sulphate of Copper, when united with ammonia, produces magnificent blue crystals. The large show bottles which are commonly placed in the shop windows of chemists and druggists have generally one of their number filled with a dilute solution of Copper, to which a slight excess of ammonia has been added. (Ammonia abounds in the soil of the Libyan desert. Sal ammoniac was prepared by the priests of Jupiter Ammon, and transmitted by them to Egypt, in baskets made of Palm leaves).

David Copperfield resolutely studied the art, and practice of stenography, so as to eke out his income when it was yet narrow. His friend Traddles would deliver the Parliamentary debate night after night, for Copperfield to follow as a shorthand reporter. "Often, and often we pursued these Debates until the clock pointed to midnight, and the candles were burning down." "The result of so much good practice was that by and by I began to keep pace with Traddles pretty well, and should have been quite triumphant if I had had the least idea what my notes were about. But, as to reading them after I had got them, I might as well have copied the Chinese inscriptions on an immense collection of tea-chests, or the golden characters on all the great red, and green bottles in the chemists' shops."

In testing bread which is suspected of containing a minute quantity of copper, a zinc plate will serve to detect this; all that is necessary is to acidify the bread with dilute pure sulphuric acid, and leave the zinc therein. The copper thus deposited on the zinc plate may be scraped off, dissolved, and tested in other ways. A dilute solution of common salt attacks copper with considerable rapidity; and thus, when pickles have been thoughtlessly boiled in badly-tinned copper vessels, or if a copper coin has been fraudulently placed in the vinegar so as to impart a fine green colour to the pickles, then a zinc, or iron plate will readily separate the copper, if this plate be digested for some time together with the pickles. Workers in copper suffer from severe abdominal colic, (with remissions); to relieve which the workman bends himself double. This copper colic differs from that to which lead-workers are liable; which latter is non-inflammatory; whereas the copper colic is attended with considerable fever.

Abundant evidence is forthcoming that the external wearing of a copper plate over the abdomen has proved singularly protective against Asiatic cholera during an epidemic of that formidable disease, which kills so rapidly. " For the choleraic cramps, which are most severe," wrote Mr. Proctor, who treated a large number of cases, in the year 1866, and with exceptional success, " copper given internally as one of its soluble salts, and applied externally, was unquestionably the best remedy " ; " and I may say for the vomiting also."

In cases which have occurred of being poisoned by copper, jaundice has been a characteristic symptom.

The ancient symbol adopted by Alchemists of old for designating the metal Copper, was a hieroglyphic character supposed to represent the looking-glass of Venus.

" The metal doth most easily contract a rust, which is called ærugo " ; " of a green colour."

A repetition of some few other particulars respecting metallic Copper, as told about among our *Animal Simples* (with which, indeed, it is scarcely in place), may be fairly allowed here. Thus, " There is abundant evidence of the fact that during the prevalence of cholera-epidemics the workers in copper have remained singularly exempt from attacks; whilst others who have worn a plate of Copper next the skin over the abdomen have likewise escaped free. In 1884, Dr. de Noel Walker found during an epidemic of cholera which was ravaging Tuscany, that among one hundred and fifty souls at the copper-smelting furnaces in Prato, not only no case of true Asiatic cholera occurred, but not even a sporadic case of such a nature; not one of the operatives was affected even by a slighter gastric disturbance of the epidemic character."

Even one workman, through having his garments dusty with Copper, served thereby to protect the other members of his family at home. "Every soldier, then, and every sailor, should be ordered to wear by day, and by night, when quartered in a district liable to cholera epidemics, a thin plate of Copper, over the front of the abdomen, next the skin, securely fastened there; or. if more convenient, across the loins behind." In Pettigrew's *Medical Superstitions* it is shown how a like curative virtue may have underlain former remedial nostrums which are now regarded as senseless, and exploded.

During the prevalence of cholera in Austria, Germany, and Italy, a certain amulet was superstitiously worn (at the pit of the stomach, in close contact with the skin). Dr. Walker tells us one of these was sent to him from Hungary; and it was found to consist merely of a circular piece of Copper, two and a half inches in diameter, and without having any characters inscribed upon it. These amulets were adopted pretty generally in Naples. Recently, again, in confirmation of the still wider curative action of metallic Copper, Dr. Clapton, of St. Thomas's Hospital, has publicly noticed that workers in Copper, though having frequently to complain of constant lassitude, with giddiness, whilst they are of sallow aspect, and dyspeptic, nevertheless show a remarkable rapidity of healing when anyhow wounded; and remain, without a single exception, free from cholera, even during the worst epidemics.

The intestinal colic from which workers in copper suffer differs again from the colic which affects workers in lead, in being attended with extreme prostration, and profuse diarrhœa. But the duration of copper colic is short, and the prognosis favourable. Frequently the hair, and beard of these copper-workers become green as grass; though the texture of the hair remains as soft, and glossy as before.

In September, 1905, Dr. J. Cavendish Molson wrote a letter, which appeared in *The Morning Post*, to the following effect, "In view of the possible spread presently of cholera to this country, it will be opportune to know of a simple, safe, and certain means of preventing infection by this formidable disease. Take a piece of pure Copper, of the size of half-a-crown; and about one-sixteenth of an inch in thickness. Perforate this, near its edge, so that the disc may be suspended by means of a silk thread, or cord, from the neck; and let it then lie in immediate contact with the abdomen, next the skin, about two inches above the navel. The attrition of the disc between the skin and the garments will ensure the absorption by the skin of sufficient Copper to render the wearer immune from attack. When cholera is in a locality, or during an epidemic, the disc should be worn continually. This piece of Copper is not a charm, or fetish, but a scientific prophylactic, and is recommended on the ground that cholera is absolutely unknown among the workers in Copper mines. "In 1894," Dr. Molson goes on to say, "I visited St. Petersburg during an epidemic of cholera, and wore a disc similar to the one I have described, without contracting the disease. I there met Baron Fredericks, who informed me that he used the same means with like immunity during a severe outbreak of cholera in Nijni Novgorod. Even if these individual experiences be regarded as mere coincidences, the hard and indisputable fact remains of the Copper workers' exemption from this 'scourge.' Suitable Copper discs for wearing on the body can be obtained from Messrs. Armbrecht, Nelson & Co., at 72 and 73 Duke Street, London."

Copper would seem without doubt to be strongly destructive of the bacteria of disease. Certain bacteria which are often plentiful on silver coins are, it is said, never found on coins of copper. Moreover, artisans in copper works are immune as regards bacterial diseases.

M. Moldini, during the 1884 epidemic of cholera in Paris, saved the lives of many soldiers in the garrison of that city by causing them to wear plates of copper next the skin, and administering to them a few drops of some salt of copper, in solution, each morning and evening. Dr. Raymond, at Gallipoli, adopted the same practice, with like success. Dr. Clapton, when physician to St. Thomas's Hospital in 1869, read a paper before the Clinical Society there, giving the results of a wide series of enquiries into the health of the workers in copper during epidemics of cholera. He found that the men engaged in various copper works had always escaped cholera, and even choleraic diarrhœa, although their neighbourhoods suffered severely during the great epidemics. Dr. Leeson, at the same scientific meeting, stated that in 1832 there was no cholera among the verdigris workers in Deptford.

In the copper mines the crude ore, in order to become a marketable commodity, has to be roasted in furnaces; it is stated that no offensive odour is given off during this process; nevertheless, some strange emanation turns the workmen's hair grass-green. Curiously enough, with reference to some of the tropical birds, it is found that traces of copper serve a highly ornamental purpose in giving brilliant colouring to certain parts of their plumage. Thus, the brilliant red of the wing feathers of the turacos is due to a colouring matter derived from the banana, (or its twin brother, the plantain,) upon which these birds exclusively feed. But, none the less, the banana, cannot be regarded as a cosmetic, whether for birds, or for human beings. The coloured races who have hitherto been addicted to this fruit as a food do not exhibit any beauty of complexion ; moreover, the scarlet pigment which obtains in the wings of the turacos, as derived from bananas, being soluble in water, is apt to be washed out by a shower. Yet the banana is certainly a remarkably wholesome fruit for our eating and, perhaps so because of the trace of copper which it contains. A little iron is essential to healthy blood ; and a little copper may likewise subserve some useful end in the human economy, particularly as a potential bactericide.

A few words as to the dietetic value of bananas will not be out of place here. Mr. Harold Crichton-Browne has written forcibly on this topic. He reminds us that the delicious fruit is a well-stocked source of real nutriment ; it supplies material for combustion, and thus for the maintenance of our animal heat ; it also serves to build up the muscular system, and to repair waste of nerve tissue. The flour made from dried bananas is equal in nutritive value to rice. (We have recently gained a practical lesson respecting the invigorating, and sustaining powers of rice, as demonstrated by the victorious achievements of the Japanese soldiers in the field). When dried, and sprinkled with brown sugar, the banana is, also, weight for weight, as nutritious as the highly sustaining fig.

But it is in its fresh state, clad in its familiar primrose tunic, that the banana chiefly appeals to the thoughtful dietist. Its creamy succulence, and delicate odour are inviting; and its pleasant sapor is a prelude to good digestion. Dependent as the said sapor is on an ethereal body which the coal-tar investigators have not yet been able to imitate by any chemical essence, it is a subtle stimulus to all subsequent alimentary processes. No sense of drowsiness, or oppression follows on a meal of bananas, though this meal of the said fruit may have been a bulky one. Mr. Browne has seen a West Indian negro consume twenty full-grown bananas at a sitting, and display unwonted vivacity thereafter. Again, it seems more than probable that this mild and gentle fruit may become a powerful auxiliary to the temperance reformer. It mixes badly with alcohol in any form, and becomes difficult of digestion when taken with any spirit; therefore the allegation is made that an habitual use of bananas as food diminishes the drink-craving where this exists. As an instance in point, Captain Parsons, of Port Kingston, (the Direct Imperial Line), told Mr. Browne that since the men on his ship, seamen and stokers, have been allowed to partake of bananas at discretion, (these fruits always forming a considerable part of the cargo,) their consumption of alcoholic beverages has been greatly reduced.

To relish the banana is not what is called an acquired taste. This fruit is acceptable at all ages. The infant sucks it greedily; children devour it with gusto; the adult appreciates it; and the toothless octogenarian blesses its tender succulence. Fortunately, too, the sense of its merits is increasing rapidly. Not so long ago this fruit was a delicacy in the menu of the rich man. To-day it is to be seen on the huckster's barrow in all our large towns; whilst we may reasonably hope that the supply of the most wholesome, and delectable esculent will increase rapidly, its price diminishing at the same time, so that an ample supply of the desirable fruit thus noticed may be within the easy reach of all persons.

Sir Ralph Moor, a competent authority, teaches that when the banana is really ripe, its skin has become almost black; and it is whilst in this condition the fruit is most fit for eating; not when it is green of skin, or even yellow. "The prosecutions," he says, "which are instituted for selling bananas thus (maturely) black of aspect are militating seriously against the industry."

Though poorer in proteids, banana-meal is richer in carbo-hydrates than the best wheat-flour. The natives of the West Indies, as preparatory to a voyage, make a paste of banana fruit, when ripe, squeezing it through a fine sieve, and then forming the pulpy paste into small loaves, which they dry in the sun, or in hot ashes, wrapping them afterwards in leaves of the flowering reed. When required for use, some of the paste is mixed with sufficient water to make a thick sort of soup, which is both pleasant of taste, and eminently nourishing. By the inhabitants of Madeira the banana is venerated as the forbidden fruit, which may not be cut with a knife, because, if thus treated, the fruit when bisected, exhibits, they say, a representation of our Saviour's death on the cross.

Some writers have formed a conclusion that the banana is the tree from which our first parents are said to have made aprons for themselves in the Garden of Eden. The leaves thereof (it being often called a fig-tree by the ancients) are three, four, or five feet long, and proportionately broad: they may easily be sewn together by the thread-like filaments which are to be peeled from the body of the tree.

Again, certain oysters likewise (notably those collected from a bed on the river Fal, Devon), which are of a green hue, owe this colour to traces of Copper which they contain. Chemical analyses have shown that the amount of Copper per oyster is only a very small fraction of a grain, so that the consumption of a reasonably moderate number of these particular molluscs would not be likely to entail any injurious consequences; indeed, under certain physical conditions, would be salutary. It being also an established fact that dilute solutions of Copper salts exercise a marked destructive action on many bacteria, for this valid reason Copper cooking vessels are, in their proper degree, excellent for use against bacterial contamination of the culinary preparations made therein. This specially holds good with regard to starchy foods, and fruits when cooked for jams and preserves.

One of David Copperfield's feats in housekeeping, (when recently married to his pretty doll of a Dora,) was "a little dinner to Traddles." When the boiled leg of mutton appeared, Copperfield wondered how it came to pass that all their joints of meat were of such extraordinary shapes: whether their butcher contracted for all the deformed sheep that came into the world; but he kept his reflections to himself. "Next came the oysters." "I bought a beautiful little barrel of them," said Dora; "the man told me they are very good." "But, I,—I'm afraid there's something the matter with them! they don't seem right." (Here Dora shook her head, and diamond tears twinkled in her eyes). "They're only opened in both shells," said I; "take the top one off, my love!" "But it won't come off," said Dora, trying very hard, and looking much distressed. "Do you know, Copperfield," said Traddles, cheerfully examining the dish, "I think it is in consequence,—they are capital oysters,—but I think it is in consequence of their never having been opened." "They never had been opened; and we had no oyster-knife; and couldn't have used one if we had; so we looked at the oysters, and ate the mutton: at least we ate as much of it as was done, and made up with capers."

In the *Encyclopedia* of Bartholomew Anglicus—1250—it is curiously related that "The crab is enemy to the oyster. For he liveth by fish thereof, with a wonderful wit. For, because that he may not open the hard shell of the oyster, he spieth, and awaiteth when the oyster openeth; and then the crab that lieth in await, taketh a little stone, and putteth it between the shells, that the oyster may not close himself. And when the closing is so let, the crab eateth and gnaweth the flesh of the oyster."

"Plant industry" has shown that water containing the germs of cholera, and typhoid, may be safely drunk after it has stood for eight hours in a clean Copper vessel. "Thus," writes another doctor, relevant to this subject, "the Copper canteen, or water-cart, may furnish in the future all the protection needed from the deadliest scourge of war; and the sources of death in many a tropic station may be cleansed of their malignancy by a Copper scavenger." "One would imagine," says playfully a journalist of the hour, " that the tinned peas of the present day offer an equivalent in Copper for anything we have lost in the copper tea-kettle of the past."

However, as far as any fear need be entertained on this score, it has been distinctly proved that a man of average weight can consume a grain of Copper daily without sustaining the slightest injury : whilst with regard to the drinking water treated as proposed, for annihilating any noxious germs possibly contained therein, ten gallons of water so metallic as to kill typhoid germs would not yield the tenth part of the quantity of Copper which is contained in a single can of tinned green peas.

Concerning the cooking utensils mentioned in the Old Testament, the Septuagint version renders the word "Brass" as "Kalkos"—Copper : and a wise provision was ordained that "Starch" foods should be prepared—" in Cupro "—in Copper utensils.

But Copper stewpans used for any such purposes must be kept highly polished as to their interior surface. else their bactericidal properties will be greatly reduced.

Mr. Norris, P.C.S., of the Technical College, Finsbury, says, " Foods cooked in Copper vessels are not thought to take up any trace of Copper, provided these vessels are kept perfectly clean. In those cases where the acids in the foods are liable to attack the Copper, the vessels must be tinned. Iron saucepans are commonly thus tinned ; but if the tin has worn off, and exposes the food to the iron, then the (tannic) astringent, or acids (e.g. of fruits) act upon the iron, and produce dark iron compounds ; even a sugar solution will thus be acted on by the iron, and turn black. Similarly fruit when cut with a steel knife dissolves some of the iron, and becomes of a dark colour where cut."

Professor Stewart states that one part of Copper is to be found in four million parts of water which has been left to stand for three hours in a Copper vessel (having the capacity of a litre). For a typhoid fever patient this very small percentage of Copper in solution has proved sufficient to kill off the "typhoid microbic guests, without doing any harm to the host." "Colloidal" Copper is the technical term applied to such Copper in solution.

"There's fevers of the mind," said Mrs. Gamp, shaking her head mysteriously, "as well as body." "You may take your slime drafts till you flies into the air with efferwescence; but you won't cure that."

In making cooking utensils of Copper, great care should be taken that acid liquors, or even water intended for drinking, or to be mixed with food, is not suffered to stand too long in any such a vessel; otherwise so much of the metal will become dissolved thereby, as to give disagreeable, and even poisonous qualities to the same. Yet, it is remarkable that while acid liquors are kept boiling, they do not seem to dissolve any of the metal. Thence it happens that confectioners, by skilful management, prepare the most acid syrups in Copper vessels without their receiving any unpleasant taste, or injurious quality from the metal. But all vessels formed of this metal, which are employed in cooking, ought to have their inner surface covered with a coating of tin.

No evidence whatever is adducible to show that Copper thus possibly ingested in small quantities for long periods has caused any detrimental effect on the health of an individual. Certain experiments have been made with the view of establishing conclusions just the opposite in character to any such view as that now refuted. These experiments are for testing the efficiency of a Copper method by which drinking-water may be purified: especially too as regards the harmful bacilli of typhoid infection. It was found that in every instance the "colon," and "typhoid" bacilli were completely destroyed in less than four hours by placing strips of Copper-foil in water containing pure cultures (prepared for the purpose in the laboratory) of these noxious organisms.

Kraemer, the scientific experimenter alluded to, considers it extremely fortunate that so effective a method has been discovered for destroying microorganisms in drinking-water, and which can be applied thus readily on a large scale, whilst so safely, by the average householder. The simple method which he suggests for domestic purposes consists in merely placing a small piece of Copper-foil (three and a half inches square) in a quart of water, and allowing this to stand overnight, or from six to eight hours, at the ordinary temperature, and then removing the foil, or drawing off the water.

Towards proving similar conclusions by other collateral means, Copper coins have been smeared by the experimental scientist with cultures of diphtheria poison, under conditions fully favourable to its development. But in a few hours every germ was dead; thus affording incontestable proof of some quality in the metal antagonistic to the propagation of the disorder. An American physician in his enthusiasm for Copper has gone so far as to attribute the surprising increase of various internal ailments (which are probably of germ origin), such, for instance, as appendicitis, to the disuse in the present generation of the Copper tea-kettle of our forefathers.

Saint Paul thought fit to tell Timothy "it was Alexander, the Coppersmith, who did him much evil." ("The Lord reward him according to his works!") But in those early days the cheery domestic copper tea-kettle of more modern times was as yet unknown. Dickens, in 1845, made his Christmas story, *The Cricket on the Hearth*, commence thus: "The kettle began it," "full five minutes by the little waxy-faced Dutch clock in the corner, before the cricket uttered a chirp." Several years previously the same genial author had described, with inimitable force of graphic, glowing, diction, a festive family tea-drinking, whereat the kettle likewise played a prominent part. It took place in Gabriel Varden, (the sturdy, jovial locksmith's) little back parlour, for the hospitable reception of his pretty daughter, Dolly Varden, and Joseph Willett, newly betrothed to one another; (he being minus an arm, "took off in the defence of the Salwanners:")—"there sat Gabriel; the rosiest, cosiest, merriest, heartiest, best-contented old buck in Great Britain, or out of it:" there he sat, watching his wife as she decorated the room with flowers for the greater honour of Dolly and Joseph, who had gone out walking, and for whom "the Tea-Kettle had been singing gaily on the hob for fully twenty minutes, chirping as never Kettle chirped before; for whom the best service of real undoubted china, patterned with divers round-faced mandarins holding up broad umbrellas, was now displayed in all its glory; to tempt whose appetites a clear, transparent, juicy ham, garnished with cool green lettuce leaves, and fragrant cucumber, reposed upon a shady table, covered with a snow-white cloth. For whose delight, preserves, and jams, crisp cakes, and other pastry, short to eat, with cunning twists, and cottage loaves, and rolls of bread, both white and brown, were all set forth in rich profusion; in whose youth Mrs. Varden herself had grown quite young again, and stood there in a gown of red and white; symmetrical in figure, buxom in bodice, ruddy in cheek, and lip, faultless in ankle, laughing in face, and mood, in all respects delicious to behold; there sat the locksmith among all and every these delights, the sun that shone upon them all; the centre of the system; the source of light, heat, life, and frank enjoyment, in this bright household world."

For soldiers in the field some method of safely sterilizing water, as by keeping it in Copper vessels, may prove of incalculable service.

David Copperfield, when he and Dora, "after several varieties of experiment, gave up housekeeping as a bad job," the house kept itself; and, "we," wrote David, "kept a page-boy." "This retainer appears to me to have lived in a hail of saucepan lids! His principal function was to quarrel with the cook; in which respect he was a perfect Whittington, without his cat, or the remotest chance of becoming Lord Mayor." "When we had a little dinner-party he would come tumbling out of the kitchen, with iron missiles flying after him." "We wanted to get rid of him; but he wouldn't go! He was always rubbing his eyes with the sleeve of his jacket, or stopping to blow his nose on the extreme corner of a small pocket-handkerchief, which he never *would* take completely out of his pocket, but always economised, and secreted."

In several of our English villages it is customary to get some of the grease (bell-comb) which gathers round the bronze "brasses," whereon the "gudgeons" of the Church bells work; such grease being reckoned curative of ringworm. This expected result is not unlikely, by reason of the fatty salts of Copper and Tin, contained in the said grease, and which are eminently destructive of such bacterial toxins as cause the complaint. "Cart-gum," from the axles of farm wagons, is likewise of rural use for remedial purposes, particularly to make whiskers grow; which hirsute purpose it is likely to advance as being intermixed, this time, with detritus of iron, always tonic.

Native Verdigris—(Chrysocolla)—was found by the ancients in Copper mines, as of a bright green colour. Nero, of old Rome, being patron of the Green Faction, in one of his fits of extravagance, caused the Circus to be strewed with powder of the said valuable mineral, instead of with ordinary sand. This was on a day when he figured there as a character clad in a livery of the same brilliant green dye.

"The common Brass," wrote Lemery, 1712, "which the workmen call 'metal,' is an alloy of Copper with Leton, or with Tin; they make divers sorts, which differ only according to the quantity of Tin that is mix't with the Copper; the mixture is from twelve pounds to five-and-twenty pounds, in the hundred weight of Copper." "They use Brass for clocks, mortars, and several other works; the best is that which gives the clearest sound when you strike it."

"Though I speak," wrote St. Paul to the Corinthians, "with the tongues of men, and of angels, and have not charity, I am become as sounding Brass, or a tinkling cymbal." After the same fashion, though told in secular terms, Charles Dickens (in *Barnaby Rudge*) has skilfully taught a useful lesson, of which the text is taken from the book of metals. His Mr. Chester, a sanctimonious humbug, of leading social position, propounds to Mrs. Varden (whom he wishes to impress as being a meek, righteous, thorough-going Christian, whilst having a base underhand design in view) "certain virtuous maxims, somewhat vague, and general in their nature, doubtless, and partaking of the character of truisms, worn a little out at elbow, but delivered in so charming a voice, and with such uncommon serenity and peace of mind, that they answered as well as the best. Nor is this to be wondered at ; for, as hollow vessels produce a far more musical sound in falling than those which are substantial, so it will often be found that sentiments which have nothing in them, make the loudest ringing in the world, and are the most relished."

Food cooked in a Brass utensil was known long since to be as hurtful as any viand cooked in an untinned Copper vessel. Amongst other proofs of this fact may be adduced a few verses from the pathetic old ballad "*The Croodlin' Doo* (as already quoted in our *Meals Medicinal*) :—

> " O, what got ye at your grandmither's,
>   My little wee croodlin' doo ?—
> I got a bonnie wee fishie ;
>   Mak' my bed, Mammie, noo.
>
> And what did she do wi' the fishie,
>   My little wee croodlin' doo ?—
> She boiled it in a brass pan ;
>   Mak' my bed, Mammie, noo.

> And what did ye do with the banes o't,
>   My little wee croodlin' doo ?—
> I gi'ed 'em to my little dog ;
>   Mak' my bed, Mammie, noo.
>
> And what did your little doggie do,
>   My little wee croodlin' doo ?—
> He stretched out his head, and feet, and dee'd ;
>   Mak' my bed, Mammie, noo."

Dickens again tells graphically (in *Barnaby Rudge*) about the "harmonious blacksmith." "From the workshop of the 'Golden Key' there issued forth a tinkling sound, so merry, and good-humoured, that it suggested the idea of some one working blithely, and made quite pleasant music. No man who hammered on at a dull monotonous duty could have brought such cheerful notes from steel, and iron ; but he might have been a Coppersmith, and still been musical ! 'Tink, tink, tink,' clear as a silver bell ; and audible at every pause of the street's harsher noises, as though it said, 'I don't care ; nothing puts me out ; I am resolved to be happy.' Who but the locksmith (Gabriel Varden) could have made such music ? There he stood ; working at his anvil, his face all radiant with exercise, and gladness, his sleeves turned up, his wig pushed off his shining forehead ; the easiest, freest, happiest man in all the world. Beside him sat a sleek cat, purring, and winking in the light, and falling every now and then into an idle doze, as from excess of comfort. Toby (Fillpot) looked on from a tall bench hard by ; one beaming smile from his broad nut-brown face down to the slack-baked buckles in his shoes. The very locks that were suspended around had something jovial in their rust ; and seemed like gouty gentlemen of hearty natures, disposed to joke on their infirmities. There was nothing surly, or severe in the whole scene. It seemed impossible that any one of the innumerable keys could fit a churlish strong-box, or a prison door. Cellars of beer, and wine ; rooms where there were fires, books, gossip, and cheering laughter, these were their sphere of action ! Places of distrust, and cruelty, and restraint, they would have left quadruple-locked for ever. 'Tink, tink, tink;' The locksmith paused at last, and wiped his brow. The silence roused the cat ; who, jumping softly down, crept to the door, and watched with tiger eyes a birdcage in an opposite window. Gabriel lifted Toby to his mouth, and took a hearty draught."

By an odd coincidence the policeman of to-day is popularly designated by the slang term of a "Copper," which epithet has nevertheless no connection whatever with the metal of this name. It owns a Latin derivation, from the verb "capio"—I seize ; and it thus actually signifies to "cop," or "grasp," anything unpleasant ; as to catch a beating, or get hold of a rogue.

LEAD.

THE metal Lead, noticeable here, not as among the "Nobles," but because of certain curative virtues which it can undoubtedly exercise, was named Saturn by the Alchemists of old. Its symbol, or representative sign, resembles the scythe of Saturn, "Old Father Time." Metallic Lead has been known from days almost immemorial. The Romans sheathed the bottom of their ships with Lead ; whilst the Romish ladies (unwisely) used White Lead—the Carbonate of Lead—as a cosmetic. Lead has not only a bad reputation for producing "painter's colic" in workmen who frequently handle the metal, whilst not adopting precautionary measures; but the poisonous qualities thereof have been unwittingly produced, says Professor Pepper (*vide* his *Play-Book of Metals*, 1877), in the cases of those unfortunate persons who have swallowed wine sweetened with poisonous "Sugar of Lead" (formerly much used by wine-merchants for preserving wines from acidity); or again by children who have partaken of "lollypops" coloured with Red Lead; or eaten "Bath buns" rendered still more injurious by "King's Yellow" (arsenical orpiment), mistaken for Chrome Yellow (Chromate of Lead), as making the confection pleasing to the eye.

Metallic Lead has a bluish-white colour; and when recently cut, or scraped, owns a brilliant lustre, which, however, fades rapidly. The well-known soft malleability of Lead enables it to be applied in sheets for serving to cover houses. An interesting proceeding for showing this softness of Lead is to be effected by placing a common sealing-wax impression between two pieces of soft sheet Lead, on an anvil, and striking them suddenly with a tolerably heavy hammer, when a correct impression of the seal is obtained on the face of the Lead, whilst other sealing-wax impressions may be taken therefrom. It is said that this was the mode employed by inquisitive Post Office authorities in olden times when they wanted to learn the contents of a letter without betraying themselves by a broken seal.

Lead is used not only to cover the houses which shelter the living, but it has also been employed from time long past in the construction of the box, or coffin, made to contain the dead. Formerly no person could be buried in a vault under a church except in a leaden coffin; but the noxious custom of putting the dead in leaden cases, liable to bulge out because of the lethal gases generated within, and then to burst, thus throwing out into the church above these deadly gases, has now been abolished; except, that is, in rare instances, when embalmed royalty, or the mortal remains of some great man, become consigned to a last resting-place in Westminster Abbey, St. Paul's Cathedral, or the Chapel Royal at Windsor.

Sweetmeats which are suspected to contain Lead as their colouring pigment may be subjected to a glowing heat together with charcoal, in the bowl of a tobacco pipe; when, after a time, the metallic Lead will finally become apparent, either in minute globules diffused through the small lump of charcoal, or collected in a larger quantity at the bottom of the bowl.

Animal albumen is sometimes found to contain a certain small amount of sulphur; (the presence of which may be readily shown by dissolving, for instance, some white of egg in a solution of caustic potash, and adding some Acetate of Lead also in solution, continuing to do this as long as the precipitate which is seen to form becomes soon redissolved. Then on boiling the clear solution, it will instantly become black by the separation of Sulphuret of Lead, thereby disclosing unmistakably the presence of free sulphur.) Seeing that the human hair is intimately allied to albumen in its composition, and likewise is known to contain free sulphur, for this reason leaden combs are frequently used to darken the colour of the hair; and likewise a hair-dye composed of Litharge (red Lead) and cream of lime has been employed for changing red hair to a black hue.

As already quoted from Warren's entertaining work, *Ten Thousand a Year;* when little insignificant Tittlebat Titmouse, a London draper's shopman, came unexpectedly, and under a mistake, (as is afterwards shown) into possession of the large annual income named as the title of this book, he resolved to dye his objectionable carroty locks, and used for this purpose a widely-advertised hair dye—" Cyano-chaitanthropopoion,"—which, sad to relate, turned his obnoxious red locks to a vivid green! Filled with concern because of such a distressing result, the mortified little cad then had recourse to another pretentious nostrum— " Damascus Cream,"—at a cost of three-and-sixpence the bottle. But, alas! this made matters worse, by changing his head of hair to purple, or violet. In indignant despair he was driven to the " Tetragmenon Abracadabra ; " vaunted, and puffed as absolutely certain of success, at nine-and-sixpence the flask; which, on being opened, furnished a fluid colourless, and with a most infernal smell. After vigorous use thereof overnight, poor little Tittlebat woke to find his eyebrows, and whiskers, white as the driven snow ; whilst—to complete the picture—his hair remained more purple than before. It being Sunday morning his landlady could not buy a bottle of ink for remedial use ; so had to suggest " blacking " ; which proved a miserable failure, as far as restoring any colour to the bleached facial appendages.

On the recognised medicinal principle of cure by any metal (or other toxical substance) which, when given in harmful quantity induces poisonous results, but which, when administered medicinally in much reduced, or diluted, and harmless doses, obviates curatively those particular symptoms characterising the poisonous effects from the larger quantity;—on this detailed principle, Sugar (i.e., Acetate) of Lead, when rubbed up, in minute proportion, with dry, inert sugar of milk, will effectively meet the same morbid symptoms (when occurring spontaneously) as signalise Lead poisoning. These symptoms are mainly colic, obstinate constipation, some forms of paralysis, especially when affecting the hands, and wrists, wasting palsy, and Bright's disease of the kidneys, in its most serious form.

For outward use as an admirably soothing lotion, which is both sedative, and somewhat astringent, in irritative, or inflamed skin eruptions, as well as for burns, the Solution of Sugar, (sub-carbonate), of Lead is a very valuable application. This solution, in a concentrated form, is known as "Goulard's Extract." It has to be diluted for external application as a lotion; from one to two (silver) teaspoonfuls to each fluid ounce of distilled water.

The so-called Black Lead with which pencils for drawing are made, and grates, etc., "blackleaded," is not Lead at all, in any sense. This substance (Plumbago, or Graphites) is merely carbon, or charcoal, uncrystallised, and mixed with some lime, together with a certain proportion of iron. When triturated by the druggist, and thus (in combination with some dry, inert, sugar of milk) powdered, up to a high degree of attenuation, the Graphites will prove admirably curative of cracked, and chapped skin (of the hands or feet); likewise effectually preventive of the hair falling off prematurely.

The metal Lead is mainly of two kinds—for remedial and other uses: Galena, or a compound of Sulphur and Lead; and White Lead (carbonate) Ore. The actual metal is easily extracted from Galena by heat, which burns away the sulphur, and leaves the Lead.

"Massicot" is the raw material which produces Red Lead; "Litharge" is the Oxide of Lead which is employed for making the Lead plaster,—of extensive use in the surgical practice of all hospitals, and a familiar appliance to cuts and wounds in most households. But, beyond this, words of grave warning are urgently needed concerning a criminal misuse to which this "Diachylon" as made and sold for Lead-plaster, is now not infrequently put when made up into pills at home, as an abortifacient, in our Midland Counties.

Water, when absolutely pure, does not act at all upon metallic Lead itself; but the oxygen of the surrounding air forms with the metal a hydrated oxide straightway on reaching it; which oxide is soluble in the water, and is a cumulative poison; hence the danger of using Lead cisterns, with the object of their continuing to contain pure water, is readily seen. If, however, such water is not absolutely pure, but contains even a small proportion of lime, (bicarbonate, or sulphate), this will prevent the water from acting on the Lead, and will make the cistern comparatively safe. Chronic Lead-poisoning, whether caused insidiously by the long-continued unsuspected use of water made pernicious by a small percentage of the metal contained therein, (as met with in the leaden pipes conveying such water), or whether by daily handling White Lead in paint, or putty, while pursuing the business of a plumber, induces what doctors call "Encephalopathy,"—a morbid condition of the brain, with gradual wasting of the body and limbs. A blue line of discoloration along the margin of the gums characterises such general toxication of the system by metallic Lead. As a practice which will operate (in some measure) preventatively, lemonade may be taken freely for a daily drink, the said beverage being made agreeably acid, partly by fresh lemon-juice, and partly by admixture with dilute sulphuric acid (which any chemist will readily supply).

When first dug from the earth, this metal, whilst still unsmelted, is Litharge, or Red Lead. It may be smelted into metallic Lead by combustion with wood, and charcoal; so that the carbonic acid (oxide) shall be driven off. As an experiment to show on a minor scale what thus takes place wholesale, a small quantity of Litharge should be mixed with some powdered coke, or charcoal, in the bowl of a tobacco-pipe (the stem of the pipe being used as a handle), whilst a dull red heat is applied to the bowl. Then the charcoal will combine with the oxygen of the Litharge, and will escape as carbonic acid gas. At the same time the metallic Lead will gradually collect at the bottom of the bowl, and can be poured off, on to a mould, or on to damp sand.

It is a remarkable fact that, after years of desertion, the Lead mines of the Peak of Derbyshire are now again attracting hopeful speculators of all sorts, thereto. Lead, like Copper, has become raised in price, and is in brisk demand. When any comer has established a claim, and settled down on it, (having the Barmaster's consent), the law thoroughly safeguards his property. All persons then attempting to purloin his Lead become liable to a heavy penalty. Formerly thieves of this kind had to undergo punishment quite barbaric. For the first, and second offences they were fined;

but, if they stole Lead for the third time, they were fastened to the " stowe " (windlass), each with a knife stuck through his hand to the haft, the only chance of getting set at liberty being to cut loose the maimed hand.

Crude Lead Ore is the Sulphide of this metal—" Galena." The fumes, or vapours, given off from Lead smelting are poisonous ; so that all the grass, and other plants around the furnaces die.

When left in the air, Lead (sheet Lead, etc.) oxidises slightly, and thus becomes self-protected from corrosion. But many kinds of water will corrode, and eat away Lead, any such water, if conveyed through leaden pipes, becoming dangerous for drinking purposes. The Chinese make sheet-Lead for enwrapping tea (within their tea-chests) by pouring melted Lead on to a flat stone, then putting another flat stone on top of the first slab, and thus pressing out the Lead thin. Snuff is enclosed likewise within similar thin sheet Lead. Whether or not these articles suffer some small measure of deterioration by continued close contact with the Lead, is an open question.

In literary association with Snuff, one calls to mind the graphic personal description among the *Benchers of Inner Temple*, by Charles Lamb (*Essays of Elia*), respecting Thomas Coventry ; " whom what insolent familiar dare have mated ? " " whose person was a quadrate, his step massy, and elephantine, his face square as the lion's, his gait peremptory, and path-keeping, indivertible from his way as a moving column, the scare-crow of his inferiors, the brow-beater of equals, and superiors, who made a solitude of children wherever he came, for they fled his insufferable presence, as they would have shunned an Elisha bear. His growl was as thunder in their ears, whether he spake to them in mirth, or in rebuke, his invitatory notes being, indeed, of all the most repulsive and horrid. Clouds of snuff, aggravating the natural terrors of his speech, broke from each majestic nostril, darkening the air. He took it, not by pinches, but a palmful at once, diving for it under the mighty flaps of his old-fashioned waistcoat pocket; his waistcoat red, and angry; his coat dark Rappee, tinctured by dye original, and by adjuncts; with buttons of obsolete gold." "And so he paced the terrace."

"Lead in powder (especially that which is in a powder almost impalpable) has some use in medicine," (*History of Druggs*, 1712,) "because it is an ingredient in several oyntments." For reducing Lead to powder, "it is to be melted in an earthen, or iron vessel; and when it is melted the dust of beaten charcoal is to be thrown in,—stirring it about. Then, to clean the Lead, i.e., to separate the charcoal from it, there is nothing to do but to wash it in water, and dry it." Red Lead ("Litharge") again "is useful in medicine because it is drying, and gives a body to some oyntments." "White Lead affords to painters the most beautiful white that we have; and of the longest duration; but then it is a very dangerous drugg, both to grind, and to beat to powder." "Balsam of Lead is composed of the Lead Salt dissolved in oyl of turpentine; it is proper to cleanse, and cicatrise ulcers because capable of resisting putrefaction." "Magistery of Lead is composed of the Lead salt dissolved in distill'd vinegar, mix'd with common water. This is precipitated into a white powder; which, after it is washed, and dried, is very useful to cure tetters, and ringworms, being mixed with some pomatum; it likewise makes, with vinegar and water, a sort of virgin's milk, that is good to allay inflammations, and to cure pimples in the face."

"Lead," quoth Dr. Schroder, "is called Saturn, because it is consecrated to the Saturn in the macrocosm, and to the Saturn, or spleen, in the microcosm." "It refrigerates, binds, and thickens; quencheth lust, fills ulcers with flesh, and cicatriseth, and takes off proud flesh from malignant ulcers, alone, or mixed with other things." "Note too what Ecgler sayes in hys Isagoge: 'Of Lead,' quoth he, 'are made medicines to prolong life.'" "A tincture of Lead, made with distilled vinegar, opens the spleen." "The Salt of Lead cools against inflammation." "Sugar (Acetate) of Lead is," according to the *Pharmacopœia Londinensis* —Dr. Salmon, 1696—"a great anodyne, and easer of pain, and is of almost infinite vertues,—if we may believe the learned Beguinus." "Outwardly, if five or six grains be dissolved in a quarter of a pint of Rose-water, and dark, or inflamed eyes be washed therewith, it helps them. By such an ablution I cured one absolutely blind." "Thibaus saith that in pain, redness, and inflammation of the eyes, as also for a redness of the face, and skin, you may dip in this lotion a thin slice of raw veal, and lay it on the part." "As to milk of Lead (*lac Saturni*), if double pledgets be dip't in this twice or thrice a day, and applied hot upon ulcers hard to heal, it will quickly cure them."

An ointment formerly much in vogue at one time for dispelling piles was made with Sugar of Lead, lard, and burnt cork (powdered). The last-named ingredient was held in much repute of old as a styptic. If hung about the neck of a nursing mother, cork was believed to possess the power of arresting the secretion of breast-milk. The dog-doctors of to-day have great faith in burnt cork, mixed with lard, as an unguent for healing mange, and other such canine skin-eruptions.

Red Lead, to be used for painting, is made by a tedious process, from Massicot. It is sometimes employed in medicine externally for abating inflammations, also for cleansing, and healing ulcers. Litharge is another kind of oxide of Lead. The Litharge plaster (or Diachylon plaster) is prepared by boiling two pints of olive oil with one pound of Litharge, adding water, and constantly stirring the mixture until these ingredients are sufficiently, and properly incorporated.

Acid liquors, if kept in leaden vessels, corrode the metal and become poisonous. The dire complaint known as Devonshire colic arose from keeping cyder in cisterns of Lead.

TIN.

"Tinn"—according to Dr. John Schroder—1660—"is a soft, white metal, of a shining blue; it is called by chymists Jupiter; because it sympathizeth with Jupiter in the Macrocosm, and so with Jupiter in the Microcosm, which is the liver. By immersion in (usually) spirit of vinegar, thence comes 'Salt of Tin.' This is an excellent, and a certain remedy against the suffocation of the mother, which it cures as by a miracle; it is good outwardly for all foul sores, and putrid ulcers."

"The greatest part of the Tin which gains use in France (wrote M. Pomet) came thither from England; and especially from the County of Cornwall. The Britannick Islands abounded so much with this Metal that the ancients gave them the name of "Tin Islands."

"Some Authors affirm that Tin may be reduced into a Calx, or Ceruse, by the help of urine; and that the urine acts upon Tin as vinegar upon Lead." The Diaphoretick Tin, which M. Lemery has called the "Jovial Diaphoretick," is made of fine English Tin, with Iron, melted together, and afterwards with Saltpetre; they draw from thence a powder which is used for diseases of the liver."

Though Tin is not to be considered worthy to rank as a noble Metal, yet it obtains such an extensive use for manufacture into homely utensils of numerous sorts, thereby retaining in immediate contact with its surface so many of our foods, provisions, stored materials for kitchen use, and preserved comestibles, that enquiry in these pages as to the properties possessed, and exercised by Tin, remedially, or prejudicially, to the bodily health, is a matter of really vital importance to us all.

It is a remarkable fact, which has been proved over and over again, that water in which tin has been boiled (or cooled, after having been first heated), is capitally hostile to intestinal worms, particularly the round worm (lumbricus). Teste declares that both lumbrici (round worms), and ascarides (threadworms), will frequently come away in large quantities after the medicinal taking of metallic Tin, in some such a form as the water thus potentialized.

Another simple method which may be reliably adopted for securing these desired effects is to reduce purest Tin-foil to powder, and then rub some of this powdered metal well together with dry powdered inert sugar of milk: one part of the powdered Tin-foil to ninety-nine parts of the milk-sugar, powdered. They must be rubbed thoroughly together in a small mortar for ten. or fifteen minutes, at least. Then a dose of the mixed powder, ten grains at a time, may be given each night at bedtime, and each morning, before breakfast; doing this for three or four consecutive days, whilst admixing the dose (it being thus for a child of eight or ten years, but to be somewhat lessened for a younger child) with a spoonful of milk, or water. The same preparation will likewise serve to exterminate a tape-worm, probably by first stupefying the parasite, and then allowing its expulsion by any simple purgative, such as a glass of some aperient mineral water.

Metallic Tin has been given in material doses by some modern mediciners, on the supposition that being insoluble it would travel along the intestinal canal unaltered, and mechanically pushing before it the bundle of thread worms, or the larger intruder, and expelling the same finally by the fundament. But this is altogether a Quixotic proceeding, needlessly heroic, and summary. The frequent causation of nervous disorders, as epilepsy, and St. Vitus's dance, by intestinal worms, first led to such an expulsive measure as giving metallic Tin medicinally as just described; but no worms have been found expelled as a result, and yet these specified nervous attacks have been much alleviated; whereby a faith in the Tin medicament as of good instrinsic service against the said nervous disorders has naturally sprung up.

The hardest alloy of tin is a composition of Tin three parts, to one of lead; the presence of the tin destroys in a great measure the noxious qualities of the lead. Copper cooking vessels tinned inside with this mixture are found to be in no respects injurious.

It is remarkable that in Cornwall the veins of tin and copper run in a direction nearly East and West: other dykes, or veins, run North and South.

The wearing of a flat plate of best Tin over the front chest and lungs by a consumptive patient has seemed to prove undoubtedly beneficial. This plate is to be worn next the skin, whilst having its sharp, hard edges well protected by a flannel binding sewn on as for a bordering along each metallic edge. The consumptive cases thus benefited have been characterised by a profuse expectoration of phlegm, greenish, and with a sweetish taste, attended also with night-sweats, and rapid wasting of the body. Similarly in minor cases of neuralgic headache, particularly in front over the eyes, it has been found speedily useful to bind on across the forehead a flat piece of pure tin next the skin, guarding this carefully as to its edges with a soft kerchief.

According to Bartholomew Anglicus (a Franciscan, who wrote, about 1250, a popular Encyclopædia, which even at that date passed through ten editions), all the metals were formerly considered to be composed of sulphur and mercury; sulphur represented their combustible aspect; whilst mercury gave them their weight, and powers of becoming fluid. Native sulphur generally occurs in the neighbourhood of volcanoes. Most of what is required in commerce is brought in this native state from Sicily. Medicinally the common brimstone is employed.

The list of seven Metals is that of the most ancient times: Gold, Electrum, Silver, Copper, Tin, Lead, Iron; but it has been clearly ascertained that the said Electrum was an alloy of Gold and Silver. A consideration of the composition of the metals shows that Tin is

—in its properties—the nearest of all metals to the precious ones; whilst Tin is precisely the metal which was chosen by the Arabian Alchemists as a starting-point in their search for the Gold-making Philosopher's Stone,—their Chrysopeia.

Tin may be rolled, or hammered into foil; moreover it is so brittle that it may be readily reduced to powder. When alloyed with Copper it constitutes Bronze. To powder Tin the Metal is first fused, and afterwards triturated in a hot Iron mortar while it cools. Tin filings have been ordered as a remedy for tape-worm since the time of Paracelsus. "But," says Kuchenmeister, "once for all I protest against the administration of Tin filings; and I am convinced no one can give the same with any pleasure who has witnessed the painful irritation of the intestine after its having been taken by living animals, or has heard them whining, or seen them writhing because of the agonising mechanical presence within them of the rough insoluble mass." "Meanwhile a harmless, and even agreeable practice is pursued in several rural districts of France, which effectually answers the desired purpose of thus exterminating the tape-worms, that of giving sweetened wine which has been kept for twenty-four hours in a Tin vessel."

Powdered Tin acts when applied externally as an astringent, even as a caustic if used to excess; furthermore it has become in some instances productive of convulsive attacks when topically employed for covering raw sores.

As is commonly known, Tin has a peculiar odour when rubbed, or handled. In the mass it does not disorder the bodily functions; but when acid, fatty, saline (saltish), and even albuminous (as flesh-meat, or fish) substances have remained openly exposed in Tin vessels for a while, before being eaten, colic, vomiting, and other symptoms of being poisoned have been known to ensue. Dr. Pareira recorded this fact in his standard large work on Materia Medica as long ago as in 1842; which bears a fourfold significance in these modern times when comestibles of every sort are "tinned," or "canned," for almost universal consumption. It must further be guardedly borne in mind that Arsenic frequently occurs combined with metallic block Tin. The Phœnicians (who were perhaps the first people who carried on commerce by sea), traded with England, and Spain for Tin at least a thousand years before the time of Christ. In Pliny's time the Romans did not realise the difference between Tin, (their *Plumbum album*), and Lead, (their *Plumbum nigrum*). The present word for Tin (*Stannum*) did not assume this meaning until the fourth century.

Of dear old England wrote Bartholomew Anglicus, even as long ago as in 1250 :—" England is a strong land, and a sturdy, and the plenteoustest corner of the world ; so rich a land that unneth it needeth help of any land, and every other land needeth help of England. England is full of mirth, and of game ; and men ofttimes able to mirth and game, free men of heart and tongue, but the hand is much better and more free than the tongue." Can as much be honestly said of our dissatisfied, democratic, peevish, factious country in the present year of GRACE (forsooth !) ?

The ordinary Block Tin is manufactured by heating crude Tin Ore, (never quite free from iron, or lead, or arsenic,) in furnaces with Charcoal; then carbonic oxide gas escapes, and the melted Tin is drawn off so as to be cooled in iron moulds for becoming Block Tin; which may be made into pure Tin, and then sold as "grain Tin." It does not tarnish in the air, and is proof against the action of acids, such as vinegar, and the like. But this pure Tin would be too costly for use in making domestic receptacles for the hundred and one articles of common daily consumption, such as biscuit tins, coffee tins, sardine boxes, tin kettles, etc.; likewise it would be too heavy, if these receptacles are to be of stable form; therefore for such vessels sheet iron (or sheet copper) is used, with a thin protective coating of pure Tin, on both the inner and outer surfaces thereof.

To make " tin plate " (in Scotland, " white iron ") the sheet-iron plates are immersed in the acidulated water, and next scoured completely bright. Each plate is then plunged into a vessel filled with melted Tin, the surface of which is covered with suet, pitch, or resin, for preventing any formation of bubbles thereupon. Some of the Tin not only covers the surfaces of the Iron, but completely penetrates it, giving to its whole substance a white colour. " Block Tin " is made by pouring the melted ore (after it has been first washed, and then roasted), into quadrangular moulds of stone, each containing about three hundred and twenty pounds weight thereof. These " blocks " are stamped by officers of the Duke of Cornwall with the impression of a lion, the arms of that Duchy. A duty of four shillings per hundredweight has to be paid, on stamping, to the Prince of Wales.

Speaking as above of vinegar, incidental mention may be made of the circumstance that at the time of the Great Plague in this country (1665–1666), Dr. Robert Uvedale caused the whole of his household to escape that dire malady by a remedy which he discovered, and which they all inhaled. It consisted of pouring vinegar over a red-hot brick, whereby the aromatic fumes given off had the desired effect when inspired. Malt vinegar was used for this purpose, as got by the acetous fermentation of wort. Vinegar is remarkably antiseptic; it is used as such in preparing pickles, though nevertheless making the vegetable albumen thereof hard, and difficult of digestion.

C. S. Calverley (*Verses and Translations*, 1894) concludes an Ode to Beer thus :—

"But what is coffee but a noxious berry,
  Born to keep used-up Londoners awake ?
What is Falernian, what is Port, or Sherry,
  But vile concoctions, to make dull heads ache ?
Nay, Stout itself (though good with oysters, very !)
  Is not a thing your reading man should take.
He that would shine, and petrify his tutor,
  Should drink draught Allsopp, in its native pewter."

The metal Pewter thus particularised is, or was until lately, an alloy of Tin and Lead, the latter forming a considerable percentage thereof. This being so, a dangerous risk has attended the standing of malt liquor (especially if at all hard), in a pewter pot, because of the poisonous acetate (or Sugar) of Lead which would become presently produced in the liquor. But now-a-days Pewter consists mainly of Tin, hardened by a trifle of Copper; being sometimes called "tin and temper." In France the percentage of Lead is restricted by law to 16·5, as securing an alloy found to be proof against the action of sour (acetic) wine. Less confidence is to be placed in the pewter pots in which malt drinks are still served at our English public-houses, inasmuch as these pots have hitherto been made of "triple pewter," an inferior metal.

British Pewter has always been considered superior to that of other countries. The "Pewterers' Company,"—incorporated 1452,—would not allow foreign apprentices, or members from abroad, among its body, lest they should learn the English composition, and manufacture of this metal. Their crest was two arms holding a pewter dish, proper; the supporters—two seahorses *per fess,—or*, and *argent;* the motto being—"In God is all my trust."

Plate Pewter is a harder variety, composed of tin one hundred parts, with antimony eight parts, bismuth two parts, and copper two parts. Pewter plates and dishes are made by hammering preferably to moulding. The records of best known old English pewter marks were accidentally burnt, and are lost.

One of our native herbal "Horse-tails" (*Equisetum hyemale*), is known as Pewterwort, from its former use by milkmaids in scouring their cans; likewise for polishing various pewter utensils. Gerarde tells that they scour their pewter, and wooden things of the kitchen therewith, and thence call it "Pewterwort;" and that the fletchers and comb-makers rubbed, and polished their work with it. Professor Davy has detected a large proportion of flinty earth in the cuticle of the plant, to which its hardness, and asperity are owing. Linnæus says it is good for horses, but that cows lose their teeth by feeding on it. Old writers called it "Shave-grass," also "Dutch Rushes."

If antimonial wine (a recognised medicinal formula made of Metallic Antimony in conjunction with white Lisbon wine) is mixed with milk, its emetic and depressing qualities are neutralised, and it becomes narcotic.

As concerning the peculiar odour of Tin, this characteristic applies likewise to certain other metals. An old classic saying of Suetonius (112) is still proverbially current regarding money, (in coin of the realm) that "*Non olet*," it has no bad odour. But, as we are now told, some money, in these modern days, *does* smell after all. Every one, says the scientist, is familiar with the smell of a penny. This is because when warmed by being handled, or kept in the pocket, it gives out radio-active emanations. The said odour is inherent in the metal, but can only be set free by the agency of heat. The ancient classic adage, "*Non olet*," therefore, no longer holds good in this twentieth century of the world's history. Nevertheless, as Juvenal puts it, in a satire, "*Lucri bonus est odor—ex re qualibet.*" Other quaint Latin proverbs had lessons to teach on the same topic of smell. "*Non bene olet qui bene semper olet*," quoth Martial, in one of his Epigrams :—" He smells not well whose smell is all perfume." Whilst Plautus (B.C. 240) has sagely remarked, "*Aliter catuli longe olent, aliter sues* "—" Puppies have one smell ; pigs quite another."

Louis XI. of France, full of sordid avarice, frequently had his meals served on pewter dishes ; his outlay in jewelry consisted chiefly in buying little "enseignes," or images of saints, with which to decorate his mean old hat ; whilst even some of these were but leaden medals.

Pewter is of three kinds : "plate," "trifle," and "ley." The second sort (formed of tin, with a small proportion of lead, and antimony) is used to-day for the quart, and pint pots of the publicans ; and the "ley" pewter (three parts of tin, and one of lead) is manufactured into wine, and spirit measures. Makers of bells (from bell-metal) sometimes pretend (falsely) that they add a certain quantity of silver to the alloy for rendering the bells more melodious of tone.

To "tin" a Copper basin is quite an easy matter. Having made this scrupulously clean, you heat it over a charcoal fire to beyond the fusing point of iron; molten tin is then poured into the basin; a little sal ammoniac is added (for removing the last unavoidable film of oxide); and then the molten Tin is spread by a bunch of tow over the inside surface of the basin, to the now purely metallic surface of which the Tin film will adhere firmly. "Tinning" wrought Iron is effected by its immersion in the molten metal, by which ordinary thin "sheet Iron" becomes "sheet Tin."

"The tinker," says a pleasant writer, "is the medicine-man of pot and kettle. Armed with a few soldering implements, and a small, smoky stove, he drives briskly along the country lanes, or tarries awhile on some grassy roadside spot, making a busy use of his hospital for metallic ailments. His cart is an anomaly; a survival from remote centuries; strangely shaped, and curiously ornamented with bright brass-work. His own private *kekaubi* hangs pendulous from the crossed sticks of immemorial vagrant usage." Leland, in his *English Gipsies*, tells of a cunning Bohemian who "bested" a lady by tinkering up an old kettle she had rejected, and selling it back to her as new.

"The tinkers are very good to their children and women-folk, and we often noticed as we met them on their journeyings, how the men and boys trudged after the carts, or herded the ponies, while the little girls and women rode at ease in the body of the carts. The children are delightfully sturdy and healthful-looking, with their curly red, or golden, locks (generally bleached, like those of their mothers, to an almost flaxen tint by the sun) laid bare to every change of wind or weather. With this rough, careless life of theirs they seem perfectly happy and content."

"I defy any man, or woman, to feel thoroughly discontented while the kettle sings." Reading again and again, always with renewed delight, Dickens' immortal story of *The Cricket on the Hearth*, never does it escape our recollection that " the kettle began it."

The mirrors of the ancients were of polished metal, as are those of the Japanese now, and of some other Oriental nations. Mirrors of smooth glass, with a metallic backing to act as the reflecting surface, did not become common until the sixteenth century. The usual method of preparing glass mirrors is to coat one side of the glass with an amalgam of Tin, and Mercury; but mirrors are now frequently constructed by depositing pure Silver on the glass behind. Keats tells, in his Poem, *Lamia*, (1820), of a young man who, having fallen in love with, and married, a serpent, (or Lamia), which had assumed the form of a beautiful woman, stooped—

> "Bending to her open eyes,
> Where he was 'mirrored' small, in paradise."

"What a quaint comment one might make," said Oliver Wendell Holmes, "on that expression of the Apostle's—'seeing through a glass darkly.' So we did in his day; and so we did seventy years ago. But, since then we have put two pieces of glass together,—a piece of flint glass, and a piece of crown glass; and now we see through our double glass clearly; how amazingly clearly!"

It has been affirmed, particularly in one instance of a hardy Breton fisherman, who had sailed much on rough, stormy seas, that suffering from *mal de mer* may be altogether avoided by the simple means of carrying a small mirror in the pocket, and gazing at it when needed. "As soon," said this old fellow, "as I felt sickness coming on, I looked steadily in the glass, and all symptoms immediately passed away." "I got the cure from my father, and I never knew it to fail."

"A werb," said Mark Tapley, who could never find adversity enough to bring out his jollity,—" A werb is a word as signifies to be, to do, or to *suffer*, (which is all the grammar, and enough too, as ever I wos taught,) and if there's a werb alive, I'm it. For, I'm always a bein', sometimes a doin', and continually *a sufferin'*."

"And continually a sufferin',—and not jolly yet?" asked Tom Pinch, with a smile.

So much for the plain, highly useful metal, Tin (*Stannum*.) But furthermore, apart from its remedial, and utilitarian aspects, this metal—Tin—has given the world a literary gem, which—"*facile princeps*" amongst its fellows—finds fond favour with young and old, as a choice jewel amongst tales, and distinguishing its lovable Author for all time: *The Constant Tin Soldier*, of Hans Andersen.

"Five and twenty tin soldiers there were, all brothers, because all made out of the same old tin spoon. They were all exactly alike except one, who had only one leg, having been melted the last of the batch, when there was not tin enough left. Yet this one was a brave, valiant soldier, standing as firmly on his one leg as the others on their two legs." Poor little "Tin Soldier!" he meets with a peck of troubles, but marches, (or rather is carried swiftly onward by the tide of war), triumphantly through them all. He falls desperately in love with a fair paper little lady dancer, who stretched out both her arms, and lifted her tiny dancing leg so high that the tin soldier lost sight of it, and therefore concluded that she had only one, like himself. After giving dire offence to a cruel gnome in a snuff-box, he gets blown out from a window, three storeys high, into a gutter of rushing water, during a torrent of rain. Some mischievous boys rescue him, only to send him adrift again on the perilous stream in a paper boat, which presently suffers shipwreck. Our ill-starred metal warrior is swallowed up by a voracious fish, which in its turn becomes caught, taken to market, sold, and cut open by the cook. Lo, and behold! there are the same room, the same children, and the same playthings from which he started. There, too, was the noble castle of pasteboard, and the elegant little dancer, still on one leg; she was likewise constant; but, sad to tell was their final fate! One of the children (impelled no doubt by the spiteful gnome) flung the helpless soldier into the burning stove. Just at the same time the room door opened, the draught blew in, the paper lady fluttered like a sylph right into the stove beside the tin soldier, and was instantly consumed by the flames. The tin soldier melted down to a lump; and, next day, when the maid raked out the ashes, she found him in the shape of a little tin Heart. Of the dancer nothing remained but the tinsel rose she had worn at her waist, and that was as black as a cinder.

When the good, honest, burly Yorkshireman, John Browdie, had married Tilda Price, the bosom friend of Miss Squeers, (an unwilling spinster, doing her best to get married), he took the ladies to "Lunnon, by stage coach, on a trip to 'joy theirselves." "Here be a weddin' party; broide, and broidesmaid, and the groom ; and if a mon doant 'joy himself noo, when ought he, hey ? Draat it all; that's what I want to know." "To have seen Miss Squeers, when, after the night's rest, she came down to a substantial breakfast at the 'Saracen's Head,' in all her maiden glory of white frock, and spencer, white muslin bonnet, (with an imitative damask rose in full bloom on the inside thereof), the bonnet-cap being trimmed with little damask roses; also wearing a broad damask belt, matching both the family rose, and the little ones ; to have beheld all this, and to have taken further into account the Coral bracelets, (rather short of beads, and with a very visible black string), which clasped her wrists, and the Coral necklace which reposed on her neck, supporting outside her frock a lonely *Cornelian Heart*, typical of her own disengaged affections ; to have contemplated all these mute, but expressive appeals to the purest feelings of our nature, might have thawed the frost of age, and added new fuel to the fire of youth."

The use of Tin-foil as a beneficial appliance over wounds, for aiding their process of healing, has found well-merited favour in Paris of late, especially with Dr. Amat. In a recent lecture which he read before the Therapeutical Association of that capital city, he advised this metallic agent for the topical treatment of open wounds, or torpid raw sores. The layer of Tin-foil is to be fastened on over the wound with an antiseptic bandage. But furthermore a novel addition to this treatment was commended in the form of "the skin which lies next within the shells of eggs." We know that this membrane is very tough, (and very indigestible). Dr. Amat orders that "six, or eight strips of the said membrane, (quite fresh of course), shall be applied over the raw flesh of a wound, a burn, or an open sore, and then covered with a small square of Tin-foil—a little beyond the margins of the wound,—this being fastened on (as already stated) with an antiseptic bandage. After four days the bandage and Tin-foil are to be removed; when it will be found, (it may be hoped), that the egg-membrane has partly grown into the sore tissues, so as to be causing the formation of a new skin. The membrane does not always adhere; but when it can be made to do this, the process of closing-over (cicatrisation) is hastened; and not only so, but the wound, or sore, heals exceptionally well, leaving but few perceptible traces behind. It may be plausibly supposed that the Sulphur which is known to form an infinitesimal constituent of this egg-membrane, helps materially to promote such speedy, and sound healing.

As a remarkable fact eggs are associated by the Jews with funerals, being eaten during the eight days of mourning. A hard-boiled egg is always laid on the supper table of the modern Jewish Passover, together with unleavened bread, bitter herbs, and a charred shank-bone of a lamb.

Similarly as to the Sulphur, it is a matter of familiar experience, that to carry a small raw potato in the trousers pocket is found to alleviate, or prevent, chronic rheumatism in a person who is physically disposed thereto. This salutary effect is due likewise to the sulphur contained in the said tuber, mainly in its skin. When a potato is peeled, as every one knows, its raw cut surface soon becomes stained with black products of the sulphur which has chemically acted on the steel blade of the knife. Furthermore, the peel, or skin of the potato, embodies a narcotic principle known as "solanin." Ladies in former times had their dresses supplied with small bags, or pockets, in which to carry one, or more such small potatoes next their person against rheumatism. But this "solanin" is dissipated, and rendered inert when the whole potato is boiled, or steamed.

IRON AND ZINC.

AMONG the Metals put to more ordinary uses, Iron and Zinc are to be classified; though not generally esteemed as "Noble," for personal adornment, or as aiding jewelry. The former of these Metals serves admirably for making handcuffs, and the latter for foot-pans; neither of which purposes comes within the range of our present treatise.

All the native Iron met with is believed to have fallen from the sky. The Iron of commerce is obtained from its ores; the Tin of commerce from Casiterite, or tin-stone, a compound of Tin with oxygen.

With respect to Iron, we have shown when treating of the Bloodstone that to wear a fragment of this stone externally on some part of the body will indisputably serve to stay any flux of blood from which the wearer may be suffering; doing so by reason of the diminutive specks of red iron oxide incorporated within its substance. This subtle effect is fully justified by the similar action which small doses of metallic Iron given internally are found to exercise. Such doses, nevertheless, are not absorbed in any degree; they pass out of the system absolutely undiminished in weight, together with the stools, which they blacken. The Iron meets intestinally with sulphuretted hydrogen generated by fermenting excrementitious matters, and a black sulphide of iron is formed. In this latter case, just as in the former, some salutary influence which materially is inappreciable must be wrought by the Iron on the blood-making organs, and functions. That such Iron proves powerfully astringent when employed by either of these methods cannot be denied; also that it will promote the increased production of red blood-corpuscles; though by what exact process is not known: most probably by some occult energy affecting the bodily part with which the metal (infinitesimally volatilised) comes into contact, whether when taken medicinally into the body, or when applied as a compound mineral to its outside. Iron was administered for curative purposes several centuries before Pliny's time. In this country Sydenham was the first (1665) to point out these very important therapeutic properties of Iron as a blood-making power. "To the worn-out, and languid blood," said he, "it gives a spur or fillip, whereby the animal spirits, which before lay prostrate, or sunk under their own weight, are roused, and excited."

Regarding Zinc: if a piece of silver wire, (or a silver probe) be introduced high up into one of the nostrils, and have its lower end brought into contact with a small strip of Zinc plate, placed under the tongue, then a sensation not unlike that of a strong flash of light will be produced in the eye on the same side. Or, a similar perception, as though of some pungent *taste*, will be produced at the moment of contact between the two said metals, if one be inserted high up between the upper lip and its gum, whilst the other is applied in like manner between the lower lip, and the lower gum, or under the tongue, the further ends of the metals being then brought into contact together in front.

The foot-pan, named as illustrating those domestic uses to which Zinc is commonly put, is one only of many such homely ends which this metal serves. Vessels of this sort are said to consist of "galvanised iron;" which is not the case. No galvanism whatever is employed in their manufacture; but they are thinly coated with melted zinc, just as similar iron vessels are tinned. Zinc in the sheet merely rusts superficially when exposed to the air and out-door elements, its substance beneath being thereby protected from any further corrosion. Because of this reason, the said metal is well-adapted for roofing, gutter-pipes, and other similar purposes. But on more than one occasion an outbreak of illness has been reported through rain-water being washed down from zinc roofing into a zinc tub, and coming into contact therein with decomposing organic matters, so that a soluble carbonate of zinc has become formed; which was more or less poisonous to its consumers.

Workers in zinc for any length of time get to suffer from spinal nervous depression, and failure of power, particularly as regards the sensory functions; also with a liability to spasmodic affections. These symptoms arise, of course, from the external effects of the metal coming into frequent contact with the skin, and the mucous linings. A like result will beneficially occur if metallic zinc is ordained, in a limited use, for outward therapeutic help against fluxes from the chest, or the kidneys, and for the profuse night sweats of consumptive patients. And similar effects may be wrought indirectly by administering powder of the oxide of zinc in doses infinitesimally small.

Zinc is the "false silver" of ancient Strabo, and

other authors. It is a bluish-white metal, of considerable lustre; fully justifying the nursery lines which serve to signalise the letter Z in the child's primer spelling-book:—

> "' Z ' is some zinc,
> So shining, and bright;
> Which makes our eyes wink
> In the Sun's merry light."

"Zachariah! blow the fire! Puff! Puff! Puff!"

EPITOME.

To summarise the remedial uses (for wear, or other personal application), of the "nobler metals," whilst specifying the bodily conditions for improving which their several influences are most salutary, will now be a profitable peroration on our part.

Gold, when employed as we have indicated, must be as pure as possible; certainly not containing more copper than the eight per cent of "Sterling Gold."—"Trinket Gold," and the "pale Gold" of jewellers, are not to be relied upon for the physical, and mental benefits which we venture to promise.

Gold, of the quality insisted on, specially strengthens a weak, or depressed heart. Moreover, it gives wisdom, and activity of sense to the brain; for each of which ends it is to be worn either immediately next the skin, or as nearly so as can be contrived. But even the latter proviso will elicit a fair measure of response to this modified contact. (We know, for instance, that the loadstone will similarly magnetise the compass needle even through the thickness of an ordinary table.) Gold, likewise, is most excellent for dispelling melancholy, particularly if dependent on constitutional causes. Its habitual wear promotes longevity; whilst its adoption in early life by children with a scrofulous taint is an assured preventive of any mischievous development thereof, as the growth proceeds, and the bodily system becomes established.

Silver, by personal wear, can indisputably repress and relieve epilepsy, and allied nervous seizures. Its employment further protects against neuralgic attacks those persons who are liable to suffer therefrom. It aids in healing sores when there is only a languid, and inefficient natural power to bring about a cure of the same. It preserves the hair, and helps to conserve its colour, even onward to advanced life. Again, it specially fortifies the bronchial membranes, and the throat, against hoarseness, and catarrhal fluxes.

The remedial activities of Gold, and of Silver (especially the former), speaking from a chemical point of view rather than in the abstract, become enhanced whilst bathing is being pursued in the sea. Chlorides of the metals, (which should be as pure as possible,) are then formed, which, being soluble, are more or less absorbed by the skin upon which these metals are being worn.

The adoption of Platinum jewelry (which is not common) will assist to operate against chronic constipation through intestinal torpor; and will thus afford help against the depression of spirits which is generally associated with this difficulty. Platinum is peculiarly beneficial to women, when chosen for personal wear.

Copper, which can be put into forms of personal ornaments without entailing singularity, is of admirable service against bacterial assaults, such as underlie typhoid fever, cholera, and harmful toxication by drinking impure water. Small convenient plates of this metal may be worn over the abdomen (as we have explained) for aiding the desirable objects thus detailed.

Lead, as a jewel, would not be handsome of appearance, nor commend itself as lending ornamental attractions. Nevertheless, it is a metal useful for maintaining the skin-surface of the body in health, and freedom from outbreaks. Likewise it is found to foster old age.

Tin, which may be easily worn as pliable light foil, is of famous promise against intestinal worms; the engendering of these it notably obviates. Much after the same fashion as Lead, it is a capital adjuvant appliance for healing indolent sores.

Zinc, made (together with Copper) into a finger-ring, will, by its use as such, obviate neuralgic rheumatism; also it will control bronchial phlegm, and profuse night sweats. Moreover this appliance will hold spasmodic affections in check.

Iron is of every-day proximity to ourselves, (and our horses,) as embedded in the fabric of our footgear. Its mystic potency within the Bloodstone (infinitesimally) against hæmorrhages gives a high remedial rank to the same for styptic wear as a jewel. To this wonderful endowment a special degree of importance is to be attached.

When the inert metallic Iron of the soil is appropriated by plants, certain complex bodies of the vegetables combine with it, and convert it into an organised iron-compound; and this affords pabulum to the blood.

We do not include Lead, Tin, Iron, or Zinc, among the "Nobler Metals." But none the less do they occupy in the mineral world a place of fundamental curative service; remarkably so, as considered in relation to the work we have now in hand. Somewhat closely do they bear out, when appraised, an analogy between their function in connection with the said "nobler metals," (of loftier aims,) and those of the Scriptural statue, which was of Gold, Silver and Brass in all its upper proportions, but its feet, when disclosed, were found to be of common clay.

The Prophet Daniel, being commanded by the King Nebuchadnezzar to interpret his ominous dreams, (which the Chaldean wise men had failed to understand), spake by inspiration thus: "Thou, O King, sawest, and beheld a great image. The great image, whose brightness was excellent, stood before thee; and the form thereof was terrible. The image's head was of fine Gold, his breast, and his arms of Silver; his belly, and his thighs of Brass. His legs of Iron, his feet, part of Iron, and part of clay." This image was a symbolism, (being still used as such), betokening a character noble, but marred by imperfection as regarding its baser features. The Image had four parts, its fourth part presenting an admixture of Iron, and Clay. Thereby was shown the inferiority of the lower parts to the head; the value, and importance of the materials decreasing from above downwards.

Mr. Quilp, the ugly, designing, dwarf (*Old Curiosity Shop*), "dropping in at Mr. Sampson Brass's office, in the absence of that gentleman, lighted upon Mr. Swiveller, who chanced at the moment to be 'moistening his clay,' as the phrase goes; sprinkling a glass of warm gin-and-water on the dust of the law, rather copiously. But, as clay in the abstract when too much moistened becomes of a weak, and uncertain consistency, breaking down in unexpected places, retaining impressions but faintly, and preserving no strength, or steadiness of character, so Mr. Swiveller's clay, having imbibed a considerable quantity of moisture, was in a very loose, and slippery state; insomuch that the various ideas impressed upon it were fast losing their distinctive character, and running into each other."

"*Quod superest?*" "*Animam manibus commendo benignis Christi salvificis; qui mihi erit*"—

FINIS.

" Thou who hast made my home of life so pleasant,
    Leave not its tenant when its walls decay;
O Love Divine, O Helper ever present,
    Be Thou my strength and stay!

Be near me when all else from me is drifting;
    Earth, sky, home's pictures, days of shade, and shine,
And kindly faces, to my own uplifting
    The love which answers mine.

I have but thee, my Father! Let thy spirit
    Be with me then to comfort and uphold;
No gate of Pearl, no branch of Palm I merit,
    Nor street of shining Gold.

Some humble door among the many mansions,
    Some sheltering shade, where sin and suffering cease;
Finding at last beneath thy trees of healing
    The river of thy peace."

" Now, when my voice is hushed, and dumb,
    The fire burnt out, the glory dead,
I feel a thrill of wonder come,
    At that which this poor tongue has said;
And think of each diviner line,
    'Only the hand which wrote was mine.'"

INDEX.

	PAGE
Abraham	26, 301
— Ruby, Light for	139
Acidity for (Coral)	292
Adamant	321
Addercop	103
Adder-stone	348, 349
Agate	311
Age, old	372, 373
Alchemists	11
— (Gold 367,) 373, 374, 375,	376, 387
Alcohol	231, 232, 244, 430
Alum, in bread	121
Alumina	278
Amber 3, 9, 263, 293, 322	
(" Black " 348,)	352
Amethyst	3, 169-173
Amethyst flower	172
Amianthus	346
Ammonia	423
Amulets 45 to 54, 294, 384	
Animals, ages of	373
Animal stones	7
Anne of Gierstein	249
Antimony	460
Antipathies (of metals)	8
— of persons	9
Apollo	102, 163
Apostle Spoon	407
— Stones	44, 45
Apples	238
Aqua-marine 116, 125, 131, 132	
— Regia	363
"Arabian Nights"	88-95
Arboreal ancestors	162
Archaus, of Helmont	265
Armenian stone	331, 332

	PAGE
Artificial stones	54, 55
— Rubies	155
— Jasper	174
Asbestos	346
Attenuations	257
Azazael	349
BACTERIA 123, 402, 428, 436	
Baddeley Cake	395
Ball at Luttrell Court	352
Banana	237, 429-432
Barilla	151
Barley	231
Bathing in sea	147, 182
Beef steaks for getting out precious stones	68
Beer	232
Beetles	110
Bellcomb grease	439
Benjamin, tribe of	173
Berenice	65
Beryl	4, 116, 125, 160
— (as oracle 202,) 304, 309, 314	
Bezoar	7, 339, 340
Biberon of crystal	164
Biblical stones	351
Bishop's stone (amethyst)	169
Black lead	446
Black puddings	186-188
Bleeding, to arrest	97
— — Topaz	166, 167
— — — Jasper	176
— — — Bloodstone 180, 184	185, 257
— — — Sard	315
Blood	185, 186, 206
— Virtue of applying	27

INDEX.

	PAGE
Bloodstone 4, 180, 184, 185,	257, 468
Blue colour 104, 114, 115,	272
— Flowers	275
— Light 85,	331
Blush	220
Books	230
— Mock titles for	327
Borax	148-150
Bottle ends for Emeralds	134
Bowl, golden	388
Bracken	238
Bran	121
Brass 439,	440
Bread	117-120
— as stone solvent	61
Breast-plate of High Priest Preface, 21-24, 45, 104,	314, 351
Brilliants	69
Burmah for Rubies	141
Burning-glass .. 198,	222
Butcher's blue dress 114,	115
Butter 189,	190
CABBAGE	236
"Cabochon, En"—stones cut 140,	158
Cæsar's blood	27
Calcination of Precious stones	8
Calf, golden	362
Camei	218
"Cancer"—sign of Zodiac	46
Cancer, the disease, Radium for	261
— — — — Silver for	405
Capitol, Roman	345
Carat 71,	75
Carbon 65, 277, 278, 281, 282,	347, 352
Carbuncle stone ..	157-159
— sore 103, 138,	157-159
Carcanet	82
Cardinal's ring	98
Carnelian	138

	PAGE
Carrots	233
Cart-gum	439
Carteret, Mr. P. (Pepys)	78
Cat's-eye stone .. 131,	311
Caustic, lunar .. 400,	404
Cerebos salt	153
Chalcedonyx	137
Champagne tablets	244
Charcot, Dr. 217,	415-418
Charles I. of England ..	273
— — — — Blood of ..	27
Charms to wear	54
Chastity, Sapphire for 102-104,	134
Chaucer—in stone 173,	312
Cheese	190-192
— skim	193
— cakes	197
— game at	195
Chemist's coloured bottles	434
Cherries 240,	241
Chest-breathing, deep ..	266
Chilblains	113
Chlorite	200
"Chlorophylle"	129
Cholera	424-427
Chrysolite 4, 166,	276
Chrysoprase 37, 64, 172,	314
Cider tablets	244
Cinnamon stone	156
"Citrine" ointment	150
Claudius, Emperor	133
Cleopatra 296, 297, 301,	302
Clotted cream	196
Clown at Christmas	90
Cochineal 330,	331
Cock Eagle Stone	344
Cockles 379,	380
Colic 293, 424, 427,	447
Colours 83, 114, 115, 260,	272
— from passion	262
Conch shell	408
Confection of hyacinth 3, 160,	161
— of scarlet grain	330
Consumptives .. 123,	124

INDEX.

	PAGE
Consumptives, Tin plate for	455
— Zinc for	468
Cooking utensils	434, 435
Copper	421, 442, 472
— in malachite	166, 422
Coral	3, 288-291, 385
Cornelian	138, 310
Corns	125
Coronation Stones	40, 41
Corundum	140, 143
Cough, coral for	291
Coutts, Mr., banker	79, 80
Crab (Cancer) eyes	46
Cramp-rings 108,109 (Loadstone 316,)	380
Cream, clotted	196, 247
"Croodlin' doo"	440
Crown, the King's	353
Crystal-gazing 15, 20, 204, 208, 219, 221	
— Balls	201
Cucumber	233, 234
Cup, San Graal	133
Curative influences of precious stones	18, 19
Currants	243
Days of week for wearing the several precious stones	38
— Jewish	43
Decay of fruit	240
Dee, Dr.	107, 203, 377
Demons, against—Onyx	314, 315
Dentist	369, 370
Denton, Professor	16, 17
Diachylon plaster	447, 452
Diamond	64-95
— and radium	260
— chief stones	73, 74, 353
— Cullinan	353
— the first	79
— generative powers of	66, 67
— imitation	54, 85
— triturated medicinally	80

	PAGE
Diamond, virtues of	9, 69, 70, 71, 352
Dickens, Charles	29, 114, 122, 193, 230, 233, 235, 242, 274, 304, 318, 361, 386, 408, 414, 424, 432, 437, 441, 464, 466, 474
"Dispensatory, the Compleat Chymical"	12
Divining-rod	397, 419, 420
Dragon-stone	136
Dreams (Onyx)	313
Drinking cups, agate	168
— — amethyst	170
Drunkenness, against, amethyst	169, 170
"Dumb animal"	245, 246
Dutch metal	423
Dwarfs	241, 242
Eagle	88, 214, 342, 345
Eagle-stone	214, 341
Earth salts	180, 403
Eating	245
Eggs	467
— membrane	467
Electricity	81, 82, 141, 323, 328
Electrides	325
Elia (Charles Lamb), Preface, 230, 243, 329, 449	
Eleusinian Mysteries	222
Emerald	42, 46, 354
— bottle ends	134
"En Cabochon," stones cut	40, 158
England	457
— lane in summer	274, 275
Ephod, to imitate	24
Epilepsy, (pearls for 308, 364)	
— (onyx for	312, 313,)
— (amber for 324,)	405, 406
Essence d'Orient	305
Essex, Earl of, ring	105, 106
Evil eye	51, 52, 289, 293
Exercise, dumb-bell	124

	PAGE
External uses of precious stones	26, 177, 256, 280, 287
Eyes, sapphire for	37
— onyx for	316
— lead for	451
FALL, turquoise saves from	265, 266, 270
False stones	56, 86
Family diamonds	49
Fatigue in metals and man	360
Fatima	92
Feld Spars	263, 334, 337
Fingers	112, 384
— nails	113
— nail-stone	312
Fire-fly (emerald)	133
Fishes, stones from	7
Five precious fragments	25
Flaws in stones	43
Fleece, golden	363
Flies in amber	324
Flint	258, 279, 284
— bottle ends	134
Flowers	230
Flummery	232, 238
Fluor-spar	147
Fluorine	147, 148, 165
Fluorescence	261
Foods	124
— light	236
— "tinned"	457
Foot bath, bran	121
Forks, silver	407, 408
Fowls' blood	186
Foxglove	123
Freckles	150
Frenzy	332
Friday	136, 138
Fruits	232, 237
Frumenty	232, 238
Fuller, Sir Thomas	79
Fur seal	179
GALACTIDES	346

	PAGE
Galen	6, 173, 175
Gamp, Mrs.	233, 234, 304
Garlick (loadstone)	319
Gems	5
— in rough	35, 46, 309
— sexual	15
Generation of precious stones	66, 67
George III. (emerald)	134, 344
German Emperor	109
Gibberish	374
Gierstein, Anne of	249
Ghosts	229, 410
Giants	242
Girasol	251
Glass	200, 201
— mirrors	463
— to etch on	148
— "burning"	159
Goat's beard	239
Goitre	148
Golcondah	66
Gold	361-399, 471
— in sea water	182
— leaf	385
— standard marks	398
— water	98
Golden bowl	388
— Calf	362
— Fleece	363
Goose	345
Gounod	
Grail, Holy	133
Grapes	243
Guinea gold	396, 397
Gunpowder	318
Gyges' ring	107, 108
HAHNEMANN	403
Hair, (auburn 327,)	444, 445
— baldness	266
— black	208
Ham House	410
Hands (and fingers)	112
Hare, sea	125
Haunted precious stones	50

INDEX.

Health, precious stones affected by 26, 265, 266, 268, 269, 270, 271, 306
—— —— affecting 20, 21, 22, 320
Heart, gold for 366
Heat, effect on precious stones 86
Heliotrope 333
Helmont, Van, superstitions 317, 318
Henry VIII., magnificence of 32
Heraldry, amethyst in .. 172
Highland superstitions 51, 52
Holy City, stones of .. 172
Honey 315
Horace Flaccus .. 2, 53
Horner, Jack .. 246, 247
Hyacinth stone 3, 160, 161, 311
Hydrofluoric acid .. 148
Hypnotism 220

Ice 201, 202
Imitation stones .. 54, 56
—— —— jasper 174
—— —— pearls .. 305, 310
—— —— rubies 144
—— —— turquoise 264, 267, 276
Infinitesimals .. 255, 256
Inglesant, John 208, 209, 210-214
Ingoldsby Legends .. 99
Insects in amber.. .. 324
Intaglios 132, 218
Invisible, to become 107, 182, 198, 248
— (by Onyx .. 313,) 335
Iona stone 287
Iron 109, 110, 152, 168, 175, 206, 257 (magnetic 320,) 468, 469, 473
Isaacs, Mr., and eyes .. 25
Issachar, tribe of, amethyst 169

Jacinth 160
Jackdaw of Rheims 99-101

Jade .. 284, 285, 286
Jarley, Mrs. 177
Jason, Golden Fleece .. 363
Jasper 3, 5, 173, 199, 263
Jester, Jack Point .. Preface
Jet 347
Jewels worn for display.. 20
— how to wear 151
Jew's eye 59
— stone 346, 351
Junket 191

Karcsay, Hungarian violinist's ring .. 307, 308
Kelly, Sir Edward .. 203
Kettle, the copper .. 437
Kidney, jade for.. .. 284
Kilmansegg, Miss, legend of .. 388 to 392
King Edward VII. .. 40
Kingsley, Charles .. 274
Kiss 220
Knives and forks (Silver) 408
Kruger ring 83

Lamb, Charles Preface, 230, 243, 329, 449
Lambert, Daniel 63
Lamp, Aladdin's 89
— stone 159
Lapidarium of Marbodeus 173, 174
Lapis lazuli 2, 96, 263, 329
Laudanum 281
Laughter 386
Lavender 225, 226
Lead 328, 442-452, 473
— black (plumbago) .. 446
Leanness 64
Lens, burning 222
Lentil 152
Life, to prolong .. 177, 382
Light, effects of 48, 83, 85, 87, 145 (polarised 154, 219,) 159, (from topaz 167,) 171, 172

31

INDEX.

	PAGE
Lime .. 333, 355, 356	
Lion, with emerald eyes	130
Liquation of stones ..	8
Liqueurs 98, 364	
Listers, the	352
Litharge .. 447, 448, 452	
Loadstone.. 9, 318, 319	
Lockyer, Lionel	259
Louis XVI.	263
— XI.	461
Luke, Saint	350
Lunar caustic .. 400, 404	
Lunatics	66
Lyncurion (amber) ..	323
MÆCENAS (and Horace)	53
Magic 10, 346	
Magicians 10, 11	
Magnesia .. 129, 146, 355	
Magnet 218, 319, 320, 321, 322	
Magnetism 143, 154, 205, 206, 208, 319	
"Maids of Honour" ..	197
Malachite, copper in 166, 263, 422	
Malt	232
— extract .. 243, 244	
Mark, Saint, ring of ..	108
Mark Tapley .. 58, 59	
Marriage, etc. (Pepys) ..	78
Martinmas	189
Marigold	258
Maund	347
Maximilian's strength ..	167
Maypole Inn .. 193, 194	
Measles	351
Meat-eating	232
Meerschaum .. 147, 355	
Melancholy (Dickens) 29, 318, 369	
Memory, antecedent ..	230
Menstruum to dissolve stones 61, 62, 63, 64	
Mental depression 29, 318, 369	
Mercury 359, 455	
Metals, to apply.. 417, 418	

	PAGE
Metals, to prepare 11, 357, 358	
— Epitome of	471
Methylated spirit ..	244
Midas 387, 388	
Milk, sheep's	195
— skim	197
Milton (carbuncle eyes) ..	159
Mind, dual 14, 216, 217	
Minerals, virtues of ..	7
— waters .. 135, 136	
Mines (Golcondah) ..	66
— (Zebarah) .. 128, 130	
— Hungary (opal) ..	252
— (Nishabour) .. 268, 271	
— (Holyhead)	423
— (Peru)	130
Mirrors	463
Mistletoe .. 393, 394, 396	
Moles (by radium) ..	261
Money, smell of	461
Monkey, ancestral ..	162
Montague, Lady Mary ..	91
Months, stones for 37, 44	
Moon, the .. 205, 404	
Moonstone, the .. 332–339	
Mottoes on turquoises ..	272
Mourning, for (the amethyst)	172
Mowcher, Miss	337
Mugwort	207
Multiplication of precious stones .. 66, 67	
Murray, David Christie ..	266
Music 273–4, 332	
Mussel 294, 298, 300, 310	
Mutton, leg of	113
NAILS, finger .. 113, 312	
Napoleon I.	83
— Louis 83, 109	
Necklace, amber.. ..	326
Needle to Pole	319
Nephritic stone (jade) ..	284
Neptune (for February)..	171
Nero	130
Nessus, shirt of .. 26, 27	

INDEX.

	PAGE		PAGE
Neuralgia, loadstone for	317	Peridot .. 163,	165
Noah in Ark	158	Peru, Mines of, emerald	130
Nonius (and opal)	251	Peter, the Apostle	198
Nose-bleeding, (topaz for 3,)	174	Peter the Great	143
November (Hood)	44	Pewter 459,	460
Nugget of gold, largest	392	Pharmacopœia, the first	305
		Philosopher's stone	203
OBJECTIVE mind	15	Photography 142, 143,	400
Occult powers 8, 9, 24, 51, 239, 259, 293		Pickles, copper in	424
		Pigs' blood	187
Ocean voyage	123	Pigeons' blood, ruby 140, 141,	165
Odours .. 224, 227,	228	Planetary influences 41, 359, 377, 378	
Odyllic force	219		
Offenbach—evil eye	51	Plants, purple	171
Oil, stone of 62, 63,	64	Platinum .. 379, 420,	472
Old age	372	Plumage, coloured	429
— Testament (revised)	341	Plumbago	446
Olfaction	257	Poisons, to detect 15, 21, 65, 101, 142, 197, 163, 340	
Onyx 179, 312, 328,	329		
Opal 4, 39, 86, 248–	253	Polariscope, tourmaline	154
Operations, under blue light	84	Polar light	219
		Polycrates' ring	316
Opium (Paracelsus)	281	Porridge, plum	238
Oracle	216	Port wine	245
Orange	227	Potash 150,	151
— flower water	227	Potato in pocket	467
Ostentation in wearing precious stones	20	Powdered stones	7
		Precious stones, properties of 2, 3, 4, 18, 19, 29, 87, 88, 151, 269, 293, 350, 354	
Oyster .. 432,	433		
— pearl .. 294, 295,	298		
		— Epitome of	352
PARIS WORKMAN	236	— Spurious .. 56,	85
Parr, Old 372,	373	— Summary of	276
Pasty	247	Prig, Betsey 233, 234,	235
Paul, Saint	350	Prince Imperial .. 83,	109
Peace pillows	227	Prometheus	104
Peacock's feather (to ruby) 139,	140	Psychometry 14, 16,	18
Pearl 3,	355	Punch	379
— (Herrick)	155	Purity of life .. 20,	21
— to restore	307	Purulent discharges	258
— mother of	300	Python, spirit of (St. Paul)	350
— white	304		
Penny, smell of	461	QUAIL	313
Perfumes 224,	225	Quarrels, against, onyx	314

INDEX.

	PAGE
Quartzes	169, 178, 199
Queen Alexandra	39
— Elizabeth	104, 105, 106
— Mary's pearls	46
Quilp, Daniel	241, 242, 474
Quinces	113
RADIUM	180, 254, 255, 258, 259, 260, 261, 419
Rain	181
— bath	181
— water	181
Raisins	233
Ray pills	259
Red colour	142
— lead	443
— light	83, 84, 85, 142, 199
Refraction	85, 154
Reichenbach	205, 218, 219
Respiration, artificial	241
Rheumatism	402
Rhubarb, garden	236
Rings	108, 111, 136, 406
— Papal	98, 99, 340, 341
— Poison	341
Rock, crystal	159, 164, 253
Roller mills, flour	118–120
Roquefort cheese	195
Rosaries	53, 169
Rose diamonds	68
Royalty (stones)	39, 40
Ruby	2, 48, 54, 87, 138–156
— superior to diamond	72, 140
— manufactured	155
Rust, copper	422, 423, 425
SALIVA	370, 371
Salt, common	153, 401
Salts, mineral	7
San Graal	133
Sandford and Merton	90
Sapphire	2, 5, 95–103, 109–115, 353
— for eyes	57
Sard	313–315
Sardonyx	4, 179, 313

	PAGE
Sardou (evil eye)	51
Saturn	328
Sausages	189
Scapulary	53
Scarabæus	110
Scent—perfumes	228, 229
Sceptical about precious stones	35
Schroder, Dr.	12
Sea air	122, 123
— hare	125
— tench	313
— water	125, 182, 307
— — gold in	397, 398
— weeds, silver in	399
Seal (of Galen)	175
Seer-ship	208
Sergius, Grand Duke, ring of	102
Serpent	130, 137, 311
— stones	56–58
Shah's jewels	33, 34
Sheep's milk	195
Sight, second	230
Signatures	239, 353
Silica	258, 279, 283
Silver	399–420, 472
— prices of old	410, 411
— cord broken	388
Sinbad the Sailor	88
Singers, public	150
Sisera	190
Sixpence, song of	411, 412
Skeleton, lines on a	144
Skin	304
— absorbent powers of	136
— precious stones next to the	151
Sleep	161, 162
— loadstone	317
— bluelight	331
Smell	223, 224
Smith, Sydney	308, 401
Snuff	233, 234, 449
Sodium (soda)	151, 152
"Soldier, Little Tin"	464, 465

INDEX. 485

	PAGE
Solomon's seal	239
Solvent for precious stones	97, 98
Somnambulism	29, 220
Sore throat (amber)	326
Souls of things influenced by precious stones	47, 48
Sparsit, Mrs.	122
Specularii	204
Spinel	142–145
Spirits in stones	49, 50, 282
Spiritual qualities of stones	48, 250, 416
Spoons, amber	327
— silver	402, 409
Spurious stones	56, 85
Stalactites, copper	167
"Stan-myln" flour	117, 119, 120
Stars, influences of	21
Statue, the Prophet Daniel	474
Stones, to dissolve	61, 97
Stone oil	62–64
— (calculus)	175
Stye, for, gold ring	368
Subjective mind	15
Sugar, triturated	80
— of lead	443, 446
Sulphur	358, 444, 455
Summary of precious stones	352
Sun, influence of, on gold	363
— flower	198
Superstitions, Highland	52
Supper, the Last	133
Surgery under blue light	84
Sweets	315
Swiveller, Dick	235, 318, 474
Sympathy	48, 230, 416
Syrupisation of precious stones	8
TALISMAN	51, 108, 109–111, 127
Tallow	113
Tamarinds	379
Tapley, Mark	58, 59

	PAGE
Tea-spoons	409
Teeth	369, 370
Telepathy	10, 16, 17, 217, 416
Temperance advocates	231
Tennyson (Arabian Nights)	95
Thackeray	231
Theodosius, Emperor	56, 57
Thousand, Ten, a Year	445
— and One Nights	91
Thumb rings	111, 112
Thummim and Urim	22, 24
Tickling	220
Tiddler's ground, Tom	413, 414
Tin	452–468, 473
— "Little Tin Soldier"	464, 465
Tinker	462
Titles of dummy books	327
Titmouse, Tittlebat	445
Toad	338, 339
Toadstone	337–339
Todgers, Mrs.	64
Tobacco	241
— pipes	323, 325
Topaz	3, 86, 163–168
Torque gold	396
Touch, royal	6, 383, 384
Tourmaline	145, 146, 154
Tree-agate	312
Trinkets	135
Triturations	80, 81, 117, 368
Tropical countries for precious stones	4
Turbith mineral	281
Turquoise	37, 263–273
Tutelary spirits of precious stones	31
Typhoid fever	433, 434, 436
Ultramarine	330
Uric acid	152, 153, 191
Urim and Thummim	22, 24
VANADIUM (topaz)	165
Varden, Gabriel	437
Varicose veins	148
Vegetables	152, 232, 233, 236

INDEX.

	PAGE
Vegetarian	152
Venus, onyx from	314
Verdigris	422, 423, 439
Vinegar	459
Violet	229
— rays of light	142, 171, 172
Viper	103
Virtuous woman	140
Volatilisation of precious stones	8
WARMING stone	393
Warts	125
Watch pendants	54
Water, drinking	135
— to purify	447
Watercress	241, 242
Weekday stones	38
Weekdays of Jews	43
Wheat	118, 238
— germs	118, 119
Whitsuntide	186, 188

	PAGE
Whooping cough (coral)	291
— — (amber)	325
Wilkie Collins (Moonstone)	333, 334–337
Wine	244, 245
Wise Men of the East	392
Women in childbed	343, 344
Witchcraft, against	70, 170
Worms, tin against	453, 454
Wortley, Lady Mary Montague	91
Wounds, loadstone for	320
— sard for	314
— tin-foil for	467
YELLOW colour	273
ZEBARAH mines	128, 130
Zinc	370, 371, 468–471, 473
Zircon	160, 163
Zodiac, signs of	45, 46

JOHN WRIGHT AND CO., PRINTERS, BRISTOL.

WORKS BY THE SAME AUTHOR.

Demy 8vo. pp. xxiv and 781. 9/.

MEALS MEDICINAL:
WITH HERBAL SIMPLES (OF EDIBLE PARTS).
CURATIVE FOODS FROM THE COOK, IN PLACE OF DRUGS FROM THE CHEMIST.

"The work has been carefully prepared; and it is of course a truth that health may be maintained by suitable diet, while as an old writer reminds us, 'a good Coke is half a Physycyon.'"—*Lancet.*

Crown 8vo. 6/-.

ANIMAL SIMPLES;
APPROVED FOR MODERN USES OF CURE.

"We must thank Dr. Fernie for having collected for the general reader a vast amount of entertaining lore."—*Lancet.*

Crown 8vo. Cloth, 6/-

KITCHEN PHYSIC:
AT HAND FOR THE DOCTOR AND HELPFUL FOR HOMELY CURES.

"All the intentions pursued by medicines might be better obtained and enforced by diet."—*Dr. Arbuthnot, 1732.*

"Dr. Fernie has managed to cram into this small book many curious and agreeable facts . . . . . Not only a vast amount of material learning with regard to herbs and meats, but a pleasant trimming of allusions and quotations, that give his book an unusual charm . . . . . A full, quiet, and scholarly work."—*Lancet.*